# In Plain Sight

THE MIDDLE AGES SERIES

Roland Betancourt, *Series Editor*
Edward Peters, *Founding Editor*

A complete list of books in the series is
available from the publisher.

# In Plain Sight

*Muslims of the Latin Kingdom
of Jerusalem*

Ann E. Zimo

**PENN**

UNIVERSITY OF PENNSYLVANIA PRESS

PHILADELPHIA

Copyright © 2024 University of Pennsylvania Press

All rights reserved. Except for brief quotations used for purposes of review or scholarly citation, none of this book may be reproduced in any form by any means without written permission from the publisher.

Published by
University of Pennsylvania Press
Philadelphia, Pennsylvania 19104-4112
www.pennpress.org

Printed in the United States of America on acid-free paper
10 9 8 7 6 5 4 3 2 1

A Cataloging-in-Publication record is available from the Library of Congress

Hardcover ISBN: 978-1-5128-2489-6
eBook ISBN: 978-1-5128-2646-3

*For my parents, Steve and Deborah Zimo,
who have always been my rock.*

## Contents

Introduction   1

Chapter 1. Geography of the Muslim Communities   25

Chapter 2. "How Many Villages of Yours Have We Emptied?": Muslims and the Economic Landscape   55

Chapter 3. "Saracens Are Also Men Like the Franks": Muslims in the Legal Landscape   85

Chapter 4. Illusory Borders: Muslims and the Political Landscape   107

Chapter 5. Shared Webs of Knowledge   143

Chapter 6. Literary Intersections   163

Conclusion   199

Notes   203

Bibliography   245

Index   261

Acknowledgments   271

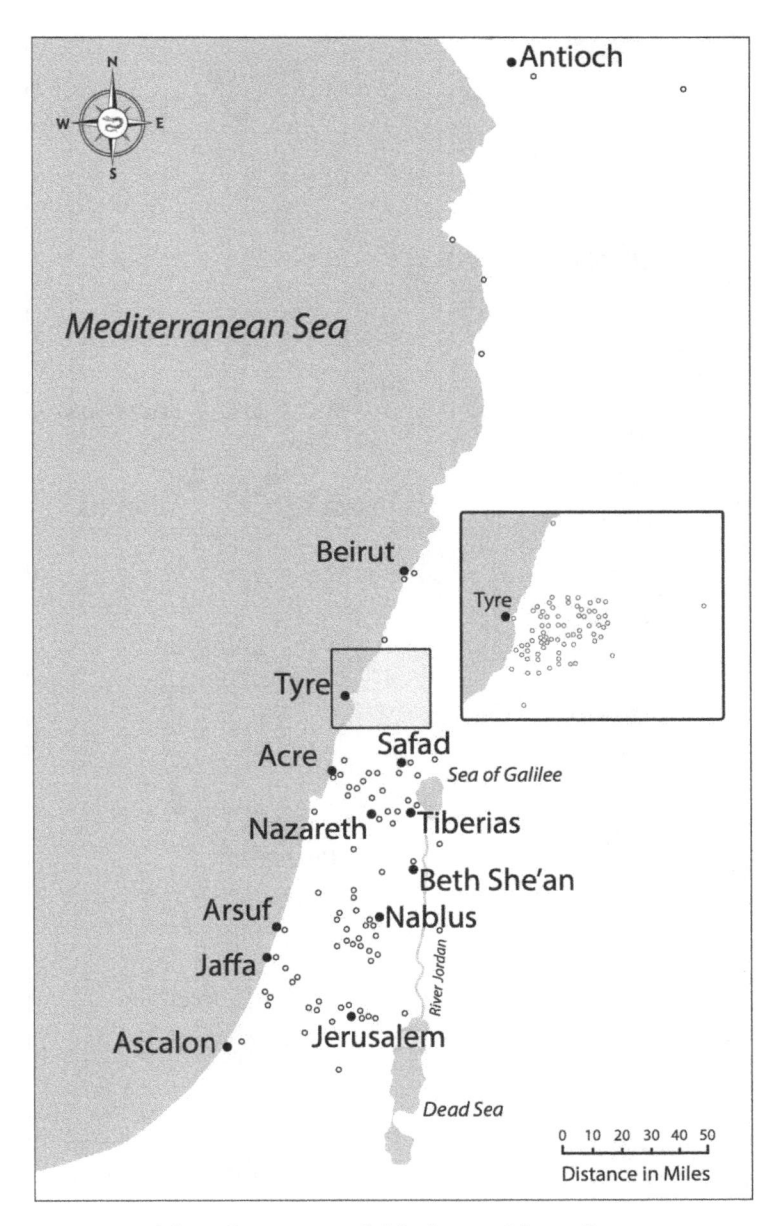

Map 1. Locations with Muslims or Islamic Sites.
Map created by John Wyatt Greenlee.

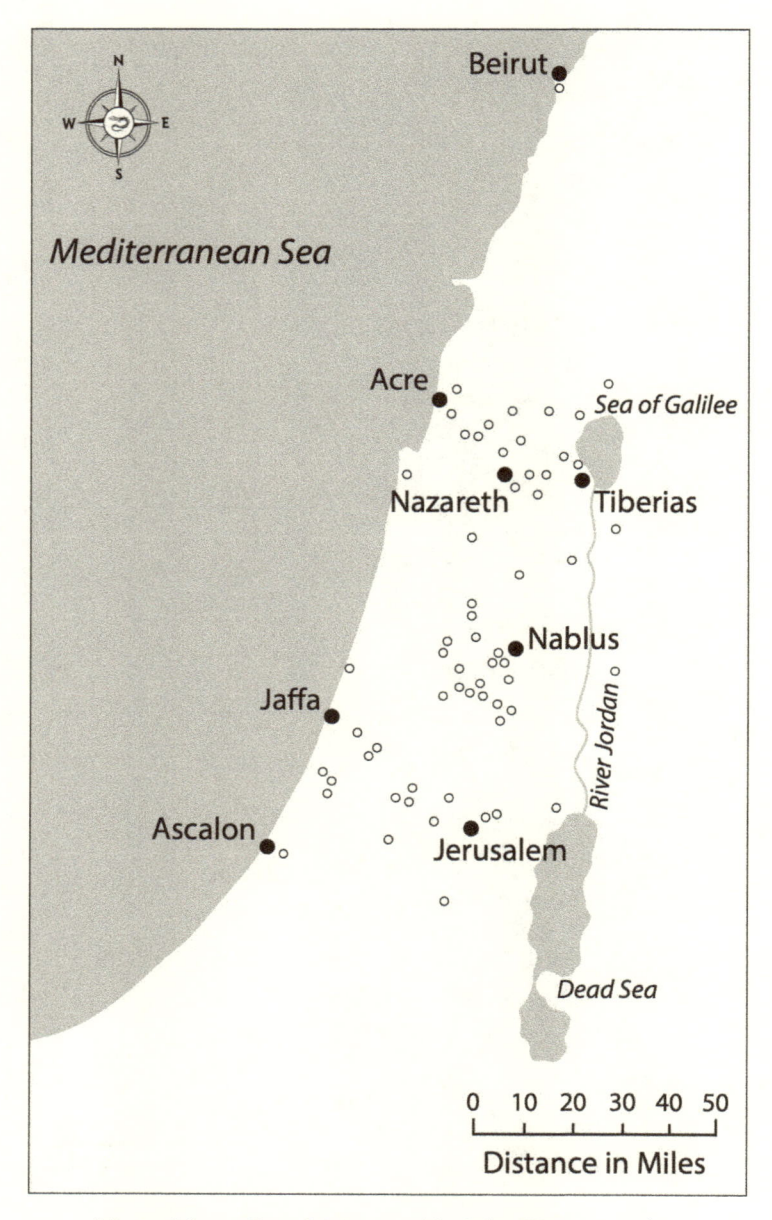

Map 2. Islamic Sites. Map created by John Wyatt Greenlee.

# Introduction

Nine hundred years ago, many thousands of men, women, and children—some armed and some not—were inspired by Pope Urban II to walk from their homes in France, the Low Countries, and Germany to Jerusalem. Their goal: to return the city they believed to have been the location of the death and resurrection of Jesus to Christian hands after four centuries of Muslim rule. It took three years, and thousands of people on all sides died in the process. In 1099, this First Crusade arrived before the walls of Jerusalem, taking and sacking the city in July. The local inhabitants who survived this initial slaughter found themselves subject to the new Kingdom of Jerusalem, established by the first crusaders in what is today Israel, Palestine, Lebanon, and Jordan. This kingdom would exist with varying geographic extents for the next two hundred years before finally being conquered by the Mamluk Sultanate in 1291.

Although we have no census data concerning the population's composition, there is no question that these locals, who included Eastern Christians, Jews, and Muslims, formed the vast majority of the population. The minority crusader immigrants, or "Franks," many of whom would never have encountered non-Latin Christians before, had to devise a system of governance and a level of coexistence with these other groups in order for their kingdom to function.

A great deal of thought and work has been put into the debate over how these political entities, which I refer to as Frankish states or the Latin East, should be interpreted. Were the Frankish states in fact the earliest examples of European colonialist expansion? What was the nature of their relationship with the European homelands? Most scholars would agree that the survival of the states depended in large part on continued military support from Europe in the form of waves of armed pilgrims. Even so, they were not politically dependent upon any one European polity, nor did they serve as mere stations of economic exploitation like the Dutch East Indies.

One approach toward determining this relationship is to investigate crusader-settlers' interactions with the populations already in place. Although perceptions of this society have changed significantly over the past century, one consistent trend has been to study the society from the Frankish perspective. Through the first decade of this century, most scholarship focused on the European crusaders. Even those asserting that the Franks assimilated with the local population base their argument on Frankish consumption patterns, not on their contacts with local people. A contention of this study is that fleshing out the lives of these subject populations is the key to better grasping the nature of this frequently invoked but poorly understood cultural encounter.

This book examines how Muslims in and around the Kingdom of Jerusalem experienced Frankish rule. I answer questions such as: Where did Muslims live and work and to what extent did they interact with Franks? What was their legal status and what kind of political power did they wield? How did Muslims and Franks interact culturally and what kind of knowledge did they exchange? I approach this study with the conception that different aspects of social life (e.g., economic, legal, political, intellectual, cultural) each present their own sets of relations that form a map of sorts. What follows is a discussion of multiple landscapes that seeks to map the communities according to not just geographic but also economic, legal, political, intellectual, and cultural spaces. From this vantage point, I reconsider the popularly accepted notion that the Crusades, and by extension the Latin East, were the locus of a monolithic clash of West and East or Christianity and Islam. I argue that Muslims did not exist merely as an external existential threat or as marginal within the Latin East. Rather they occupied important, often central places in the economic and political landscapes, and lived not at the outskirts of the kingdom but at its very spiritual and political cores.

This study explores both centuries of the kingdom's existence but leans heavily upon evidence from the so-called second kingdom that emerged in the wake of conquests of Saladin in the 1180s and the Third Crusade of the 1190s. I do this first because there are more sources from which to draw, particularly in the number of charters, letters, and other documents that have survived in various European archives as well as in later compendia in Arabic. Furthermore, the first half of the kingdom's existence has received far more attention than the second and the evidence for the society is better known, even if Muslims in that period are relatively neglected. A new study touching on Frankish society of the thirteenth century will therefore not be a redundancy. The twelfth-century situation is not ignored, however, and as the subject allows, I do attempt to trace changes over time, although this is not always possible.

## A Brief History of the Kingdom of Jerusalem

The Kingdom of Jerusalem was established in the wake of the First Crusade with the conquest of Jerusalem from the city's Fatimid defenders in July 1099.[1] The kingdom was actually the third of the Frankish states to be formed, with the County of Edessa and the Principality of Antioch created in 1098 by Baldwin of Boulogne (d. 1118) and Bohemond of Taranto (d. 1111).[2] After the crusade most of the crusaders returned to Europe, but small groups remained and carved out lordships for themselves in the hinterland. Bohemond's nephew, Tancred of Taranto (d. 1112), for instance, took the area of Nablus, Beit Shean, and Tiberias, creating his own Principality of Galilee as a lordship within the Kingdom of Jerusalem. The last of the Frankish states was formed in 1109 with the conquest of Tripoli and the formation of a county centered in that city and controlling the northern Lebanese and Syrian coastline. The first ruler of the kingdom, Godfrey of Bouillon (r. 1099–1100), never took the title of king, but his brother and successor Baldwin I (r. 1100–1118) did and had himself crowned in Bethlehem on Christmas Day 1100.

At the time, the major local political players were the Byzantine Empire, the Seljuks of Rum based in Anatolia, and the Fatimids of Egypt. The Byzantines had helped the crusaders in exchange for the promised return of conquered cities that had once been part of the empire. This promise was only kept with Nicaea, although they had ongoing relations with the Principality of Antioch. The Seljuks were active also in the north and posed a potential threat to the County of Edessa and Principality of Antioch. The Fatimids were the primary adversary of the kingdom in the south. However, the many cities of Syria were largely independent of their nominal overlords and it was the process of unification that would define the encounter between Muslim lords in Syria and the Franks.

The military history of the kingdom in the twelfth century has been divided into three segments. The period from 1099 to 1115 was a period of insecurity and securing the kingdom. From 1116 to the mid-1160s, the kingdom experienced its greatest security and growth. Finally from the mid-1160s to 1187 there was constant military pressure, large territorial loss, and almost complete collapse.[3] Baldwin I was responsible for guiding the nascent kingdom through its tumultuous beginnings. He did so in part by securing most of the southern and western boundaries and by gaining control of both sides of the Jordan River in the east and most of the coastal cities except for Ascalon and Tyre. His successors continued to consolidate and gain ground, with Tyre taken with the help of the Venetian fleet in 1124, and Ascalon taken by Baldwin III (r. 1143–1163) in 1153. The conquest of Ascalon effectively eliminated the Fatimid ability to raid into the hinterland or to send navies up the coast.

The Frankish concern was the consolidation of power in Syria by their neighbors, first begun by ʿImad al-Din Zengi (d. 541/1146) the *atabeg*, or governor and regent for a child, of Mosul. Over the course of his career, Zengi consolidated power in Syria and upper Mesopotamia, coming to rule also over Aleppo, Hama, and eventually Edessa. He was responsible for the end of the first Frankish state when he conquered the city and much of its territory in 1144. His repeated attempts to gain control of Damascus pushed that city closer to the Frankish polities and they maintained an alliance up until Zengi's death. Zengi's sons—Sayf al-Din Gazi and Nur al-Din (d. 1174)—split the inheritance, with the elder, Gazi, getting Mosul and the younger, Nur al-Din, getting Edessa. Nur al-Din immediately set his sights on Antioch, attacking and taking many castles and eventually crushing the Antiochene army in the Battle of Inab in 1149, killing the prince Raymond of Poitiers. Damascus finally sought an alliance with the Zengids at this time and in the face of the Second Crusade (1147–1150).[4]

Although the situation in the north was looking difficult, the Kingdom of Jerusalem continued to thrive for the next decade under Baldwin III (r. 1130–1163) and his brother Amaury (r. 1163–1174). Baldwin III managed to secure Ascalon, and he and his brother took advantage of the political chaos of Fatimid Egypt. Both kings invaded Egypt, seeking to secure its resources and wealth. Neither were successful and ultimately it was an agent of Nur al-Din, Saladin (Salah al-Din Yusuf b. Ayyub, d. 1193), who managed to seize control of the caliphate.

Although Nur al-Din did much to unify Syria under his control, it was Saladin who brought Syria and Egypt under a single ruler and nearly drove out the Franks.[5] Saladin came to Egypt in the service of his uncle Shirkuh, one of Nur al-Din's generals. He became close to the Fatimid caliph, who eventually appointed him vizier, or chief minister, in 1169, after the old vizier was assassinated and Shirkuh died. Saladin abolished the Fatimid caliphate after the last caliph, al-ʿAdid, died in 1171 and had the Abbasid caliph al-Mustadi's name proclaimed in the Friday prayer. Saladin, although nominally subject to Nur al-Din, was now essentially in command of Egypt. He made ongoing raids against the Franks until Nur al-Din's death in 1174 caused him to turn his attention toward conquering Syrian strongholds. After defeating the remnants of the Zengid army in 1175, the Abbasid caliph proclaimed Saladin the sultan of Syria and Egypt.

Saladin spent the rest of the decade mopping up Syrian holdouts, including the independent Ismaʿili strongholds in the mountains near the coast. The first part of the 1180s was spent alternately in truce and in skirmishes with the kingdom. Saladin took the periods of truce as times to extend his rule into the Jezira and notably to add Aleppo to the territory under his control. On the Frankish side, it was decided that Baldwin IV's sister Sibylla would become queen and whoever she married would be regent on her behalf, as the king had contracted leprosy as a child and could not have children of his own.[6] She married a rather divisive man named Guy de Lusignan. In 1185, Baldwin died, and Sibylla and Guy became regents for their young son Baldwin V, and then king and queen in their own right when their son died the following year.

In 1187, in response to Frankish attacks on caravans, Saladin sent a large army toward the kingdom, provoking the Frankish forces into an attack in the heat of July at a place called Hattin.[7] The army of the Franks was utterly destroyed, and the kingdom was left open to Saladin. In quick succession the cities of Ascalon, Acre, and even Jerusalem itself fell. In the end Saladin almost drove out the Franks entirely. By the end of the decade, only Antioch, Tripoli, and Tyre remained in Frankish hands.

Despite near total collapse in the wake of Saladin's conquests in the 1180s, by the second decade of the thirteenth century, the Kingdom of Jerusalem was in a stable and secure position. The Third Crusade (1189–1192)—led by the king of France, Philip II Augustus, and the king of England, Richard I the Lionheart—ended in a three-year treaty that recognized the Frankish holdings along the coast from Tyre to Jaffa, and gave Muslims and Christians free access to travel to Jerusalem and throughout the land.[8] It also added the new kingdom of Cyprus that would eventually be joined with the Kingdom of Jerusalem under King Hugh III of Cyprus (I of Jerusalem, r. 1268–1284).[9]

After the death of Saladin in 1193, the combined Sultanate of Egypt and Syria quickly disintegrated into a loose confederation of city-states ruled by members of his family, the Ayyubids.[10] The fragmented political situation was ideal for the reduced kingdom, and its leaders inserted themselves into the complex web of regional diplomacy and political maneuverings that developed. Thus in 1228 when Frederick II Hohenstaufen arrived to fulfill his crusading vows and to lay claim to the kingship of Jerusalem by virtue of his marriage to the heiress Isabella/Yolande, he was able to negotiate a favorable treaty with Sultan al-Kamil of Egypt. This Treaty of Jaffa returned Jerusalem, Bethlehem, Nazareth, and surrounding lands to Frankish control for a period of ten years.[11]

The Ayyubids were not the only decentralized political power. For much of the century, the Kingdom of Jerusalem was ruled by a series of regents and absentee kings. Frederick II held the regency for his son and heir to the throne (through Isabella who tragically died in childbirth) Conrad and sent lieutenants with armed contingents to maintain his interests in the kingdom. They were deeply unpopular and helped divide an already fractious Frankish aristocracy. Not only were the lords of Antioch and Tripoli independent, as they had been in the twelfth century, but now the other great magnates within the kingdom also acted on their own, contracting treaties with the Ayyubids and Mamluks to their own advantage. These included the lords of Jaffa, Tyre, and Beirut as well as the military orders whose land holdings only expanded as secular lords found themselves less able to defend their lands and sold them off. Additionally, the Italian communes, especially Venice, Genoa, and Pisa, held a great deal of power in the kingdom by virtue of their mercantile activities and the concessions of property and privileges granted to them in return for their naval assistance. The war that erupted between Venice and Genoa in the 1250s, commonly referred to as the War of St. Sabas, over a property of that name in Acre, came to involve much of the Frankish aristocracy and evolved into a kind of civil war that only officially ended in 1270.[12]

Crusading as an institution hit its stride in the thirteenth century. Pope Innocent III launched two crusades intended to aid the Latin East, the Fourth (1202–1204) and Fifth (1213–1221), only the second of which actually reached its intended target and neither of which provided any particular benefit to the kingdom. The Baron's Crusade (1235–1241) continued the diplomacy initiated by Frederick II and resulted in further territorial concessions from the Ayyubid al-Salih Ismail of Damascus.[13] As a result, his rival al-Salih Ayyub of Egypt invited the Khwarazmian Turks, who had been pushed out of their holdings between the Caspian Sea and Oxus River by the Mongols, into Palestine.[14] They agreed to join him and ravaged Jerusalem and the surrounding region in 1244. In October of that year, the armies of Egypt and the Khwarazmians met and devastated the armies of Syria and the Franks of Jerusalem at the Battle of al-Harbiyya/La Forbie. The Frankish military never really recovered, and Jerusalem never again fell under Frankish control. King Louis IX's crusade (1248–1254), which, like the Fifth Crusade, targeted Egypt, was a mixed blessing. On the one hand, it ended in spectacular failure with him and his magnates imprisoned and ransomed only at great cost. On the other, the years he spent in Palestine afterward resulted in the rebuilding and fortifying of the kingdom's defenses.

The most significant outcome of Louis's expedition was the toppling of the last Ayyubid Sultan of Egypt, Turanshah, in 1250 by his own mamluk (slave) soldiers. These Mamluks in turn established their own Sultanate that would reunite Egypt and Syria and last until 1517.[15] It would be the Mamluks who succeeded in conquering the entirety of the kingdom and driving the Franks entirely from the Levantine coast. As shall be argued in chapter 2, certain of the Mamluk Sultans, especially al-Malik al-Zahir Baybars (r. 1260–1277) and al-Malik al-Mansur Qalawun (r. 1279–1290), followed deliberate policies of alternating truces and undermining the Frankish economy in order to facilitate their overthrow.[16] Baybars conquered large swaths of Frankish territory including Safad and Caesarea (1265), Jaffa and Antioch (1268), Crac des Chevaliers and Montfort (1271). By the end of Qalawun's reign, none of the hinterland remained to the Franks, who continued living in the coastal cities of Acre, Tyre, Sidon, and Beirut. The murder of Muslims in Acre by recently arrived crusaders in 1290 provided the Sultan with a reason to initiate the city's final conquest.[17] The incensed Qalawun began assembling the siege engines and armies following this breach of truce but died shortly thereafter. It was his son al-Malik al-Ashraf Khalil who led the siege and conquest of Acre a year later and oversaw the quick mopping up of the rest of the Frankish holdings.

## Historians Model Frankish Society

The historiography of the Crusades has been described well and does not need to be re-trodden here.[18] Instead I will focus on presenting what I see as the main trends in the work focusing specifically on the Latin East itself. The trajectory of the scholarship on the society in the Latin East is a prime example of the hazards of disciplinarity. Traditionally approached from the single vantage of European medieval history and accordingly privileging texts written by the Franks or Europeans, the image of what society in the Latin East was like has suffered distortion over the century and a half of modern study. It has only been with the greater acceptance and integration of the information provided by other disciplines and sources that we have, first, seen just how distorted the picture of society has been, and second, have begun to perceive the complexity involved in such a diverse population living together.[19]

The scholarship of the last seventy-five years has largely been dominated by two "genealogies" of historians headed by R. C. Smail and Joshua Prawer. By force of personality, and that of their immediate students such as Jonathan Riley-Smith and Benjamin Kedar, these two schools fostered a relative conservatism of the field that has been bound by Latin texts; oriented toward political, legal, or economic history; and less affected by emerging trends in other historical fields. This is most obviously exemplified by the near absence until the twenty-first century of any work in the field of gender.[20]

The conception of Frankish society has been similarly bound by Frankish texts until very recently. Like a pendulum, the models for the construction of that society have swung from complete Frankish assimilation with the locals to complete segregation from them. At the height of French colonial expansion in the nineteenth and early twentieth centuries, French scholars promoted the idea that Franks formed a perfect Franco-Syrian society as a means of demonstrating their suitability for rule in Syria and North Africa. Although there were several key German scholars such as Heinrich Hagenmayer and Reinhold Röhricht whose work in compiling and editing primary sources has remained useful to today, the narrative that gained currency was produced by French historians.[21] Emmanuel Rey's *Les colonies franques de Syrie aux XIIe et XIIIe siècles* articulated a vision of Frankish society as a vibrant mix of Frankish (read French) and local Syrian institutions linked implicitly to France's contemporary interests in North Africa and later the Levant, through the label of "colony."[22] This symbiotic image in which the Franks intermarried and produced children who identified more with the East than with the West continued into the early twentieth century with René Grousset's three-volume *Histoire des croisades et du royaume franc de Jerusalem* published in the 1930s.[23] Even though the idealized view of the French colonial experience has since dissipated, Grousset's work continues to be republished.[24]

The Second World War, the onset of the Cold War, and the creation of the state of Israel all combined to result in substantial reversals and revisions throughout crusades scholarship. R. C. Smail's *Crusading Warfare (1097–1193)* sounded the death knell for the general acceptance of the Franco-Syrian assimilationist model of society in the Kingdom of Jerusalem.[25] As part of his discussion of twelfth-century military tactics in the Levant, he argued forcefully for the complete segregation of the Frankish population from the native Christians and Muslims due to the insecure nature of their hold on the territory. He contended that the crusaders brought with them the western feudal system, which, above all, required sufficient territory in order to be sustainable.

It is difficult to overstate the importance of the work of Joshua Prawer, whose scholarly contributions paired with those of Smail to put an end to the idea of Frankish assimilation. Approaching the states from an institutional perspective, his work proposed a view of a largely urban Frankish population with its own courts of law and ecclesiastical system. His 1972 book *The Crusaders' Kingdom* articulated the model he had been advocating for the previous two decades.[26] Like the French school before him, he viewed the Frankish polities as colonies, but instead of being symbiotic, they were rather characterized by apartheid with urban Franks exploiting the rural indigenous populations economically. Building upon Smail's observations, he highlighted the complete separation of administrative institutions as a particularly colonial characteristic, with imported European models serving the Frankish population and established Islamic ones serving the indigenous. This society he further characterized as being devoid of cultural innovation and not even functioning as a conduit for cultural exchange between East and West as Sicily and Iberia had. Although by no means all historians agreed with Prawer's deployment of the term *colonial* in the twelfth- and thirteenth-century context, there was an overall agreement with his assessment of, and emphasis on, Frankish institutions, which continued to preoccupy the major historians for the next several decades.

For the last twenty-five years of the twentieth century, the bulk of the scholarship continued to focus upon the Frankish element of the Latin East. Jean Richard, Jonathan Riley-Smith, and his student Peter Edbury in particular focused upon the nature of Frankish government and the nobility. In his *Feudal Nobility and the Kingdom of Jerusalem*, Riley-Smith joined Prawer in presenting a view of feudalism as administered by absentee landlords, and added what he saw as the gradual rise of power of the local barons at the expense of the monarchy.[27] Of particular importance to his line of argument was a close study of the development of the courts and legal system and the nobility's monopoly on these institutions by the thirteenth century. Peter Edbury turned his attention to the thirteenth-century situation in his study of one of the most important Frankish legists, John of Ibelin, editing his treatise the *Livre des Assises*.[28] He, as well as Myriam Greilsammer through her study of another important legal text, the *Livre au Roi*, have sharpened scholarly awareness of the break in the legal systems in place in the Latin East on either side of Saladin's conquest.[29] They have traced the means by which nobles, in the context of dynastic crises and the absentee monarchy of the Hohenstaufen, essentially recreated and reinterpreted the law in order to wrest power out of the hands of the king.[30]

Despite its conservatism, crusades scholarship has not been entirely cut off from broader trends in medieval history. The increased interest in identity studies particularly since the 1990s drew some crusades scholars' attention to Frankish noble self-perception and culture within the Latin East. Peter Edbury and Jean Richard have convincingly shown that legal literacy and the ability to plead well in court came to dominate Frankish expectations of the nobility.[31] Furthermore, David Jacoby argued that by 1200 the Frankish nobility in the eastern Mediterranean had developed a class consciousness based upon French language and literature. He cited ongoing relations with family members back in Europe, the circulation of romances, and the importance of jousting and falconry as leading to a pan-Mediterranean noble culture.[32] In his own work, Conor Kostick has also championed the concept of emerging class distinctions among the crusaders and within Frankish society.[33] Alan Murray, on the other hand, eschewed the notion of class or colony, preferring to argue that the Franks as a whole developed a sense of belonging to a distinct race.[34] He analyzed major twelfth-century chronicles written in the Levant, paying attention to the use of the words *Latini* and *Franci* for settlers, and argued that Frankish society was not riven by regional origin; in fact, it had a burgeoning new identity based in part on origin myths contained in those chronicles.[35]

## The Perspectives from Other Disciplines

While the work of historians, bounded as they were by Frankish sources, led them to construct a model of societal segregation, scholars in other fields came to different conclusions.[36] Art historians had been investigating the impact of cultural contact among crusaders, Franks, and the local populations on artistic production since the 1950s. Kurt Weitzmann established this field of inquiry with his discovery and publication of the "crusader" icons bearing Eastern and Western characteristics in the monastery of St. Catherine's in the Sinai. His work inspired subsequent art historians to try to understand who created these icons, where, and for whom. Studying the icons, manuscript illuminations, and monumental art from the Kingdom of Jerusalem, Jaroslav Folda has maintained that rather than being produced by orientalized Westerners, the art created in the Levant was created by local craftspeople responding to Frankish demand.[37] Annemarie Weyl Carr, while focusing primarily upon Cyprus, has proposed that many of the characteristics deemed to have been western were already present in the art of the Eastern Christian communities in Lebanon and gained popularity due to common cultural values with the settler Franks.[38] Meanwhile, Anthony Cutler has highlighted that most of these pieces of art were used by members of differing communities. He has consequently probed symbols and styles that might have been meaningful in different ways to all in conjunction with identity creation and maintenance.[39] Through their research, these art historians have implicitly undermined one of the main contentions of the Prawer model of Frankish society, by demonstrating significant cultural interaction between the Frankish settlers and the "indigenous" inhabitants as well as an unmistakable level of artistic production and consumption.

From the 1990s on, the work of archaeologists and those who study remains in the physical environment made a greater impact on the narrative that historians tell of Frankish society.[40] Denys Pringle's earlier work explored fortified sites and the role they played in settlement, but his most weighty project has been a complete catalog of churches used in the Latin East.[41] His work reintroduced the notion that Frankish presence was not confined to the coast and urban centers.[42] Pringle's student Andrew Petersen has undertaken the task of compiling gazetteers devoted to Islamic sites and non-Frankish archaeological remains from pre-Ottoman Muslim rule.[43] More recently, Bogdan Smarandache has compiled evidence for Muslim sites and compared them to Frankish settlements, arguing that Muslims were present in substantial numbers in regions the Galilee and Samaria, and that Franks seem to have focus their settlements on locations of pilgrimage.[44]

Meanwhile, the work of two Israeli scholars, an archaeologist and historical geographer, who entered the field in the years following, significantly, the death of Joshua Prawer, brought new scrutiny and challenges to the segregation model. Both Adrian Boas and Ronnie Ellenblum have surveyed surviving buildings from the crusader period, attempting to establish those built and/or used by Franks through isolating diagnostic plans or building techniques.[45] As a student of Benjamin Kedar, Boas in his dissertation and later published works has simultaneously upheld certain elements of the model, such as the notion of indirect administration through the local official known as the *ra'is*, while demonstrating the clear presence of Franks in the hinterland and theorizing the role of fortified farms in rural settlement. He likewise has developed typologies of Frankish buildings, noting in the face of the segregation model that urban buildings actually tended to display a greater level of "eastern" architectural influence than those in the hinterland.[46]

Ronnie Ellenblum's 1998 book *Frankish Rural Settlement in the Latin Kingdom of Jerusalem* has entered the academic canon for any serious study of the Latin East.[47] Publishing a comprehensive survey of the locations in which Franks lived in the hinterland of the Kingdom of Jerusalem and establishing the villages for which the documentary evidence shows a mixed population, Ellenblum destroyed the thesis that the Franks were exclusively urban and lived separately from the local populations. Instead he proposed that the Franks deliberately settled in areas that were predominantly Christian and only started to spread into Muslim areas at the time of Saladin (1138–1192). In this fashion, they created a Franco-Eastern Christian frontier society. Ellenblum also staked a claim in the debate over Arabization and Islamization of the Levant by arguing that there remained significant portions of Palestine that had not yet converted to Islam.[48]

Unlike the work of earlier scholars from outside the discipline of history, Ellenblum's *Frankish Rural Settlement* came to be incorporated by crusades historians and accordingly the state of the field changed. Nevertheless, the process for determining what concepts about Frankish society should be kept, discarded, or reinterpreted, and just how they should be reassembled, is ongoing. For instance, Jonathan Riley-Smith in an article on the relationship between the Frankish governmental institutions and the local population, agreed enthusiastically with Ellenblum yet offered the correction that the Franks did also assimilate in some degree with the local Muslim population. As evidence he presented examples of shared places of worship, independent Muslim courts, and the Frankish adoption of the *dhimma* system for taxation.[49] It is significant, however, that evidence of separate court systems and the dhimma system were used by scholars in support of the opposite contention, that is, the utter separation of governmental structures of the colonizers and the colonized.[50] The trend in the scholarship of late has been toward a view in which cultural closeness does not exclude social distance and intergroup violence.

## Scholarship on the Rest of the Population

It should be clear by now that the people who had been living in Syria-Palestine prior to the Crusades have received comparatively less attention by historians of the Latin East. Joshua Prawer devoted his last book to studying the Jews in the Kingdom of Jerusalem and it remained the only monograph on the topic for over thirty years.[51] Drawing heavily upon the research of S. D. Goitein, as well as the travel literature of medieval Jews (not to mention the usual Latin sources), Prawer carefully analyzed the tension between eastern Jewish groups and more recent arrivals from the West, especially when it came to the debate over the perceived obligation to settle the Holy Land. Although Jewish communities enjoyed prosperity and intellectual vigor in thirteenth-century Acre, Prawer contended that they had very little to do with the Christian or Muslim communities in the Kingdom of Jerusalem. Brendan Goldman has recently challenged Prawer's assessment of the Jewish community, arguing that rather than being predominately of European background and isolated from other communities, Jews of the kingdom were largely local Arabophone Syrian Jews who were intimately connected with people throughout Syria as well as the Mediterranean and Europe.[52]

To date there has been no comprehensive treatment of the Muslims living in the Latin East.[53] Benjamin Kedar has made the greatest contributions in this area. A former student of Prawer, Kedar has consistently presented a balance between following and challenging Prawer's lead. In his important article "The Subjected Muslims of the Frankish Levant," Kedar showed that although Muslims were forbidden from living in Jerusalem, they were still permitted to worship openly.[54] Even so, he argued that they were irreversibly separated from the settler Franks due to the Franks' "low brow religiosity" that prevented them from having any desire to assimilate or engage with the local populations.[55] On the other hand, he has also made a foray into the realm of demography, arguing against the opinion supported by Prawer that medieval Palestinian Muslim families were small.[56] Similarly, a considerable thrust of his work on the Muslim population challenges the idea that the Latin East did not serve as a cultural conduit.[57] Taken as a whole, therefore, Kedar's scholarship on the local populations has tended to temper the more extreme elements of Prawer's model.

In recent decades some of the most theoretically sophisticated approaches to the issue of intercultural contact in the Middle Ages have come from scholars of medieval Iberia and al-Andalus. While the historiography of *convivencia* is long and beyond the scope of this discussion, several recent contributions should be highlighted for the useful models they offer for the study of the Latin East.[58] David Nirenberg's *Communities of Violence* illuminated both the historical specificity of violence against Jews and Muslims in France and the Crown of Aragon in the fourteenth century, as well as its potent symbolic content.[59] Brian Catlos has also thoroughly explored relations between the different religious groups in Aragon, particularly between Christians and Muslims in the centuries prior to Nirenberg's study. Catlos developed the theory that what governed the relations between Christian rulers and the subject Muslim *mudéjar* populations was not tolerance in the modern sense or convivencia, but rather what he calls *conveniencia* or the Principle of Convenience.[60] Drawing from archival materials, he noted a discrepancy between the official legal stance against Muslims within Christian society and the reality on the ground in Aragon in which Muslims, Christians, and Jews frequently lived together. He generated a schema that visualized the levels of interaction between Christians and Muslims and their ritual content. It shows how "low complexity" activities such as farming could more easily withstand sectarian difference and compromise while "high complexity" activities with high ritual stakes such as justice or sexual relations would be incompatible and liable to cause friction or violence.[61] What held this society together was a mutual need, or conveniencia, and once this mutual need receded in the sixteenth century, then the total oppression and suppression of the mudéjars took place. Catlos has since turned his attention to the experience of all Muslims under Latin Rule, including a chapter about the Muslims under Frankish rule.[62] By necessity for such an ambitious project, Catlos relied heavily on secondary works to generate his narrative. While offering an interesting "outsider" perspective on the scholarship, there are unfortunately some gaps in his coverage, which results in mischaracterizations of the society and scholarship and some factual errors.[63]

It is within the context of this turn within Iberian studies that one should understand the work of the most recent scholar to engage the topic of Frankish society, Christopher MacEvitt. MacEvitt's book *The Crusades and the Christian World of the East* is the only work within crusades historiography to focus specifically on the relationship between the Frankish settlers and the local Christian populations. In it he brought texts written by members of the Melkite, Jacobite, and Nestorian communities into direct conversation with the Latin sources to develop a model for interaction and coexistence that he called "rough tolerance."[64] Influenced significantly by the work of David Nirenberg as well as Ellenblum, MacEvitt argued that the Frankish ecclesiastic and secular elites practiced a form of willful ignorance toward the specifics of religious difference of the Eastern Christian groups in order to accommodate cohabitation. Despite instances of violence or discrimination against Eastern Christians, MacEvitt maintained that these were never perceived as systematic or as being perpetrated against a religious community as a whole, merely against individuals. Contra Prawer, he likewise contended that this rough tolerance allowed a significant level of integration among the Christians at all levels of society including the level of governance, that the locals were not serfs in a western sense, and that there was not a strict legal separation among the communities.

There has been important push back on the perception of a more integrated society in the Latin East. Johannes Pahlitzsch, a Byzantine historian whose work has focused on medieval Melkite Christians broadly, but who has examined Eastern Christians specifically in the Latin East, has argued against the idea that society there was integrated.[65] He takes as a given the idea that the Franks were confused by the peoples they found in Palestine and were uninterested in understanding them and, in line with Riley-Smith, adapted the dhimmi system to their own use. Apart from the Armenians, he argues that the social structure of the Latin East that relied on religious and ethnic identity for advancement severely hindered Eastern Christians, and entirely prevented Jews and Muslims from integrating unlike the case in Spain. Indeed, he dismisses entirely the idea that the Latin East was multicultural society at all.[66] As will be seen, I believe that by reexamining the textual and material evidence for the variety of activities that encompass social life, we can find a greater level of connection and influence than this view allows.

The impact of opening up the historical narrative to consider the information provided from other disciplines has been enormous and positive. The texts produced by the Franks and their European co-religionists are vital, but clearly leave significant gaps. As has been shown, and will be further examined in this book, they can mislead us when they are not analyzed critically in comparison with evidence from Arabic and other textual sources and archaeology. Furthermore, while the Crusades were certainly an institution born in Latin Europe, the Frankish states belong firmly in their Near Eastern context.[67] The Latin East cannot and should not be studied from the single vantage point of Europe or texts, just as it cannot be completely understood only from the vantage point of Islamic Syria or Egypt or archaeology. It warrants truly interdisciplinary and inter-field collaboration. It is in this spirit that this book has been written.

## Sources

The book can be thought of as a series of concentric circles, investigating ever larger, more abstract spheres of society. It begins by placing Muslims within the kingdom itself, both those living in and moving through it. In subsequent chapters, it progressively broadens to include those not necessarily resident but wielding administrative and political power within the kingdom, finally ending by discussing cultural elites, men of letters called *udaba* (sing. *adib*) whose work was part of a larger, shared cultural landscape. It is a truism to say that illuminating the experience of non-elites, which most of the Muslims who lived in the kingdom were, in the distant past is a challenge. Both the Frankish and the Arabic narrative sources for the kingdom of Jerusalem are frustratingly, but predictably, reticent about non-elites, including Muslims. In the Frankish narratives, Muslims tend to exist on the surface only as the enemy. The Arabic sources similarly have little direct concern for peasants or merchants. Non-elites usually exist in these texts only as foils for a larger program to make the Franks look bad or the author's patron look good.[68] Getting at their experience, as I do especially in the first chapters of this book, therefore requires creativity and a wide array of textual and material sources.

Published archaeological reports are particularly important for the first and second chapters, on the geographical distribution of Muslims and their contributions to the economy. Archaeology is the single fastest-growing body of source material for the crusader period and has already helped illuminate aspects of daily life that did not make it into the documentary record. As archaeological work especially in Israel and Lebanon expands and is published, there is no doubt that we will gain greater insight into where and how people lived as well as what goods were produced locally and where they circulated.

The textual sources I draw from fall into two categories: those produced by the Franks in Latin and Old French, and those produced by Muslims in Arabic. For the twelfth century, the chronicles of Fulcher of Chartres (ca. 1059–c. 1127), the *Historia Hierosolymitana*, and William of Tyre (ca. 1130–1186), the *Chronicon*, are vital.[69] Both men of the church, their narratives represent well-informed and often firsthand accounts of the period of the creation of the states through about 1184. Of the narrative sources, I rely most heavily upon the thirteenth-century chronicle written in Old French by the author known only as the Templar of Tyre.[70] Although the author remains anonymous, we know that he was in the entourage of William of Beaujeu, the Master of the Knights Templar from 1273 to 1291. Probably born in Cyprus around 1255, the author reported that he was in the service of Margaret of Antioch-Lusignan in Tyre, before becoming an adviser—although whether he was a member of the order remains unclear—to William in 1285.[71] The text remains the major narrative source for the last decades of the existence of the Kingdom of Jerusalem, and the author was himself an eyewitness to the fall of Acre in 1291.

There are a number of Arabic narrative sources important for the crusader period. For the twelfth century, I draw from ʿIzz al-Din Ibn al-Athir's (1160–1233) *al-Kamil fi'l Ta'rikh* and Usama Ibn Munqidh's (1095–1188) *Kitab al-I'tibar* (Book of contemplation), the latter featuring prominently in the final chapter on the cultural landscape.[72] These works are well known to scholars of the Latin East and available in good, recent English translations. Ibn Munqidh has long been used by crusades scholars as a mine of stories about the Franks. I on the other hand am taking it as a whole and analyzing it as evidence of literary exchange. Of the thirteenth-century Arabic narrative sources, I draw most heavily from the works by Mamluk-period authors including Jamal al-Din Ibn Wasil's (1207–1298) *Mufarrij al-kurub fi akhbar Bani Ayyub*;[73] ʿIzz al-Din Muhammad Ibn Shaddad's (1217–1285) *Ta'rikh al-malik al-zahir*;[74] Baybars al-Mansuri's (ca. 1247–1325) three works: *Mukhtar al-akhbar, Kitab al-tuhfa al-mulukiyya fi al-dawla al-turkiyya*, and *Zubdat al-fikra fi ta'rikh al-hijra*;[75] Muhyi al-Din Ibn ʿAbd al-Zahir's (1223–1292) *al-Rawd al-zahir fi sirat al-malik al-zahir*;[76] and Nasir al-Din Muhammad Ibn al-Furat's (1334–1405) *Ta'rikh al-duwal wa-l-muluk*.[77] Ibn Wasil and Ibn Shaddad, also known at least in fragmented form from their partial English translations, both came from well-to-do Syrian families. Ibn Wasil, born in Hama in 1208, traveled widely throughout the region, witnessed the crusade of Louis IX to Egypt, and was sent as an ambassador to Manfred Hohenstaufen. Ibn Shaddad came from Aleppo but was forced to abandon the city when it was attacked by the Mongols in 1260.[78] He traveled to Egypt, entered the service of the Sultan Baybars, and lived there until his death in 1285.[79] Ibn ʿAbd al-Zahir and Baybars al-Mansuri are less known by crusades scholars since their works are available only in Arabic editions although they are staples for scholars studying the Mamluks. Both authors were themselves Mamluks and contemporaries of the events they recorded. Ibn ʿAbd al-Zahir was the head of the state chancery (*sahib diwan al-insha'*), and wrote what was essentially the official biography of the Sultans Baybars and Qalawun.[80] Baybars al-Mansuri was one of the Sultan Qalawun's mamluks before being freed, and participated in several campaigns against the Franks, including the siege and conquest of Acre in 1291.[81] Unlike Ibn ʿAbd al-Zahir, he wrote his works in the decades after the fact.[82] Ibn al-Furat's *Ta'rikh* is also known to crusades scholars through a partial English translation and edition. Though significantly later than the rest, it is an important source because it combines many of the contemporary and near contemporary accounts of the period, clearly citing them, and represents, as the English editors commented, "the main stream of this tradition."[83] To crusades scholarship, this book is bringing into the conversation a number of important narrative sources that have been previously unused since they are available only in Arabic. To Islamicate history, this book offers a new view since I am analyzing these sources with an eye toward a society, the Latin East, that is usually seen as outside of the main trajectory of the field.

Other important narrative sources for this project include biographical dictionaries and pilgrimage accounts. The biographical dictionary is a genre distinct to Arabic literature in which an author compiled biographies of people of varying lengths according to a particular theme. For example, I draw from the biographical dictionary written by the Aleppan Kamal al-Din ʿUmar Ibn al-ʿAdim (1192–1262), *Bughyat al-talab fi taʾrikh Halab* (Everything desirable about the history of Aleppo), which contains the biographies of thousands of men and women connected to that city in some fashion.[84] This work is regularly used by social historians of the Middle East given the wealth of prosopographical information and details about daily life that it contains.[85] Another, much shorter work preserves much wonderful detail about peasant life of the Muslim Hanbali community around Nablus in the mid to late twelfth century: Diyaʾ al-Din al-Maqdisi's (1173–1245) *Al-Hikayat al-muqtabasa fi karamat mashayikh al-ard al-muqaddasa*, edited and translated by Daniella Talmon-Heller.[86] From entries that contain anecdotes and stories from these people's lives, one can gather many insights into mundane experiences that do not normally make it into the chronicles. The pilgrimage literature, especially ʿAli ibn Abi Bakr al-Harawi's (d. 611/1215) *Kitab al-isharat ila maʿrifat al-ziyarat* (A lonely wayfarer's guide to pilgrimage), was particularly useful in identifying places where Muslims traveled and worshipped.[87]

Legal treatises and treaties also inform discussions of the economic, legal, and political landscapes. The Frankish sources, all surviving from the thirteenth century and written in Old French, include the *Assises de la Cour des Bourgeois* and the *Livre des Assises* of the High Court.[88] The former work, created by an unknown compiler, presents the rules and customs of the burgess court at Acre, which was the main economic center of the kingdom.[89] As such, it deals quite a bit with people of differing religions, but usually within the context of commerce. The latter work, composed by John of Ibelin (1215–1266), Count of Jaffa, around 1265, is a comprehensive and weighty treatment of the laws and customs of the High Court, similar to, but far more extensive than, the *Livre au Roi*.[90] As in the earlier work, Muslims continue to be viewed as an external threat, a group prone to ruining crops intended for payment of vassals, or to capturing kings.[91] Perhaps due to the reduction in Frankish territory and the accompanying reality of intensified contact among people of differing religions, the *Livre des Assises* pays more attention to interpersonal violence and its consequences, as well as the process for including non-Franks within court procedure. From among the Arabic literature I make use of some *fatwas* (nonbinding legal opinions), and the texts of treaties surviving in narrative sources, especially those of Ibn 'Abd al-Zahir and Baybars al-Mansuri as well as the large encyclopedia of chancery documents titled *Subh al-a'sha fi sina'at al-insha*, completed in 1412 by Ahmad bin 'Ali al-Qalqashandi.[92]

In comparison to other places in the contemporaneous Mediterranean, the Latin East does not have many surviving documents of practice like charters, bills of sale, legal decisions, trial transcripts, and so forth. Still, compilations of surviving charters do exist, especially from the Hospitallers, the Teutonic Knights, and the Chapter of the Holy Sepulchre.[93] Those touching on the kingdom itself are compiled in Reinhold Röhricht's *Regesta Regni Hierosolymitani* and expanded upon in the more comprehensive *Die Urkunden der lateinischen Könige von Jerusalem* of Hans Eberhard Mayer.[94] Also of great use in pinpointing where Muslims lived and what contributions they made to the economy are the inventories of Venetian possessions and the people who lived in them compiled by the *bailo* Marsilio Zorzi in 1243–1244.[95]

## Methodology and Chapter Outline

Society is a complex thing that shapes and is shaped by many factors. Up until now, the place of Muslims in Frankish society has been largely approached through Frankish law. But the law is far from the only means to understand the relations between different communities. Accordingly, I have studied Frankish society from the perspectives of geographic distribution of people, the economy, political power, and culture in addition to the law. Although Frankish law is relatively well-known among crusades scholars, I have chosen to revisit the topic in order to add a discussion of Islamic law and thereby examine the complete array of legal discourses that Muslims in the kingdom had to navigate and in order to offer a new reading of the Frankish texts. Each of these aspects of society, what I call landscapes, is invariably intertwined with the next, but offers particular opportunities for participation or exclusion of members of a society. Analyzing these categories is thus an important means of accessing just how Muslims fit into the society of the Kingdom of Jerusalem as a whole.

Because some of the types of possible interactions between Muslims and the rest of Frankish society depended upon physical proximity, I begin the book by discussing the geographic distribution of Muslims within the kingdom. Drawing together archaeological and textual evidence for Islamic buildings as well as textual references to individual Muslims and Muslim communities dating from the eleventh through the early fourteenth centuries, I have generated a map of where Muslims likely lived and worshipped. Unlike the distinctive Frankish architecture mapped by Ellenblum, which can be securely dated to the period of Frankish occupation, most medieval buildings in the region are very difficult to date precisely by themselves. Even using ceramic evidence can be fraught as very few types are diagnostic to a tight chronology.[96] It is usually necessary to compare medieval remains with references in the textual sources to determine when a building was in use. Unfortunately, even the textual coverage leaves much to be desired. The earliest systematic census data is from the sixteenth century, when the Ottomans took over the region from the Mamluks. Scholars have long had to make do with the chronological imprecision of the evidence, comparing what evidence can be gathered from the patchy narrative sources with the early Ottoman census records to try to understand the population changes in Palestine and Syria from the collapse of Byzantine rule in the seventh century until the sixteenth century.[97]

Taking my lead from the scholars who have studied the issue of the Arabization and Islamization of the region, I operate with the governing assumption that drastic changes in population were not the norm.[98] Rather, change was usually gradual with some historically verified exceptions, for instance, the destruction of the Muslim population of Caesarea. Thus, if there is evidence for Muslim residence in an area in the eleventh century, barring textual evidence to the contrary, I assume that there continued to be Muslims there, even if in reduced numbers, in the twelfth and thirteenth. Similarly, when there is concrete evidence for Muslims in a location in the early fourteenth century, I assume they were there in the previous two centuries as well unless texts describe an immigration to the area.[99] I place the map that I have created in direct conversation with Ellenblum's work on Frankish settlement and find that there were Muslims living in most of the places where he found Christian and Frankish settlement. I argue that while it is true that the Kingdom of Jerusalem was a Christian society under Frankish hegemony, as Ellenblum asserted, it was not so because of a lack of Muslim residents.

Continuing with the more material aspects of society, Chapter 2 discusses the economic landscape. In particular it investigates Muslims' roles as merchants, laborers, and agriculturalists and demonstrates the important part they played within the kingdom and the larger regional economy, especially in the thirteenth century. Looking first at commerce, I note a tendency of the Mamluk Sultanate to attempt to break down the Frankish dominance of commercial activity by strengthening the protections for Muslim merchants in treaties. Turning to the agricultural sector, I argue that the Mamluks pursued a deliberate policy of depriving the Franks of the peasantry necessary to maintain the kingdom. This often meant killing the peasants or removing villages that Chapter 1 established had Muslim residents. Thus Muslims within and without the kingdom were important to the kingdom's economic health, and were key to the Mamluk ability to eventually conquer it.

The next two chapters move from material to more conceptual realms of human activity. Chapter 3 addresses the legal landscape. Much of the support for the segregated model of Frankish society came from readings of the Frankish texts. In this chapter I draw Islamic law and legal systems into the conceptualization of the legal landscape, to explore the totality of the legal systems Muslims navigated in the kingdom. The chapter offers a reappraisal of the Frankish legal materials by tracing not only the ways these systems attempted to segregate different communities, but where they ultimately failed to do so. It argues that while maintaining boundaries between the different religious groups was important and Muslims were theoretically marginalized, what often took precedence was separating peoples of different social statuses.

The fourth chapter starts where the previous one left off and addresses the role of Muslims within the political and administrative landscape of the kingdom. Analyses of Frankish sources have left scholars with the idea that the overwhelming majority of the administrators in the kingdom were Franks or Eastern Christians.[100] By using evidence of diplomatic activities and the treaties they produced, surviving mostly in Arabic sources, I show that Muslims, especially Ayyubid and Mamluk agents, actually played important administrative roles within the kingdom. Thus while the *assises* of the High Court attempted to keep Muslims out of positions of authority, in reality Muslim administrators in shared lands (*condominia/munasafat*) and even within Frankish territory held a great deal of power. Indeed, the notion that any of the polities, including the Kingdom of Jerusalem, was a self-contained and sealed off political entity just does not fit the evidence. The chapter ends with the argument that it is better to look at how power was distributed within the region, rather than within individual polities.

The final two chapters examine the intellectual and literary landscapes. As by far the broadest and least concrete of the topics under discussion, neither attempts to provide a comprehensive discussion of the entirety of intellectual or cultural production connected to Muslims and the Kingdom of Jerusalem. Instead they note points of overlap and sharing. Chapter 5 focuses on intelligence and knowledge exchange, showing the roles Muslim informants played or were thought to have played in the dissemination of military and other kinds of information. It also explores the field of medical and scientific knowledge, discussing how it was shared between the Islamicate and Frankish worlds, largely through Eastern Christian intermediaries.

The final chapter explores the shared cultural landscape as evinced in literary production. In particular, it examines the impact the Frankish presence had on Muslim authors such as Usama Ibn Munqidh and others, and how they understood the Franks to fit into their realm. It advances the argument that rather than being a disruptive element, Muslim litterateurs easily incorporated the Franks into preexisting tropes, such as the hunt or courtly literary competition. Not only were the Franks absorbed and their presence impactful in Arabic literature, but there is tantalizing evidence of a shared literary culture among the Frankish and Muslim elites. Although the evidence for Frankish participation in these same realms is sparse, an analysis of the evidence for the letters exchanged among the regional elites suggests that Latin Christian and Muslim rulers participated in a shared cultural of literary competition.

In the end, this project is intended as a corrective. By exploring the experience of Muslims, it attends to a major gap in the conceptualization of society in the Kingdom of Jerusalem. It argues against the implicitly and occasionally explicitly articulated vision of a Frankish society in which Muslims were unimportant. On the contrary, the combined evidence from the Frankish, Arabic, and archaeological sources demonstrates that Muslims were central in many facets of Frankish society. Accordingly, my findings should prompt a reevaluation of the model proposed by Ellenblum and supplemented by MacEvitt. There is no compelling reason to think MacEvitt's "rough tolerance" applied only to interactions between Franks and Eastern Christians. At work, I suspect, was a process similar to what Catlos found in medieval Aragon, of the Christian and Muslim communities dealing with differences in ritual content and complexity through compromise and "mutually recognized administrative and social conventions."[101] A future study of shared religious spaces would be able to probe perhaps just how far a willful ignorance of religious difference, as required by "rough tolerance," extended. Regardless, what this study demonstrates is that Mediterranean societies like that of the Kingdom of Jerusalem cannot be satisfactorily explored within the confines of traditional geographic disciplinarity. Instead, they must be approached using a combination of the tools used separately by scholars of Europe, the Middle East, Byzantium, and Judaic Studies. Not to do so results in an unnecessarily distorted narrative.

## Note on Names and Dates

For the sake of clarity I have chosen to use the English rendering of all Frankish names, so I use John of Ibelin and not Jean d'Ibelin. Medieval Arabic names could be quite long and complex, involving a formal title or titles, a personal name and those of male ancestors designated by *ibn* (son of), a *nisba* or term referring to place of origin, and even a nickname, often calling the person "the father of" his first-born son. Particularly with the authors, I introduce the person by a generally accepted version of their longer name, and then proceed to refer to them by the part that usually is used as their "family name" in library catalogs. For example, I introduce Baybars' biographer and chancellor as Muhyi al-Din Ibn ʿAbd al-Zahir and then subsequently refer to him as Ibn ʿAbd al-Zahir. Even so, for simplicity I have opted to use the more widely known English renderings for some individuals such as Saladin, as opposed to Salah al-Din.

For transliterations of Arabic into English, I have generally followed the conventions from the *International Journal of Middle East Studies*; however, I do not incorporate macrons or dots as these serve only as a distraction for non-Arabic readers and are not usually necessary for those who do know Arabic to recognize the original. An exception is when I quote from someone else's published transliteration.

When I introduce a person or event featured in the Arabic sources, I give dates in both the Islamic and Julian/Gregorian calendars. For places, I use the common modern English version—for example, the word *Acre* and not *Akko* or *Akka*. For smaller locations, I use the name found in the source under discussion and give the alternate name in parentheses.

When I refer to Syria or Syrians, I am using the expansive meaning of greater Syria from the Arabic *bilad al-Sham*, which includes modern day Syria, Lebanon, Israel, Palestine, and Jordan.

I occasionally use the word *Islamicate*, a term coined by Islamic studies scholar Marshall Hodgson to refer to aspects of culture from the Middle East dominated by Muslims but in which peoples of all faiths participated.[102] Thus Islamicate medicine was medicine as practiced by all physicians in the part of the Middle East ruled by Muslims.

In this work I use the terms *mamluk* and *Mamluk*. I use the lowercase version to indicate slave soldiers, part of the mamluk system whereby boys, principally from the steppes of central Asia, were enslaved and trained into corps of soldiers. When capitalized, it refers to the regime that ruled Egypt (and later Syria) from 1250 to 1517.

Finally, I divide the Europeans involved in the Latin East into two primary categories, crusaders and Franks. Crusaders were those from Europe, who took the crusading vow and ultimately returned home if they survived. It was a special status conferred by the Latin church akin to being a pilgrim, and in fact the earliest crusaders were simply called pilgrims. The Franks are those Europeans who lived in the Latin East, either who came as immigrants or who were born there. Many Frankish immigrants arrived as crusaders but, having fulfilled their vow and decided to stay, no longer had that status.

*Chapter 1*

# Geography of the Muslim Communities

In the conclusion to his paradigm-shifting book *Frankish Rural Settlement in the Latin Kingdom of Jerusalem*, Ronnie Ellenblum offered this explanation for the lack of reference to non-Christians in Frankish documents: "This concept [I propose] of a mixed Franco-Eastern Christian society can perhaps provide the reason for the fact that the Latin documents and chronicles ignore the existence of Muslim inhabitants. It would appear that the settlement and social relations map had an effect on the mental map of the Franks, with the result that it included only Christian regions and Christian inhabitants."[1] Prior to the publication of his work, the scholarly consensus among Crusades specialists had been that the Frankish minority of the Kingdom of Jerusalem lived largely separate from the rest of the population, safe behind the walls of the coastal cities. Ellenblum upset this model by demonstrating the significant extent to which the Franks did in fact live in the rural hinterland of Palestine, principally in areas, he argued, that still possessed a majority Christian population. The groundswell of support for this new interpretation, however, while resituating the various Eastern Christian communities within the landscape of the kingdom, did not have the same effect upon the Muslim communities.[2] Undoubtedly an unintended consequence of the renewed appreciation for the role of Eastern Christians within Frankish society has been a continuation of this "mental map of the Franks" that Ellenblum recognized.

This chapter focuses on the physical landscapes in which Muslim communities resided, traveled, and worked. Although it is intended to illuminate the human geography of the crusader period, it draws from a wider chronology than what will be discussed in subsequent chapters because of the nature of the evidence and the state of the field. A broader sense of where Muslims lived in the eleventh through early fourteenth centuries is necessary to establish the background against which the discussions of the economic, legal, political, and cultural landscapes were set.

The goal here is to place on the map known Islamic institutions, and villages and towns in which Muslims resided or regularly stopped at (as in the case of pilgrimage). In this, I am joining and expanding upon the work of Bogdan Smaradache, whose groundbreaking chapter first sought to literally put Muslims on the map of the Latin East.[3] This chapter similarly seeks to reinscribe Muslims onto the map of the Latin East, but expands the range of locations to include evidence of thirteenth-century use as well as sites that may have been visited by Muslims but were not necessarily a place of permanent residence. The map reveals that Muslims could be found not only in regions that Ellenblum's model allows for, such as Samaria/Jibal Nablus, but also those it implicitly precludes, such as Jerusalem and the western Galilee. In reality, the evidence of the combined textual and archaeological sources indicates that there were few places in the kingdom in which Muslims were not visible parts of the landscape, even if they were only passing through. Supporting Smaradache's findings for the twelfth century, my work shows that while it may be true as Ellenblum argues that Frankish society was a Christian-dominated one, it is not true that Muslims were absent from it. This argument has broader implications for our understanding of Frankish society as a whole. The physical presence of Muslims throughout the kingdom requires us to reassess our own mental map of the Kingdom of Jerusalem to ensure that we do not remain content to passively reflect that of the Franks.

## Development of Muslim Communities in Palestine

In order to explore the state and experience of Muslim communities in the twelfth and thirteenth centuries, it is necessary to understand the growth of Islam in the region from the previous centuries. The timeline of this process, as well as its mechanisms, are vague and not well understood.[4] The process and pace of Islamization and Arabization in Syria and Palestine, which are issues with high stakes with regard to modern politics, are highly contested. There have been two schools of thought concerning the Islamization of Syria and Palestine. One held that the region had reached a Muslim majority sometime in the tenth century; the other held that it was only following the Crusades and waves of anti-Christian sentiment that accompanied them that large segments of the non-Muslim population, mostly Eastern Christians but also Jews and Samaritans, converted to Islam. The debate concerned mostly evidence from narrative histories, which tend to ignore commoners as a rule and to speak in generalities when they speak of them at all.[5] This led to a situation where many prominent scholars of the Middle East considered it likely that non-Muslims formed a substantial percentage of the population on the eve of the First Crusade, while others, including prominent Crusades historians R. C. Smail and Joshua Prawer, held otherwise.[6]

Richard Bulliet made an important attempt at overcoming the limitations of the narrative sources by performing quantitative analysis on name data derived from a sixteenth-century biographical dictionary. Looking at changing name-patterns of individuals mentioned in the dictionary, Bulliet argued we could see rates of conversion in various regions and determine when the majority of people who would convert to Islam did so.[7] In graphs of names over time in a region, he discerned two peaks in "Muslim names," the first representing people from the initial wave of Arab conquest, and the second representing the peak time of conversion. For Syria (which includes Palestine), Bulliet determined that the second peak concluded by the end of the tenth century.[8]

Scholars quickly noted that the processes of Islamization and Arabization varied by locality. For example, Nehemia Levtzion has argued that the most important factors in an area's conversion were the establishment of Islamic institutions and the presence and settlement of Arab nomads. In the latter case, those regions in which they settled had higher and earlier rates of conversion as the intensive contact with the nomadic lifestyle disrupted that of the settled, non-Muslim populations, leading to emigration and conversion.[9] He suggests that in northeastern Syria, including the Jazirah and Diyar Bakr, there was a Muslim majority, while in northwestern Syria, including Antioch and Edessa, Christians were more numerous and probably held the majority at the time of the Crusades. As for southern Syria, there were fewer Christians except in Lebanon and around Christian holy places like Jerusalem, Bethlehem, and Nazareth.[10]

The question of the population composition of Syria and Palestine at the turn of the twelfth century naturally concerned Crusades scholars, but it was not until Benjamin Kedar that they attempted to answer it. Confronting crusade-period sources directly, Kedar further narrowed the geographic units under discussion. In his study of the status of Muslims under Frankish rule, Kedar reconciled seemingly contradictory witnesses claiming the land was either still Christian or Muslim. On one hand, the Muslim scholar Ibn al-ʿArabi lived in the region of Jerusalem just prior to the arrival of the first crusaders and wrote that the country was still "theirs," meaning Christian. However, the Syrian notable and author Usama Ibn Munqidh and the Andalusi traveler Ibn Jubayr both testified in the later twelfth century that there was a Muslim majority in Palestine. Kedar reconciled them by noting that they were discussing the realities of the particular areas in which they lived or traveled. Thus, Jerusalem and its environs were still majority Christian, while the region of Acre had more Muslims.[11]

Despite these efforts to refine the understanding of the state of Islamization in Palestine, it was Ronnie Ellenblum's work in the late 1990s that moved the debate firmly from simply evaluating the reliability of particular texts and what they indicated about the population, to something more definitive. In *Frankish Rural Settlement in the Latin Kingdom of Jerusalem*, Ellenblum incorporated the tools at the disposal of archaeologists—that is to say, evidence from surveys and excavations—to check and strengthen the theories based upon the narrative sources. Ellenblum mapped all the known Frankish buildings found in Palestine (modern-day Israel and the West Bank) and then compared this map with maps of settlements from the Byzantine period with Christian or Jewish populations. He noted two areas in particular where there are fewer known Frankish sites than elsewhere: notably in northern Samaria north of a line made by the villages of ʿAbud, Sinjil, and Khirbet Istuna and south of Nablus; and the upper eastern Galilee.[12] Important to his interpretation of why this might be is the work of Levtzion and especially Speros Vryonis who postulated the key role of nomadic Turkish and Arab settlement in the rapid Islamization of an area.[13] For Ellenblum, areas such as north central Samaria and the Eastern Galilee were deserted due to nomadic pressure during and immediately following the Islamic conquests of the seventh century. In turn, due to the vacuum left by the lands' abandonment, those nomads settled the deserted regions, thus Islamizing them. Samaria's Samaritan population had been ravaged in the Byzantine period and thus the area was empty and available for settlement.[14] For the eastern Galilee, Ellenblum suggests that weak central government and nomadic pressure were responsible for the abandonment of settled lifestyles by the population in favor of transhumance. Again, this vacuum in settlement permitted increased number of Muslim nomads to enter the region.[15]

Christian populations were able to hold on in greater numbers in the areas around Jerusalem, Nablus, and Nazareth, and the western Galilee up to the advent of the First Crusade. Returning to the archaeological evidence for Frankish settlement, Ellenblum then demonstrated that (1) the Franks did in fact settle outside of the major coastal cities, and (2) they did so in areas that still had significant Christian populations, thus creating a Franco-Christian society. While on the whole a very convincing argument, the model ought to be checked against direct evidence for areas of Muslim habitation. Of primary concern is the assumption that the ongoing presence of Christians meant a lack of Muslims. The trouble from the beginning with the issue of population conversion is that it is not zero sum. An unfortunate result of the power of Ellenblum's argument has been the assumption that Muslims were at the margins of Frankish society because Franks only settled in areas with strong Christian populations. But what is strong? Ellenblum cites Kedar, who believed that Nablus, which has upward of sixteen different extant Frankish sites, already had a Muslim majority.[16]

Since Ellenblum's study, there have been two publications that have made important contributions to the issue of demographics in Palestine. Gideon Avni's 2014 *The Byzantine-Islamic Transition in Palestine* brings an archaeological approach to settlement and population between the sixth and eleventh centuries.[17] Through careful examination of the material remains from excavations across Palestine, Avni concluded that the transition from Christian majority to Muslim majority was in fact a slow process that involved considerable regional variation and also depended on the type of settlement involved. The transformation occurred differently in large urban centers than it did in agricultural hinterlands.[18] The archaeological excavations and surveys he analyzed indicates that across the board, however, Palestine in the eleventh century had experienced population and urban decline in the form of contraction of urban centers and towns and abandoned settlements.[19] Jerusalem and its surroundings did have a significant population decline, but it maintained a diverse populace in which the Christian communities survived alongside Jewish and Muslim residents. Among other things, he points to evidence of shared shrines in which small mosques were built within or next to existing Christian places of worship as signaling population diversity.[20] Ramla was a newly constructed city and capital of the region in the early Islamic period in which the early residents were almost certainly majority Muslim. Over the time, other villages in the region also came to have a Muslim minority. Although Ramla itself appears to have been completely abandoned by its original residents, who fled to Ascalon following the crusader conquest, it's possible that Muslims from surrounding villages who were dependent on agriculture for their livelihoods may have remained.[21]

Although most of the work focuses on the issue of population as a whole, rather than the issue of the religious or ethnic composition of that population, Avni does make some statements about the religious groups living in Palestine at the start of the crusader period. He notes that the coastal plain exhibits the greatest change in settlement patterns of all the regions, due to the construction of fortifications to protect from Byzantine naval raids. While the previous Christian, Jewish, and Samaritan inhabitants remained stable, there was the deliberate construction of Muslim infrastructure and the settlement of Muslims in the area.[22] In the Judean lowlands and Hebron Hills to the west of the coast, Avni points to the networks of villages and farms continuing between the Byzantine and early Islamic periods with clear evidence of Christian populations thriving until the tenth or early eleventh centuries, when there is increased evidence for new Muslim populations in the form of mosques or the abandonment of churches.[23] Even so, he argues that the majority of the population continued to be Christian.[24] In the southern Hebron Hills where there were larger numbers of Jewish villages, it seems by the tenth century a new, Muslim population had developed alongside or in some cases replacing the Jewish one.[25] In the southern regions of the Negev, Avni identifies two patterns of religious change. In the urban areas such as Nessana and Shivta, Christianity had replaced pagan practices, and Islam only slowly manifested in the form of small mosques in the ninth or tenth centuries. However, large-scale raids by Bedouin from Arabia destroyed the connections between town and farms, and so by the time of the arrival of the crusaders, the Negev settlements were completely abandoned. In rural areas where nomadic peoples lived, they continued to practice pagan worship until seemingly converting to Islam in the later 700s when standing stone shrines were replaced by open-air mosques.[26] He sums up his findings by stating, "In contrast to previous assessments that mass conversion was complete before the eleventh century, the survey of sites shows that most Christian settlements in Palestine and Jordan preserved their identity up to the crusader period. . . . Despite the language change from Greek to Arabic, the majority clung to Christianity until Crusader times."[27] It was only after the defeat of the Franks by Salah al-Din in 1187 that Islamization proceed apace.

Bogdan Smarandache has further explored the issue of Islamization. In his work focusing on Muslims in the twelfth century, he has applied ratios to his data for Muslims living in the kingdom to estimate the prevalence of Muslims in different region. He argues that while Eastern Christians were still the majority in many places, Muslims were "predominant" in central

Samaria between Sinjil and Nablus, and in the Galilee between Acre and the Hawran.[28] Moreover, based on his statistics from evidence from a charter concerning the village of Bayt Surik, he concludes that even in the area about Jerusalem, Muslims continued to live "in considerable numbers" during the Frankish period.[29] Rather than Frankish settlement patterns being dictated by the presence or absence of Muslims, Smarandache argues persuasively that the Franks favored settling near locations of pilgrimage.[30]

I argue along with Smarandache that mapping the archaeological remains of Islamic sites from the crusade period in addition to the Christian ones clarifies the distribution of the various peoples in the kingdom. While Ellenblum created maps of churches, synagogues, and Samaritan sites in the period before the Islamic conquest, and Frankish buildings from the crusade period, he did not map parallel indicators of Islamic worship. Instead, he relied on textual accounts from Frankish sources describing the presence of nomadic groups in Samaria and the Galilee to demonstrate their presence there, and the lack of reference to Muslims elsewhere as indicative of their absence.[31] The presence of mosques, tombs, and shrines surely also are important indicators of local Muslim populations.

In the next section I build upon Smarandache's work and present a map of the Levantine coast in which I locate sites with Islamic buildings dating from the mid-eleventh to the early fourteenth centuries as well as locations known to have Muslims associated with them from textual sources. This map, like Smarandache's, adds to Ellenblum's work by providing this information for locations in modern-day Lebanon that also belonged to the Latin Kingdom. The map shows that Muslims were living in the areas that Ellenblum argued had Muslim majorities, but also in areas where Franks settled.

## The Geographic Distribution of Muslims in the Crusade Period: Methodology

Drawing from both primary textual sources and published archaeological material, I have been able to identify over sixty places of Muslim worship, a hundred pieces of land with Muslim inhabitants or administrators, and three hundred individuals. As mentioned, I have deliberately broadened the chronological scope of the discussion. In part, this is because it can be very difficult to date archaeological remains precisely and the textual coverage of regions varies considerably. As with Ellenblum's data, accidents of survival, recording, and politics play an enormous role in what evidence is available. Thus, in order to discuss an area as large as the Kingdom of Jerusalem, it was necessary to cull evidence from the mid-eleventh through the early fourteenth centuries. This breadth is essential to help us gain a sense of the distribution of Muslims in the region. Just as with the majority of the scholars investigating the process of conversion, I assume that changes in population generally came slowly, and so an area that had Muslim communities in the eleventh century would have likely had some Muslims in the twelfth and thirteenth centuries.

It has been argued that the way an area was originally conquered largely determined the fate of the Muslim and Jewish populations. Cities such as Jerusalem, Haifa, or Beirut, which were taken by storm, had their Muslim and Jewish residents decimated and the survivors permanently fled.[32] Even so, as will be shown, these populations did not leave, but returned or never completely disappeared. Similarly, if there is evidence for non-elite Muslim presence in locations in the early fourteenth century, then I assume that it predated the fall of the kingdom as well, unless evidence suggests otherwise.

Looking at the overall map of the region, one can notice concentrations of entries in the vicinity of Nablus and Tyre (Map 1). This is due to the important documents prepared by the thirteenth-century Hanbali scholar Diya' al-Din al-Maqdisi concerning the villages and holy people around Nablus from which his parents and community fled in the early 1170s, and the inventories of Venetian possessions around Tyre compiled by the *bailo* Marsilio Zorzi in 1243 and 1244.[33] Wonderfully detailed, both sources give information concerning the names of villages or *casalia* and some of their male inhabitants. Unfortunately, such coverage does not extend to other areas that also had Muslim inhabitants—for instance, the region of Safad—but for which no correspondingly helpful documentary evidence survives.

Another caveat to keep in mind is that given the fluctuations in territorial control in the first half of the thirteenth century, it is not always possible to know whether a small village fell under Frankish control during certain treaties or not. Nor is it always possible to tell merely from architectural features whether a given shrine was early Mamluk or Frankish (or earlier). In keeping with other scholars of the region's population like Gideon Avni, I have included some of the ambiguous locations under the assumption that there was relative continuity in populations over the Frankish period. If there were substantial numbers of Muslims in a location in the period immediately prior to the arrival of the first crusaders, I assume that there continued to be at least some Muslims in the area during it (even if their numbers may have declined). Exceptions would include a few places like Caesarea where we know from historical sources that there was a significant Muslim population in the eleventh century but that they were killed or evicted, or fled upon conquest; there is no evidence for later Muslim habitation until after 1291. Nevertheless, such places were extremely rare. Even Jerusalem, which is so frequently held up as having been entirely depopulated of Muslims (and Jews) after the conquest of 1099, clearly did have Muslims resident in and near the city even in the twelfth century.[34] Similarly, for archaeological remains, if we know that a particular *maqam* (a mausoleum shrine dedicated to a revered figure or saint) was reendowed in the Mamluk period, I assume that it continued to be a part of the sacred landscape for Muslims and that they, at a minimum, continued to visit, whether or not they lived there. The point is, if we accept that Islamization and Arabization of Syria and Palestine was generally a slow process, with some areas changing more quickly than others, then so too should that have been the case during the Frankish period. Thus what the map represents are the locations where Muslims lived, worked, and traveled through throughout the crusade period from the late eleventh through the end of the thirteenth centuries. These are places where they would have been a visible part of the landscape.

## *Islamic Institutions and Venerated Places*

An important means for identifying locations in which Muslims lived is through finding buildings tied to Islamic worship or practice in published archaeological material.[35] These buildings could include mosques, maqams, and cemeteries. Such institutions are distinct in the archaeological record because of their orientation and special features. For instance, in this part of the world, mosques are buildings oriented along a roughly north–south axis with a *qibla* or special niche in the southeastern wall indicating the direction of Mecca. They are thus distinct from, for example, churches that were oriented toward the east generally, or domestic rooms that had no rule for orientation. Maqams, in addition to containing a room with the tomb of the revered person(s), also usually contain a mosque room. Islamic cemeteries similarly are oriented north–south, with the graves east–west and the bodies placed without a coffin directly in the soil on their sides facing south. Contemporary Christians tended to be buried on their backs with their feet toward the east, and often in stone-lined cists and with more elaborate tomb markers.[36] Besides these distinctive features, all the surviving Islamic structures included in the map also have corresponding evidence from textual sources that help identify them.

As with many areas in academia, however, a major limitation in this aspect of research is publication. The eastern Mediterranean has a long history of archaeological exploration, especially in British Mandate Palestine and modern Israel. However, Islamic archaeology, and crusader archaeology, often treated as a subset of Islamic archaeology, has received significantly less attention when compared to sites and levels associated with the biblical and Second Temple periods.[37] This has been changing in recent decades, with several prominent academic archaeologists such as Adrian Boas, Denys Pringle, and Katia Cytryn-Silverman excavating Frankish sites, and other academic and salvage excavations taking careful note of all levels encountered. Given the extraordinary volume of work being done, publication of results lags behind. Thus, for example, relatively recent articles from the journal *'Atiqot*, the journal of the Israeli Antiquities Authority (IAA), describe results from excavations in the 1990s.[38] It can be expected, though, that additional evidence for Muslim habitation will be revealed in time.

Another familiar issue is survival of the sites themselves. There have been several travelers to the region over the centuries who have mentioned Islamic religious buildings they encountered. However, many of these did not survive to be subjected to scientific or reliable examination. For instance, the eleventh-century Persian traveler Nasir-i Khusraw visited the shrine of Dhu'l-Kifl located in the village of Damun (Frankish Damor).[39] In the 1850s, the British vice-consul Edward Thomas Rogers visited the village and mentioned it having two mosques. However, the village was destroyed in 1948 and so excavation would have to be conducted in order to determine whether those or some other Islamic structures were in use during the Frankish period.[40]

Even when sites survive until today, the fact of continued habitation complicates matters. During the British Mandate period (1923–1948), a survey of the village of Kabul (Frankish Cabor) was made and two maqams recorded, that of Banat Yaqub and Shaykh Rum. Today only a mosque, called "the old mosque," survives, along with a photograph of the maqam of Shaykh Rum from the Mandate files housed at the IAA. The location of the two maqams is unknown, and finding them would involve invasive excavation into the fabric of the inhabited village. Similarly, Andrew Petersen, who visited the village in 1994, could determine that the *qibla* wall of the mosque was old and that there was some trace of an arch below the current ground level that might indicate an underground vault or earlier structure. However, he makes no indication of the period of construction, presumably because he was unable to do so without further excavation.[41] Because of these issues, it is very likely that the data I have collected underrepresent the communities in existence during the crusade period.

The archaeological evidence that does survive positively testifies to the visible presence of Muslims in the landscape. The mosques and shrines with their domed rooms were obvious markers of Islamic practice. So were cemeteries such as the Mamilla Cemetery outside of medieval Jerusalem. They served as markers of communities that could not be overlooked. By placing them on the map, we can see a minimum of the locations where Muslims performed their Islamic identities in plain sight of everyone, whether they be Frankish, Eastern Christian, Jewish, or otherwise.

Another important source of information for finding buildings associated with Islamic worship are travelers' writings, and especially pilgrimage literature. Just as medieval European pilgrims, such as Seawulf or John of Wurzburg, left itineraries of the holy places they saw or learned about, so too did Muslim pilgrims. One example has already been mentioned, the *Safarnama* by Nasir-i Khusraw about his travels to the Mediterranean and Arabia from Balkh in central Asia from 1046 to 1052.[42] The work I have drawn from the most is the travelogue of ʿAli ibn Abi Bakr al-Harawi (d. 611 AH/1215 CE), edited and published in Arabic with facing English translation under the title *Lonely Wayfarer's Guide to Pilgrimage*.[43] Al-Harawi was born in Mosul to a Sunni family perhaps originally from Herat in today's Afghanistan. He was an ascetic, scholar, preacher, and counselor over the course of his life. Besides his travels, he became known in his own time as an envoy and counselor to the Abbasid caliph al-Nasir li-Din Allah and the Ayyubid sultan Saladin. Al-Harawi was given the position of preacher (*khatib*) at the congregational mosque in Baghdad in the mid-1180s before leaving to serve a host of Ayyubids in Syria, including Saladin. He eventually settled in Aleppo where his patron al-Malik al-Zahir Gazi built a *madrasa* for him and he remained based there until his death in 1215. We know that he did enter Frankish lands on diplomatic missions prior to the conquests of Saladin in the 1180s, principally that he visited Jerusalem in 569/1173 and Ascalon in 570/1174.[44] In his work he also mentions that he was ambushed by some of Richard the Lionheart's men on the Third Crusade, who seized some of his notes for the *Lonely Wayfarer's Guide*. Richard apparently asked to meet al-Harawi, indicating he was a known quantity, and offered to return his documents in exchange, but al-Harawi was unable to do so.[45]

Despite heading his own *madrasa*, al-Harawi's biggest impact was on the genres of geography and travel writing. Scholars from his day down to the eighteenth century frequently quoted from the *Lonely Wayfarer's Guide*, including important thirteenth-century writers such as Muhammad Ibn Shaddad (d. 684/1285), Yaqut al-Hamawi (d. 626/1229), and Kamal al-Din Ibn al-'Adim (d. 660/1262).[46] In fact, Yaqut's *Kitab muʿjam al-buldan* (Compilation of countries) which frequently gets cited before al-Harawi, actually derives much of its information from the earlier source. The work, as the recent editor and translator has noted, functions as a memory aid and not as an instruction manual for how to perform pilgrimages.[47] Much of the information presented by al-Harawi reflects popular local beliefs, rather than the consensus of theologians. He will often write "it is said (*qila* or *yuqalu*)" and will give conflicting traditions before adding his own remarks about the true location of a place. For instance, he was informed of and reports two different locations for Joseph's Well in the guide, the village of Jubb Yusuf north of the Sea of Galilee and Sinjil in Samaria, but he writes that the true one is at Sinjil.[48] This is useful because it means that one can trust that the information he presents about the holiness of a place represents contemporary beliefs. It also indicates that his informants were participating in those Islamic practices in some capacity.

A potential danger in taking shrines as evidence for Islamic practice is misidentifying Jewish or Christian places of veneration for Muslim ones. There were and are many revered persons and places that Muslims share with Jews and Christians, after all. Al-Harawi departs from the approach taken by other contemporary pilgrimage guides by referring to places specifically holy to Jews and Christians. For the sections on holy places in Syria and Palestine he very rarely distinguishes a location based on who worshipped there or who was in control; rather it is assumed that anything he presents would be of religious interest to his intended audience, Muslim scholars. There are exceptions, though, where he clarifies that a location was venerated by Jews or Christians but not by Muslims. An example comes with two different homes for Mary the mother of Jesus. In the entry on Nazareth, al-Harawi writes, "Nazareth (al-Nasira) is a city that contains the home of Mary, daughter of Amram. She was from there, and it is for this reason that Christians are called 'Nasara.'"[49] Later in the entry for Ludd (modern Lod, or Lydda to the Franks), he also writes, "It contains Mary's house, which the Franks venerate."[50] Mary (Maryam) is a revered person and an important figure in the Qur'an. In fact, the Qur'an refers to Jesus as "Isa son of Maryam," which may explain why al-Harawi attributes the name "Nazarene" to her origins as opposed to Jesus's.[51] That al-Harawi specifies that the place in Ludd was venerated by the Franks suggests it was not venerated by Muslims. That he does not make a similar comment for the home in Nazareth, which must have been the location within the Church of the Annunciation, suggests it was also revered by Muslims. Accordingly, based on the fact that he does occasionally demarcate places that Muslims do not venerate, I have assumed that all other places were venerated by some, in most cases local, Muslim groups.

Al-Harawi's handling of Muslim, Christian, and Jewish sacred space also hints at how the Muslim communities adapted to Christian hegemony. In the above example of the Church of the Annunciation, we see al-Harawi's simultaneous acknowledgment of the Christian holy landscape, and erasure of its immediate political and physical manifestation in the form of the church built around the location. In other words, he ignores the Frankish building in order to "see" the Muslim venerated space of Mary's home. This resonates with Christopher MacEvitt's model of rough tolerance by which Franks and Eastern Christians were able to coexist through, in part, a process of willful ignorance.[52] Al-Harawi as he moved through the sacred geography appears to have been engaging in willful ignorance as well.

Combining the structures for which there are archaeological remains and those which we know only from texts, I have found over sixty locations of Islamic veneration and worship reasonably datable to the Crusades era (Map 2). Drawing from this map, one can make two related observations. The first is that evidence for Islamic places of devotion is evenly spread throughout the Galilee. The second is that these places of Islamic worship occur evenly in areas with high numbers of Franks and low numbers of Franks. These observations suggest that while it may have been true that Christians lived more in the western Galilee, it did not mean that they did so because there were no Muslims. As mentioned earlier, Bogdan Smarandache has argued that the rationale for Frankish settlement in this and other regions had more to do with associated biblical sites of pilgrimage than who was already living there.[53] Remember also, al-Harawi traveled through these areas in the 1170s and later, a time when the Franks would have had the greatest say in where people lived. That sites in areas with a relatively high proportion of Frankish presence had similar numbers of places of Islamic devotion to regions with a relatively low Frankish presence suggests that the Franks were not a decisive factor in where Muslims lived. Nor, conversely, were Muslims per se the deciding factor in where Franks decided to settle. Rather I suggest that the biggest difference, one to which Ellenblum also points, was the prevalence of nomadic groups in the east. It makes sense that the transition of the populations of eastern Galilee and central Samaria from being predominantly sedentary to nomadic, however that may have occurred, would have impacted all the sedentary residents, regardless of their religion. If Christians moved west to continue an agricultural lifestyle, so too would Muslims. Since major arteries connecting Syria and Egypt passed through the western Galilee, it holds that even if nomadic peoples lived there, shrines and other revered places would have continued to receive Muslim pilgrims or devotees as they traveled.

Where Muslims lived and traveled among Franks provides further evidence of their interaction. From among the religious buildings, there are several that continued to be used in some capacity despite being located in areas inhabited by Franks. This geography includes the towns of Jerusalem (al-Aqsa mosque, maqam of Rabi'a al-'Adawiyya), Hebron (Cave of the Patriarchs), Nazareth (house of Mary), Arsuf (maqam Sidna 'Ali), Acre (congregational mosque, and 'Ayn al-Baqar), Beirut (tomb of al-Awza'i), and Baysan (Jami' al-Arba'in Ghazawi). It includes the villages of Kafr Kanna (maqam Yunus), Kabul (tombs of Rubin and Simon), Ibelin/Yibna (tomb of Abu Hurayra), and Emmaus/Imwas (tomb of 'Ubada ibn al-Samit). These towns and villages were sites of some of the holiest places to Christianity. And yet the current model of Frankish settlement patterns holds that the Franks and Muslims did not mix. Ellenblum wrote, "The Franks did not refer to the Muslim population because they did not settle among them."[54] By naming areas such as Jerusalem and the Judean Hills and the western Galilee—including their cities—as predominantly Christian, Ellenblum implied that Muslims were absent.[55] The evidence presented here, demonstrating that Muslims lived or worshipped in these places, undermines this understanding of Frankish settlement. Even if Muslims did not always live where they worshipped, they went to those locations and maintained them. They were a presence.

Of the sites with mixed populations, it is worth discussing Jerusalem in some depth. Ellenblum and others have shown convincingly that the region of the Judean Hills around Jerusalem was still occupied predominantly by Eastern Christians at the time of the First Crusade. This, taken in conjunction with the detailed and bloody accounts of the sack of Jerusalem in 1099, has prompted the assumption that Jerusalem was completely depopulated of Muslims and Jews throughout the twelfth century, and only reinhabited following the conquest of Saladin in 1187. Even the Muslim noble and observer of the Franks Usama Ibn Munqidh's well-known account of his visit to al-Aqsa

Mosque and his encounter with a Frank fresh from Europe, who tried to orient his prayers east instead of south, had not prompted a reconsideration until recently.[56] Drawing statistical data from twelfth-century charters, Bogdan Smarandache has argued that a 2:3 ratio of Muslim to Eastern Christian names found in charters suggests that a large minority population of Muslims may have still lived in the Jerusalem region in the twelfth century.[57]

To Smarandache's statistics, we can add discussion of descriptive evidence from the textual sources. Ibn Munqidh was not exceptional in the use of the holy places in Jerusalem, however. Al-Harawi visited the complex in 1173 and left a detailed description of the Dome of the Rock, noting the aspects that the Franks did not change.[58] For example, he noted that the gates around the Dome were inscribed with the names of caliphs and suras from the Qur'an and the Franks had not made any alterations.[59] He also noted that they had not changed the *mihrab* of the Caliph ʿUmar ibn al-Khattab at al-Aqsa Mosque. In fact the only modifications he mentioned were Christian icons hung in various places and the location of priests' lodgings. He described the stables below al-Aqsa, used by the Franks during their residency, but in the context of their connection to the biblical figure of Solomon: "Beneath al-Aqsa is a stable that tradition maintains used to be for Solomon son of David's riding animals. It contains a wondrous rock, and the [mangers] of the riding animals exists down to this day. Therein is a grotto which it is said contains the cradle of Jesus son of Mary, [May Peace Be Upon Him]."[60] Given that the entire complex, as we understand it, was largely repurposed for Frankish use as the headquarters of the Templars, it is odd that al-Harawi mentions so little about this. However, it is also intriguing that much was apparently left unchanged and was readily acceptable for continued Muslim use. Al-Harawi gives no indication that he dismissed the veracity of the claim concerning Jesus's cradle or reviled the presence of icons in the Dome of the Rock. For him, these were just aspects of the accumulated religious landscape in which he was participating.[61]

Besides charters showing Muslims living in villages near Jerusalem, evidence exists that also points to Muslims actually living and working in the city. We have the biography of a shaykh from Mardin in southeastern Turkey named Rabiʿ b. Mahmud (d. 602/1205–1206), who lived for a time in Jerusalem prior to 1187.[62] He told his biographer Ibn al-ʿAdim that he lived there with some Eastern Christians that he knew from Mardin and worked as a laborer for monks. He liked working for them because they did not mind him praying, and because he made enough so that after rent he could go to the gate of the Dome of the Rock and bribe the guard there "who always took the bribe from Muslims" to let him in. He evidently continued to live there until his death because he is buried in Mamilla Cemetery. This aspect of Rabiʿ b. Mahmud's biography indicates that Muslims could and did live in Jerusalem, albeit under the clear domination of Franks. They could find employment among the Christians. Even further, they could worship in the Aqsa complex (i.e., the buildings on the Temple Mount).

Another person was the Sufi ascetic Hasan b. Ahmad al-Iwaqi, who also lived and died in Jerusalem and was buried in Mamilla in 1232.[63] He actually spent much of his life in border areas living for a time at a *ribat* (originally an Islamic frontier outpost, but by the thirteenth century it took on the meaning of a Sufi lodging) in Acre, followed by a stint at al-Khadra', an institution endowed by Saladin in Ascalon before it was destroyed in 1191, settling afterward in a Sufi monastery at the Aqsa complex.[64] His biography notes that he continued to live there even after the city was handed over to the Franks in 1229 and many people left. This reference to people leaving probably had more to do with the earlier destruction of the city's walls by the Ayyubid ruler of Syria al-Muʿazzam in 1218 during the Fifth Crusade. Ibn Wasil informs us that it was after their destruction, which the Muslims in particular regretted, that most of the inhabitants left.[65] Another figure who resided in Jerusalem during its period of Frankish rule in the thirteenth century was the onetime imam of the Dome of the Rock, al-Burhan Ismaʿil b. Muhammad al-Maghribi.[66] We are told that he had held the prestigious position up until the city was returned briefly to the Franks again in 1244, and that nevertheless he continued to live in the city "immersed in pious activity."[67]

It is telling that some Muslims continued to live and worship in the most holy of places to the Franks when Frankish power was at its apogee (twelfth century) and most able to enforce its will or when safety concerns would have been most prevalent (1230s). The annihilation of the city's Muslim and Jewish populations following the conquest of the city in 1099 is so frequently invoked that the possibility of the return of those communities is rarely considered.[68] Taken together, these individual cases do not contradict the idea that Jerusalem and its environs were mostly inhabited by Christians, Latin or otherwise, during the crusader period. What they do show is that even in what was the most contentious and politically and religiously significant location, where there was the greatest pressure for religious segregation and exclusion, there were still Muslims present. They were almost certainly few and far between, but they were there. Some Muslims did continue to live, work, and worship even in the city that the first crusaders had struggled to free from its associations with Islam. Jerusalem continued to be exceptional in both the sacred geographies of Christianity, Frankish and Eastern, and of Islam. The imposition of Frankish rule did not erase the Muslim presence from the region's sacred geography.

One interesting example of Muslim activity in a less religiously charged area for the Franks is the maqam of Sidna ʿAli immediately south of Apollonia-Arsuf, in what is now the northern outskirts of Herziliya, Israel.[69] Dedicated to a holy man by the name of ʿAli b. ʿAlim who was buried in or near Arsuf in 1081, the current structure dates no earlier than the late fifteenth century according to Petersen, although historical sources inform us that the place had been revered prior to that period.[70] The story is that ʿAli b. ʿAlim (or sometimes ʿAlil) was a great leader of jihad and a scholar and descendant of the second caliph ʿUmar ibn al-Khattab whose tomb had long been known to be the site of miracles in which even the Franks believed. In 1265, the Mamluk Sultan Baybars camped there, prayed for victory against the Franks, and endowed the tomb (i.e., granted it as a waqf, pl. *awqaf*), after which he conquered Arsuf and Jaffa.[71] Hana Taragan, who has studied the building and associated texts, argues that ʿAli was most likely a *murabit* or someone who lived at a *ribat* or frontier outpost fighting the enemies of Islam. In this case, the ribat would have been Arsuf, a border post against the Turcomans who moved into the region with the Seljuqs in the late eleventh century. Taragan proposes that among the locals ʿAli's tomb gained a reputation for *baraka* or blessing in association with ʿAli's status as a holy fighter and thus became a site of veneration and pilgrimage.[72] The Sultan Baybars's visit is confirmed by his biographer and contemporary, Muhyi al-Din Ibn ʿAbd al-Zahir, who mentions that pigs (belonging to the nearby Franks) refused to enter the maqam and that one time, the Frankish lord of Arsuf Ibn Balyan (son of Balian?) entered the compound and drank wine near the tomb, and in retribution his hand withered and he died three days thereafter.[73] However skeptical one might be about the reality of these miracles, Ibn ʿAbd al-Zahir definitely demonstrates that the maqam existed and was used when it was under Frankish control. Whoever worshipped at the maqam, whether they lived in the vicinity or traveled from further afield, must have rubbed shoulders with Franks and others since they were only a kilometer from the inner keep of Arsuf and half of that from the town's outer walls. Given Arsuf's likely status as a ribat in the time leading up to the establishment of the Kingdom of Jerusalem, it is also possible, if not probable, that Muslims lived in the town itself.

Visiting the maqam and seeing its proximity in the landscape to Arsuf, one cannot help but consider the political statements it could represent. Hana Taragan herself interpreted Baybars's adherence and endowments as a means of tying himself to the image of jihad and a fighter of the Franks to bolster his legitimacy. She also read the endowment of the maqam at the doorstep of Arsuf, followed by its conquest, as Baybars laying claim to rectifying the massive defeat Saladin endured at Arsuf in 1191.[74] Its existence prior to Baybars's activities while it was still under Frankish rule, however, also bears hefty symbolic resonance. Whether it was venerated prior to the Third Crusade or only afterward, it represented at the very least an ongoing commitment by Muslims under Frankish rule to their religious devotion, a commitment that the Franks apparently tolerated.

The data shows us that there were active locations of Islamic veneration and practice in the kingdom. They existed in areas of high and low Frankish settlement. Although these sites are much fewer in number than the known churches and other places of Christian practice, given that research into Islamic archaeology of the crusade-period Palestine is still in its infancy, it is reasonable to assume that there were more mosques, cemeteries, maqams, and so forth in use at the time than we are currently aware of. Those we do know are frequently in very visible, prominent locations such as Jerusalem and Arsuf, but even more so at Acre, the actual capital of the kingdom in the thirteenth century. Muslims were present and publicly practicing Islam in the spiritual heart of the Frankish territories, the actual heart of the kingdom, as well as in other kinds of Frankish holdings. The Kingdom of Jerusalem may have been Christian under Frankish domination as Ellenblum posited, but it was not due to a complete absence of Muslims.

### Muslim Villages in the Plain of Acre and Western Galilee

Each of the Islamic structures located outside of a city on Map 1 does not automatically indicate the site of a Muslim town or village. Some may have been stand-alone shrines like Jacob's Well. Some, however, do correspond with Muslim villages. In this section, I discuss the evidence for Muslim residence and work in places within the Kingdom of Jerusalem. I focus on the areas of Acre and the western Galilee because these remained under Frankish control the longest and, importantly, speak directly to the idea that Muslims lived only at the eastern peripheries of the kingdom. To begin, I will return to one final example from the list of locations with archaeological evidence for Muslims.

The village of Kabul, located fourteen kilometers southeast of Acre, belonged to the kingdom until at least 1272. Ellenblum has identified the remains of a Frankish barrel vault and fortifications there, which he has interpreted as belonging to a manor house. He further investigated the Frankish administration of this village, arguing that the lords of the village were actually resident in the village and not absentee.[75] Even so, the Arabic sources contradict his suggestion that the village was inhabited exclusively by Christians. An old mosque exists at the site, but it is of undetermined date and therefore one could be excused for thinking it post-dated the crusade period. However evidence from the Arabic literature supports the opposite conclusion. Al-Harawi also visited the village and recorded that the maqam of the Banat Ya'qub was located there.[76] Given that the maqam was actually located in the village and not at a crossroads or beside a major road, it is reasonable to assume that at least some of the villagers were Muslim and that the maqam was not exclusively used by transient pilgrims. Consequently, Kabul should be seen as an example of Frankish direct administration of a mixed village rather than of a purely Christian one.

The map I generated contains several lands associated with Muslims in the western Galilee and the bastions of the Frankish presence along the coast (Map 1). If Jerusalem was the spiritual heart of the Frankish kingdom, then these coastal cities, especially Acre and its environs, represented its political and economic heart. These are also the lands where, according to the prevailing image of Frankish settlement, one would expect to find few to no Muslims because of the relatively strong Eastern Christian presence. In contrast, Bogdan Smarandache found the region of Galilee to have been predominately Muslim in the twelfth century.[77] To his data I can contribute additional locations. Besides Kabul, there are several other villages with Muslims in the near vicinity of Acre. The contemporary Frankish chronicler known only as the Templar of Tyre reported that the villagers of Caroublier (modern al-Ruways), a few kilometers west from Kabul, were all Muslim. In 1265, they attacked the drunken remnants of a failed Frankish raiding party and stole their armor and clothing.[78] Just to the north of Caroublier was the village of Damun mentioned earlier. In the mid-eleventh century, Nasir-i Khusraw visited a shrine there dedicated to the Islamic prophet Dhu'l-Kifl.[79] Thus it appears that a Muslim population lived in this particular area, among this cluster of villages near Acre.[80]

Further north of Acre were located a couple of other places with Muslim inhabitants. The modern town of Shaykh Danun is the combination of two older villages, one by that name and the other called Shaykh Dawud. Both of these villages contained maqams for the shaykhs that lent their names to the villages. The maqam for Shaykh Danun might date to the Mamluk period according to Petersen, which would indicate a Muslim population in place to use it. The maqam for Shaykh Dawud also at least predates the Ottomans, and villagers informed Petersen that according to tradition Shaykh Dawud died fighting the Franks.[81]

Even further to the northeast lies the village of Tarshiha. The Mamluk chronicler and official Ibn ʿAbd al-Zahir reports that in 664/1266 Franks from Acre went out and raided the village and hanged four of the inhabitants.[82] This village, about twenty kilometers to the northeast of Acre and a few kilometers from Montfort and two from Miʾilya (Frankish Chastiau du Roi) would have been contested between the Teutonic Knights who ruled the region and the Mamluks who were pressing their advantage and would eventually conquer it in 1271. No particular reason was given for this raid or the selection of the victims. It is tempting nevertheless to suggest they were targeted because of the village's contested nature and proximity to the beleaguered castle, the richness of the land, and the fact that they were Muslim.[83]

Combining the evidence from archaeological surveys with contemporary Frankish and Arabic sources, we thus see that there were clusters of Muslims in the western Galilee and region of Acre. Muslim communities were not sequestered at the outer borders of the kingdom, but within a day's travel of its capital. Moreover, at least in the case of Shaykh Danun and Tarshiha, we have evidence of Muslims residing in areas that were directly and intensively administered by Franks in the thirteenth century. Were Muslims in the majority? Bogdan Smarandache argues yes for the twelfth century. For the thirteenth, with Mamluk efforts at depopulating the country and greater concentrations of Franks in the remaining cities, maybe not. For the purposes of reinscribing Muslims into our idea of the kingdom, it does not necessarily matter so long as the point remains that Muslims were there, and they were clearly visible.

### *Muslims in the Cities*

The textual sources also provide some information concerning the Muslim presence within the coastal cities themselves, including Acre. It is challenging, however, to find or isolate individual residents. Even though some documents survive that list names, it can be difficult, based on a person's name alone, to determine religious affiliation, since many names could be used by Muslims and Christians and Jews (e.g., Ibrahim, Abraham, Avraham). The issue can become even murkier when the name coming from Frankish sources was rendered into a Latin or French form. For instance, we know that there was a homeowner in Acre by the name of Beloais because his house (*domus*) was mentioned in a transaction recorded in 1206.[84] The name is probably Arabic, but it is not clear what that name was or whether it belonged to a Jew, a Christian, or a Muslim. However, because of the prevailing idea that Muslims and Franks did not mix, these ambiguous names are often assumed to belong to Christians.

Jacques de Vitry also noted the presence of Muslims in the city. In a letter he wrote to Europe from Acre in 1216 or 1217, he complains that Franks in Acre refused to allow their Muslim ("Saracen") servants to be baptized.[85] One should not discount the role of sincere belief in these requests, but it is likely that many such requests had more to do with economic or legal standing, since Christians were not supposed to be held as slaves according to canon law.[86] Pope Urban IV himself expressed concern about this situation in Acre in the 1260s when he forbade the patriarch of Jerusalem from permitting Jews and Muslims seeking baptism to convert.[87] He reasoned that they were doing so only out of a desire to escape extreme destitution because they no longer had the wherewithal to obtain the necessities of life. He commented that once they received the provisions they required, they returned to their usual "errors." Accordingly, he suggested that those who were sincere be placed in a church or monastery in Acre in order to firm up their knowledge of the Christian faith.

As it happened, the Muslims of Acre were part of what sparked the final conquest of the city in 1291. According to both the Templar of Tyre and the contemporary Muslim chroniclers, Ibn ʿAbd al-Zahir and Shafiʿ b. ʿAli, a group of crusaders went on a rampage in the city, killing Muslims there selling produce.[88] This in turn prompted the Sultan Qalawun to prepare for an attack, although he died shortly thereafter, leaving the final siege and conquest to his son al-Ashraf Khalil. In an interesting twist, given the concern about destitute Muslims in Acre from Urban IV, the Templar of Tyre reports that those killed were "poor Saracen peasants" who had come to sell goods "as they were accustomed to do."[89] Shafiʿ b. ʿAli calls them merchants and others.[90] Both sources provide ample evidence that Muslims were in the habit of being in Acre whether staying there in the merchants' facilities (*funduq*) or living in the nearby villages and traveling there to sell produce. In fact, according to Shafi' b. 'Ali's account, the Sultan Qalawun explained in 1283 that it was important to conclude a treaty with Acre, "because this Acre is a *funduq* (marketplace/warehouse). Our merchants go to and from it, a place from which comes a wider range of choice for us."[91]

From the biographical literature we learn of some of such individuals. For example, Muhammad b. 'Abd al-Rahim Sharaf al-Din al-Dimashqi was a merchant and hadith scholar (*muhaddith*). He was born in Cairo in 641/1243 and died in 720/1329, and we are told that he traveled for commerce.[92] At this time if he were engaged in commerce in Syria, he very well may have gone through Acre given its importance as a regional hub.

As one of the goals of this work is to trace the experience of Muslims within the kingdom, it is important to note that not all the Muslims in Acre were there voluntarily. Indeed, depending on the time, it may well be that in cities like Acre that served as collection points, there were as many or more Muslims in captivity and/or servitude than those there voluntarily or as residents. Yvonne Friedman's investigations have shown the Franks and their Muslim peers held large numbers of captives and slaves, with the boundary between the two statuses frequently blurred.[93] As Frankish political power was quite fragmented in the thirteenth century, many of the major lords and the military orders maintained their own sets of captives to be either ransomed or sold into slavery. Lords frequently opened treaty negotiations with "gifts" of released prisoners, and once concluded, treaties frequently contained clauses stipulating the release of more. For instance, the count of Jaffa, John of Ibelin, exchanged his slaves with the sultan in 1263, thus successfully concluding a treaty with Baybars.[94] We know that many Muslim slaves and prisoners lived in Acre from the frequency with which they are mentioned in the narrative sources. Frankish and Mamluk sources record that the Sultan Baybars raided the neighborhood of Acre and held tense conversations with the representatives of the Frankish powers in 661/1263 concerning their failure to produce Muslim prisoners that they had promised to release.[95] The Templar of Tyre goes so far as to explain that the reason the Templars and Hospitallers refused to release the promised prisoners was because "their slaves brought them great profit, since they were all craftsmen, and that it would cost too much to hire on other craftsmen."[96] It was not unusual, while the prisoners were awaiting their fate, for the Franks to put them to work. We know that the Templars used, according to Ibn al-Furat, a thousand Muslim prisoners to build their castle at Safad in 1240–1241.[97] When these prisoners recognized that they vastly outnumbered their captors, they decided to write to the nearest Ayyubid lord, Sayf al-Din ʿAli, the lord of ʿAjlun castle, asking for him to write to his overlord, al-Nasir Daʾud of Kerak, to send troops to attack the Franks and seize the fortress. When Daʾud got the letter, he sent it to his (nominal) lord al-Malik al-Salih Ismaʿil of Damascus, who had given Safad to the Franks in the first place. Ismaʿil then forwarded it back to the Templars. The Templars were unsurprisingly displeased when they learned what their captives were plotting, marched them back to Acre, and killed them all, perhaps as warning to the other Muslim prisoners not to try such a maneuver.

Another story about Muslim prisoners in Acre is notable in part because we learn of it only from Arabic sources and in part because of the details evoked about the landscape as experienced by prisoners.[98] This incident centers on the captains from the Mamluk fleet of eleven to fourteen ships that broke up on the reefs of Limassol in an attempt to attack Cyprus in 1271. Most died and those who survived were seized and sold into slavery or ransomed. Everyone, that is, except for the captains who were sent to Acre where they stayed in what is described as a pit for over three years before the Sultan Baybars decided to have his lieutenants arrange for their escape in 1274.[99] Ibn Shaddad provides the names of those captains who survived: Raʾis Shihab al-Din Abu al-ʿAbbas al-Maghribi; Raʾis Shihab al-Din Muhammad b. al-Raʾis al-Muwafiq of Alexandria; Zayn al-Din his brother; and Raʾis Sayf al-Din Abu Bakr b. Ishaq. The prison break involved a bribe, the smuggling in of tools, and a late-night escape through a barred window to a waiting boat. The captains rowed the boat to a designated spot where horses were waiting for them, and these they rode some fifty kilometers through Frankish territory, most likely the lands belonging to the Teutonic Knights of Montfort, to the safety of Safad, which was now in Mamluk hands. With its details of the pit, the iron bars, the sea, and the land, this story provides a rare and gripping account of the built environment and Frankish landscape as experienced by prisoners. It is a reminder that for the many Muslims within the kingdom who were captive or enslaved, life was hard and uncertain.

### *The Northern Kingdom*

The textual sources reveal the presence of Muslims in the north as well, outside the scope of Ellenblum's study within the boundaries of modern-day Israel and Palestine. The most evidence we have comes from Tyre. As previously mentioned, this is due to the survival of two inventories of Venetian possessions in and around the city. We thus have a very detailed understanding of the villages and lands (*casalia*) of Tyre and have a great number of names of individuals. One such person is the man Homo Dei, who Marsilio Zorzi's 1243 inventory reports as being a royal scribe at Tyre.[100] As Riley-Smith has noted, this must be the rendering of the Arabic name ʿAbd Allah. But despite this being a very common name among Muslims (in fact, often it is a name taken by converts), he calls this man an Arab, leaving open the question of his religion.[101] The explanation for this is because it is thought that Arabic scribes employed by the Franks were Syrian Christian as a rule. Be that as it may, Marsilio Giorgio's inventory amply demonstrates that there was a significant population of Muslims in the city and surrounding villages of Tyre. He records men named Muhammad and ʿAli, certainly Islamic names, in the villages of Maharona, Betheron, Femom, and Aiffit.[102] Taken with the other more ambiguous ones, some of whom must also have been Muslim men, and assuming that they had families who were also Muslim, we have a substantial community or communities in the neighborhood of Tyre. That said, it does not seem out of the question that there may have been Muslims in the royal administration, and perhaps this ʿAbd Allah was one such example.

Looking at the men recorded from the *casale* of Aiffit (Aatit), we can see perhaps another example of where preconceptions about the relationships between Franks and Muslims can and should be problematized. For *Aiffit* the Ventian consul recorded three *raʾises* (Arabic sing. *raʾis*, headman in charge of governing local villages and reporting to the lord or his underlings) named Rays Sade (Saʿdi?), Rays Haindoule (ʿAyn al-Dawla?), and Rays Meged (Majid?).[103] Given that there was a Muhammad and Nur al-Dawla also in Aiffit, we know that there was a Muslim presence in the village. Other men with more ambiguous names who could have been Muslim include Baym (Ibrahim), Seid (Saʿid), and Selem (Salim). That the villages around Tyre included Muslim inhabitants is confirmed by a less specific reference to "Saracen archers" helping to defend the city from Venetian attack in 1264.[104] Although it is possible these men were Christians, it is just as likely that one or more of them were Muslim because of the strong Muslim presence in the village. Perhaps these three raʾises are examples of Muslims who formed part of the local administration.

Like Acre, Tyre was also a locus of Muslim imprisonment; the sources can provide insight into the experience of being imprisoned and the role freeing them played in regional politics. Ibn ʿAbd al-Zahir records that in Ramadan 665/May–June 1267, messengers from Tyre arrived at the sultan's camp before Safad requesting a continuation of the treaty.[105] Baybars explained to the messengers that he had ordered a raid on the city earlier that year because they had killed his servant (*ghulam*) al-Sabiq Shahin and his brothers, who presumably were in or near Tyre. The parties negotiated a blood price, and the representatives from Tyre released a group of prisoners from the Maghreb being held in the city. These were probably people seized while at sea as this seems to have been a regular occurrence, and one often covered in treaties.[106] Indeed, just before this diplomatic encounter, Ibn ʿAbd al-Zahir records that messengers from another city in the kingdom, Beirut, arrived bringing Muslim traders they had imprisoned and their goods.[107]

This was not the only encounter between Frankish Tyre and Baybars concerning Muslim captives. Again Ibn ʿAbd al-Zahir records that in 1269 Baybars encountered a woman around Safad, who informed the sultan that she had been a slave in Tyre. She managed to buy her own freedom and then secure funds from an endowment (waqf) in Damascus devoted to freeing imprisoned Muslims to purchase her daughter. She received a document "with writing in Frankish script on it" confirming this purchase and was nearly to Safad before being overtaken by Franks from Tyre who seized her daughter and "forced her to turn Christian."[108] The story enraged the sultan, who immediately sent to Tyre demanding the girl's release, but the Franks declined, citing her status as a Christian. This sparked a series of military and diplomatic responses, but for the purposes here, the story provides further evidence for Muslim prisoners/slaves in Tyre. It also provides some insight into their circumstances, that it was possible for them to purchase themselves and that there was an Islamic charitable system established to help free Muslims in the kingdom. Freed persons could then expect to receive a document that in theory was supposed to guarantee and authenticate their freed status, although this clearly was not always respected.[109] It also shows that Safad in the later part of the thirteenth century served as the major crossing point between Frankish and Mamluk territories. The woman and her daughter made their way to Safad (and not Damascus), which required that they cross Frankish territory, principally the land still under control of the Teutonic Knights of Montfort.

For a while, Tyre served as a diplomatic node with Acre and Cyprus as well. We learn that in the early 1270s the emir Fakhr al-Din al-Muqri al-Hajib was sent to Tyre to negotiate the release of the imprisoned ship captains from the fleet that had foundered off of Limassol in 1271. Although it is not recorded how long deliberations dragged on before being abandoned, these negotiations, which included many messages sent back and forth, would have certainly required that the emir be in residence for several weeks at least.

There must have been facilities in the city that fulfilled the needs of a Muslim emir, including halal cooking, bathing facilities, and places to pray. While individuals like the emir or the many Muslim merchants passing through port would have been temporary residents of the city, the staff required to maintain these facilities would have been permanent.

By the 1280s, Tyre had been under significant political pressure from the Mamluks, and many territories belonging to the city came to have the status of a *condominium* or *munasafah* (pl. *munasafat*, meaning "jointly held land"). Although the importance of *condominia* for the administrative landscape of the kingdom will be discussed in greater depth in Chapter 4, they belong in this discussion as indicators of the presence of Muslim administrators. In 1285 Lady Margaret of Tyre contracted a treaty with the Mamluks, now ruled by the Sultan Qalawun, which established some sixty-six named lands in the territory of Tyre as condominia.[110] I have mapped these locations with help from Maurice Chéhab's two-volume work devoted to Tyre during the Crusades (Map 1).[111] From at least 1285 until Tyre's conquest by the Mamluks in 1291, these lands were administered jointly and would have been subject to tax collection and judicial oversight by both Frankish and Muslim officers. These Muslim administrators would have worked closely with their Frankish counterparts and traveled from village to village in the daily conduct of their duties. These villages therefore represent, at a bare minimum, places where Muslims exercised authority, while still within the confines of Tyre and by extension the Kingdom of Jerusalem.[112]

Unfortunately, nothing so detailed as Marsilio Zorzi's inventory exists for the other northern cities. For Beirut, we know that Lady Isabel released Muslim captives to the sultan in 1267, thereby maintaining the peace between her holdings and the Mamluks.[113] Jacques de Vitry, in his letter to the Parisian masters, described his journey from Tyre to Beirut around 1216, generally giving the impression that much of the coast had Muslim inhabitants. He reports that on the way he stopped at Sarepta (modern Sarafand) and preached to the Christians he found there living among the Muslims. He writes "In the city of the Saracens (Sarepta) the [Christians] were particularly corrupt, and to the best of my ability I revealed to them the lies of Muhammad . . . because some of them were hesitant and uncertain as to what constituted Christian religion and what Saracen."[114] While there are levels of translation here, and it is possible that what Jacques took for corruption was actually a matter of confessional difference between his Latin Christianity and an Eastern Christian sect, it bears noting that he considered the area to be filled with Muslims.

In fact, at this point, the coastal strip was not yet entirely under Frankish control and was rather lawless. Although the German crusade of 1197 occupied Beirut and Sidon, when they left it seems Sidon was abandoned again and not really under any control until it was officially ceded to the Franks with the Treaty of Jaffa in 1229.[115] Jacques de Vitry reports he felt the need to send ahead to Sidon "which the Saracens control," requesting an escort through the territory to Beirut. They complied, sending soldiers who took him and his people "through the land of the Saracens."[116] While the account is a little confusing because he does not differentiate between the Saracens, what it suggests is that while Sidon itself was under some official Ayyubid control, the hinterlands were not and that there were independent bands who attacked or extorted money from travelers. Whatever the political situation, it seems that the strip between Tyre and Beirut at the start of the thirteenth century was home to a fair number of free Muslims with possibly large numbers of unfree especially in the city awaiting ransom or sale.

## Travelers and Asylum Seekers

Thus far I have presented evidence for long-term and permanent Muslim residents, voluntary and involuntary, within the kingdom. Another set of people for whom there is evidence are Muslims traveling through and seeking refuge within the kingdom. Principally this consists of accounts of Muslims fleeing the Mongols in the 1240s and 1260s. For instance, the papal legate Thomas Agni wrote a letter to Charles of Anjou—the brother of the king of France—in April 1260, reporting that refugees from Damascus, which had just been taken by the Mongols, fled to Frankish lands and "immersed our borders like a rising flood."[117] In another letter he wrote that Muslims who did not choose to capitulate to the Mongols "fled with their families, children and belongings to the seashore like birds fleeing before a hawk; there they entrusted themselves to the Christians."[118]

Arabic sources, particularly the biographical dictionaries, also refer to these refugees. So, for instance we know that the Majorcan shaykh Rajih b. Abi Bakr b. Ibrahim al-Mayyurqi fled to Egypt from Aleppo in 641/1243 out of fear of the Mongols. He passed through Baysan (Bet She'an) on the road from Damascus to Egypt at a time when this road was partially under Frankish control.[119] Around the same time a Hanafi *faqih* (legal scholar) named Ahmad b. Yusuf b. ʿAli also fled Aleppo to Egypt; only we are told he later returned to the city where he died in 1250–1251.[120] Jamal al-Din b. al-Ruhbi was a doctor who worked at the hospital (*bimaristan*) in Damascus and fled to Egypt because of the Mongols in 1258–1259 where he died two years later.[121] Another shaykh, al-Fadl Zayn al-Din ʿAbd al-Malik, left Aleppo in 1261–1262 seeking refuge in Damascus, and then fled to Egypt via Banyas because of the Mongols.[122] A further example is Mubarak b. Yahya Abu al-Khayr al-Himsi, a shaykh and literateur (*adib*) who fled from the city of Homs to Jabal Lubnan, traveling through lands partially in control of Tripoli, where he died in 1260.[123]

Transit by Muslims through Frankish territories was so commonplace that it was part of the routine administrative machine. Ibn al-ʿAdim provides some insight into this process in his biography of the doctor Abu Bakr b. Yusuf b. Muhammad al-Hakim al-Rasʿani.[124] He informs us that Abu Bakr was a frequent messenger between the Seljuks and Abbasids in Syria and was in Damascus when the Mongols arrived there in 1259. He apparently wrote to the Franks asking for protection for himself and his goods as he traveled through their territory to Egypt. This permission was granted, but Abu Bakr died before receiving it.

Muslims also looked to the Frankish territory as a refuge from their own political adversaries. For instance, four *mamluks* (slave-soldiers), belonging to the Sultan Baybars sought refuge in Acre in 1269. In essence they defected, and the sultan wrote to the kingdom demanding their return. Like the story with the mother and her daughter, the Franks refused this request on account of the mamluks having apparently converted.[125] There were thus many Muslims crossing the landscape of the kingdom on the major roads of the region. Far from being hidden away in separate villages or neighborhoods, they were traveling the very arteries of the land.

## Conclusion

Although this is changing with the work of new scholars, the current conception of society in the Latin Kingdom still largely excludes Muslims. The effect of mapping Frankish and Eastern Christian communities and noting their overlap has been to promote the implication that Muslims lived elsewhere. Through the suggestion that the regions without Christian communities, such as Samaria and the Eastern Galilee, were the sites of nomadic, Muslim incursion, it has been implied that Muslims were where the Christians were not.

While Eastern Christians have some space as villagers or low-level bureaucrats and translators within the usual accounts of Frankish society, Muslims exist almost entirely as external entities and existential threats to the kingdom. This is especially true for the narrative of the thirteenth-century kingdom, which tends to be described in terms of inevitable decline.

The data I have collected and added to the work of Bogdan Smarandache suggests quite a different picture. In general, although probably an overall minority in numbers compared to other groups in the kingdom, Muslims lived and traveled in the same places where Eastern Christians and Franks lived and traveled. This included both the religious and political hearts of the kingdom. Muslims lived and worshipped in Jerusalem throughout the crusade period in significant numbers even in the twelfth century when the Franks were most able to exclude them.[126] They were regularly given admittance for a fee to the Temple Mount, their Haram al-Sharif, despite it being the headquarters of the Knights Templar. They continued to use the Mamilla Cemetery to bury their dead right outside the city's walls along the road to the coast. So too were they a constant presence in the political and economic heart of the kingdom, Acre, where they may have even been a slight majority in the twelfth century if not in the thirteenth.[127] There is evidence of clusters of villages belonging to the city with significant Muslim presence. Both the ʿAyn al-Baqar shrine and the portion of the congregational mosque that contained the tomb of Salih continued to be used by Muslims in and around Acre.[128] Tyre likewise was surrounded by villages populated by Muslims.

Muslims of all stripes lived and traveled within the kingdom. Many were captives or slaves who spent their lives in Frankish prisons or performing labor, at times actually building elements of the Frankish landscape like the castle of Safad. Others were refugees fleeing from the advancing Mongols, using Frankish ports as transit points to Egypt or even staying for longer periods. Muslim merchants brought their goods to the markets of Acre and Tyre from Syria, Egypt and further afield. They were neither hidden nor entirely segregated from the rest of the kingdom's population. Why does this matter? It prompts a reflection on what it means to say that society in the Kingdom of Jerusalem was Christian under Frankish hegemony. Given the density of points Ellenblum found in his own map, it is entirely possible that more Christians of all kinds lived within the confines of the Kingdom of Jerusalem than non-Christians. In that sense, perhaps it was a "Christian society." But again the kingdom and its society must be thought of regionally. It is unfortunate that Ellenblum was unable to extend his work into the parts of the kingdom that are currently in Lebanon, given the evidence we have for Muslims living in and sharing the administration of lands around Tyre and Beirut. Despite perhaps existing as a minority, Muslims were an ordinary and visible presence throughout the kingdom and should not be ignored or deemed insignificant in our accounts of its society.

The process of mapping the evidence for Muslim habitation in the kingdom not only reinscribes Muslims onto the physical landscape, but also serves as a visual reminder that they were not simply external entities threatening the existence of the kingdom. Rather, Muslims themselves formed a substantial part of society. The next chapters will explore the ways the Muslims functioned within the economic, legal, political, and cultural networks of that society. It will continue to trace the points of contact between Muslims and Franks, outlining the ways Muslims were integrated into the society. Ignoring them has skewed our view of the kingdom itself.

Chapter 2

# "How Many Villages of Yours Have We Emptied?"

Muslims and the Economic Landscape

## Introduction

In an entry describing the events of 1290, the Templar of Tyre recorded: "Poor Saracen peasants came into Acre carrying goods to sell, as they were accustomed to do. It happened one day [in August], by the agency of the Enemy from Hell (who desires to arrange evil deeds between good people), that the crusaders, who had come to do good and to arm themselves for the succour of the city of Acre, brought about its destruction, for one day they rushed through Acre, putting all the poor peasants who had brought goods (both wheat and other things) to sell in Acre to the sword. These were Saracens of the villages around Acre."[1] On the same events, his Mamluk contemporary Muhyi al-Din Ibn ʿAbd al-Zahir wrote: "And when it was confirmed to the Sultan the betrayal of the Franks in Acre and their outrage, and what they did, that they sanctioned the killing of Muslims in Acre, and the plundering of their goods, letters from deputies from every side kept arriving concerning what they authorized and what they committed. Their letters arrived saying: 'This matter was done by Franks of the West, we have already hanged all of them.' And they apologized with this plea which the Sultan did not accept, and he dismissed those who brought them, he resolved and submitted himself to his Lord, and he informed the enemy of his fury."[2] This attack by recently arrived crusaders on Muslim peasants and merchants in the streets of Acre marked the beginning of the final conquest of the Latin Kingdom of Jerusalem. The Sultan Qalawun in response ordered the preparation of his forces and the movement of his siege engines to Acre. Although he died before the siege began, his son al-Khalil, upon ascending the throne, continued what his father started, and in May 1291 he captured the city. Shortly thereafter the remaining Frankish cities of Tyre, Sidon, Beirut, Tortosa, and Château Pèlerin also fell.

These stories describing the events that immediately prompted the final conquest of Acre emphasize the role of Muslims as victims of broken Frankish treaties, while also marking the presence of Muslims in economic affairs. The victims of these rampaging crusaders were Muslim peasants and merchants going about their business of selling their produce in the economic hub of the kingdom. They were not exceptional. Indeed, as the Templar of Tyre himself noted, Muslim peasants routinely brought their produce into the city to sell. Muslims performed a variety of roles within the Frankish economy, from agricultural producers to mercantile investors. In this chapter I will explore the roles Muslims played in the economic landscape of the kingdom and argue for their importance not just in terms of generating income, but also for the kingdom's very survival. As noted in Chapter 1, Muslims may have even formed the majority of the rural population around Acre in the twelfth century. In the thirteenth century, when the population of the city itself surely expanded with the dwindling territory of the kingdom, the city would have become even more reliant on the produce of the countryside still under Frankish control. Without its Muslim economic players, the kingdom could not survive, a fact that the Mamluks exploited.

Any attempt to discuss the roles of a particular group within the Frankish economy is hampered by the absence of a comprehensive study on the topic. A great deal of scholarship has been conducted on particular facets of the economic history of the crusades. Michel Balard and David Jacoby have explored the Italian communes and their activities in the Levant and broader Mediterranean.[3] Their perceived primacy in the economic sphere was eloquently expressed by Balard, who, in a debate concerning the status of the kingdom as a European colony, went so far as to call the Italians its "economic lungs."[4] Besides the studies focusing upon the Italian mercantile activities, there has been work on the military orders and their land management and industrial activities.[5] Ongoing archaeological projects have also contributed significantly to our understanding of the industrial production in the kingdom, especially in the areas of ceramics and sugar.[6]

In this chapter I point to areas in which Muslims likely participated in the economy. It is an attempt to describe the economic landscape as perceived and experienced by Muslims. Accordingly, not every aspect of commerce, industry, or service is discussed, nor are they discussed in equal measure. Rather the emphasis is on the evidence for the economic activities of Muslims and Muslim communities. Due to the spotty nature of the evidence concerning people of non-noble status, this discussion will involve speculation and extrapolation based on what we know about Muslim population distribution and economic activities taking place in those areas. The chapter is organized by economic sector and roughly adheres to the division between urban and rural activities, with the understanding that many activities took place in both rural and urban areas. The evidence shows that Muslims participated in such key economic roles as merchants, laborers, captives, and agriculturalists. I argue that the Mamluks recognized this and deliberately sought to weaken the kingdom by cutting into its economy, both by enhancing the role of Muslims within commerce and by divesting it of its agricultural capacity through depopulation.

## Merchants and Commerce

David Jacoby has argued that the economic framework of the Levant remained largely continuous following the establishment of the Frankish states. Largely self-sufficient in food stuffs, there were also preexisting industries such as sugar, cotton, and glass manufacture that the Franks saw fit to maintain and develop further.[7] Indeed, the Franks in the twelfth century were clearly very wealthy as they were able to consistently recruit soldiers to fill out armies that dwarfed those of their Latin European contemporaries.[8] Over the course of the Frankish period, it seems that the economic landscape of the cities came to be dominated by the Italian mercantile communities. During the twelfth century, frequently providing critical naval aid in their conquest, they negotiated and vied for the best quarters and terms of access to the markets of Acre, Tyre, and the other coastal cities. By the thirteenth century, the Venetians and Genoese were so powerful that they were able to upend the domestic politics of the Kingdom with their own war in the 1250s during the so-called War of St. Sabas.[9] Even so, the Italians, though dominant, were not alone in their activities in the kingdom, and evidence points to a significant presence of Muslims within the mercantile sphere.

The degree to which Muslims were engaged in commerce across and within Frankish territories can be deduced from the frequency with which protection for merchants occurred in diplomatic agreements. Treaties concluded between Mamluk and Frankish elites nearly always included provisions covering merchants from Mamluk territory and their goods. The religion of these merchants was rarely specified and thus included Christians and Jews as well as Muslims. However, the likelihood remains that many of the merchants to and through Frankish territory were Muslim. The treaty concluded between the Sultan Baybars and the Hospitallers in 1267 stipulated that "merchants, travellers and wayfarers from all these said places (i.e. territories controlled by the two parties) shall be safe from both parties . . . in respect of their persons, chattels, beasts and whatsoever pertains to them." The merchants and travelers were also guaranteed safety on any of the roads they chose to take within the territories covered by the treaty.[10] The 1269 treaty between Isabel, the Lady of Beirut, and Baybars held similar guarantees and added stipulations that "no new and unaccustomed duty shall be levied on any of the merchants who come and go, but they shall proceed according to the regular customs dues and the rules established by both parties."[11] The narrative sources confirm that these stipulations did work. Baybars al-Mansuri noted that following the treaty concluded in 1261 with John of Ibelin, Count of Jaffa, the roads became safe and imports (to Mamluk territories) increased while merchants traveled back and forth.[12]

Mamluk merchants were traveling not only by land but also by sea, as evidenced by stipulations concerning shipwreck in the treaties. The renewed treaty between the Hospitallers and Baybars in 1271 included the usual provisions for the safety of travel by land, and added several clauses concerning what should happen to the property of shipwrecked merchants. It stipulates that a shipwrecked merchant would be entitled to maintain possession of his goods without hindrance other than paying the necessary duties. If the precise owner of the goods was unknown other than that he was a Muslim or any resident from the sultan's territory, then the goods reverted to the Mamluk treasury. Likewise, if the owner were a Christian from Frankish territory, then the merchandise would revert to the Hospitallers.[13] The Templar-Mamluk treaty of 1282 similarly stipulated that if a ship from the sultan's territory should be wrecked or stranded in the Templar's territory, in this case Antartus, all persons and goods therein would be safe. If the owner were found, the goods and ship would be returned to him, and if he were lost, the property would be kept and delivered to the sultan's representatives.[14] As will be discussed in

Chapter 4, by this point it seems like there were a number of Mamluk administrators working within Frankish territory. Accordingly, it would not have been difficult for goods to be returned in the way described in these treaties.

The fact that merchant vessels could be also used for piracy or other violent endeavors was also recognized and accounted for in the treaties. The 1281 treaty between the Sultan al-Mansur Qalawun and Bohemond VII of Tripoli specified that the galleys of each party would be safe from each other.[15] It would not make sense to include such a provision unless Mamluk merchant galleys were frequently crossing paths with those of Tripoli.

The specificity in the treaties concerning the safety of merchants from Mamluk lands crossing into Frankish territory and the regularity with which such items were included suggests a high level of mercantile activity. Indeed, in the last several decades of the thirteenth century, there were a number of incidents of Franks seizing Mamluk ships or Muslim merchants. Ibn ʿAbd al-Zahir reports that in 1265–1266 a ship belonging to the *atabek* ʿIzz al-Din al-Hilli with Muslim merchants on board was sailing to Cyprus but then required repairs.[16] According to the account, the merchants requested safe passage from Isabel of Beirut's brother, who granted it, then arrested them and seized their goods.[17] They apparently remained in custody until April 1268 when Baybars took up the issue with Isabel's messengers who had come to negotiate peace terms. They agreed to release the merchants, repaying their money, and to make up the ship's value.[18] In 1272 some people from Marseilles seized a ship on which traveled an embassy to Baybars from the Golden Horde along with a Mamluk interpreter. Their goods were confiscated and the people on board sent in captivity to Acre. There was a peace treaty in effect at the time and so the sultan sent to Acre, demanding their release. The Franks agreed to release the Mamluk interpreter, but declined to free the Mongols since they had been taken on high seas, not in Frankish waters, and because they had been seized not by Franks of the kingdom, but rather by subjects of Charles of Anjou. The sultan only managed to gain the release of the ambassadors when he threatened to close all Egyptian ports to merchants from Marseilles.[19]

The Mamluk efforts at safe-guarding Syrian and Egyptian merchants, their property, and their ships were successful and the evidence suggests a considerable presence of Muslim merchants in Frankish cities, especially Acre in the thirteenth century. The Mamluk historian Shafiʿ b. ʿAli recorded that shortly after Sultan Qalawun's conquest of Tripoli in 1289, agents of the kingdom from Acre approached him about extending the treaty they concluded in 1283. According to him, Qalawun agreed because of Acre's function as a market and the implied number of Muslim merchants (the text reads "our merchants") who traveled back and forth from it.[20] Acre even appears to have served as a sort of off-shore account for Syrians wanting to avoid Mamluk extraordinary taxation. Over the period of several years, 686–688/1287–1289, the Mamluk emir in charge of the sultanate's fiscal administration, ʿAlam al-Din Sanjar al-Shujaʿi, orchestrated a series of confiscations of goods and property from elites of Damascus.[21] According to the historian al-Jazari, when they learned about this and fearing they would be next, people from Nablus, Ramla, and the general area in between—locations with Muslim populations—sent their goods to Acre and themselves fled to Frankish territory.[22] They thus preserved their wealth from Mamluk appropriation. This remarkable incident demonstrates the comfort that Muslims of means had with the Frankish economic milieu and suggests a familiarity with its markets and cities. They knew, after all, where to send their capital and to whom. It also implies that the Frankish economy had the wherewithal to absorb such investments.

Because the detailed treaties we have for the Mamluk period do not have extant counterparts from the Ayyubid or Fatimid periods that preceded it, it is difficult to make comparisons between Mamluk and earlier policies and how they changed over time. But among the Mamluk treaties, there does appear to have been increasing concern over the fate of Muslim merchants. If this is true, then that would suggest Muslim merchants were a growing component of the regional economic landscape or that the Mamluk sultans decided they wanted to help them to become so. In either case, it means that at the very time that the Frankish hold on the land was in decline, Muslims were putting themselves in ever more advantageous positions within the economic sphere at the expense, to whatever degree, of the Franks.

## Industry

Two of the major non-food-related industrial products of the Kingdom of Jerusalem were glass and ceramics. Most of what we know about industrial activities comes from archaeological excavations, which do not tend to include concrete indications for those laborers involved. What follows is a discussion of industries in areas that we know from the previous chapter had Muslim populations and so Muslims may have been involved. This is admittedly a tenuous connection, but it's worth exploring so that we have a clearer idea of the possibilities for Muslim and other residents to contribute to the economic landscape. Knowledge of both industries continues to expand with ongoing archaeological excavations, and so any analysis must necessarily be preliminary. In both cases, the industries appear to have been based in and around the major coastal cities. There is evidence that glass was produced in Tyre, Beirut, and Acre, as well as Antioch outside of the kingdom.[23] Several furnaces were excavated in the 1940s and '50s in Tyre, which revealed massive industrial production of raw glass.[24] At the village site of al-Sumayriyya (Frankish Somelaria), just five kilometers north of Acre, archaeologists discovered a small glass furnace intended not to produce "raw" glass but to work glass into finished products, probably tableware.[25] Although Muslims did live in the vicinity of the places we know were associated with glass production, the documentation we have, namely the itinerary of Benjamin of Tudela, associates the industry specifically with the local Jewish communities.[26]

Like the glassworks, the ceramics industry similarly appears to have been situated in and near major cities, principally Beirut and Acre but also Tiberias, although it was not limited to the Jewish communities.[27] While the coastal cities appear to have been major production sites supplying the larger region, Tiberias seems to have been more locally oriented. However, studies comparing ceramics produced during the Fatimid period with those from twelfth-century crusader contexts indicate continuity, which in turn indicates that the same workshops and people continued to work in the industry despite the change in regime.[28] Accordingly, it is reasonable to conclude that any Muslim families involved with ceramics production in the period before the advent of the First Crusades continued to produce ceramics afterward under Frankish rule.

Excavations in the last decades have given us a clearer idea of industrial activities in Beirut and thus what any Muslims involved would have been producing. In the 1990s following the end of the civil war and as a prelude to a citywide reconstruction program, a number of Lebanese and international excavations took place in Beirut. These projects uncovered two important locations of medieval ceramics production at the Place des Martyrs and Souks quarter, both within the northwest confines of the old city.[29] The excavations in the Souks area revealed the long-term heavily industrialized purpose of the area, exposing many deposits of waste products of not just ceramics but glass and metallurgy as well.[30] Regarding the ceramics, el-Masri interprets the finds to suggest there were three main phases of production in the medieval period, pre- and post-dating the Frankish presence. The first period he dates to the Fatimids, the second to the Franks, and the third to the Mamluks. The focus in the second phase was on the production of common kitchenwares such as pots and baking pans, and more refined tablewares.[31]

The excavations in the Place des Martyrs revealed a site more specifically oriented toward ceramics production. In addition to waste dumps, they also unearthed an industrial furnace and at least four other, less well-preserved furnaces.[32] From the waste dumps the archaeologists were able to determine the kinds of vessels the workshops produced—again principally tableware and cooking wares, with some storage vessels and lamps. They compared what they found in Beirut with examples of ceramics from other Frankish-period sites in the region, demonstrating the wide circulation of these products. For instance, cups and bowls like those produced at Beirut have been found at Acre.[33] Glazed tablewares similar to those from Beirut were found to the north at Tell ʿArqa and Tripoli in the Country of Tripoli, to the south at Acre and Caesarea, and even at Paphos on Cyprus.[34] To further strengthen the argument that Beirut was a major ceramics production center, the archaeologists had the clay fabric of their finds analyzed. Since soils have distinct chemical compositions, the chemical composition of the clay can be used to isolate its source, and the results substantiated the fact that it was locally sourced.[35]

Acre, another city with a documented Muslim population surrounding it, was another area of ceramics production. Edna Stern in particular has worked extensively on the ceramics finds from Israel and is responsible for helping to identify the "Acre ware," which is a ceramics type principally produced in the city.[36] Originally, Acre ware was identified as consisting only of simple, unglazed, and mass-produced bowls. A large cache of them was found in the courtyard of the Hospitaller Complex in Acre, and thus it is thought that they were used by the brothers, pilgrims, and patients.[37] Moreover, wasters were also found there, suggesting that they were not only used but produced nearby.[38] The Acre bowls seem to have been less widespread than the Beirut ceramics, being found only in the city and in villages, such as Horbat ʿUza, Lower Horbat Manot, and Horbat Sefat ʿAdi.[39] Chemical and petrographic analyses were conducted on the Acre bowls and glazed bowls and cooking wares common to Frankish sites by Yona Waksman and her colleagues, similar to the study conducted on the Beirut ceramics. They found that the Acre bowls were indeed made from local clay while the glazed wares were not. In fact, the glazed wares matched with the ceramics made in Beirut, indicating that that is where they originated.[40] Subsequent study has revealed that while the Acre bowl may have been limited to Hospitaller contexts, other simple wares using the same clay were also made and more widely consumed in the area.[41] These wares include jars, sugar vessels, and lamps that are found in quantities in most excavations in and around Acre.

Unfortunately, the textual sources have little to say about the ceramics industry. It does show up in the assises of the Cour des Bourgeois, which stipulated tariffs for ceramics imported and exported from Muslim lands.[42] The archaeology amply demonstrates both the significant local production of these wares and their regional circulation. It is therefore clear that this industry was an important part of the economic landscape. The principal production sites we know of were Beirut and Acre, both of which had significant Muslim communities, including unfree workforces. According to a recent survey of the published material, nearly all the glazed cooking ware found in areas that were part of the kingdom originated in Beirut, reflecting continuity with what was produced prior to the conquests of the First Crusade. This suggests that the workshops and their workforce producing ceramics in the Fatimid period continued operating under the Franks.[43] As noted, similar continuity in production is found at Tiberias. Additionally, we know, for instance, that the Hospitallers maintained large numbers of captives whom they would set to work. They easily could have been involved in the production of the large quantities of cheap bowls required to serve the pilgrims and patients of the hospital. Given their proximity, it is entirely reasonable to think that Muslims participated in the production and circulation of these wares, either as merchants buying and shipping the wares to the interior, artisans, or laborers doing the hard work of maintaining the furnaces and moving the product.

## Slaves and Captives

An unfortunate reality confronting Muslims in the region was the serious risk of enslavement. Many of the Muslims traveling through or living in the kingdom did so as captives or slaves. The slave trade became an ever more important aspect of commercial activities in the Mediterranean over the course of the Middle Ages. In the thirteenth century, the Frankish cities of the Kingdom of Jerusalem functioned as key ports of call in the shipping of enslaved peoples from the Black Sea region to Egypt to become mamluks. The cities would have been full of these enslaved people during the spring and fall sailing seasons as the Venetians, and after 1261, the Genoese, transported their human cargoes.[44] Although not all the slaves living in or traveling through the kingdom would have been Muslim, a large percentage of them were—or, in the case of the mamluks, were destined to become so.

While hundreds or even thousands of enslaved people passed through Frankish ports to Egypt, many Muslims resided within the Kingdom as captives. Yvonne Friedman, who has written on the history of captivity and ransom in the kingdom, noted that despite a well-developed system of ransom between the Byzantine Empire and the Seljuks and Abbasids, the Franks were slow to join in the practice of captive taking. Even after coming to understand the advantages of taking captives in the twelfth century, they were used more for prisoner exchange rather than for monetary gain. This seems to have changed in the thirteenth century when ransom became more frequent.[45]

There can be little doubt that throughout its existence there were considerable numbers of local captives in the kingdom, most of them Muslims, awaiting their ransom. Usama Ibn Munqidh paints a picture of a regular system of captive taking and ransoming in his *Book of Contemplation*, noting that the Franks "used to bring their captives before me so that I might buy their freedom," which involved both direct payment in cash on the spot and guarantees for later payment.[46] He ransomed captives not only on his own behalf but also for others as an act of charity. Many of the captives were peasants seized during Frankish raids as part of the booty. Two examples from the thirteenth century were the Hospitaller raid on Hama and another on Homs, both in 1204.[47] It is telling that the lord of Homs' reaction was to launch his own raid that resulted in seized cattle. It is unclear whether this was by choice or circumstance, but it shows that both peasants and cattle were seen in material terms and as such could face a precarious existence. Like cattle, captives had monetary value in their ransom price, and like cattle they were often put to work. Many people also were sold to Franks by the Mongols as they pressed into Syria. Although the number must be exaggerated, Ibn al-Furat reports that as many as a hundred thousand women and children were captured by the Mongols when they took Aleppo in 1260, and most were sold to the Franks and Armenians.[48]

General references to captives appear regularly in the narrative sources. A release of prisoners was a routine "gift" brought by emissaries seeking to open treaty negotiations. For instance, the lord of Hama sent a group of prisoners to the Franks in 1214–1215 in order to smooth the way for a cessation in the raids referenced above. Ibn Wasil reports that they were pleased by the prisoners and were reconciled with him.[49]

Prisoner release was also frequently invoked in the conclusion of treaties and could be a significant sticking point in carrying out those treaties. The Muslim historians frequently complain about the Frankish failure to release prisoners as they had agreed. For instance, the failed release of Muslim prisoners was a major source of contention in the negotiations between Baybars and the Franks of Acre in 661/1262–1263.[50] In 1275 Baybars used the death of Bohemond VI and the regency of his teenage son Bohemond VII as an excuse to press claims on the city of Latakia. Over the course of negotiations, the Franks agreed to release two hundred Muslim prisoners and to make a tribute of 20,000 dinars.[51] The Hospitallers agreed to release all their Muslim captives to secure a continued truce with Qalawun in 1281.[52]

So widespread was the problem that freeing Muslim prisoners became a major focus of charitable works. As noted, it seems that Usama Ibn Munqidh engaged in this form of charity when he passed through Frankish territory. Often Muslims from outside of the kingdom created special waqfs or endowments for the purpose of helping to ransom their coreligionists held captive by the Franks.[53] For instance, from the biographical dictionary of Kamal al-Din Ibn al-ʿAdim, we know that on his deathbed Abu Bakr bin Yusuf al-Hakim al-Rasʿani, who was discussed in the previous chapter, willed that a third of his property be used in charity for the release of prisoners.[54] In 1265, following the Mamluk conquest of Arsuf, the Mamluk Fakhr al-Din b. Julban along with other Muslims were released from Frankish captivity thanks to money from a waqf established by the emir Jamal al-Din al-Nujaybi. We are told the released prisoners made their way to Damascus where a qadi arranged marriages for the women, again with the help of the waqf.[55] Ibn Shaddad relates the story of a man whose generosity was exemplified by sending money to Frankish lands in order to purchase the release of Muslim prisoners in 1273–1274.[56] He also presents the obituary of Faris al-Din al-Salihi al-Mustaʿrib who helped negotiate a treaty between the first Mamluk Sultan al-Malik al-Muʿizz Aybak and the Franks, and whose contribution included the release of Muslim prisoners.[57] Ibn Wasil highlighted the charitable nature of the general al-Malik al-Muʿazzam Muzaffar al-Din Kukburi (d. 630/1233) by emphasizing the vast amount of dinars and dirhams he sent to the Franks for the purposes of freeing Muslim captives.[58]

Unsurprisingly, given the unhappy circumstances under which people most often found themselves subject to captivity, the Arabic sources tend to paint the Franks in a negative light when it came to their treatment of

Muslim prisoners. In his account of the capture of Safad in 1266, Ibn al-Furat comments that the surrendering Templars attempted to pass off some of their Muslim captives as Christians so that they could be taken with the retreating order as they made their way to the coast. He adds that this was "a thing that they also did with the children of the Muslims whom they had as prisoners."[59] This was not the only attack leveled against the Franks concerning their perfidy when it came to Muslim children. Philip de Montfort, lord of Tyre, in particular was criticized for treating Muslim captives poorly. A story provided by Ibn al-Furat and mentioned briefly in the previous chapter relates that in 1268–1269 when Baybars was traveling from Egypt to Syria, he came across a former captive woman who complained to him about her treatment at the hands of the Franks of Tyre. He reports:

> On Baibars' arrival in Syria he was approached by a woman who said that she had been a prisoner in Tyre: she had bought her own freedom and she had got a ransom price fixed for a daughter of hers; she had then obtained a sum from the waqfs of Damascus and with this she had bought the girl from Tyre, getting a document with writing in Frankish script on it: after she had brought the girl out, when they had nearly reached the territory of Safad (Saphet), a band of men who had been sent after her from Tyre took the girl and forced her to turn Christian. When the Sultan heard this story, his anger was stirred in the cause of Almighty God and he wrote demanding the girl. The Franks, however, excused themselves (from complying) on the ground that she had become a Christian.[60]

The account of the girl snatched away from her mother upon nearly reaching the safety of Safad paints a particularly cruel picture of the Franks. In contrast to the pious industriousness of the mother, the Franks are faithless animals willing to break their own laws as well as that of the bond between mother and daughter in order to gain a convert. While surely deployed here in order to emphasize the righteousness of the Sultan Baybars's response, the story also reflects an anxiety felt by Muslims about forcible conversion.

The story provides a number of other vital pieces of information about the experience of Muslims in captivity. One is that the line between captivity and slavery was blurred. The woman purchased her own freedom presumably through her own labor. Given the lengths to which she subsequently went to free her daughter, one might suppose that had she access to her own funds, she would have used them to free her daughter first. Regardless, we know that she didn't have access to funds of her own for her daughter after she freed herself, but was able to secure the release of her daughter through money from a Damascene waqf. That she was able to contact the agents of the waqf from Tyre indicates there were open lines of communication between the cities. Perhaps there were even agents operating in the Frankish cities in order to administer the ransoms as there were in contemporary Iberia.[61] We also learn that freed Muslims could then expect to receive a document declaring their free status, which would in theory allow them to pass through Frankish territory on their way home.

Captives were routinely used for their labor, further blurring the line between imprisonment and slavery. Ibn Jubayr mentions seeing captives in chains put to work and Yvonne Friedman suggests that the reason Salah al-Din was able to free so many captives upon conquering the unfinished castle at Jacob's Ford was their use in its construction.[62] In 1263 the military orders jeopardized a truce with Baybars because of their reluctance to release Muslim prisoners. The Templar of Tyre reports that the agreement was for two Muslims to be released for every Christian, which "seemed to [the Christians] good" but the Hospitallers and Templars refused "saying that their slaves brought them great profit, since they were all craftsmen, and that it would cost too much to hire on other craftsmen."[63] Ibn al-Furat corroborates, relating an exchange of letters between Baybars and Hugh Revel, the Master of the Hospitallers. Baybars complained to Hugh that they and the Templars avoided returning Muslim prisoners by transferring them back and forth among themselves. He accused them of showing no pity for their coreligionists by failing to make the exchange "lest the work done for you by the Muslim prisoners you held might have to be abandoned."[64] The Franks clearly valued the economic contribution of these Muslim captives.

The work these captives were put to varied. The mother, based in Tyre, might have worked in a domestic or service setting. In 1266 Baybars refused to renew a treaty with Jaffa because, among other things, he heard rumors that Franks were forcing Muslim women to work in taverns in the city.[65] Others were made to labor on massive construction projects. In addition to their likely use in building the castle at Jacob's Ford, as mentioned in the previous chapter, Ibn al-Furat tells us that nearly a thousand prisoners were sent to Safad to build the castle there. They were able to send word to Sayf al-Din ʿAli bin Qilij al-Nuri, the ruler of Ajlun, that their Frankish overseers were greatly outnumbered and suggested he write to his lord, the ruler of Kerak, asking for permission to attack. This came to naught because a treaty was in place and the letter eventually was forwarded back to the Templars who took the prisoners back to Acre and killed them.[66] In this story, we see Muslims contributing to the economy through their labor in castle building, actually erecting the kingdom's infrastructure, while also embodying the potential revenues accrued from ransom. Like the case of the mother trying to recover her daughter, this example also signals the ease of communication between Muslims of even the lowest status, in this case slaves and captives, with Muslims outside the kingdom.

As captives and slaves, Muslims functioned within the Frankish economy as both agents and objects of value. Because of the blurred line between captivity and slavery, they embodied revenue both as slaves for sale, and captives for ransom. Their labor also contributed to the economy in various ways, whether by building infrastructure or performing service activities. Given the constant flow of taking and exchanging prisoners, the impact of these people on the economy must have been considerable.

## Peasant Farmers and Agriculture

Trade and commerce were important aspects of the kingdom's economy, but its foundation, like those of its European peers, was agriculture. Life was not easy for peasants of any community in the kingdom. Even so, they had the advantage over their European peers with regard to legal status and obligations. As Christopher MacEvitt has convincingly argued, peasants in the crusader states were tied to the land, but did not have the same status or obligations as European serfs. They did not have to pay a servile head tax (*chevage*). They could have heirs of the body and so their possessions did not revert to their lords upon death like those subject to *mainmort*. Finally they did not have to perform *corvée*, obligatory, unpaid labor on lords' estates.[67] As a point of comparison, Ibn Jubayr famously lamented following his visit in the 1180s that the Muslim peasants in Frankish Syria had a better deal than their counterparts living under Muslim lordship.[68] He reports that they paid half their crops, a head tax, and some of their fruits. One must be cautious when using Ibn Jubayr's comments because he paints a broad picture, and we know that taxation varied from lordship to lordship.[69] Moreover, he was likely interested in shaming the local Syrian Muslim lords with whose relative inaction against the Franks he was displeased. Nevertheless, it gives a sense of the relatively decent treatment Frankish peasants received.

Landholding at the peasant level in Palestine and Syria is not well understood until the Ottoman period. Studies for the crusader period have often focused on Tyre, from which some generalizations can be extrapolated.[70] Overall, it seems that land belonged to a given village and was divided among the villagers in a system called *musha'*.[71] We do know that during the crusader period, the basic agricultural land unit was the village or *casal* and that land was measured in *carrucas*, the amount of land that could be plowed by a team of oxen in a day.[72] Arriving at numbers of *casalia* for each town and who owned them is tricky. Best known are the lands around Tyre thanks in large part to Marsilio Zorzi's inventory. Joshua Prawer calculated that Tyre possessed around a hundred twenty villages, of which the Venetians held sixteen to twenty-one outright in their entirety and another fifty-one of which they held a third.[73]

As David Jacoby has argued, the crusader states were fully integrated into the wider regional economy, participating in the circulation of goods and foodstuffs around the Mediterranean region and beyond. Further, he contended that the agricultural sector changed little in the immediate aftermath of the creation of the Kingdom of Jerusalem.[74] The Frankish arrival did not disrupt rural infrastructure and the previous kinds of agricultural production continued unchanged. The Franks "were careful to preserve their rural workforce" and inserted themselves into this rural framework using extracted incomes to support themselves.[75]

The political realities of the thirteenth-century Eastern Mediterranean meant that the Latin Kingdom had ever-dwindling arable lands. While the area would have been largely self-sufficient in foodstuffs during the eleventh and twelfth centuries, in the thirteenth and especially following the conquests of Baybars in the 1260s, the Latin Kingdom's ability to feed itself fell dramatically.[76] Instead the Franks became dependent upon imports from Muslim-ruled lands and Sicily. The small size of the Frankish strip of coastal territory is often one of the first descriptors used when discussing the thirteenth-century Latin East in order to point to the decreasing ability to support domestic military forces. Instead, the kingdom became more reliant on externally funded military forces such as those under Geoffrey of Sergines, left by King Louis IX of France when he returned to the West in 1254, and those by Frederick II under the leadership of Richard Filangieri. At the base of this problem was decreased economic output. As the borders of the kingdom collapsed from the 1260s on, the territory that remained grew in importance. At the same time, and perhaps encouraged by this diminishment of arable land, landlords, especially the military orders and Italian communes, transitioned to cash and industrial crops like sugar and cotton. This required investment in irrigation and mill infrastructure and prompted some significant litigation over river use.[77]

Crops varied by region, so it is worth discussing these with regard to the areas in which Muslims lived as presented in the previous chapter. Samaria, the mountainous region bounded on the north by the Jezreel Valley, the east by the Jordan Valley, and the south by the Judean hills, now largely falling within the Palestinian West Bank, contained an important Muslim population.[78] In central Samaria around the city of Nablus where many Muslims lived, products included olives and orchards as well as cattle, sheep, and goats.[79] Daniel the Russian, who traveled through on pilgrimage in 1106, likened the groves surrounding Nablus to dense forests.[80] Nablus itself was a major center for olive processing, making olive oil and soap. Although the Franks never recovered the city after it fell in 1187, the farmers of the region, regardless of where they lived with respect to political borders, would have continued to harvest their olives and process them.

To the north of Samaria lies the Galilee, ending in the north with the Litani River (modern-day southern Lebanon) and bounded on the east by the Jordan Valley and the west by the Carmel range along the coast. In both Samaria and the eastern Galilee lived significant numbers of nomadic peoples, such as the Bedouin and Turcomans. Although invoked often as brigands or sources of instability, they also participated in the economy of the kingdom and the region at large, particularly in their capacity as herders, raising sheep, goats, and cattle. From early on in the twelfth century, efforts were made to monitor, control, and extract taxes from these groups, with the military orders coming to play the predominant role as the century wore on.[81] The assises of the Cour des Bourgeois had a tariff on goats imported from Muslim territory, indicating the licit role these nomadic groups probably played in the regional economy.[82] More often, though, Bedouin and Turcomans enter the historical record as the victims of cattle rustling. Ibn al-Furat reports a Frankish raid against the territory of Homs in 1204–1205 that resulted in a counterattack by al-Malik al-Mujahid, the lord of the city, that drove the Franks back to Crac des Chevaliers and in the process seized sheep and cattle.[83] Ibn Wasil reports another raid by the Franks at Baghras in 1237–1238 against the Turcomans of the region that included seizing their cattle.[84] In 1239 the crusader contingent led by Peter Count of Brittany, operating out of Jaffa, raided a caravan on its way from Egypt to Damascus, seizing among the plunder a great quantity of livestock.[85] Later, in 1271, there was a major Frankish raid against the castle of Caco. It failed to take the fortress, but the Franks did attack nearby Turcoman bands, killing many and seizing "a great number of large and small animals."[86] Finally, Turcomans in the region of Chastel Blanc had the misfortune of crossing paths with Hospitallers on their way home to Margat in 1277. The Hospitallers attacked, slaying many, and seized a large number of animals and other loot.[87] The Franks were not the only ones to engage in cattle raiding. Ibn ʿAbd al-Zahir reports that a group of Turcomans raided around Haifa in 1266 taking a lot of cattle.[88] From these examples it is clear that cattle rustling was a common way for a side to extract economic gain from the enemy, and more often than not, it seems to have been at the expense of the nomadic Muslim groups of the region.

Concerning plant agriculture in the Galilee, vine growing and wine making were important parts of the local economy.[89] From tariff lists for the market at Acre, we know that Galilee was a major source of wine. The *Assises de la Cour des Bourgeois*, which lists tariffs placed on merchandise bought and sold in Acre, names Nazareth specifically as a producer of wine, requiring that for every camel-load the market takes two small kegs and fourteen *drahans*.[90] It also places a tariff on wine from Muslim-controlled territory, what it labels *Païenime*, at three and a half drahans for each wineskin.[91]

It might come as a surprise to think of Muslims participating in the wine industry because of the Islamic prohibition against drinking it, and yet across the Islamic world, viticulture continued apace.[92] Pauline Lewicka, in her study of alcohol production and consumption in medieval Egypt, found that it was only in the later thirteenth century and even after, that ideologies against drinking alcohol became internalized by the local Muslim populations. Prior to the Mamluks, the enforcement of the prohibition was sporadic, torn between the desire to oppose vice and the desire to reap the financial benefits of taxation.[93] The Cairo Geniza documents of the Jewish community suggest that society operated along a sort of compromise. People would purchase (or grow) their own grapes to be turned into wine. They would take their grapes to a professional presser (*ma'sara*) who was often a Jew, and then they would take the juice and ferment it themselves.[94] In this way, they would not be purchasing wine; they would be producing their own under the radar, so to speak. Even so, there was a "wine-sellers' street" in both medieval Fustat and Cairo, where wine was openly sold not just by Christians and Jews but by Muslims such as "Ahmad the wine-seller."[95] It is possible that a similar kind of system operated in the crusader states. In this case, it is likely that the pressing facilities were controlled by the local landlord similarly to how they controlled ovens and mills.[96] This is the conclusion that Rabei Khamisy has proposed for the large wine press he excavated at Miʿilya.[97] People would have brought their grapes there to be pressed in exchange for a fee and then ferment them at home. Even the relatively conservative Hanbali community living around Nablus, which rejected playing music as haram, engaged in growing grapes, although they probably consumed only the fruit.[98]

The Galilee was also an important grain-growing region.[99] Archaeologists and scientists have tied the settlement and population of the region to rainfall. During the first centuries after the Arab conquest, evidence suggests that annual rainfall was less than the average 600 millimeters, which may have caused an abandonment of settled agricultural life for transhumance. This changed during the crusader and Mamluk periods with annual rainfall increasing, and there is a corresponding increased evidence for settlements in the region and its development into an important breadbasket.[100]

Along the coastal plain from Caesarea and Acre up through Sidon and Beirut, especially along the rivers, sugarcane was grown and processed.[101] Requiring ample water for irrigation and milling, these sites are found in along the banks of the Naʿaman, Litani (classical Leontes), and Kziv rivers. We know of mills at Lanahia/Lanoye (modern Khirbet Yanouhieh),[102] Kurdana/Recordane (Khirbet Kurdani),[103] Cabor (Kabul),[104] and Manueth (Horbat Manot).[105] Of the large cities, Tyre and its vicinity seems to have been particularly involved in sugar.[106] Although the preeminent role in trade that it had enjoyed since antiquity was superseded by Acre by the thirteenth century, Tyre continued to be a major site of commercial and mercantile activity.[107] We know from the documents produced by Marsilio Zorzi that Venice operated plantations around the city from 1191, from which they derived considerable revenue.[108]

In brief, making sugar involved cutting the cane into segments that were crushed twice by a water- or animal-powered wheel. The juice was boiled in large cauldrons, and something would be added to aid the separation of the sucrose. The thicker syrup produced would then be poured into conical pots with perforated tips set on top of a molasses jar. The sugar crystals hardened in the cone while the jar collected the remaining molasses. The crystals would be dissolved in water and undergo the process two or three additional times to produce ever more fine grades of sugar.[109]

It is very likely Muslims engaged in the strenuous raising and processing of sugar. We have direct evidence for Muslims living in Cabor and Tyre. We also know that sugar was grown and processed throughout the Acre region. Surveys in the western Galilee conducted by Rafael Frankel and Edna Stern revealed a system of presses, including a distinctive sugar mill that they named the Manot Press.[110] In 1995 this sugar mill at Lower Horbat Manot (below crusader Manueth) in the plain of Acre underwent a salvage excavation.[111] Manueth belonged to the Hospitallers in the thirteenth century but was leased to the Teutonic Knights in 1270. It continued to be in Frankish possession through the 1280s since it was included in their possessions in the 1283 treaty with the Mamluks.[112] The surviving remains of the site consisted of a large building, an aqueduct from the Kziv River, and the base of a screw press. The archaeologists found that from the level dating to the thirteenth century, the majority of the pottery was associated with sugar production, principally consisting of sugar pots and molasses jars, thus strongly indicating that it was a sugar production facility.[113]

The large, two-story building would have served multiple uses. During production, it was where the cane juice from the mills would have been taken and boiled in copper pots at as many as six fire chambers and twelve fireplaces at the northern walls. The rest of the space, though unexcavated, might have been where the pots in which the refined molasses was poured, soaked, and washed. The second floor, based on its proximity to the mill, might have housed the laborers and a steward and could have also served as a collection and storage facility during the spring and summer.[114] The archaeologists also found a surprisingly large number of oil lamps, which they suggest might indicate that sugar production took place at night.[115] If true, it would mean that workers labored extensive hours during the autumn and winter, the sugar production season.

Fruit growing was also prevalent along the coast. S. D. Goitein in his investigation of the Cairo Geniza documents found evidence to suggest, in fact, that dried fruit was a major export of the region throughout the Middle Ages. For example, he found reference to five camel loads of dried plums sent by sea from Acre to Egypt in the 1030s or '40s.[116] The thirteenth-century sources frequently mention gardens (Old French: *jardins*) and trees (Old French: *les arbres*, Ar: *al-ashjar*) near cities, most likely referring to fruit orchards.[117] For the most part, these references occur in descriptions of their destruction. The Sultan Baybars, in particular, seemed to favor cutting down these orchards rather than investing a city directly. For several years in a row in the 1260s, whenever passing through the region from Syria to Egypt and back, raids would be launched against Acre and its environs, including the chopping down of orchards. The two most serious raids were those of 1263 and 1267. The former involved the destruction of the Templar mill at Doc and the latter the destruction of the Hospitaller installation at Kurdana (Recordana).[118]

Thus far, for the contributions Muslims made in agriculture, we must rely principally on evidence that certain products were raised in an area where they lived to make a connection between them. Logically, if Muslim peasants were living in an area where olives were grown, it makes sense that they would have participated in raising and processing olives. The documents prepared by the Venetian *bailo* Marsilio Zorzi, which inventory the Venetian possessions in and around Tyre, can help us make more direct connections between Muslims and how they participated in the agricultural economy.[119] Zorzi recorded that Venetian lands produced diverse agricultural products including sugar, wheat, barley, pulses, olives, and grapes. As already mentioned, sugarcane would have been planted near the river, while the vines and olives could have been planted in the hills, with the plain reserved for the grains.

The taxes owed also inform us of what these peasants raised. There were twelve households of the casal Aiffit, which included Muslim families, since men named Muhammad (Mahomet) and Nur al-Dawla (Nor el doule) were recorded. Each household owed one hen, ten eggs, and twelve besants at Christmas, Lent, and Easter for each *carruca* of land. For the latter two holidays, peasants also had to give a round of cheese.[120] Thus it is clear that in addition to whatever plants they tended, peasants also raised chickens and livestock for dairy. These taxes are fairly standard across the board and do not appear to discriminate against a peasant's religious background.

The documents also present evidence that Muslims worked vineyards. Zorzi called one of the archbishop's peasants Sideomfi son of Boali—the latter part of the name is certainly the Islamic name Abu ʿAli—who worked a vineyard that belonged to the Venetians.[121] Another peasant belonging to the Venetians named Maummet (Muhammad) worked a vineyard of the archbishop in return for an annual rent.[122]

Elsewhere in the inventory, we get information about the labor and income involved in tending olives. The casal Betheron, shared between the Venetians and the Archbishop of Tyre, contained a plot of land planted with forty olive trees and is described as being two carrucas in area and able to be worked by two pairs of oxen in a day.[123] The returns (*reddictus*) of the land amounted to five besants annually. Another plot of land worked by a peasant named Belhala—possibly a rendering of the likely Muslim name Abu al-ʿAlaʾ—contained twenty-five olive trees, was able to be worked by a pair of oxen in a day, and returned four besants annually.[124] Another plot of land held only four olive trees and two fig trees and could be worked in a single day by one ox, yet owed about two besants a year, thus suggesting that fruit trees, or at least fig trees, produced more income than olives.[125] On top of these returns, these peasants, like those mentioned above, also owed a hen, ten eggs, and twelve besants for wood at the three major holidays.

The evidence from the Venetian inventory thus suggests that at least along the coast, peasants participated in a mixed agriculture, tending fruits (grapes, olives, figs) and grains as well as engaging in some limited animal husbandry. It also suggests that Christians and Muslims participated in the same agricultural activities and so were equally important to that part of the economy. Looking closer at the Arabic sources, in fact, reveals just how important agriculture was to the survival of the Kingdom of Jerusalem. In the next part, I will discuss the evidence that the Mamluks and the Franks were very much aware of the precarious economic situation the kingdom faced and the very key role that peasants played in keeping it sustainable.

## Peasant Stealing and the Conquest of the Kingdom of Jerusalem

The year 1271 was an eventful one in the history of Frankish relations with the Mamluks. In late spring of that year, the Sultan Baybars sent a fleet against the island of Cyprus. The fleet foundered on the reefs of Limassol with all the ships lost and all survivors taken prisoner. The exultant Hugh de Lusignan, King of Cyprus and Jerusalem, sent a letter to the sultan informing him of this event. Baybars's response, so we are told by his biographer Muhyi al-Din Ibn 'Abd al-Zahir, was to thank God that nothing worse happened.[126] Shortly thereafter on June 23, the sultan accepted the surrender of the Teutonic castle of Montfort and sent his own taunting letter to King Hugh in response.[127] In it he wrote among many things, "You may have seized a broken ship's yard of ours, but how many populous villages of yours have we emptied of inhabitants? You may have taken a rudder, but how many lands of yours have we emptied of inhabitants?"[128] With these rather pointed rhetorical flourishes, Baybars brought to Hugh's attention the Mamluk dismissal of seafaring and prioritization of the land and warfare. The Mamluk aversion to the sea is well documented, and it would be tempting to read no further into the letter.[129] However, the second part of those sentences, the image of emptied villages, bears further scrutiny. Rather than reading this merely as a boastful claim to land superiority, these images of depopulated lands read true and can be corroborated by other Arabic and Frankish sources. I contend that these phrases are indicative of a Mamluk attempt to weaken the Latin East through a deliberate plan of divesting it of its peasant populace. This practice would have served to deprive the Franks of an important economic engine and destroy any possibility of it supplying itself with food.

The sources from both sides are rife with references to destruction of crops and looting. Of course, by themselves they do not necessarily indicate that there was a deliberate or special Mamluk policy of crippling the enemy through its agricultural production. It tends to be a regular feature of war after all. Moreover, looting and cattle rustling were important parts of the performance of elite identity on all sides. John of Brienne followed his wedding with Maria de Montferrat in 1210 with a raid on the village of Iusse, collecting considerable booty and draught animals.[130] Oliver of Termes, Marino Sanudo also tells us, led men of Acre into raids against Bethsan and other villages: "Wasting the land roundabout he took away a great booty of men and pack animals."[131] Raiding was usual practice among the Muslim military too. The contemporaneous qadi and mufti ʿAla al-Din Yahya al-Nawawi (1233–1277), who trained and worked in Damascus, in fact was questioned concerning the proper division of loot and issued a legal opinion or fatwa on the issue.[132] The problem was so common that the legal treatise *Le Livre au Roi* dating to the beginning of the thirteenth century, included a clause dealing with what should happen should "God's ire, or pestilence that kills all the wheat . . . or if Saracens come and take all that the king ought to pay." It asserts that in these cases, the king is not bound to pay his liege men except in proportion to what he has been able to collect.[133] This same clause was reincorporated into Philip of Novara's legal treatise of the latter half of the century, indicating that the raids Muslims unleashed against agricultural lands were still taking a toll.[134]

What stands out from the routine reports of destruction are the references to population movements, particularly the seizing or killing of peasants and demands for their return. Indeed, Hugh Kennedy in his book *Crusader Castles* suggests that the Sultan Baybars used this strategy in his conquest of the Frankish fortifications in the region of Tripoli in 1270–1271. In particular, Crac des Chevaliers, one of the most formidable of the Frankish castles, was more easily taken because the area around it had been controlled and destroyed by the sultan for a year.[135] Kennedy cited a letter written in 1268 by Hugh Revel, Grandmaster of the Hospitallers, to Brother Faraud of Barras, prior of

St. Gilles. In this letter, Revel described the devastating effect Mamluk raids had on Hospitaller finances. Nothing remained to them outside the walls of Acre, he wrote, and they have had to pay "many, immense, and unreasonable expenses" following the sultan's many raids.[136] Moreover, and this gets at the issue of the peasantry, the Hospitallers had lost ten thousand inhabitants who used to provide for the brothers of Crac des Chevaliers and Margat.[137] In fact, this displacement of peasants continued until the final conquest of the castle. The Syrian historian al-Yunini (1242–1326), in his continuation of Sibt Ibn al-Jawzi's chronicle, *Mir'at al-zaman*, noted that when Baybars's forces descended upon Crac de Chevaliers in 1271, they seized the peasants and mountain folk (*al-jabaliyya*) of the area.[138]

There is evidence for the long-term concern over agricultural labor beyond this one letter, however. In treaties concluded between the Hospitallers and Mamluks in 1267 and 1271, we are witness to a negotiation and struggle for control over the peasantry. The 1267 treaty between the Sultan Baybars and the Hospitallers explicitly provided for the settlement of thirty households of Arabs (by which they mean nomadic Bedouin) and Turcomans in the territory of Rafaniyya and Barin, belonging to one of the last remaining Ayyubid lords, al-Mansur Muhammad II of Hama (642–683/1244–1284). These people were allowed to settle in order to transport grain to the castle of Barin.[139] The same treaty at multiple points made specific provisions for the care of the peasantry. In the section devoted to the shared territory around the city of Homs, both parties agreed not to prevent any peasants recognized as living in the condominium from "returning and dwelling there," suggesting they had fled or had been removed at some point.[140] Moreover, they agreed to release "the common goods" from the realm of private property "so that the destitute may obtain subsistence from them." These common goods in Prophetic tradition were water, fire, and fodder.[141] In other words, the parties agreed to make it easier for the peasants of the region to raise their animals without being subject to extraordinary taxation on the right of pasturage or watering. Likewise, in the section on the Isma'ili territories, it was confirmed that the peasants belonging to Hospitaller territory would be permitted to "go and come, sell and buy in security." No one would attack them, and so also for the peasants from Isma'ili territory.[142]

The issue of the return of individuals continued even following the loss of the Hospitaller Syrian castles, as seen in the treaty concluded in 1271. In a lengthy clause, both the Hospitallers and Baybars agreed that any Muslim "or any nation" who fled "whether a mamluk or not, a freedman or not, whoever of the Muslims he may be, of whatever degree, a servant or not; he shall be sent back with everything found with him."[143] In a shorter clause, they similarly promised that any Frank or Christian who fled would be returned to his or her proper territory with all his or her goods. Given the disparity in detail and length, it seems these two clauses are most concerned about the Hospitallers giving refuge to fugitive Muslims, especially under the excuse that they had converted to Christianity. The treaty stipulates, "Even if the fugitive enters the church and sits in it, he shall be taken by his hand, brought out, and delivered to [the sultan's] representatives with all he has with him."[144] The sultan was evidently hoping to block those of his subjects who sought to escape his rule, his taxes, or so forth by seeking refuge with the Hospitallers. It is also not impossible that the Hospitallers might have encouraged them to do so and claimed peasants were Christians when they were not, simply to augment their workforce.

Another section directly points to the idea that both sides understood that their prosperity was tied to their peasantry. In a discussion about the joint investigation of crime, there is a sentence that reads: "None of them [the parties] shall show favour in the taking of a peasant in this or otherwise in the interest of the prosperity of the territory, the levy of dues, the sharing of crops, and the search for the disturbers of the peace by night and day."[145] The passage emphasizes that neither side would infringe upon the process of justice to enhance their own position. In so doing, it gives examples of how the agents of both sides might compromise their duties in bringing crime to justice, and one of those, tellingly, is that they might seize a peasant to make their own territory more prosperous.

The narrative sources confirm that the Hospitallers had been given to seizing or purchasing peasants unlawfully from the area in the years preceding their loss of Crac des Chevaliers. Baybars al-Mansuri recorded that in 1266 while the sultan was making his way from Damascus to meet up with his army in Sis (Armenia), he traveled through the village of Qara. There people from the surrounding lands approached him, complaining that the villagers of Qara had taken to seizing and selling them to the Hospitallers of the castle Gibelacar (Hisn 'Akkar).[146] According to Ibn Jubayr, who visited in 1184, the village was inhabited entirely by Christians and was the location of a major caravanserai since it was located on the main road between Damascus and Homs.[147] That the people from outside Qara came to the sultan to complain, rather than to the Hospitallers, suggests that they were Muslim, unlike the people of the town itself. In this instance, Baybars became incensed, we are told, and punished the people of Qara by attacking the village, seizing the women and children and relocating them to Egypt where they were raised and incorporated into the Mamluk system.[148] The question remains as to what the Hospitallers were going to do with these Muslim peasants. It is possible that they were destined to merely be sold off elsewhere as slaves, though I suspect that they were just as likely to have been used to work the fertile lands in the coastal plain the castle controlled.

Thus there is ample evidence to support the idea that the loss of peasantry and the devastation of the lands around Hospitaller castles in Syria were key to the Mamluk conquest of those areas and were not accidental. I believe this thesis should be pushed further to include the entirety of the Frankish and Armenian coastal possessions and not merely the strongholds of the military orders. In the same letter of 1268, Hugh Revel complains that the Hospitallers had not been able to receive any sustenance from the Armenian plain because of drought and because of the land "having been emptied of people out of fear of the sultan."[149] Accordingly, it appears that Baybars similarly sought to weaken his Armenian enemies who had allied with the Mongols through dispersing their peasantry.[150] Even more to the point, after the conquest of Crac des Chevaliers, Baybars moved his forces to the vicinity of the city of Tripoli itself. Al-Yunini informs us that the lord, Bohemond VI, sent to him, asking why he was there, to which the sultan replied, "To use your fields as fodder and destroy your lands and return next year and besiege the city."[151] Given how removal of peasantry was part of the destruction of the land elsewhere, I suspect that was also part of the plan here. Fortunately for Bohemond, Edward of England arrived at the time, and Baybars decided to negotiate a new peace treaty instead.

Not every effort to relocate Muslims came at the point of the sword or within the body of a treaty. As will be discussed in more detail in Chapter 4, the Sultan Baybars felt he possessed the authority to compel any Muslims living within Frankish territory to move. As part of his 1275 negotiations following Bohemond VI of Tripoli's death, he went so far as to have his deputy in charge of Balatunus castle order the Muslims of Latakia to leave and move to his lands.[152] The Muslims of the city apparently felt this carried sufficient weight that they asked the Frankish deputy of Latakia for help, and so he wrote to the sultan saying they were holding to the treaty and the Muslim residents were finding it difficult to leave.[153] The matter was of such concern that King Hugh also wrote to the sultan on behalf of the Muslims of Latakia and the city itself. This episode demonstrates the seriousness of the problem posed by the Mamluk attempt to weaken the Franks through depopulation. It also hints at the real dilemma faced by the Muslim communities who were being fought over and pulled between wanting to remain in their homes and the authority they recognized in the Mamluk sultanate.

This is an outlying episode though, and the sources more often record the violent means used to move or remove peasants. One of the most graphically depicted acts of violence against the peasantry comes from the Templar of Tyre. According to the chronicle, on May 2, 1267, Baybars led his army to the plain before Acre, taking the commoners working the fields by surprise. He wrote, "[Baybars] advanced to the gates of the city, and killed more than five hundred of the common people whom he had taken prisoner, and spilled the bile from every one of their bodies. And he sliced all the hair off their heads, to below their ears, and carried it back to Safad, where he strung the scalps on a cord and hung the cord around the great tower at Safad."[154] Later, on May 16, Baybars returned and devastated the mills and gardens and cut down the orchards and olive groves in the immediate vicinity of Acre.[155]

Ibn ʿAbd al-Zahir likewise reported these raids, although he did not emphasize that those killed were peasants. Instead he mentioned that the heads of those killed were carried back to Safad on spears. Later, when Frankish messengers arrived asking for a truce, the sultan brought out some of those taken prisoner in the raid and had them killed too, and told the messengers that the raid was in response to the Frankish raid on lands around Beaufort.[156] What is particularly instructive is that following his description of Baybars's second round of destruction around Acre, Ibn ʿAbd al-Zahir included an aside providing an excuse for such behavior: "The ʿulamaʾs [sic] consider it permissible to burn the crops of the enemy and to fell their trees if the leader of the Muslims approves this as a method of weakening them. For the Apostle of God, may God bless him and give him peace, cut down the vines of the people of al-Taʾif, which led to their acceptance of Islam, and in his campaign against the Banuʾl-Nadir he ordered the felling of the so-called 'yellow palms' whose date stones can be seen through the flesh of the dates."[157] This aside, taken in conjunction with the particular violence against the agriculturalists, demonstrates the sultan's intention to cripple Acre economically through the destruction both of the crops and of the people necessary to tend them. Not only did Acre lose the labor of those who died, but seeing their terrible fate would almost certainly have proven ample justification for the survivors to abandon their lands to move someplace safer.

With the increased Mamluk attention on the Frankish kingdom, life for the local peasantry became progressively more difficult. A year after the attacks that garnered Ibn ʿAbd al-Zahir's apologetic remarks, Baybars took Jaffa and "killed many of the common people," letting the rest go with their goods and a safe conduct.[158] Neither here nor in the account of the May 2 attacks did the Templar of Tyre specify the religion of the peasants. Given the diversity of the population around Acre, as discussed in the previous chapter, it is likely that both Muslims and Christians fell victim to these attacks. If Baybars had targeted Christians specifically, the Templar surely would have remarked upon that fact. As the Mamluks conquered Frankish territories, peasants of all stripes inevitably became a target.

The kingdom would negotiate and win the return of some of those who had moved in the treaty concluded with Baybars in 1272.[159] Ibn ʿAbd al-Zahir tells us that the Franks asked for and were granted the lands and village of Shafarʿam (Le Saffran), Kabul (Cabor), and half of Iskandaruna. Moreover, he states "[Baybars] allowed the return of the peasants belonging to those parts specifically apportioned to them in the truce terms."[160] The area of the plain of Acre already had a high percentage of Muslims, and there is direct evidence for Muslim residents in both Iskandarouna and Kabul. These people apparently had been removed from their lands by Baybars's forces when they conquered the areas and their return was necessary for the villages to be productive again.[161]

Clauses in which the parties contracting the treaty promised to return peasants continued with the sultan Qalawun. The 1283 treaty between the sultan and the Latin Kingdom went into great detail explaining that neither side would keep peasants that did not belong to it. It specifies that peasants, either Christian or Muslim, who used to live in Muslim territory would be returned there and vice versa. Further, any peasant who declined to move would be expelled. They promised, "The peasants of the territory of the Muslims shall not be enabled to stay in the territory of the Franks to which this truce applies, nor the peasants of the territory of the Franks to stay in the territory of the Muslims to which this truce applies."[162] A similar provision was contained in the treaty concluded two years later with Leo III (d. 1289), king of Cilician Armenia, another major antagonist of the Mamluks.[163] Again, reading between the lines we see a situation in which peasants were recognized as valuable, and had been moved either forcibly or through means of enticement.

The Franks engaged in seizing peasants as well in an attempt to offset these losses. In late 1268 or the first part of 1269, Philip de Montfort, lord of Tyre, set aside the truce he concluded with Baybars in 1267. Baybars had sent to him demanding the return of the Muslim girl from Tyre seized from her recently freed mother, already mentioned. Philip excused himself, saying that the girl was a Christian, although the Arabic sources accuse the Frankish captors of having forcibly converted her. Then Philip followed this refusal by sending his men out to seize Muslims at al-Nawaqir (Passe Poulain).[164] Baybars again sent demanding their return, but Philip declined.[165] So on May 23, the sultan set out and attacked the outskirts of Tyre, seizing a number of men, women, and children. At this time, a slave-soldier (mamluk) belonging to Jamal al-Din Aqush al-Rumi ran away to Tyre and was granted refuge by Philip once he converted. The sultan now reiterated his demand of the return of the girl and added the request for this mamluk. To offer encouragement, Baybars sent back the women and children, but to no avail. This series of incidents echoes the situation indicated in the Hospitaller treaty of 1271 and shows that it was not merely the military order that tried to prevent the return of Muslims to the Mamluks through conversion (willing or coerced). Although ostensibly about the return of unjustly held subjects of the sultan, this episode demonstrates how the seizing of peasants was used as a means of coercion just as their release was used as an enticement and sign of good faith.

It was not only the Mamluks who used violence against the peasantry to hurt the Franks. During the 1240s we hear of several occasions on which nomadic peoples exacted vengeance through the peasants. Ibn Wasil recorded how in their sweeping attacks across Frankish lands, the Khwarazmians in 1242 attacked Ras al-'Ayn, and its people holed up with the soldiers and archers there for a while before surrendering upon being granted assurances of their safety.[166] The Eracles continuation of the chronicle of William of Tyre described how in 1247 Turcoman tribesmen exacted vengeance on the people of Antioch who had done them injury by "sweeping across country, looting the villages and killing the peasants."[167]

The difference between the Mamluk and Khwarazmian or Turcoman use of such devastation, however, is that the latter used it in a limited manner for specific purposes of exacting revenge or gaining loot. The Mamluks, I contend, used it more or less continuously in various areas of Frankish control as part of a long-term strategy to weaken their enemy. The rather constant uncertainty of safety among the peasantry, even in times of truce, would certainly have had a demoralizing effect. We know that Saladin similarly used ravaging the countryside as a means of weakening besieged Frankish forces in the 1180s. With the countryside destroyed and no help in sight, most of the Frankish cities and forts capitulated relatively easily. Those that resisted, he passed by and returned to later.[168] The Mamluks, especially under the leadership of Baybars and Qalawun, took their lead from Saladin but had the advantage of time. They were able to succeed where Saladin was not by slowly chipping away at the kingdom's productive capacity, decreasing its land and workforce until it could no longer support or defend itself.

## Conclusion

Although the precise proportion is not possible to calculate, the evidence shows that at least some Muslims participated in the Frankish economy as merchants, investors, farmers, laborers, and slaves. They could be seen working orchards, stoking kiln fires, bartering in the market, and sailing into port on a merchant galley. They formed a part of every sector where one could find Franks, Eastern Christians, and Jews. Given the communal nature of agricultural production, Muslims even participated in growing grapes and making and selling wine. There was no area of the economy in the Kingdom of Jerusalem that was cut off from Muslims. In fact, the evidence does support the fact that they made up the majority of the captives and slaves moving through and residing in the kingdom. As such, they functioned within the economic landscape both as actors and commodities.

In later stages of the kingdom's existence in the thirteenth century, the Mamluks, I argue, waged a sophisticated attack upon the kingdom's economy in order to achieve its ultimate collapse. In the treaties we see them increasingly emphasizing the rights of their merchants in Frankish territory and waters. The documentary evidence shows Muslim merchants and investors working within the regional commercial circuit. These were not hypothetical Muslim merchants that the Mamluks were inventing for the treaties; they were real. At the same time that Muslims were making headway into the regional commercial sphere, the Mamluks were systematically eroding the Frankish agricultural sector. They not only conquered territory but destroyed orchards and agricultural installations, while seizing the peasant workforce needed to keep it all productive. It is fair to say that while conditions may have improved for Muslims of middling means in the kingdom, they worsened for the peasants. Subjected to raids, killings, and even forced removal, they slipped away from the kingdom, leaving it with a failing economy. The Italian communes might have been the kingdom's economic lungs, but the peasants, Muslim and Christian, were its heart, and it was the heart that stopped beating.

*Chapter 3*

# "Saracens Are Also Men Like the Franks"

## Muslims in the Legal Landscape

### Introduction

So far I have discussed the physical and economic landscapes in which the Muslim communities in the Latin Kingdom of Jerusalem lived their lives. In this chapter I turn to a more theoretical kind of landscape—the law. Inhabitants of the Latin East had recourse to a number of legal systems, each with its own imperatives in attempting to shape people's lives. Medieval law was both personal and territorial. The judicial system that applied to an individual was determined both by his or her identity and by where he or she happened to be. With regard to how law was personal, in Europe, one's relationship with the Latin Church dictated the laws one had to follow. If one were a member of the church, a nun or a priest for example, one was liable to ecclesiastical courts. If one were lay, the local secular legal institutions had jurisdiction with exceptions in cases that touched upon spiritual matters like marriage. Non-Christians in Europe—mostly Jews, but Muslims also in Iberia—were allowed to administer justice for themselves except in cases which involved Christians, in which case the local secular lord would step in.[1]

The Muslim communities in the Kingdom of Jerusalem lived at the intersection of three forms of law: Islamic, Latin ecclesiastical, and Latin secular. The latter two were impositions that their coreligionists in Syria or Egypt did not have to navigate. Indeed, in Islam there was not such a hard distinction made between the secular and the religious. Rather, the basic premise of Islamic law (*shariʿa*, literally "the way/path") is that it exists entire and complete in the Qurʾan and the hadith, the sayings of or concerning the

Prophet Muhammad. *Fiqh* is the body of law generated from the interpretation of the Qur'an and hadith when dealing with situations and practices not directly referenced in either source. Fiqh covers not only religious but also secular law as it does not make a clear distinction between the two. Jurists (sing. *faqih*, pl. *fuqaha*) derive their rulings according to principles established by particular schools of jurisprudence (sing. *madhhab*, pl. *madhahib*) involving processes of consensus, analogy, and reasoning.[2]

The Frankish legal system has been studied in great depth by numerous important crusades scholars such as Joshua Prawer, Jonathan Riley-Smith, and Peter Edbury and is the aspect of the non-Frankish experience of Frankish rule that has received by far the most attention.[3] The idea of Muslim marginality and disenfranchisement has rested largely on an analysis of the sources for the Frankish legal apparatuses.[4] It has been posited that the Muslim communities experienced the imposition of new Frankish governance as the unfortunate, but predictable, reversal of the dhimmi system they used with their Jewish and Christian subjects.[5] Moreover, for the peasant majority of this population the indignity was taken yet a step further with the imposition of the European model of serfdom. However, Christopher MacEvitt's reexamination of this issue has persuasively shown that serfdom is neither an accurate nor particularly helpful model by which to understand non-Frankish peasant legal status.[6] The only similarity, he argues, was being tied to the land, in the case of the Latin East, in order to ensure a sufficient workforce. MacEvitt's work exemplifies the rewards that new approaches to well-trodden material can reap.

In this chapter I discuss the legal systems at work in the Kingdom of Jerusalem and how Muslims were supposed to interact with them. I analyze the Frankish and Islamic legal texts in light of the roles they afforded Muslims and the kinds of interaction they permitted and sought to prohibit. This chapter considers the theoretical place of Muslims in the legal landscape since the sources at our disposal are all prescriptive. In the following chapter on politics, I will discuss how justice was practiced in reality. Here, I argue that although each legal system functioned in some capacity to separate communities from each other, there was nevertheless space in each for significant interaction. We also find that while clearly placed in a second-class position, Muslims were not very much more legally disadvantaged than the other non-Frankish subjects. Moreover, in the Frankish courts that so often have been read as prioritizing religious affiliation as the primary means of identifying individuals, we often see social status taking precedence in determining access.

## Legal Systems of the Kingdom of Jerusalem

In the twelfth century, the Franks established three main law courts that continued to function and evolve over the course of the kingdom's existence. These were the ecclesiastical court, the High Court, and the Burgess Court. The ecclesiastical court administered canon law and had jurisdiction over the professed religious in the Latin rite and cases of religious import such as marriage or heresy. The High Court was the domain of the nobility, was presided over by the king, and dealt largely with issues concerning landholding, the nobility's prerogative. The Burgess Courts, which existed independently in several cities throughout the kingdom, handled cases for the rest of the populace. These courts were intended to be primarily devoted to the legal needs of the Frankish populace, with the subject religious communities being free to administer justice among themselves. The Muslims would have had a *qadi* (judge) or *ra'is* (headman) to adjudicate intra-faith disputes. As will be seen, however, even in theory, the communities were not envisioned as being completely segregated from each other.

Six major works of Frankish law composed in the Kingdom of Jerusalem survive. These are the Canons of the Council of Nablus dating to 1120, the *Livre de la Cour des Bourgeois* from around 1200, the *Assises d'Antioche* dating from 1201 to 1219, the *Livre au Roi* from around 1240, Philip of Novara's *Le Livre de Forme de Plait*, dating to the 1250s, and John of Ibelin's *Le Livre des Assises* composed around 1264.[7] Although law texts, these, with the possible exception of the Canons, do not represent actual legislation of the government. At this time in Europe, much of the law was customary and not written down. Legislation was created by the lords for their domains (including the king) or through assemblies like the Burgess Court where precedent was followed and evolved as different situations arose. As Peter Edbury has explained, sometimes elements of court procedure were enshrined as an *assise* in personal handbooks of law, granting it some official status, but the lines were vague at best. When the assises were lost or forgotten, as was the case following the collapse of the first Kingdom of Jerusalem after the military successes of Saladin in 1187, the distinction between the two vanished completely.[8] Jurists then were put into the position where they could start afresh, presenting their own agendas by expressing their legal opinions as traditional, regardless of whether they were or not. Accordingly, the views represented in the assises collections most likely reflect attitudes from the thirteenth century and not necessarily positions adopted in the twelfth.

## Islamic Law

Religion was an important identifier in the legal world constructed by and envisioned in these sources. In fact, the Old French texts often label people by religion. Law and faith were essentially synonymous to these authors. Because of this identification, if a conflict arose between two Muslims, the theorists held that it should be handled internally by the community itself. Although we can not be certain exactly how this worked, there are two main possibilities. John of Ibelin in his *Livre des Assises* discussed the institution of the *Cour des Suriens* and related the supposed story of its creation in the early years of the Kingdom of Jerusalem after the Syrians approached Godfrey of Bouillon asking to be permitted to govern themselves.[9] It is possible that the *Cour des Suriens* then became responsible for not just the Syrian Christian, or Melkite Christian, communities, but all the non-Frankish ones. It is more likely, though, that each religious community—Christian, Muslim, Jewish—had its own judicial oversight.[10] For Muslims, this meant either recourse to a local judge, a *qadi*, or more likely especially on the village level, to the local headman called a *raʾis* or *shaykh* in the sources. While a raʾis in Arabic means "leader" and has a secular sense of person in charge, a shaykh could be an elderly local leader or someone with religious authority, as in the leader within a Sufi order. At the village level, the same person could be call both a raʾis and a shaykh. The following sections will discuss Islamic jurisprudence, its institutions, and how it approached the kinds of questions Muslims living under non-Muslim rule might have confronted. Although the imposition of Frankish governance disrupted formal Islamic institutions in Palestine, Muslims were still able to live according to the principles of Islam.

The qadi and his court form the basic legal institution under Islamic law, but evidence for qadis in the Latin Kingdom is scarce. We know that one of the stipulations from the 1229 treaty between Frederick II and the Egyptian sultan al-Malik al-Kamil was that Muslims would retain full control over the Haram al-Sharif (Temple Mount) and be able to continue the full range of religious practice. This would include justice according to Islamic law.[11] To my knowledge, there is only one qadi, Mansur bin Nabil from Jabala, mentioned in the sources as living under Frankish rule, in this case the Principality of Antioch. He is noted as being instrumental in negotiating the town's surrender to Saladin in 1188.[12] For the thirteenth century, the only evidence is of several who are named as working in Jerusalem under the Ayyubids, shortly after its conquest, and potentially when it belonged to the Franks between 1229 and 1244. Yusuf bin Ibrahim bin Abd al-Wahid was known as al-qadi al-Ashraf, and served in Jerusalem under Saladin's son, al-Malik al-Aziz Uthman, around the year 591/1194.[13] Another qadi, Taqi al-Din al-Raqi Muhammad bin Hiya bin Yahya (d. 676/1277), governed in Jerusalem early in his career before eventually becoming a chief judge (*qadi al-qudat*) in Damascus.[14] We do not have a precise date for when he served in Jerusalem, so it is possible he was there during the period of Frankish rule. The biographer Ibn Taghribirdi associated him with the Sultan Baybars, writing that the sultan knew Taqi al-Din from a long time back, which suggests that they were roughly peers in age.[15] It is thus likely Taqi al-Din would have been too young to be a qadi in Frankish-held Jerusalem. Nevertheless, given the presence of qadis in the city before and after Frankish rule, it stands to reason that there would have been one during the treaty at the Haram al-Sharif. Alternatively, Ibn Wasil wrote that along with maintaining control of the Haram al-Sharif in Jerusalem, the governor of the lands would maintain a seat at the well to the north of the city, which could also have been the site of a court.[16]

The lack of reference to qadis in Frankish territories in the biographical dictionaries is worth thinking about in light of what we know about contemporary centers of culture. Palestine in the crusade period is generally considered to have been a cultural backwater both from the European and the Middle Eastern perspectives.[17] Although this attitude has been contested lately from the European side,[18] the centers of cultural production in the twelfth- and thirteenth-century Islamicate world were such places as Cairo, Damascus, Aleppo, and cities in Al-Andalus. Palestinian cities had long paled in importance in comparison to those in Syria.

At the heart of cultural production in the Islamic world were the ʿ*ulama*, a term that encompassed the learned intellectual and religious elite. The majority of the ʿulama were supported through positions in government or in Islamic institutions like *madrasas* (schools), *zawiyas* (Sufi lodges), or other foundations supported through pious endowments called *awqaf* (sing. *waqf*).[19] For instance, on the basis of the reports of Ibn al-ʿArabi, a Muslim from Seville who lived from 1092 to 1095 in Jerusalem, we know that there were twenty-eight scholarly circles and two madrasas, one belonging to the Shafiʿi and the other belonging to the Hanafi school of legal thought.[20] Benjamin Kedar has connected these two, which were located near the Gate of the Tribes and the Church of the Holy Sepulchre respectively, with the Salahiyya *madrasa* and *ribat* (Sufi institution) founded by Saladin following his reconquest in 1187. With the conquest of lands by the Franks, these endowments were erased and had to be reendowed once they returned to Muslim control. It is likely then that the majority of the scholars and judges, who relied upon these *awqaf* for support, left after the Franks took over in their cities. Moreover, qadis were traditionally appointed by rulers, so without a Muslim ruler to appoint qadis in Frankish territory, there would be none.[21] Those Muslims who remained to render justice among the Muslims were more likely to be the local headman (*ra'is*) and *shaykh*, an honorific usually designating an older man with a reputation for holiness and wisdom, who had to support himself in other ways.

If examples of qadis are scarce, there is ample evidence for the continued presence of shaykhs in lands controlled by the Franks that demonstrate their role in the legal landscape. Diya' al-Din al-Maqdisi's biographies of religious leaders or shaykhs from the Nablus region in the twelfth century, translated into English as *The Cited Tales of the Wondrous Doings of the Shaykhs of the Holy Land*, gives us a wonderful view into the lives of rural Muslim peasantry.[22] The sole surviving manuscript of the text preserves accounts of thirteen shaykhs who lived in the greater Nablus region in the mid-twelfth century, a third or less of the original number of biographies.[23] As the text's editor and translator Daniella Talmon-Heller observes, the biographies provide a wealth of detail about Muslim village life at the time.[24] For our purposes, they reveal that the important personages on the village level were the shaykhs, imams (prayer leaders), and ra'ises. Islamic life continued despite Frankish rule, and the people were even able to maintain their allegiance to their preferred Islamic juridical school, in this case, the Hanbalis. In the biography of 'Abd Allah bin Ahmad bin Muhammad bin Bukayr we are told that one day his disciples came to him describing a different shaykh who was consulted on earthly matters, and 'Abd Allah replied that he himself could distinguish between good and bad men.[25] At one point he was consulted on the correctness of praying behind a man suspected of being a swindler. He replied that the day of judgment would only come after many swindlers appeared, which mollified the villagers who in turn accepted the man in question.[26] There is another story of the shaykh 'Abd Allah bin 'Umar Abu Musa of the village of Salmiya, which describes how the shaykh relieved his village of the burden of providing food for all the many people coming to visit him. He performed a wonder, or in the terminology of the text, *karama*, of making a bowl of stew and bread suffice for lots of people.[27]

These stories, and the others like them contained in Diya' al-Din al-Maqdisi's work, put a face on those Muslims who remained under Frankish rule. Indeed, evidence from this source was important in helping to construct the maps discussed in Chapter 1. They also demonstrate that shaykhs remained important authorities on matters of religion and law. They suggest that in the rural villages, where perhaps qadis were unlikely to live or travel through, shaykhs could fulfill an important role in the operation of Islamic law. If issues or conflicts arose, people could go and solicit the advice of the local shaykh, or perhaps several given the number referenced by al-Maqdisi. Thereby Muslims could go about their lives assured of living according to Islamic principles.

## Islamic Law and the Obligation of *Hijra*

The migration of the Hanbali community of the Nablus region recounted by al-Maqdisi is an exceptional instance of mass migration of Muslims from Frankish territory. During the initial conquest of the kingdom in the twelfth century, Muslims were permitted to leave cities if they had capitulated. Even so, it seems that most of the people of lesser status remained.[28] According to al-Maqdisi, his family only decided to move from Nablus to settle in a Damascus suburb when the Frankish lord decided to kill the author's grandfather, the shaykh Ahmad bin Qudama, because his Friday sermons took the peasants from their work in the fields. The author's informants sum up the story by saying "*shaykh* Ahmad was the first to emigrate both out of fear for his life and because he was unable to practice his religion."[29]

The issue of whether it was mandatory for Muslims to emigrate if the place they lived became subject to non-Muslim rule is one that gained increased importance in the twelfth and especially the thirteenth centuries.[30] Latin Europeans were pushing their way south into Iberia, into Sicily, and obviously into the eastern Mediterranean, but it grew even more urgent upon the Mongol conquests of vast swaths of Asia. The four schools of Sunni Islamic jurisprudence, Hanafi, Maliki, Shafi'i, and Hanbali, came to different conclusions. The Maliki school, which prevailed in the western Mediterranean and is considered to be among the more strict, was itself not entirely consistent. Ibn Rushd (d. 520/1122), the foremost Maliki jurist of the time and grandfather of the famous philosopher known in the west as Averroës, held that it was never permissible for a Muslim to reside or even enter territory controlled by non-Muslims since by doing so, he would be subjecting himself to non-Muslim law. Another Maliki jurist, al-Mazari (d. 536/1141) held that while it was preferable for Muslims to live under Muslim political rule, it was valid for them to live under non-Muslims if their motivation for doing so was correct. For instance, someone could stay if he or she intended to restore the territory to Islam or if the person in question dedicated him or herself to spreading Islam to non-Muslims.[31]

A key difference between the Maliki school predominant in the western Mediterranean and the Hanafi and Shafi'i schools predominant in the eastern Mediterranean was the definition of what constituted the *Dar al-Islam*. The Malikis took the strict political view that the *Dar al-Islam* was the land under political control of Muslims and all other lands, the *Dar al-Harb*, were not usually permissible for Muslims to reside in. The other schools had a more flexible view, which allowed for land that had been under Muslim political control, but was subsequently conquered by non-Muslims, to keep its status as in the *Dar al-Islam*. The Hanafis held that as long as prayer was allowed or Muslim judges remained in office, a territory was part of the *Dar al-Islam*. By implication, not only were Muslims permitted to stay; they were encouraged to do so if they could do so safely in order to maintain the land's status as part of the *Dar al-Islam*.[32] The Shafi'i and the Shi'a schools concurred. These held that what was important was the ability to express one's religion. Emigration (*hijra*) from non-Muslim-controlled territory therefore was only obligatory if the person was unable to express his or her religion and feared its loss.[33]

The Hanbalis, a smaller school of jurisprudence to which the biographer al-Maqdisi belonged, held that hijra was only mandatory if Muslims were in danger and were unable to practice their religion.[34] The jurists still recommended emigration so as to avoid enhancing the material wealth of non-Muslims, but if Muslims were to experience physical or financial hardship from such a move, they were excused from migration. We see the Qudama family and their followers pursuing just these lines of interpretation, when they moved from Nablus to Damascus following the Frankish lord's attempt on their shaykh's life. The shaykh in question, Ahmad b. Qudama, arrived in Damascus, we are told, with his nephew Muhammad Abi Bakr, his brother-in-law 'Abd al-Wahid b. Surur, and another nephew and father of the author 'Abd al-Wahid b. Ahmad. When he reached the city, he wrote a letter back to his followers telling them to leave Nablus and join him in Damascus. When his relatives returned to their ancestral village to deliver the letter, they were met with resistance and were forced to hide because the villagers apparently did not want to leave and went so far as to inform the Frankish authorities. The Franks, as discussed in the previous chapter, had to be wary of maintaining their labor force to work fields and lords did what they could attract or at least keep their peasants. Although the Frankish army was sent after Ahmad's followers, the soldiers were unsuccessful in preventing them from leaving Frankish territory once again.[35]

The episode highlights the conflict that confronted every Muslim community within the kingdom—whether or not to emigrate. The Hanbalis of Nablus decided by 1156 that their position was no longer tenable since their safety and ability to practice Islam was no longer secure. As a result, they left. It is important to note, though, that they were clearly a minority since they had to evade the rest of the community intent on preventing them from leaving. Since the area around Nablus was majority Muslim at this time, we can assume that most of these opponents were fellow Muslims, people who chose to remain in the land despite being under Frankish dominion.[36] Within the Islamic juridical landscape, therefore, these people probably adhered to the Shafi'i or Hanafi schools of thought.

## Fatwas and Intercultural Contact

Besides the particular case of the Hanbalis of the Nablus area, it is difficult to determine what school most Muslims in the Frankish territory would have belonged to or made use of. At the elite level, we do see a continuing strength of the Shafi'i school in the region as a whole that might suggest that it was also favored by Muslims in the kingdom. Both of the qadis associated with Jerusalem mentioned above, Yusuf b. Ibrahim b. Abd al-Wahid and Taqi al-Din al-Raqi, belonged to the Shafi'i school. There was also Muhammad b. Ahmad bin Khalil, chief qadi Shihab al-Din Abu Abdallah (626–693/1228–1294), who governed the qadis of Jerusalem before 1260.[37] The Shafi'i qadi Jamal al-Din b. Sa'd Muhammad (620–694/1223–1294), studied in Jerusalem, and later governed there in addition to Nablus.[38] In addition to them, there was Badr al-Din b. Jama'a Muhammad bin Ibrahim (b. 639/1241), who was a Shafi'i qadi and *khatib* in Jerusalem before 1291.[39] Of course, just because the elites tended to be Shafi'i does not mean that the peasants were. They could have been drawn elsewhere like the Hanbalis of Nablus, or even made strategic use of different schools given the context or availability of legal authorities.

Even though the documentary sources skew toward reflecting the legal-religious opinions of the elites, fatwa literature has the advantage of potentially reflecting concerns of a wider range of Muslims. The qadis' courts did not produce, or at least did not maintain, records in the manner that ecclesiastical and secular courts in Europe were beginning to generate at this time, but fatwas grant insight into the sorts of rulings they made.[40] A fatwa is and was a nonbinding legal opinion made by a *mufti* (a legal scholar and jurisconsult), deemed to be an expert in his legal school. In theory, someone would pose a question to the mufti, he would choose to respond, and sometimes these questions and responses would be collected.[41] The questions could, however, be hypothetical and not necessarily reflect questions posed by other people. Even so, when read critically, these fatwas are good sources for social history and provide information about the kinds of situations that confronted Muslims in their daily lives.

The compilation of al-Nawawi can help us understand what sorts of questions Muslims, living in religiously diverse circumstances such as those in the kingdom, may have had and brought to their local shaykh, if not actually sent to a mufti in Syria or Egypt. Muhyi al-Din Abu Zakariyya Yahya al-Nawawi was born in 631/1233 in the small Syrian town of Nawa, but was educated in Damascus and lived his short life there before dying in 676/1277. He too was a Shafi'i qadi and mufti and wrote on a wide range of topics, including a selection of forty hadiths for ordinary believers.[42] His collection of fatwas, organized by his student Ibn al-'Attar, offers several questions posed by Muslims living in a multi-faith setting that are of relevance to this discussion.[43]

Two concern clothing. One person inquired into the permissibility of wearing non-Muslim dress: Did it impinge upon his religion and his prayers? Did the Prophet Muhammad wear what contemporary soldiers wear in terms of a long-sleeved outer garment (*qaba'*) and other things when he set about an ambush?[44] Al-Nawawi answered that it was indeed forbidden to imitate a non-Muslim in dress and so forth, and that to do so rendered the person's prayers imperfect. He added that in the *Sahih al-Bukhari* hadith collection, it is said that Muhammad wore the qaba' in some battles and in another collection he wore a Syrian *jubba* (another long-sleeved garment with an opening in the front) while waiting in ambush.[45] In this scenario, the questioner clearly had been involved or planned to be involved in raids on Frankish controlled lands. There are recorded instances in which Muslims did disguise themselves as Franks prior to attack. In addition to individual assassination attempts made by the Nizaris who would not have followed Shafi'i law, the most well-known instance was the failed attack on Cyprus in 1271. The leader of the Mamluk fleet, Ibn Hassun, proposed that the galleys be painted black and crosses be put on the sails to resemble Frankish ships.[46] This example demonstrates that while fatwas reflect the legal opinion of a qadi, they do not necessarily indicate how people on the ground behaved in response to that opinion. Since they were nonbinding, and different muftis might have conflicting views, we cannot assume that all opinions were actually followed. We know only that the question was posed, and thus the situation was an issue to someone at the time. The fatwas therefore indicate the kinds of concerns Muslims might have had about their practice and the different directions in which the law tried to pull them with regard to their practice.

Another question of attire was whether it was permissible for a Muslim woman to reveal her face and other parts of her body to Jewish, Christian, or other kinds of non-Muslim women.[47] Al-Nawawi replied that according to Shafi'i jurisprudence, it was not permitted unless the non-Muslim woman were the slave of the Muslim woman. If actually followed, this ruling would have serious practical implications for shared, public spaces such as the *hammam* (public bath). Typically, hammams were (and are) gender-segregated with women and men going at separate times during the day or week or using different facilities. Separating female attendance by religion as well would have involved a further division of the schedule not necessary for men. While perhaps feasible in non-Frankish Syria, it seems unlikely that the Franks in power would recognize the need for further complicating a schedule to serve the needs of their female Muslim subjects. We know that some Franks at least adopted the habit of going to the public bath from, among other things, their archaeological remains found in Jerusalem, Acre, and, tellingly, the castles at 'Atlit and Belvoir.[48] Tales of Frankish bathhouse deportment from Usama Ibn Munqidh in the twelfth century suggests their tendency to neglect what he would have considered proper gender boundaries and modesty.[49] Again, the fatwa represents an attempt to pressure Muslims, specifically women, to behave in a way that may have not even been possible under Frankish rule.

Other concerns of Muslims living among non-Muslims involved more intimate contact. For instance, the question was posed as to where to bury a non-Muslim woman who died while pregnant with the child of the Muslim man, since the child would be considered Muslim under Islamic law. Al-Nawawi believed that the best practice was to bury her midway between the tombs of the Muslims and the tombs of the unbelievers (presumably those of whichever faith to which she belonged), but he noted that others said to bury her on the paths among the graves of the Muslims. Yet others said to pay the people of her religion to wash and bury her among their graves, but to position her so that her back was to the *qibla* (the direction of Mecca), because the face of the fetus is to the back of its mother.[50] Yet another person or the mufti himself posed an extraordinary question concerning baby identification. Someone asked what to do when a Muslim man has an infant son whose mother has died so he is given to a Jewish wet nurse who also has an infant son. The Muslim man leaves for a period, and when he returns he finds the wet nurse also dead; he cannot tell which infant is his and no one around can tell either, and no one knows who the Jewish child's father is. What is to be done?[51]

The general health of community relations also found its way into the fatwas. In a section on sin, one person inquired what to do to someone who called a Muslim a dog or a swine. Was it a sin? Yes, and he should be punished and repent.[52] Another inquired whether it is permitted to curse a Jew or a Christian among others generally. Al-Nawawi replied yes, it is permitted, but rather pragmatically adds that it is better not to do so.[53]

Of a financial nature are questions concerning the proper division of booty and oath-taking. In Sunni tradition, one-fifth (*khums*) of all booty seized while raiding or in battle with non-Muslims was to be given to the caliph or sultan as the representative of the Islamic community. Someone inquired what should be done if the sultan gave an emir the entirety of the booty without having kept the khums. Should the emir still render a fifth? The answer was yes, the emir must not touch any of his portion until the khums is paid either from the total booty or from the portions allotted to each of the participants in the raid.[54] One person asked whether someone committed the sin of oath-breaking if he swore that he did not eat meat, and then ate carrion, or pork, or wolf, or donkey or some other forbidden meat. Al-Nawawi replied that no, the person did not sin through oath-breaking, although there were differences of opinion.[55]

Although there is no evidence that these queries came from Frankish territories, they do offer a fascinating window into the kinds of interactions that could occur between Muslims and non-Muslims as well as the anxieties they could provoke. Although some clearly originated or were only fully enforceable in lands controlled by Muslim lords, these questions help color our appreciation of how life engaging with or even subjected to Frankish domination would have impacted Muslims vis-à-vis their own sense of Islamic law. Muslims sought out advice on a whole range of circumstances from interpersonal relations, distribution of goods, clothing, oath-taking, to best burial practices. While many if not most of the Muslims in the kingdom, especially peasants, may not have had the ability to actually write to a qadi in Damascus or Cairo, they would have been able to pose the same or similar questions to their shaykh. Muslims under Frankish rule would have wanted to live in accordance to their understanding of Islamic law. While almost certainly modified from its shape in *Dar al-Islam*, Islamic law did exist within Frankish territory, if only in the concerns Muslims would have had about how to live appropriately. Through the fatwas we can see what those concerns might have been, especially given the multireligious environment, and the directions Islamic law may have pushed them.

## Frankish Law

Muslims in the Kingdom of Jerusalem of course were not only subject to Islamic law, but rather existed at the intersection of multiple legal frameworks and understandings of law. Unlike their Syrian or Egyptian counterparts, they were subject to imported Latin systems of secular and non-secular law. In what may have been seen as a perplexing state of affairs, Muslims in the Latin East had not only secular laws applied to them but Latin Christian laws as well. They thus needed to navigate a more complex legal landscape than their Syrian or Egyptian peers.

Although different religious groups were allowed to administer themselves, there were contexts in which the Frankish legal system would intervene in the lives of Muslims, or in which Muslims would have recourse to the Frankish system. Perhaps what would have been most perplexing to Muslims was that they came under the purview of Latin ecclesiastical law. The earliest set of laws surviving from the Kingdom of Jerusalem were actually church canons that dealt extensively with the issue of sex between Franks and Muslims. The Canons of the Council of Nablus (1120) were promulgated in the wake of a shattering Frankish defeat at the Battle of the Field of Blood (Ager Sanguinis, 1119) near Antioch. The preamble to the canons explicitly stated that the framers made these rules to counteract the sins that led to the defeat. In that text, sex between Franks and Muslims was the only kind of interaction given any recognition, and it was strictly forbidden as profoundly damaging to the spiritual well-being of the Frankish polity, in the same fashion as adultery and sodomy.[56] Although punished in the same manner as adultery between Franks, Canons 12–15 specified that sexual relations between a Frank and a Muslim should be punished by castration and rhinotomy (nose cutting) and enslavement of the Muslim participant by the state. Canon 16 prohibited

Muslims from wearing Frankish clothing, to prevent the Franks from mistakenly wooing or being wooed by someone considered inappropriate by the Church.[57] Imagined here is a community of Latin Christians whose integrity has come under extreme duress from military losses to Muslim forces. Such losses were evidently considered to be the direct result of sexual misconduct such as the specifically mentioned sex with Muslims. These canons continued to apply in the thirteenth century, although no records survive of them being implemented. Nevertheless, as far as the ecclesiastical legal landscape was concerned, Muslims posed a threat to the Franks with their sexuality or sexual availability, which the Frankish establishment sought to limit.

In the Frankish secular legal sphere, as noted earlier, there were two main court systems that were predicated largely on social status. The High Court led by the king and attended by his vassals managed the governance of the kingdom and grievances among the nobility. The Burgess Courts governed matters concerning lower levels of society including issues pertaining to trade and mercantile activities. The lords also had the right to exercise justice in courts of their own, but there are very few texts surviving that detail their laws, and it is likely that they functioned similarly to the High Court.[58] In the High Court and the Burgess Court, the Franks reserved the right to practice justice on Muslims in cases that also involved Franks. Specifically they made laws regulating violence, commerce, testimony, and conversion.

Primarily, Muslims had a place in the proceedings of the High Court when land was involved. Since one of the distinguishing features of lordship was landholding, it comes as no surprise that disputes or issues concerning land that involved Muslims would be adjudicated in the High Court. In the *Livre au Roi*, a reference work on customary law written around the beginning of the thirteenth century at the behest of King Amaury II, we see as many as three chapters referring to the illegality of selling one's land to Muslims.[59] This implies that it was not out of the realm of possibility that there were wealthy Muslims within or near the kingdom who were able and might have wanted to purchase a fief. Hypothetically, this would have risked the loss of the fief from the kingdom, if the Muslim lord decided to move his allegiance from the king to the local, nearby sultan. The loss of land would be followed by the loss of manpower, since each fief owed a certain number of knights and soldiers to the king's army, as well as revenues in the form of taxes.

Another aspect of the effort to keep fiefs out of Muslim control comes in the chapters from the *Livre au Roi* dealing with the apostasy of Franks who converted to Islam. If a noble went into lands held by a Muslim without prior approval, his lord could legally seize the fief. Moreover, if a year and a day passed before the noble returned, in order to get the fief back he had to prove in court that he had not apostatized while away. In the case that the noble "went to the land of the Saracens" and assumed their law (i.e., Islam), there was no trial and the land was lost to his family forever. Legally, this would have constituted a double transgression against the faith as well as the kingdom since the king would have lost another warrior and would have gained, presumably, an enemy.[60]

Taking these cases a step further, we can say that by trying to preserve the integrity of the physical landscape of the Kingdom of Jerusalem, the High Court had to preserve itself as an all-Frankish space. Only major fief-holders would sit in the court. By prohibiting the sale of fiefs to Muslims, the High Court was reiterating that Muslims had no place sitting among its members.

The legal texts for the High Court assert this principle time and again, by strictly controlling who was allowed to participate in legal matters.[61] An important role in the practice of justice was the guarantor—someone who would back up a party, guaranteeing as truth what he said in court. John of Ibelin (d. 1266), count of Jaffa and Ascalon, wrote his own legal treatise on the procedures of the High Court and included a chapter devoted to who could not serve as a guarantor. He provided a long list, including "renegades" or Christian converts to Islam, and "people of any nation not obedient to Rome: neither Greek, nor Syrian, nor Armenian, nor Jacobite."[62] Only if litigation was brought against them or someone of their religion could they speak in the court.

Muslims might make an appearance in the High Court in litigation against bodily harm.[63] In the case where a Frank hit someone not of the "law of Rome"—that is any Eastern Christian, Jew, or Muslim—that resulted in a visible wound, and did not deny the fact, he would owe the High Court fifty besants and the claimant fifty sous. In the case of the claimant being a Frank who was not a knight, the penalty was one hundred besants to the court and one hundred sous to the injured party.[64] If the victim were a knight, and the batterer not a knight, then the latter would be sentenced to lose his right thumb.

The presence of Muslims in the High Court was perhaps most acceptable when they served as witnesses. For instance, John of Ibelin described the scenario where a lord had been summoned to court on a particular day, but for some reason he found that he could not make it. Normally, failure to show up would have been grounds for loss of the lawsuit, but the lord could send someone to swear that he was held up, and the absence would be excused. John of Ibelin allowed for that person to be a Muslim, as long as he swore "according to his law."[65]

Without a doubt, an embedded agenda in the legal texts of the High Court was the institution and maintenance of a social hierarchy with Franks, or followers of the law of Rome, at the top, other Christians in the middle, and Jews, Samaritans, and Muslims at the bottom. John of Ibelin in the above-mentioned passage said the delayed lord can send one man "of the law of Rome" to make his excuses and "if he does not have a man of the law of Rome, and he countermands his day [in court] by another Christian, it is valid. And if he does not have a Christian and he finds a Jew or Saracen by whom he countermands his day, it is valid."[66] This judicial ranking occurred in even greater detail in a passage originally from the Cypriot jurist Philip of Novara, but which was also included in some versions of John of Ibelin's work, potentially by Ibelin himself.[67] In the case of a dispute over the boundaries between fields, the agents of the court were instructed to look for, in order of preference, a man (*Franc*) of the law of Rome, then a Syrian, then a Greek, then any other kind of Christian, and lastly a "Saracen."[68]

The area of the domestic legal landscape of the Kingdom of Jerusalem that offered Muslims the most space was the *Cour des Bourgeois* or Burgess Court and especially its subsidiary, the *Cour de la Fonde*, or the Market Court.[69] The Burgess Court of a given city was where free men and women who held property would go for legal satisfaction.[70] The Market Court was the arena specifically where commercial dealings took place. It was also the place where all non-Franks had to take their legal business—except in the cases of murder, treason, blood, or theft, which would be heard before the Burgess Court. The texts providing the regulations for these two courts only survive for the city of Acre; however, Prawer found in surviving Hospitaller documents evidence that there were Burgess Courts in Caesarea (twelfth century), Haifa (thirteenth century), and Jaffa (thirteenth century).[71]

Here the laws describe a venue that, given the context, might strike the reader as surprisingly fair-minded. The assises of the Burgess Court of Acre devoted five chapters to outlining the procedures for who is and is not able to be a witness against someone. They outlined situations between Franks and Greeks, Greeks and Armenians, Armenians and Syrians, Syrians and Nestorians, Nestorians and Jacobites, Samaritans and Jacobites, Samaritans and Muslims, Muslims and Jews, and Jacobites and Syrians.[72] In each of these situations, the laws stipulated that when someone wishes to prove a case against someone of another religion, he must provide two witnesses belonging to the defendant's religion. Suppose a Samaritan loaned money to a Muslim and there was no court record. Later the Samaritan decided to take the Muslim to court for failure to repay the debt, but the Muslim denied it. In order to prove his case, the Samaritan had to provide two Muslim guarantors. No other guarantors would be sufficient.[73] Unlike for the High Court, the assises of the Burgess Court espouse no hierarchy of trustworthiness based on religion.

The law also outlines how oaths were to be taken—on the texts holy to the person's faith. So Jews were to swear on the Torah and Muslims on the Qur'an; Armenians, Syrians, and Greeks swore on the cross and the Gospels written in "their letters"; and the Samaritans on the five books of Moses.[74] So again we see accommodation for religious diversity in this court.

Nevertheless, the Burgess Court was not an entirely egalitarian space. The viscount or *bailli* (bailiff), who sat at the head of the court, had to be a knight or a burgess, statuses that probably served as a means of ensuring only Franks held the position.[75] Under him there were six jurists, loyal men, four of whom were to be Syrian Christians and two Franks. While it is interesting that the majority of the jurists deciding cases were Syrian Christian, it still meant that most of the other groups living in the kingdom were ultimately being judged by people outside their group.

The law does also specify that the bailli should "like to ensure the rights of all kinds of people."[76] Moreover, he should judge "the Saracen like the Syrian, and the Syrian like the Jew, and the Jew like the Samaritan, and all other kinds of people also like the Christians" since they are men "like the Franks."[77] While clearly holding Franks up as the standard marker for humanity, and assuming that some Franks at least might not see others as equals, it does advocate for justice being administered equally among people of all religions. Within the context of the busiest port in the Latin East, even against the backdrop of the misfortunes encountered by the Frankish elites, religious pluralism was accommodated in order for commercial exchange, and the financial benefits the administration reaped from it, to function.

Thus far I have discussed the procedure and composition of the court, but what do the contents of the laws have to tell us of the legal landscape regarding Muslims? The assises of the Burgess Court reiterated, for example, the canonical prohibition of carrying arms and armor into Muslim-controlled lands with intention of selling them.[78] This law echoed canon law also when it prohibited the marriage of a Christian man with a Muslim woman. The reasoning, though, is different. Rather than focusing on the spiritual problems of interfaith marriage, instead the law disapproved of it because the wife was entitled to half a man's property.[79] The assises therefore were trying to minimize the amount of Frankish war materiel and property, movable as well as immoveable, acquired by Muslims.

Another issue related to property in which Muslims suffered a disadvantage was their association with enslavement. The Burgess law clearly attempted to create or enforce a system in which slaves were by default Muslim. One assise referred to Muslims owning slaves, which was not a problem. It continued on to say that if a slave escaped his Christian, Jewish, Samaritan, Syrian, or "Saracen" master by going into "Païenime," or Muslim-held territory, and then returned to the "land of the Christians" in order to become Christian, he would gain his freedom.[80] Thus in line with canon law, the Burgess Court operated according to the premise that it was forbidden to enslave *Christians*. Another chapter explained at some length the punishments for the sale of Christians into slavery.[81] Even if a Christian sold him or herself voluntarily, if he or she did it "as a Saracen," that is to say, if he pretended to be a Muslim in order to circumvent the prohibition against Christians being slaves, and took part of the purchase price, upon discovery she or he would become a perpetual slave. On the other hand, if he did not take any money and the buyer knew he bought a Christian, upon discovery by the court the man would be returned to freedom and given part of the purchase price while the buyer lost his money. The would-be seller would become a servant of the local lord. Furthermore, if the seller knowingly sold a Christian to Muslims, the seller should be dragged around the city and then hanged.

Marwan Nader has explained how the assises attempted to limit this manner of manumission through baptism and the rights enjoyed thereafter, but what bears on this discussion is that despite being otherwise concerned with property relations (deferring to the ecclesiastical court for issues concerning spiritual matters), here the burgess law took a stand on something not entirely material in nature.[82] True, it concerned slaves, a form of property, but the compilers saw fit to uphold on its own the religious distinction advocated by the church. Slaves, in the imagining of the text, were assumed to be non-Christian, which is why they were permitted to return after flight if they desired to be baptized and join the "true religion." Christians, in turn, were not supposed to be slaves; therefore, willingly entering into that condition for monetary gain constituted a virtual abandonment of their status as Christians as evinced by the prescribed punishment of perpetual servitude. We see in the handling of slaves this dichotomy in which Christians had to be free, while slaves had to be non-Christians. It should be noted that in theory, it was possible that some of the slaves were Jews or Samaritans or a member of a non-Abrahamic religion; however, legal texts do not account for this possibility and only refer to Muslims when discussing the religion of slaves.[83]

## The Legal Landscape

Geography would have been key in influencing how Muslims could interact with the systems within which they lived. Those living in or near urban areas such as Acre, Beirut, and Tyre would have had more opportunity to encounter and make use of the Burgess Courts and especially the Market Courts. In the case of the latter, there has been speculation that the court was actually segregated by religion. Chapter 243 of the *Assises* opens: "Know well that the king and the knights and all other people established together that no Syrian, not anyone who the law obliges to provision in the Market Court just as with the Syrians and Greeks and Nestorians and Jacobins and Samaritan and Jews and Muslims, all these people must stay in the upper (*en amont*) market in Acre; and they should never be in the lower (*en aval*) market of Acre, by law and by assise."[84] Some of the scholarship, notably Prawer, has taken this to mean that within the city of Acre there were two market courts, an upper and lower, and that the non-Franks were consigned to the upper one.[85] However, David Jacoby rejected this, arguing persuasively that the market court was located near the St. Nicholas land gate in the northeast, and that in *en amont* and *en aval* rather refer to the flow of people and the goods they purchase inside or outside the city gates. He suggested that the assises meant to ensure that non-Franks living inside the city would not go elsewhere for justice, thus losing the king or his administrator revenue.[86] The Frankish secular law courts therefore strove to prevent non-Franks from moving outside their jurisdictions, thereby avoiding having to pay their fees.

It is unlikely, however, that Muslim peasants living in more rural areas would have had as much interaction with such a court. Rather, it would have been the role of the ra'is appointed by the local lord to ensure that any justice reserved for the secular authority (i.e., his boss) made its way to his court. Peasants, on occasion, would have also been called upon to serve the High Court as witnesses concerning land boundaries or their lord's inability to attend court, as discussed. In those, presumably rare, occasions, they would have had to travel to Acre or wherever the High Court was being held.

## Conclusion

Much of the image of the experience of non-Muslims in the kingdom has been based on the Frankish legal texts discussed here. Scholars of Frankish administration like Prawer, Riley-Smith, and Kedar have pointed to the great extent that Muslims, and non-Franks in general, were shut out of and disenfranchised by the kingdom's elite court systems, and concluded that they held a strictly marginalized position in the kingdom. Christopher MacEvitt, who has demonstrated this was not true for Eastern Christians in the twelfth century, posits that the case in the thirteenth century might have been different and actually segregated.[87] Although both the Islamic and Frankish legal texts discussed here were born out of some actual practice, whether questions posed to a qadi answered in a fatwa or situations arising before a Frankish court resulting in the writing of an assise, ultimately these documents represent prescriptive discourse. They do not represent actual court cases. We do not know whether or to what extent what they prescribed was actually followed. When we think about the position of Muslims in the kingdom under the law, therefore, this must be kept in mind.

In this light, Muslims in the kingdom can be seen as occupying a marginal position in the discourses of *both* Islamic and Frankish jurisprudence. The Frankish legal discourse, especially that of the High Court, did indeed discriminate against Muslims, placing them at the bottom of the hierarchy of trustworthiness. Even in the Burgess Courts, there was the direct association of the enslaved with Muslims, and the privileging of Christianity by mandating the enfranchisement of Christian converts as well as the prohibition of commerce in military paraphernalia with Muslims. Moreover, both Islamic and canon law sought to constrain sex across religious divides. The very permissibility of Muslims living under non-Muslim rule was questionable. The Muslim residents of the kingdom must have felt a certain amount of pressure to move, even if they had a legal case not to do so.

Despite the segregationist leanings of the various legal discourses, none of them was completely successful, nor was religion necessarily the identifier by which the court was most preoccupied. Neither canon nor Islamic law could ignore the reality of intercommunal contact. At the very point of trying to exclude nonmembers, the law makers recognized their existence and made room for them within the system. Both Islamic and Frankish laws sought to regulate the practicalities of intercommunal behaviors by punishing violent behavior or trying to prevent conflict from developing in the first place. The

High Court was far more interested in maintaining the elite political status of Frankish lords than spiritual purity. Accordingly, most of the population, regardless of religion, was barred from its proceedings. While it did disadvantage Muslims as well as Jews and Eastern Christians, the assises of the High Court were far more interested in preserving the privileges of nobles than the privileges of Franks over others. The Burgess and the Market Courts prioritized the smooth functioning of commerce over maintaining particular privileges of the Franks. Moreover, there, even more clearly than for the High Court, Eastern Christian groups other than the Syrians were just as disenfranchised as the Muslims were. None of them could serve as jurors.

Besides the segregationist intentions of the legal discourses in the kingdom, this chapter has also explored the totality of the legal options available to Muslims. The usual legal context of Muslims in the Kingdom of Jerusalem was the local court of the ra'is, or the Burgess Court or especially the Market Court. Muslim peasants would have been tied to their village, and so almost all their legal issues would have been taken up by the ra'is or local shaykh. For Muslims living in a city or for those passing through engaged in trade and commerce or just traveling, they would have been subject to the Burgess and Market Courts. Unlike the High Court or ecclesiastical court, here Muslims were not at such a legal disadvantage. True, Franks and Syrian Christians were privileged by being the ones who filled court positions; nevertheless, in ordinary proceedings the field was level. Everyone's ability to serve as a guarantor was equal. Nor is there any sense that Muslim participation in these courts would have been considered unusual.

What perhaps distinguished the Muslim communities in the kingdom the most from the Jewish and Eastern Christian communities was the extent to which they must have had to adjust their legal practices under Islamic law. Although permitted to adjudicate among themselves issues concerning only Muslims and not involving capital offenses, there were, in all likelihood, very few qadis available to administer justice. At least, very few survive in the sources. Dependent upon governmental appointments and waqf payments, the overwhelming majority of the men who served as qadis must have abandoned regions no longer under the political control of a Muslim. It is possible that individuals took advantage of opportunities to solicit opinions from scholars traveling through Frankish territories, on their way to Acre and the sea for instance, after making the pilgrimage to Mecca, as the Andalusi litterateur Ibn Jubayr did in 1184, or as refugees from the Mongols in the 1240s and 1250s. It is also possible that some, the wealthy and independent, traveled to Syria or Egypt and made inquiries there. Or perhaps they wrote a letter requesting a fatwa. But for the majority for whom that would probably not have been an option, they had to adjust by creating a system that included unofficial legal authorities such as shaykhs or ra'ises.

Although this means of implementing Islamic law stood in stark contrast to that in the *Dar al-Islam*, Muslims rarely emigrated en masse. Instead they navigated the legal options available to them. They were discriminated against by the Frankish legal discourses, but they were not at a complete disadvantage compared to the other non-Frankish communities of the kingdom. The Frankish authors of the legal texts created a theory that privileged first of all the position of elite Franks that rested atop a large sublevel consisting of Eastern Christians, Jews, and Muslims. This was the theory. The next chapter will explore in part how justice was practiced in the context of the larger regional political landscape.

*Chapter 4*

# Illusory Borders

## Muslims and the Political Landscape

### Introduction

When surveying the monographs on the Crusades to the Eastern Mediterranean and the Frankish states established there, one perceives an imbalance in the coverage between the twelfth and thirteenth centuries.[1] The earlier period has the allure of seemingly stable territory, relatively centralized power in the king, and the only incontrovertibly successful crusade in the First Crusade. The Kingdom of Jerusalem as an entity in the thirteenth century, however, offers serious challenges to anyone wanting to describe it. It was smaller, more fragmented, and with seemingly less stable territory and more contested leadership than its twelfth-century self. Furthermore, the Crusades of the later period are easily caricatured as a terrible comedy of errors: the Fourth bringing down the Christian Byzantines, the Fifth succumbing to the well-known hardships of the Nile, the Seventh replicating the failure of the Fifth. The kingdom simply appears to be more like what we think a kingdom should look like in the twelfth century with relatively strong monarchs and sufficient territorial control that we can draw a contiguous line around it. Even so, as scholars investigating the nature of power, kingship, and sovereignty in the Middle Ages have argued, this vision of medieval kingdoms is an anachronistic projection of the modern state backward in time.[2] Rather than being defined by geographic space, medieval kingdoms or other political entities are better understood through common association with a ruler, which may or may not comprise contiguous territories and over which the ruler will exert differing levels of control.[3]

Another tendency in the scholarship has been to present the Franks and their Muslim neighbors as permanently antagonistic and thereby perpetual outsiders to each other. As discussed in the introduction, crusades scholars have relied primarily on Frankish sources, which were mainly written by men of the church with specific religious purposes that inclined them to presenting the sides as oppositional. In the last decades there has been another side, often called the Islamic history of the crusades, in which scholars from Middle East Studies have turned their attention to what medieval Muslim sources have to say about the Crusades. These too have tended to be organized around opposition. Carole Hillenbrand's groundbreaking monograph *The Crusades* explicitly seeks to address the imbalance in sources, by providing a thematic study of the Crusades, and to a lesser extent the Franks, using exclusively Muslim sources.[4] Although synthetic, she provides numerous translations of Arabic sources, which opened many of these to traditional crusades scholars for the first time. The book serves as a touchstone for anyone wanting to understand Muslim perspectives on the Crusades, but in its mirroring of contemporary Europeanist crusades scholarship, it largely focuses on the oppositional nature of the relationship between Franks and Muslims. Only two of the nine chapters engage with nonmilitary topics, and one of them is about negative stereotypes. A more recent example of Islamic history of the Crusades is Paul Cobb's *Race for Paradise*, which provides a chronological narrative of European crusade activity in Muslim sources from the tenth to the fifteenth centuries.[5] Addressing important historiographical questions like the use of jihad and whether memory of the Crusades was a modern phenomenon, Cobb similarly presents a narrative of conflict and focused on the ways Muslims and Franks were externally opposed to each other. These works and others like them that draw from Arabic and other eastern sources have enriched the discussion of the Crusades to the eastern Mediterranean and the Latin East. This chapter will build upon and then depart from these studies by drawing from (largely) Arabic sources to investigate relations between Franks and the Muslim neighbors with an eye to how they worked together rather than against each other. Instead of presenting Muslims as default outsiders, it will seek out and illuminate the ways that Muslims were integral to what has been considered Frankish space.

Investigating the legal, administrative, and political landscapes of the Kingdom of Jerusalem and how Muslims intersected with them further undermines the notion that the kingdom functioned in a way similar to the modern nation-state. As we have seen, the Muslims in the kingdom were not exclusively subject to the legal systems contained within it. They had the possibility of turning to other political powers, such as Ayyubid and Mamluk rulers, who in theory were invested in assuring their well-being in hopes of one day ending the non-Muslim Frankish regime. This sense of having recourse to alternate and competing powers in legal affairs could only have increased as the thirteenth century progressed and the balance of power in the region shifted decidedly toward the Mamluks. Ironically, since this political landscape in no way resembles that of today's nation-states, we do see a sort of "international" or, more properly, "inter-sovereign" law at play in the form of officially recognized diplomatic and oath-swearing protocols, treaties, and jointly administered territories, in addition to the legal systems predicated on religion.

This chapter considers the diplomatic process and the treaties concluded between the Frankish lords and their Turkish and Arab counterparts to understand the totality of the political and administrative landscape in which the kingdom was situated. These treaties mostly survive in Arabic sources and have not been incorporated into discussions of Frankish administrative practice, which, as a consequence, have allowed for some participation by Eastern Christians, but practically none for Muslims or Jews.[6] Shaping and shaped by the region's political and legal frameworks, these treaties constitute key pieces of evidence. Investigating the Arabic chronicles and administrative manuals reveals a situation in which Muslims could be found in any given area of the legal landscape, even when that went against the understood jurisdiction or privilege of the court. The sources show political actors from both sides enforcing their will across local boundaries without the use of direct military action. Moreover, the treaties established systems of joint administration of lands called *condominia* or *munasafat* that permitted—in fact, required—that Muslims work at the very heart of the kingdom's administration. In effect, we see the complete permeability of the legal and political boundaries that the legal texts discussed in the previous chapter attempted to establish. The evidence provides further support for the argument that the notion of a kingdom with geographically defined borders within which a sovereign exercised uniform control is not applicable to the Kingdom of Jerusalem.

Although the fragmented nature of the kingdom is most obvious in the thirteenth century, even studies of earlier treaties have revealed that the political powers of the twelfth century drafted treaties with the intention of diffusing power, rather than concentrating it. Michael Köhler's *Alliances and Treaties between Frankish and Muslim Rulers in the Middle East* remains the most comprehensive treatment of these documents and traces the changes they underwent over the crusade period.[7] Köhler proposes that a "no place" (*la maqam*) policy lay behind the negotiations and alliances among the rulers of the region in the twelfth century.[8] The concern was to maintain independent Syrian city-states, lest imposed unity leave "no place" for the Franks. Regional politics were not dictated by religious animosity; rather, Frankish, Turkish, and Arab leaders dealt with each other in such a way as to maintain the status quo and permit their continued independence. The autonomous emirs and lords of Syrian cities participated in a shifting set of alliances that crossed religious and ethnic boundaries in order to deny a place to a superpower to impose its hegemony upon the rest. The idea was that if any one side were allowed to conquer the other, the third would lose its place as well.

Köhler saw a change in the thirteenth century. Principally, in the second half of the twelfth century, he marked a rise of the ideology of jihad under Nur al-Din, and especially Saladin, which led to the abandonment of the "no place" doctrine by the thirteenth century. Used, as Köhler argued, to bolster Saladin's claim to authority, jihad ideology demanded that Saladin wage continuous wars of conquest against the Franks or those Muslim rulers who opposed him.[9] Confronted with a unified Ayyubid front that succeeded in crushing their army in 1187, the Franks were no longer able to sustain the previous system of relatively small, politically autonomous power centers. Moreover, with Saladin's successes, the Franks became totally dependent upon recruits and supplies from outside the kingdom. Thus even in the half century between Saladin's death in 1193 and the advent of the Mamluks in Egypt, treaties were no longer concluded according to the "no place" policy, but along more defensive lines.[10] Köhler has argued that from 1255 until 1282, the balance of power shifted decisively to the Muslim leaders—that is, the last Ayyubid in Syria, al-Nasir Yusuf, who ruled until 1260—and the Mamluks in Egypt starting in 1250 and Syria from 1260. He emphasizes that treaties were no longer concluded between the Kingdom of Jerusalem and the Muslim leaders, but rather with a host of smaller lords and ladies, and corporate groups, ranging from the Knights Hospitaller to the count of Jaffa. No longer agreements between peers, these treaties were one-way tools to serve Mamluk purposes and that the Mamluks were at liberty to break as soon as they were so inclined.

Implicit in Köhler's analysis of the treaties concluded in the thirteenth century is the narrative of inevitable decline that has characterized accounts of the second half of the Frankish presence in the Levant.[11] He argues that while alliances in the first several decades of the twelfth century were made between equals who could act independently of other powers and were at liberty to intervene in each other's affairs, in the last decades alliances were practically imposed by the crushing might of the Mamluks upon the ever shrinking and insignificant Frankish outposts. Their dwindling territory notwithstanding, the Franks at the time would have been shocked to learn that their defeat was inevitable, and despite what the political realities may seem to us today, we should endeavor to read them as the participants would have.

The hold that the inevitable-decline narrative has upon crusades scholars is illustrated by Köhler's own admission that treaties throughout the Frankish period in the Levant were conducted as if between equals. He notes that one fundamental difference between the treaties made between Christians and Muslims in the Levant and those made contemporaneously in Sicily or Iberia is that the treaties from the latter areas tended to establish one party's sovereignty over the other. In Sicily and Iberia it was commonplace for a Muslim to enter into the service of a Christian lord as a vassal and vice versa.[12] Again, as Köhler himself notes, there is no evidence of such events occurring in the Levant.[13] Although political and military power shifted over time, and certainly by the latter thirteenth century the Mamluks clearly dominated in exerting their will militarily and within negotiations, nevertheless in treaties the contracting parties were legally equals. This fact warrants further investigation as it has a direct impact on the reality of the region's political landscape and should prompt us to reconsider how we understand the nature of the kingdom as a kingdom for the entirety of its existence.

The state of equality on the level of this "inter-sovereign" law created by treaties had important ramifications for the Muslims in the kingdom. In the previous chapter, we saw how carefully the different Frankish court systems attempted to separate and subordinate Muslims to Christians and especially those of "the law of Rome," just as Islamic law simultaneously separated and subordinated non-Muslims to Muslims. Nevertheless, these systems were never entirely successful in achieving either end. The implementation of these regional agreements only served to undermine further the attempts to marginalize Muslims within the kingdom. As will become clear, this was especially true on the highest social level. While the assises of the High Court were perhaps the most successful in creating a legal framework discriminating against Muslims and preventing them from participating in it, the practical necessities of engaging with political equals through the creation and implementation of these treaties only served to open elite Frankish spaces to their Muslim peers.[14]

## Chapter 4

## Ayyubid and Mamluk Treaties and Territory

In this section, we will examine treaties concluded between the Franks and the Ayyubids and Mamluks. This examination offers us an opportunity to see not only how territories were (re)constituted during, primarily, the thirteenth century but it will also offer insights into the power dynamics as constructed by those treaties. As discussed, there is a tendency to view the second half of the Latin Kingdom's existence as one of weakness. Examining the treaties, however, shows us how those concluding the treaties constructed themselves in the moment, usually with the Franks having equal footing with their contracting partners. By the end of the discussion, we will also see how Muslim leaders, so frequently discussed as part of entirely distinct polities from those of the Franks, were in fact very much involved in the daily running of parts of what we consider to be Frankish territory.

We know more about the treaties concluded between the Franks and the Mamluks in the latter part of the thirteenth century than we do about those concluded with the Ayyubids. In contrast to their Ayyubid precursors, redactions of the Mamluk treaties were preserved in Arabic literary sources by authors with close connections to the sultan.[15] These treaties had a significant impact on the political landscape. Most obviously, they helped define the areas of political control, and although the source imbalance does make fraught a comparison between the Ayyubid treaties and the Mamluk treaties, one can note greater territorial concessions on the part of the Ayyubids than the Mamluks. A good deal of the reconstituted kingdom emerged diplomatically, with treaties of 1198 and 1204 between al-ʿAdil and King Aimery of Lusignan adding to Frankish holdings along the coast, notably Beirut and Jubayl with shared revenues from Sidon, Lydda, and Ramla.[16] Ever present in the background of these latter Ayyubid treaties is the threat of renewed crusade as well as the internal strife among the Ayyubids themselves, which played a part in motivating them to come to terms with the Franks.

The most favorable treaty the Franks made with the Ayyubids, the Treaty of Jaffa (1229), came on the heels of the threat of renewed crusade. Concluded in February 1229 between Frederick II—the Holy Roman Emperor and sometime king of Jerusalem through his marriage to the heiress Isabella of Brienne—and the sultan of Egypt al-Malik al-Kamil, the treaty returned Jerusalem, Lydda, Bethlehem, and the villages between them, as well as a corridor of villages between Jerusalem and Acre.[17] The groundwork for this treaty was made in the years prior when al-Kamil endeavored to use Frederick against his brother al-Mu'azzam in Damascus, promising these lands in exchange for aid. While by November 1227, al-Kamil's political troubles were resolved by al-Mu'azzam's death, Frederick's arrival in the Kingdom in 1228 with a large army in tow provided sufficient pressure for al-Kamil to honor the negotiations and conclude the treaty.[18] From 1226 when al-Kamil first broached the potential peace, to 1227 with the death of his brother, the treaty was viewed in practical terms by the sultan as a means of extending his power in Syria while temporarily neutralizing a potential enemy on his flank. Afterward, it was a convenient way to avoid a potential threat from the Franks. As Ibn Wasil reports, al-Kamil himself replied to his detractors following the treaty with a dismissive comment on how he had merely given up some churches and broken towns, while the Haram al-Sharif remained in Muslim hands.[19]

Köhler was not wrong when he pointed out that a difference in treaty-making between the mid-twelfth century and the early thirteenth is that in the latter period the Frankish threat was seen to emanate from (potential) crusader waves rather than their standing military resources. Nevertheless, it is incorrect to read this as a disregard for Frankish forces on the ground or that legally the Franks were on unequal standing vis-à-vis their Muslim counterparts. Although the treaty of 1229 was concluded with Frederick, who left shortly thereafter, the Franks were expected to and did maintain it.[20] In 1240, shortly after the treaty expired, al-Kamil's brother al-Malik al-Salih Isma'il, now in control of Damascus and seeking a partner against Egypt, renewed the treaty, this time with Thibaut of Champagne who had come on crusade.[21] In addition, al-Salih Isma'il threw in the hinterland of Sidon, the fortress of Beaufort, Tiberias, and Safad. Again, this treaty must be read against the backdrop of internal Ayyubid politicking making use of the latest wave of crusaders. Moreover, just as with the treaty of 1229, the Franks who remained in the kingdom after Thibaut's army left continued to keep the treaty. It was the Khwarazmian Turks, invited by al-Salih Isma'il's nephew and rival al-Salih Ayyub, who conquered Jerusalem and defeated the Franco-Ayyubid coalition in the Battle of La Forbie/Harbiyya. The newly dominant al-Salih Ayyub of Egypt would later capitalize on the defeat of his Ayyubid rivals and their Frankish allies by retaking Tiberias in 1247.[22]

The analysis of treaties between Franks and Ayyubids thus shows us how dynamic political power was and how political lines were not determined by religious affiliation. Franks and Ayyubid Muslim leaders forged alliances to suit mutual purposes. In so doing, they continuously reshaped the political geography of the region, usually by granting Franks more control. The key takeaway is that the Franks were not outsiders, nor were they being handled as inconvenient nuisances, but full partners in the game of regional geopolitics. In a real way Franks and their Ayyubid partners shaped the Latin East together.

The treaties concluded between the Franks and Mamluks had a different tenor. The Mamluks presented themselves to the Franks as a united entity, not fractured among city-bases like the Ayyubids. Moreover, the Franks had less crusader support in the latter half of the century than in the first. Following the defeat of King Louis IX's crusade to Egypt in 1250 and his return to Europe in 1254, there was only one major wave of crusaders until the conquest of Acre in 1291. This last wave consisted of the remnants from Louis's abortive crusade against Tunis in 1271, including a contingent sent by his brother Charles of Anjou and that of the young Prince Edward of England. This incident will be discussed in greater length in the final section of the chapter, but briefly, the Sultan Baybars, rather than attempting to negotiate a truce, elected to try to distract the Franks by sending a fleet from Egypt to attack Cyprus.[23] When that ended in failure upon the reefs of Limassol, Baybars then turned to negotiation and agreed to a ten-year treaty with Edward and King Hugh of Cyprus in 1272, which also included territorial concessions, albeit ones of lesser importance.[24]

In contrast to the earlier period that extended land to the Franks, the majority of the treaties the Mamluks served instead to stabilize land control, provide for the safe passage of merchants and others, and establish or confirm revenue-sharing mechanisms. The way land was handled in the later treaties is most likely the greatest difference between those treaties the Franks conducted with Ayyubids and those with the Mamluks. In a way, the Mamluk treaties acted to legalize Frankish territorial losses. For instance, the treaty concluded between the Knights Hospitaller and Baybars in 665/1267 was initiated a year earlier in the face of Baybars' ravaging of the area around the castles of Alba (Halba) and Coliath (al-Qulayʿat) on the approach to the Hospitaller castle of ʿAkkar. When it was finalized, it granted the demolition of a Hospitaller mill near Acre that had already been destroyed by Baybars' campaign in May 1267.[25] Similarly, the treaty the Sultan Qalawun entered with Bohemond VII of Tripoli in 680/1281 served to ratify his predecessor Baybars's conquest of ʿArqa. Bohemond's ambassadors traveled to Damascus in 1281 to renew a treaty concluded in 674/1275 and attempted to argue that ʿArqa was simply acting as collateral until the lord of Tripoli fulfilled the terms of the earlier treaty and should therefore still be considered part of

Tripoli's holdings. The young clerk Shafi' bin 'Ali Ibn Asakir al-'Asqalani, the nephew of Baybars's biographer Muhyi al-Din Ibn 'Abd al-Zahir, was present and, as he reported in his own biography of the Sultan Qalawun, he argued that 'Arqa was not held in collateral but rather conquered in light of the breach of the previous truce. He exclaimed to the Frankish ambassador: "Al-Malik al-Zahir occupied 'Arqa only as an act of war against you, not as an act of kindness by taking instalments [sic]. The oxen in this settlement, the seeds and the peasants belong to him, not to you, through his representatives, not your representatives. Its soil became his possession by the sword, as indeed did everything, since the truce lapsed through your breach of the condition."[26] According to Shafi' bin 'Ali's logic, the failure to fulfill the terms of the 1275 treaty permitted Baybars to legally conduct war against Tripoli during which campaign he conquered 'Arqa. This new treaty of 1281 therefore would reestablish the territories now under Tripolitan and Mamluk control, taking that conquest into consideration. The treaty of 1281, in short, acted to formalize the conquest. Treaties concluded between the Franks and Mamluks continued to serve as instruments defining the geopolitical contours of the land. The Mamluks did not rest on de facto control of a castle; they continued to use treaties to make that control legal. Whereas earlier in the century, the Franks could rely on the military threat of a new crusade to push Ayyubids into granting them territory via treaty, the Mamluks conquered first and then subsequently legitimized the conquest through treaty. The analysis reveals that the political landscape was not shaped only by military conquest, or its threat, but by a joint belief in the necessity and existence of shared law as created by treaty.

## Treaties and Shared Social Status

Treaties not only show the more complicated manner in which the political landscape was defined; they also testify to, while simultaneously helping to shape, the relative standing of each of the contracting parties. As the discussion in this section will show, counter to the idea of the Franks inevitably being in the weaker position compared with the Mamluks, the Franks were treated in the documents as equals. Whereas in the twelfth century, we believe treaties were conducted for the most part between the King of Jerusalem or his regent and the rulers of individual city-states or smaller polities, in the later thirteenth century we see the situation reversed.[27] The Mamluk sultan concluded treaties with not only the King of Cyprus and/or Jerusalem but also the magnates as well as the military orders.[28] The situation in the twelfth-century treaties coincided with what crusades scholars have long noted as the period of greatest strength for the Frankish monarchy, when its suzerainty was most widely recognized, whereas for much of the thirteenth century, the king was absent in Europe or split his time between the coastal mainland and Cyprus. The period also saw significant internal political unrest with several civil wars boiling up between the Venetians and Genoese during the 1250s and '60s, and another, related one between the Embriaco lords of Jubail and the princes of Antioch-Tripoli. The political playing field therefore was peopled by a relatively larger group of Franks who operated independently in contracting agreements with their Muslim peers. In effect, the Frankish lords gained status regionally, since by the 1260s the only Muslim with whom they did contract treaties was the sultan.

This functional state of equality was recognized by the Mamluk leadership. One of the most important sources we have about Mamluk administration and diplomatics is the treatise *Subh al-a'sha fi sina'at al-insha* by Ahmad bin 'Ali al-Qalqashandi (756–821/1355–1418) who worked in the Mamluk chancery in Cairo.[29] In this fourteen-volume treatise, al-Qalqashandi discussed different kinds of administrative documents and the philosophy behind them using actual documents, many from the thirteenth century, as exemplars. As he began the section on truces, al-Qalqashandi noted that while technically the Arabic word for truce (*hudna*) indicated unilateral action of one party granting another, subservient one a period of peace, in fact two parties were involved.[30] When read in the context of truces made with the Latin Kingdom, hudna signals two parties of relative equality in importance, which contrasts with the situation in contemporary Iberia where treaties between the Christian kings and the Muslim rulers were concluded in terms of clientage.[31] In fact, al-Qalqashandi went on to explain that another condition of truces was that the status of the contracting parties varied. That is, if on one side was a region like Anatolia, then the Muslim equivalent was the Great Imam, or caliph, which functionally meant the sultan was his executor.[32] When there is a truce with the sultan as the contracting party it meant that the other party was of equal importance. Although al-Qalqashandi provided for the potential of treaties being concluded between lesser individuals, we do not have evidence for this from the treaties with the Franks. Rather, in the treaties he preserved, it was always the sultan and some personage or institution on the Frankish side. Thus, we may conclude that these Frankish lords and ladies of the Latin East were seen as having the same importance as the hypothetical lord of Anatolia or other major region from al-Qalqashandi's explanation.

The language used in naming the parties in the treaties itself is suggestive of this broader equality among the Frankish magnates, the Frankish king, and the sultan. The description of the treaty between Hugh III and Baybars in 667/1268 compares favorably with those made with the Frankish magnates, like the lady of Tyre, in content and terminology. The text identifies those lands under possession of each signatory and those that were shared. It also underlines that Muslim prisoners were to be freed as a precondition, and that the truce would not be lifted in the event of a new crusade. The treaty was equally meticulous in naming the Frankish parties involved. Ibn al-Furat gave the most detailed presentation of Hugh, with a lengthy explanation of how he became king as cousin and *bailli* for Hugh II, while naming him in Arabic fashion by calling him "Hugh, son of Henri, king of Cyprus and Akko."[33] In Baybars' 684/1285 treaty with King Leo of Armenia, a Frankish ally, the king was called *al-malik al-jalil layfun* or "his Majesty King Leon." It later designated him as the son of King Hetoum and the grandson of Constantine, mirroring genealogical naming practices among the Arab elites.[34] In direct parallel with this, the 1285 treaty between the Sultan Qalawun and Margaret of Tyre referred to her as "al-malika al-jalila dam mar[g]arit bint sir hari bin al-ibrins bimond malikat sur" or "her majesty Queen/Lady Dame Margaret, daughter of Sir Henri, son of the Prince Bohemond, Lady of Tyre."[35] Similarly, in the 667/1269 treaty with Isabel of Beirut, Isabel was called "the exalted, virtuous, and glorious Lady [Isabel, daughter of John,] the Queen/Lady of Beirut and of all its mountains and lowlands."[36] Not only is the sultan contracting treaties with Frankish lordships, elevating them to a high status, but he is doing so with women leaders, who in the text are being identified with elaborate names and titles. True, they are not as lengthy as those of Muslim rulers, but they are fairly extensive, showing that the effort is being made to indicate their worthiness to be on equal footing with a sultan.

It is interesting that these two ladies get such lofty titles in the treaties. The leaders of Tripoli do not tend to be treated as well, at least according to the treaty summaries in the narrative sources. For instance, in the treaty between Bohemond VI of Antioch-Tripoli and Baybars in 669/1271, Bohemond was called "the Prince" (*al-brins*), Lord of Tripoli (*sahib Tarabulus*).[37] Ten years later his son Bohemond VII was called by Baybars al-Mansuri the "*de facto* ruler (*mutamallik*) of Tripoli, Bohemond son of Bohemond" in the description of the 1281 treaty with the Mamluks.[38] The princely title of the elder Bohemond clearly hearkens to his title as Prince of Antioch prior to its capture in 1268, but instead of being called the *malik* of Tripoli, the masculine equivalent to *malika* as Isabel and Margaret were called, he was merely referred to as its *sahib*. It is curious that Ibn ʿAbd al-Zahir also retained the princely title here even though Bohemond no longer held Antioch at the time of the treaty. The taunting letter the Sultan Baybars sent to Bohemond after the city's conquest informing him that he would no longer be prince, but merely a count, underscores that the Mamluks understood "Prince" to be a title and not some strange Frankish name.[39] Still he is referred to as the Prince—perhaps as a means of distinguishing him from the many other Bohemonds with fathers named Bohemond—but merely the "lord" of Tripoli. His son was demoted further to being *mutamallik*, or someone who took possession by force, obviously indicating a less-than-legitimate lord of Tripoli.[40]

The treaties concluded with the military orders again demonstrated this incorporation of transliterated Frankish titles in addition to more traditional Arabic sobriquets. In the 665/1267 treaty between the Hospitallers and Baybars, the Master Hugh Revel was called "the gallant [*al-humam*] Grand Leader X., Leader of the house of the Hospital such and such in Acre and the lands of the coast."[41] Later in the 669/1271 treaty between the two, Hugh Revel was called: "his majesty Leader [Master] Brother Hugh Revel, leader of the entire House of the Hospital of St. John in the land of the coast and all the Brothers of the Hospital."[42] The Master of the Templars William of Beaujeu received similar titles in the 681/1282 treaty with Qalawun.[43]

What we see from these examples is twofold. First, there was a clear effort to incorporate the Franks into Arabic models of naming. Although not nearly as long as the combined names and titles of the sultan, they certainly were mirroring them, by listing the individual as so-and-so son/daughter of so-and-so, along with a sobriquet like *al-jalil(a)* or *al-humam*, in addition to their Frankish titles like *al-mastar* or *dam*. This shows the incorporation of these Frankish elites into the Arabic elite political sphere, recognizing them as individuals with power with whom one contracts treaties, and possessing a recognizable dignity. Although it might seem obvious, given the habit of modern scholars to describe the thirteenth-century Latin East in moribund terms, it is important to recognize that diplomatically, they were still seen as people possessing status and power. Second, the examples demonstrate that these Frankish elites were seen by the Mamluks, and probably the Ayyubids before them, as functionally equal, each possessing individual power over his or her own territories, independent of the actual king or regent. Remember, the sultan was the executor of the caliph and so worthy of contracting treaties only with the most powerful people. That he was contracting with the lords of Tripoli, Tyre, and Beirut signals that they were seen as possessing prestige and power on par with the sultan. In the process, it confirms that at least for the thirteenth century, power among the Franks was distributed widely as not only an internal reality but one externally recognized as well.

One treaty that might show a more traditional indication of priority among the Franks is the treaty of 1283. The last of the treaties concluded before the conquest in 1291, it was between the sultan and "the authorities of Acre, Sidon, ʿAthlith." It proceeded to list who those authorities were: "the Seneschal Odo, *Bailli* of the kingdom in Acre, the Master Brother William of Beaujeu, Master of the Order of the Templars, Master Nicholas Lorgne, Master of the Order of the Hospitallers, the Marshal Brother Conrad, Deputy Master of the Teutonic Order."[44] A letter written by William II of Agen, Patriarch of Jerusalem, and others of the kingdom's leaders in October 1265 to King Louis of France demonstrates that in documents among Franks, the Templars had precedence over the Hospitallers.[45] The recording therefore of the Templar Master, followed by the Hospitaller Master in the treaty, followed Frankish sensibilities of precedence. Nevertheless, this ordering in all likelihood stemmed from the Franks themselves, rather than the Mamluks. We know that these treaties were constructed after much negotiation over the contents and the wording. What we see in this arrangement of precedence is an accommodation of Frankish mores, similar to the transliteration of Frankish titles, which in no way undermined their functional equality to each other in the eyes of their Muslim counterparts.

## Shared Processes, Shared Spaces

The texts of these treaties shaped and were shaped by the mental geography of the regional political landscape. As far as the Mamluk sultans were concerned, the Frankish elites were equally available to contract and negotiate agreements. While there was only one acceptable partner, the sultan, on the Muslim side, there were multiple partners on the Frankish side. This situation, as it existed in the latter half of the thirteenth century, represented a long-term shift from what it had been before. Although we do not have the texts of the treaties, we do know that in the twelfth and early thirteenth centuries, treaties were concluded between the Kingdom of Jerusalem and the heads of other Frankish polities and individual Syrian city-based and Egyptian powers. In this next section, we will examine how the process of seeking, negotiating, writing, and swearing treaties also had a practical effect of opening up spaces to Muslims in the Kingdom of Jerusalem. While domestically the Frankish High Court attempted to exclude everyone but the highest ranks of Frankish nobles, the realities of the regional political landscape undermined this effort.

Muslim messengers and envoys frequently crossed the roads between the major Levantine cities seeking access to Frankish lords and vice versa. Some of these were seeking safe conduct (*aman*) for travel through Frankish lands, others were seeking to initiate longer peace treaties, while still others were simply delivering letters or other forms of information. Aman requests were temporary passes of safe conduct that had become a routine matter in intraregional political dealings. These seem to have been the usual first step in opening negotiations. For instance, in September 659/1261 negotiations between John of Ibelin, Count of Jaffa, and the Sultan Baybars opened with the Count sending a messenger to Baybars with gifts and a request for a safe conduct for the Count to come to the sultan's camp at al-ʿAwjaʾ. The request was granted, and the *atabek* (commander of the army) Faris al-Din Uqtay al-Salihi rode out to meet him and escort him to the sultan to negotiate an agreement. Similarly we learn of a messenger traveling to Damascus with the request for safe conducts for envoys from the military orders.[46]

One famous, not to mention contested, example of an aman request on the part of the Egyptians occurred in the lead-up to the Battle of ʿAyn Jalut in 1260 that marked the halt in Mongol advances into the Middle East. The death of the Great Khan Möngke the previous year prompted the leader of the Persian Mongol contingent, Hülagü, to withdraw with the majority of his forces to Mongolia in order to participate in the selection of next Great Khan. When the Mamluk sultan Qutuz learned of the significantly weakened state of the Mongols in Syria, he assembled his military and moved into Palestine to retake land now nominally under Mongol control. According to contemporary Mamluk historiography, the army moved quickly and unnoticed through the territory until it approached Acre. The accounts of what transpired next differ. According to the Templar of Tyre, the sultan requested permission to pass through Frankish territory in order to fight the Mongols, which was granted, given the Franks were fresh off a Mongol retaliatory raid on Sidon.[47] The *Rothelin* continuation of the history of William of Tyre gives a slightly different account. It does not mention whether the Mamluks requested permission to cross Frankish territory, but instead records that they requested Frankish aid after having assembled in Damascus. It was only through the counsel of the Master of the Teutonic Knights that the Frankish lords decided to decline the offer to participate. Instead, they promised not to harm the Mamluk forces and to provide supplies.[48] According to Ibn al-Furat, however, it was the Franks who sent gifts and offered their aid upon seeing the Egyptian host outside of Acre. The Sultan Qutuz declined the offered Frankish reinforcements and asked instead that they swear "that they would be neither for him nor against him."[49]

Besides the obvious posturing and reimagining of the roles played in what was then and is still now seen as a major check in the Mongol advance, this story does illustrate the kind of high-level interactions that took place between the Frankish and Mamluk (and Ayyubid) elites on a regular basis. Muslim emissaries came and went from the Frankish courts, and the Frankish elites visited the sultan as well as his representatives. In fact, this particular episode led to the Mamluk army crossing through the Frankish landscape to meet the Mongols at ʿAyn Jalut, in addition to the penetration of the very heart of the kingdom by not just a handful of Mamluk representatives but large numbers of them. While the exchanges were taking place, or perhaps while the decision of whether or not to join forces was being made, Mamluk soldiers were permitted to enter the city of Acre. According to Ibn ʿAbd al-Zahir, who was present at the time, one could overhear Franks from the city ramparts calling "Hey Muslim! Show us someone!," which the author interpreted as meaning they wanted to see the sultan. Of even more consequence in retrospect is the fact that the soon-to-be sultan Baybars, at this time a general in the Mamluk army, was among those who entered and walked around Acre.[50] The significance of this was not lost upon the Templar of Tyre who also noted Baybars's entrance into the city and the fact that he later "did an enormous amount of harm." He also reported that there were so many Muslims in Acre that the inhabitants became afraid and "drove them out both by force and by persuasion."[51] Given that the coerced exit was not mentioned by Ibn ʿAbd al-Zahir who was there, one suspects that this part of the tale was added to emphasize in hindsight the ominousness of the presence of the man who would be responsible for so much Frankish territorial loss.

With the emphasis on impending disaster contained in many of the narratives concerning the kingdom during the thirteenth century, one might also assume that the majority of the messengers were in fact Franks seeking out an audience with the sultan. There is, on the contrary, plenty of evidence for

Muslim messengers and envoys. Often these were directed at Acre, which was the seat of government. For instance, we know of al-Malik al-ʿAdil sending envoys to the city in 1210 to discuss renewing the treaty from six years prior; an attempt that was rejected thanks to the Grand Master of the Templars, and was not successful until July 1212.[52] King Louis IX received many envoys from Muslim leaders while he was in residence at Acre in 1250. Upon the assassination of the last Ayyubid sultan of Egypt, Turanshah, in May 1250 by the Mamluks, the emir of Damascus and Aleppo, al-Malik al-Salih Yusuf, sent to Louis seeking an alliance against the new rulers of Egypt. This initiated a diplomatic exchange that eventually fell through in favor of an alliance with Egypt.[53] The leader of the Nizari Ismaʿilis (pejoratively known as the Assassins), ʿAlaʾ al-Din Muhammad (d. 653/1255) also sent envoys to King Louis IX while he was at Acre. He sought to intimidate the king into asking the Hospitallers and Templars to stop their demands of tribute from them. This, according to Joinville, was unsuccessful.[54] The author of the *Rothelin* text complained about how Frankish leaders were "constantly [receiving] envoys from the princes of the unbelievers, who gave them lavish retainers and payments" in 1239–1240.[55] Al-Salih, in 1240 when he was ruling Damascus, sent envoys to the heart of the Frankish army, then led by Thibaut of Navarre, to offer an alliance against his Ayyubid rivals in Egypt.[56] Thus we have plenty of evidence for Muslim envoys being received and performing their communicative and diplomatic duties in Frankish courts. This on its own is not terribly surprising as messengers were how political leaders communicated among themselves at this time. If one were inclined to believe that the Latin East metaphorically walled itself off from the rest of the region and that once it was in unrelenting decline in the thirteenth century, all communication would have been outward desperately trying to stave off neighboring attack, then it would be easy to forget that messengers would travel frequently in the other direction.

Nor were these messengers necessarily lowly or anonymous. We can return to the example of Abu Bakr bin Yusuf al-Hakim al-Rasʿani (d. 657/1259) already discussed in Chapters 1 and 2. The biographer Ibn al-ʿAdim recorded that al-Rasʿani was not only a doctor but a frequent messenger between the Abbasids and the Seljuks of Rum.[57] He wrote that al-Rasʿani was in Damascus when the Mongols were threatening to attack and he decided to proceed to Egypt and sail from there home to Anatolia. He accordingly wrote to the Franks of Acre for permission to travel through their territory and protection for himself and his goods. He fell ill and died before the letter granting permission arrived and it was delivered to Ibn al-ʿAdim instead. Ibn

Wasil informed us of another emissary, the emir Fakhr al-Din bin al-Shaykh who executed the exchange of letters between al-Malik al-Kamil and Frederick II during the latter's time in the Levant. At this period, Fakhr al-Din was toward the beginning of what would end up being an illustrious career that would conclude with commanding the military forces of the Egyptian sultanate under al-Malik al-Salih and acting as regent with his widow Shajar al-Durr before his death in 1249.[58] The leaders had a lively intellectual exchange in which, among other things, the emperor posed questions concerning governance, engineering, and mathematics to the sultan in order, so Ibn Wasil suggested, to determine who was the most learned.[59] Ibn Shaddad provided us with the name of another emissary. Faris al-Din Aqtay al-Musta'rib al-Salihi (d. 673/1274) was appointed by the first Mamluk sultan, al-Malik al-Mu'izz Aybak, to conduct negotiations with the Franks for the release of the prisoners from King Louis IX's crusade.[60] Faris al-Din was one of the key Mamluk commanders involved in the rout at al-Mansura during Louis's crusade, holding at the time the rank of emir but soon to be elevated to atabek after he aided in Aybak's assassination in 1257.[61]

We see, therefore, that in the course of normal political dealings between Franks and non-Franks, there was an active movement of personnel from one court to another. These envoys literally and figuratively traveled through the landscape in order to deliver messages and requests, making their presence felt both as they traversed the territory of the kingdom and as they negotiated in the courts. They were regular features of the political landscape and consisted of people of elevated position. Again, this is not by itself shocking, but should remind us of the frequent presence of Muslims of status within Frankish spaces. It also further shows the way the Latin East was very much integrated into the political and diplomatic practices of the larger region and not exclusively oriented to Europe.

## Shared Protocols

In order for this intertwined political and legal landscape to function, there had developed a series of shared protocols. This shared political culture involved mutually recognized behaviors seen as requisite for particular interactions to take place. For instance, above we have already seen that when John of Ibelin wanted to initiate diplomatic discussions with Baybars, he first sent an ambassador requesting permission for him to come into the sultan's camp.[62] Yvonne Friedman, in her study of captives and captivity in the Kingdom of Jerusalem, discussed the shared protocols involved in handling captives.[63] She argued that by the time of the First Crusade, there had already developed along the Byzantine-Seljuk frontier a mutually recognized system of treatment and exchange of captives. This system involved both official diplomatically arranged exchanges and individual efforts at ransom. It was to this system of ransom that the newly arrived Franks eventually came to accommodate themselves.

These sorts of shared political behaviors also necessarily led to interpenetration of spaces. As we have already seen, the process of initiating and negotiating treaties involved exchanges of high-ranking personnel.[64] The conclusion of treaties was no different. After the terms of a given treaty were agreed to, the contracting parties had established means of rendering them official through oath-swearing ceremonies. Al-Qalqashandi pointed out that it was customary to write out the oaths that each party was to swear to at the end of the treaty documents. He wrote assuming that the negotiations took place in the presence of the sultan and that either the sultan or his delegate would swear to it before the Frankish delegation and then the Frankish delegate would so swear if he had a letter confirming his ability to do so. If not, a copy of the treaty would be sent to the Frankish party in question for him to swear upon and sign which would then be returned to the sultan.[65]

This oath-swearing seems to have been regularly done without both named parties present, thus requiring high-level deputies to travel to the court of the one absent. Evidence suggests that prior to the administration of the oath, the contents of the treaty would be read aloud before an array of notables, highlighting the dispersed nature of power in the kingdom. The Patriarch of Jerusalem, Gerold of Lausanne, complained bitterly in his letter of March 26, 1229, to Pope Gregory IX of infractions in these protocols when Frederick II concluded his treaty with al-Kamil. He protested that Frederick swore before the sultan's envoys "in secret," by which he meant without representatives of resident nobles from the kingdom. Moreover, the contents of the treaty were not read aloud to the barons or masters of the military orders, key holders of power, which struck the Patriarch as scandalous.[66] Even so, we know that it was very common for envoys from the Muslim powers to travel to the Frankish courts to administer these oaths. Ibn al-Furat recorded that for the 665/1267 treaty with the Hospitallers, Baybars sent the emir and chamberlain (*hajib*) Fakhr al-Din al-Muqri and the qadi Shams al-Din Ibn Quraysh, a state secretary (*katib al-darj al-sharif*), to administer the oath to the Master Hugh Revel.[67] Fakhr al-Din al-Muqri made regular appearances in various Frankish courts. He is also recorded as being part of the delegation, along with the state secretary al-Sadr Fath al-Din Ibn al-Qaysarani, sent to administer the oath to King Hugh III in April 1272 (670).[68] In this particular oath-swearing protocol, the sultan swore before the leaders of the military orders, and we are told that the sultan had them swear separately from the king on their own behalf. Undoubtedly this was done with the understanding that they operated independently, and therefore needed to swear that they would be beholden by anything to which Hugh swore.

For the Mamluks, these ambassadors were functionally equal to those to whom they administered oaths. Ibn ʿAbd al-Zahir related the story of the administration of the 666/1268 treaty with Hugh III.[69] In Shawwal/July of that year, Baybars sent Ibn ʿAbd al-Zahir and the emir Kamal al-Din bin al-Shith to Acre and instructed them not to humble themselves to Hugh either in seating or address. When they arrived at the court they were given a lavish reception. However, when it came time for the oath-swearing, the king and the barons were seated and the ambassadors, according to Ibn ʿAbd al-Zahir, declined to sit until they were given places before the king. The ambassadors likewise declined to hand over the treaty until the king deigned take it himself with his own hand.[70] This episode encapsulates a number of threads under discussion in this chapter. It demonstrates that Muslims entered ostensibly Frankish-only elite spaces such as the High Court on a regular basis. As we have seen, the Franks were in frequent diplomatic contact with their neighbors so such ambassadors were not exceptional. It further demonstrates that these Muslims were themselves high ranking, and that they were to be seen as functionally equal to Frankish monarchs and his barons. That the emissaries were able to enforce this equality by refusing to be seated anywhere but before the king, and by refusing to hand the treaty to anyone but the king, in the very heart of Frankish political power, the High Court at Acre, demonstrates that the idea of a segregated High Court as proposed in John of Ibelin and the other Frankish legal treatises reflected more of an idealized state of affairs than the reality.

The reach of Muslims into the Frankish political sphere is best exemplified by the very curious episode involving Isabel of Ibelin (1252–1282), the Lady of Beirut.[71] In 1273 Isabel's second husband, Hamo l'Estrange, an English noble from the entourage of Prince Edward, died while away from Beirut.[72] In order to secure a replacement, King Hugh III occupied the lordship and sent Isabel across to Cyprus. Isabel resisted his attempt to remarry her. Somehow, either through a message from Isabel herself or through other intelligence networks, news of this reached Baybars, and in 673/1275 the sultan wrote to Acre contesting Hugh's activities. He declared that the lordship was under his protection by way of the treaty between him and the Lady and that her husband had entrusted her to his protection before he left.[73] Moreover, he wrote: "and it was her custom, if she travelled, to commit her land to me. On this occasion she has sent me no ambassador. She must be produced, and my ambassador must go and have sight of her; otherwise I have the best right to her country."[74] Thus Baybars put forth the claim that he was the rightful protector of the lordship of Beirut and was seeking to ensure the interests of Isabel. Should Hugh refuse to return her, Baybars would implicitly be moved to take Beirut himself.

Ibn 'Abd al-Zahir recorded that Hugh was disquieted by this message, knowing that he was also opposed by the Templars at the time.[75] He argued with the emir and *dawadar* (supervisor of the Mamluk chancery) Sayf al-Din Balaban, saying that the treaty he had concluded with the sultan in Ramadan 670/April 1272 put Beirut under his protection as King of Jerusalem. The delegation held firm that Hugh had to produce Isabel. The sultan next took the step of writing to the Papal Legate in Acre, Thomas Agni of Lentino, telling him and the Franks to write and decide the matter according to their religion. Eventually Hugh backed down and permitted Isabel to return to Beirut and she remained unmarried and in sole control of the lordship until after the death of Baybars.

These exchanges have to be interpreted against the backdrop of Baybars's series of conquests starting with Jaffa, Beaufort, and Antioch in 1268, and Chastel Blanc, Crac des Chevaliers, Gibelacar, and Montfort in 1271. Although he subsequently turned his attention to Armenia and the Mongols, he continued to involve himself in internal Frankish politics. In March 1275, immediately prior to the contretemps with Isabel, he became embroiled in the succession of the county of Tripoli. Bohemond VI died that month, with his son Bohemond VII only fourteen years old. King Hugh claimed the regency, however, Bohemond's widow, Sibylla, took over the guardianship together with Bishop Bartholomew of Tortosa. Baybars, on the march in Cilician Armenia, took the dissension as an opportunity to lay claim to half of Lattakia, which he argued ought by right be held as a *condominium* (*munasafa*), and he moved his troops to the nearby castle of 'Arqa (Arcas) to emphasize his point.[76] According to Ibn 'Abd al-Zahir, Hugh requested that Baybars send someone trustworthy with whom he would negotiate on behalf of the lordship of Tripoli. So Baybars sent the dawadar Sayf al-Din Balaban, whom we have already met, to ʿArqa and negotiations began. These came to a standstill after Baybars retired to Damascus around June 1275, and King Hugh retired to Tripoli, requesting the Mamluk delegate to accompany him.

This is the context in which the intrigues over Lady Isabel occurred. Sayf al-Din Balaban entered Tripoli July 4, 1275 (8 Muharram 674), carrying Baybars' letter concerning the Lady of Beirut, having been summoned by Hugh to conclude negotiations on the status of Lattakia.[77] In these negotiations he was able to get Hugh to agree to release twenty prisoners and pay 20,000 Tyrian dinars.[78] Although the threat of Mamluk force was not distant, and in fact was an unavoidable fact of political dealings, both parties were nevertheless operating as independent sovereigns creating a kind of regional law and diplomacy. The Mamluks were not merely external forces applying pressure to an insulated Frankish political landscape; they were themselves players within it. At the same moment when treaties were being concluded between Frankish and Muslim elites, those very same supposedly external Muslim elites were in the position to serve as protectors for Frankish lordships. They maneuvered within Frankish systems of administration and law, as well as negotiating "inter-sovereign" or regional laws in the form of treaties.

## Condominia/Munasafat: Shared Territories and Administration

The epitome of this shared political landscape was the institution of condominia or munasafat (sing. *munasafa*). This was the system of holding lands in common between a Frankish and a Muslim lord; a system that seems to have distinguished Muslim relations with Franks in the Levant from encounters elsewhere.[79] Although they were used in the twelfth century, most of the evidence for them comes to us from thirteenth-century Arabic sources.[80] In particular, the treaties concluded with the Mamluks go into extensive detail on the munasafat. The details of a given condominium, whether it was sovereignty or revenues that were shared, varied.

Köhler, in one of the only treatments of this system, has argued persuasively that it was largely an import from European landholding traditions. Although there was some precedent in Islamic jurisprudence in the field of personal property, in the realm of the administration of justice and sovereignty, such condominia did not exist prior to the twelfth century, while certain Arabic writers complained of them being imposed by the Franks.[81] He further pointed out that Franks in the Levant arranged condominia among themselves, and that the administrative provisions for justice—for instance, requiring a village to be held accountable if the one responsible for committing a given crime failed to be discovered—hearkened back to Western legal traditions like the Salic law.[82] Moreover, the evidence we have suggests that lands held as condominia tended to remain so regardless of the vicissitudes of politics, following a more Western approach to custom and landholding.

Although condominia seem to have largely come from European administrative custom, they quickly became an established element of the regional political landscape and another factor tying together the Frankish and Muslim elites. Condominia imbricated their territories no matter how much their rulers might have desired a distinct separation. Income from the area of the Golan was shared from perhaps has early as 1108.[83] Sidon had been a condominium until Frederick II had its walls rebuilt in 1228, and the Franks took it over entirely, although the surrounding mountain territories remained under Muslim control.[84] Tiberias was held jointly after an agreement was reached with al-Nasir Yusuf of Damascus and someone referred to as "the Constable" until Baybars took it in 1260.[85] Lydda and Ramla were made condominia as part of the treaty between King Richard of England and Saladin, and continued to be so through the successive Ayyubid sultans until the Franks seized them entirely from al-Malik al-ʿAdil Muhammad (d. 645/1248) during his brief reign as sultan of Egypt.[86] In a treaty concluded in 669/1271 between the lord of Tyre, John of Montfort, and Baybars, we know that they agreed that Montfort would hold ten of the villages belonging to the city, Baybars would get five of his own choosing, and the rest would be held as munasafat.[87] Ibn ʿAbd al-Zahir related that in another treaty worked out the next year in Ramadan 670/April 1272 between Hugh III and Baybars, the sultan granted half of Iskandarun and half of one of the city's estates, as well as permitting the return of its peasants.[88]

What exactly was shared or how condominia were administered varied. Condominia often seem to have been used as a means of keeping vulnerable lands, lands at a remove from centers of control, productive. For example, we have the instance when the Franks sought out the sultan's deputies in Syria in Safar 662 (December 4, 1263–January 1, 1264), requesting a truce until the next harvest in order to cultivate lands. This was granted, so we are told by Ibn al-Furat, because they promised to do so out of their own resources, which would mean that they would deplete a large amount of their seed stores. This in turn, would be in the Muslims' interest since it would ultimately weaken them.[89] Unfortunately, the specific location of these lands was not mentioned, but Riley-Smith interpreted this as a request to open up wastelands. I would suggest, though, the fact that the request was made in the first place and the fact that the Frankish envoys specified it would be entirely out of their own resources, indicates that these were lands traditionally held jointly with the expectation of shared expenditures of resources. As noted, lands held jointly tended to continue to be so regardless of changes in political circumstance. This indicates that while the lands had fallen into disuse because of their peripheral nature and the military dangers in the 1260s, in spite of this, they still existed as condominia. Therefore the Franks were making a concession to the Syrian deputies by offering to plant them entirely out of their own seed provisions.

While some condominia involved sharing the burden of provisioning and the harvest, others were more oriented toward revenues. We know that over the course of his sultanate, Baybars received shared revenues from al-Marqab/Margat (Hospitallers), Baniyas, and Antartus/Tortosa (Templars).[90] The treaty of 665/1267 between Baybars and the Hospitallers went into great detail concerning how the condominia of the area around Homs would work. Here they were to share evenly "their summer crops and winter crops, the herd-tax and all sources of profit."[91] In fact most of the treaty dealt with how the herd-tax (*'idad, 'adad*) would be administered, emphasizing that everybody entering the area, whether peasants, nomadic peoples (Turcomans, Arabs, Kurds) or others entering with animals, should be liable and that no one would seek to prevent anyone from entering the territory with their animals. Moreover, it emphasized that the tax should only be collected if half of it would go to the sultan and half to the Hospital.[92] As should be clear, this herd-tax was seen as the major source of revenue and the two parties were very keen to ensure that it was split between them. The truce also provided for the division of "whatever may be levied from the Greek fishery" and all the other fisheries on the west bank of the Orontes. The straw, however, would go entirely to the sultan while the Hospital would receive fifty Tyrian dinars in lieu of their portion.[93]

Things changed four years later in the new treaty following the capture of Crac des Chevaliers on April 8, 1271. The lands that had been held as condominia around the castle of Balda, including its fisheries, salt-pans, orchards and other installations or sources of revenue, became the property of Baybars "until the end of the" truce, and the Hospital and specifically those at al-Marqab would "have no right or claim therein on any pretext or for any reason until the lapse of this truce."[94] The language here again shows that lands designated as condominia continued to be viewed as such until something extraordinary, such as outright conquest, revoked that status. Balda would return to its status as a condominium after the expiration of the truce. Similarly, the Isma'ili territory around al-'Ullayqa, as well as Masyaf, al-Kahf, al-Maniqa, al-Qadmus, al-Khawabi, al-Rustafa would cease to be held jointly and pass entirely to the purview of the sultan's treasury. The language here, though, is less explicit about whether they would return to shared status after the end of the treaty.

Although abandonment did not seem to change a land's status as *munasafa*, conquest did. We see examples of the offer of turning lands into condominia as enticement for peace or to ease the bitterness of defeat. The same treaty stated that all the territories of al-Marqab had been conquered "and were thereby established in the Blessed and August fisc." Even so, those lands would be shared equally as condominia, while the castle and its suburb would be released to Hospitallers.[95] Like the earlier treaty, the terms of the condominia were mostly concerned with revenues. Here they focused on harbor dues, specifying that all the harbors and anchorages of al-Marqab, Balda, al-Qantara, located on the coast of modern Syria, and their dues raised from merchant activities would be shared. The treaty did exempt levying taxes on traffic related exclusively to the Hospitallers and their servants, however. The shrewdness of the negotiators emerges when it specified that the Hospitallers had to promise not to cheat the sultan by falsely labeling property as their own, "even were he the Brother closest to the Master or the Master's son," nor to hide any of the crops from al-Marqab.[96] Returning to the way munasafat were used, we see here how the Mamluk negotiators used the offer of making lands conquered from the Hospitallers into munasafat as a way of ensuring revenue went to the sultan while making the peace treaty more palatable to the Hospitallers.

Earlier in this chapter, we encountered another similar example showing a preoccupation with securing revenues when Baybars seized on the internal strife between King Hugh III and the Templars as an opportunity to press the case for renewing the condominium of the city of Lattakia. While he was unsuccessful at that time, opting to receive a one-time payment of 20,000 Tyrian dinars and the release of Muslim prisoners, the issue was not dropped and would eventually result in the placement of Mamluk personnel in Frankish territory as part of the munasafa agreement. By 1281, the current sultan Qalawun agreed to a treaty with Bohemond VII of Tripoli that established the city of Lattakia as belonging to the court, but its revenues would be shared. The treaty reads: "Provided that the city of Latakia and what is newly constructed therein shall be established as the Prince's domain; and the representatives of both parties in the city and harbour of Latakia shall be established for the levy of the dues, taxes, produce and so forth as shared revenue."[97] Moreover, these representatives were to reside within the city. This was not the only example of the sultan's agents residing within the count's territory. The treaty also stipulated that the bridge crossing the Nahr al-Barid at Artusiyya on the road between Tripoli and 'Arqa would also have sixteen of the sultan's agents for the purpose of collecting dues and produce. It is further provided that "they shall have houses on the bridge in which to dwell as is customary," but would not prevent the count's subjects from moving nor do them harm. They would only take dues on goods crossing from the sultan's territory into that of the count.[98]

The provisions of this treaty touch upon two items of emphasis. First, that condominia did not necessarily entail a division of sovereignty. Often the focus was on administration, justice, and especially the extraction of produce and taxes. Second, condominia present a clear example of the interpenetration of supposedly external Muslim political elites into the Frankish landscape. The sultan had agents inside the city of Lattakia, which was explicitly described as part of Bohemond's domain. Nevertheless, they worked to enforce the stipulations of the treaty, "inter-sovereign" law, in this case by collecting revenues. So we can see from this analysis that while acting to stabilize political centers and ensuring the productivity of the lands between them, condominia complicated the political landscape by creating spaces of shared administration, occasionally shared sovereignty, and otherwise shared dominance. They forced open spaces to Muslim elites that the Frankish elites endeavored to keep closed.

An outgrowth of this proximity and imbrication of land administration was the opportunity it gave Muslim observers to criticize Frankish rulership. For instance, Ibn Wasil discussed King Leo II's brief take-over of Antioch in 1216: "In *Shawwal* of this year (22 Jan.-20 Feb 1216) Ibn Leon, the king of the Armenians, ruled Antioch, and he benefited its people, and he showed justice in the city, for the Prince its lord was unjust, while Ibn Leon improved the position of the people of Antioch. He also released a group of Muslim prisoners from the city and conveyed them to Aleppo."[99] One is inclined to suspect that a significant reason for Ibn Wasil's high opinion of Leo II was the king's beneficence toward the Muslim prisoners, but that was probably not the only reason. We know that Bohemond IV was disinclined to reside in Antioch, preferring Tripoli, and had therefore become unpopular.[100] Ibn Wasil's estimation that Leo returned justice to Antioch, therefore, might be based on these sentiments, as well as Leo's inclination to make peace with the neighboring Ayyubid elite and son of Saladin, al-Malik al-Zahir of Aleppo.

Ibn Wasil also revealed some of the practicalities of life with Frankish neighbors and that munasafat were double natured. On the one hand, they stabilized land, helping to ensure it would be exploited. On the other, they represented areas open to potential enemies. In 630/1232 al-Malik al-Muzaffar Mahmud made the request to his uncle, the Sultan al-Malik al-Kamil, that he be permitted to take Baʿrin (Montferrand) from his brother al-Malik al-Nasir for fear he could not hold it from the Franks.[101] The explanation given was that the Franks of Crac des Chevaliers and Safita (Chastel Blanc) were his neighbors and that some of the lands between them were condominia. The Muslims meanwhile held Baʿrin in fee, and so the Franks were "all the time seeking to gain it."[102] In light of this situation, the sultan became convinced of his nephew al-Nasir's weakness and permitted al-Muzaffar to take the fortress over. We see here that while condominia were used to stabilize relations between the castles, they nevertheless remained precariously held, and posed a potential point of attack on Baʿrin, which itself seems to have been rented in some form from the Franks.

This potential threat posed by condominia was exploited later in the century when the Mamluks used them as entry points into their conquest of Frankish territory. Baybars al-Mansuri gave multiple versions of the story of Tripoli's conquest by the Sultan Qalawun in 688/1289. In *Zubdat al-fikra* he wrote that they did not follow the treaty presumably regarding revenues and prevented the movement of Muslims on the roads.[103] If we recall the treaty of 1281, there was special attention paid to the collection of duties from the ports and the bridges. Baybars al-Mansuri reported that Qalawun no longer saw fit to hold to the treaty, because the authorities of the country were themselves no longer holding to it by correctly collecting or sharing the condominia revenues. For what it is worth, the commune of Tripoli claimed that the previous counts had been unjust and would only allow Lucy, the sister of Bohemond VII and claimant to the title, to enter if she swore to permit the commune's continued existence.[104] Given the political disunity and outright civil war between the factions of Lucy's brother Bohemond VII and the "Roman faction," the Templars, and the Embriaco lords of Jubail, it would not be surprising if taxes and other duties became irregularly collected and (re)distributed.[105]

Much of the case for condominia therefore rested on revenue. Although undoubtedly, lords would have preferred to hold lands outright, when that proved untenable, they would create munasafat that would ensure the land could continue to be exploited and some benefit would be enjoyed, even if shared. Territories within the sovereignty of a Frankish lord would still have Muslim agents exerting power within it on behalf of the sultan. In the process, it created a political and administrative landscape that was far more complicated than modern maps would allow for.

## Shared Justice: The Theory

Although the Mamluks conquered Tripoli and Acre in the name of broken treaties, failures to keep the letter of the law in the day-to-day administration of these legal instruments did not inevitably lead to violence and conquest. Thus far we have seen how the creation of treaties and the body of regional or "inter-sovereign" law required an interpenetration of elite political spaces by emissaries and negotiators. Similarly, they fostered and reinforced a shared, regional elite identity. Just as they established shared lands in the form of condominia, so too did they institute shared instruments of justice. Breaches or perceived breaches in law were most often handled peaceably and were resolved by Frankish and Muslim administrators and elites working together. Investigating clauses within treaties that detail how resolutions were to be made, as well as accounts of disputes from the narrative sources, can help clarify further how administration by Franks and Muslims in and around the kingdom actually functioned. In them we see three interrelated systems aimed at joint tax collection, joint policing, and joint justice.

Establishing clear tax-collecting policy was a priority in these treaties, and they all emphasize the necessity of cooperation. The treaty of 665/1267 between Baybars and the Hospitallers created a system of shared administration with the sultan's agent in the dominant position. It stipulated that the peasants in the jointly held lands of Homs would be under the jurisdiction of a representative of the sultan with the agreement of a representative of the Hospital in matters concerning his or her freedom or taxation. The condominia of the mill of Kurdana (Recordane) and the nearby orchard would also be jointly administered. In this instance, though, the language suggested that the two deputies would have equal say, perhaps because, as the treaty noted, the Hospitallers built the mill and planted the orchard.[106] Qalawun and Lady

Margaret of Tyre worked out a similar system. Their treaty listed seventy-eight estates to be held as condominia and from which all revenues were to be evenly divided. It further declared that the sultan's representatives were his fiscal officer (*mubashir*) and tax collector (*mustakhrij*) and that they would work together with those of Lady Margaret to ensure that no one acted unilaterally in the levy.[107]

The Hospitallers and Baybars outlined in detail the parameters of the herd-tax levied in their condominia. The treaty again provided for the existence of tax collectors from both sides, and imagined that they would often be present together at tax-collecting spots, presumably on roads along the area's main access points. Furthermore, it outlined what should happen should one of either party not be present:

> when anyone liable to herd-tax enters the condominia and withholds it, if the tax-collector of either party is present, either the tax-collector of the office of [Sultan Baibars] or the tax-collector of the Order of the Hospital, then the representative for the herd-tax of either party being present shall take from that person withholding the herd-tax or leaving the condominia a pledge for the amount of the herd-tax for which he is liable, in the presence of one of the headmen of the condominia. The pledge shall be left on deposit with the headman until the representative of the other party is present, and the due share of the herd-tax shall be remitted to each party.[108]

We have here a situation in which someone declined to pay the tax on the spot and instead gave a pledge for what he owed in front of the tax representative and the headman (ra'is) of the condominia. The ra'is represented a neutral agent of sorts since he was given the responsibility of keeping the pledge and, although this is ambiguous, paying out the tax halves to the tax collectors when both were present to redeem them.[109] That it came down to the ra'is is supported by another clause discussing the case of the ra'is 'Abd al-Masih of the village of al-Mushayriqa in the Hospitaller territory of Marqab. 'Abd al-Masih had apparently mortgaged (*rahna*) the estate, but the treaty specified it would be safe as long as he settled his mortgage by the end of the period of truce and that he bore responsibility for its dues.[110]

These administrators had to work closely together, along with the local headmen directly responsible for each village. If not always directly stated, a subtext in these treaties outlining the administrative responsibilities of each party was providing for a shared system of keeping the peace. Another responsibility borne by these representatives was to inform the other side of large movements of people into the condominia. The representatives of the sultan were required to get the approval of the Hospital should nomadic Turcomen, Arabs, or Kurds wish to enter the condominia. In lieu of permission, they could personally "sponsor" (*yakfuluhu*) the groups, taking responsibility that no harm come from them to the condominia or Hospitaller lands, provided that they informed the Hospital of this situation by the next day.[111] The subsequent treaty of 1271 with the Hospitallers strengthened this sense of shared policing. It stated outright "the Sultan shall order his representatives to keep the condominia of al-Marqab ... from disturbers of the peace, robbers and thieves" and that the Master Hugh Revel would be similarly bound.[112] Beyond simply assuring each other that they would not attack the other's lands, they committed themselves to protecting them from internal disrupting elements in the form of known lawbreakers. They took co-responsibility for keeping the peace within the condominia, but also in part for the other's sovereign lands by acting as gatekeepers to people and groups wishing to pass across the borders.

A necessary complement to the joint policing was joint judgment and punishment. The treaty of 1267 provided that the sultan's representative would judge a peasant from their condominia according to Islam if he were Muslim and according to "the regime of Hisn al-Akrad," that is according to the justice of the Knights Hospitaller, if she were Christian.[113] Presumably in the latter case, it would be heavily influenced by the representative of the Hospitallers whose agreement would be necessary in any case. The treaty Baybars and the Hospitallers agreed to in 1271 also emphasized that people in their condominia would be judged according to the dictates of their religion. A Muslim who committed a crime in Hospitaller lands, or those held jointly, would be judged and punished according to Islamic law, and the sultan's representative would apply a sentence of hanging or mutilation as necessary. This would also be done in the presence of a Hospitaller representative who would be informed of the offense and give confirmation. Any fees extracted would be divided evenly.[114] The exact same conditions were included in the 1285 treaty between Qalawun and Lady Margaret of Tyre: a criminal would be judged and punished by a representative of his or her religion; however, it would be witnessed and confirmed by the other party.[115]

The treaties actually went into specifics for the conduct of the investigation into crimes. For instance, in the border area between the Hospitallers and the Ismaʿilis in and around Masyaf, al-Rusafa, and the mountainous area around Bahra and al-Lukkam (central Syria), it was agreed that if any attack were made on a road or market, there would be a fifteen-day grace period in which to find the culprit and make restitution. The treaty was more vague about what was to happen should the culprit not be found. It only stated, "A person who is placed on oath shall swear. He who has not done so shall be sworn, otherwise he shall redress the damage."[116] This seems to suggest that a person who was unable to swear to his innocence would be held accountable for reparations.

The treaty clarifies how this worked later in the document. We learn that the headmen were key figures in the dispensation of justice in the condominia provided that the agents of the "Islamic party and the Frankish Hospitaller party" agreed.[117] Claims of theft were to be made to the raʾis who would then initiate a forty-day "strenuous and energetic" investigation. If the property were found, it would be returned, but if not, the claimant would choose three persons to swear to what they know about the matter. If that produced the property, then the matter again would be settled, and if the claimant had already received compensation, it would be returned. If the accused person refused to swear on his own behalf, then the claimant would swear and be entitled to compensation according to its kind.[118] If the forty days expired and the accused had not submitted to an oath, he would be obliged to make compensation to the accuser. If, however, he had, the accuser had ten days to renew his oaths (presumably with new witnesses) in which case he would still be compensated, and failing that the claim would drop. The same procedure would hold for homicide, and compensation would be valued according to the rank of the victim (knight, foot soldier, turcopole, peasant).[119] These values were recorded in another treaty as 1,100 Tyrian dirhams for a knight, 200 dirhams for a turcopole, and 100 dinars for a peasant.[120] Although not stated explicitly, it is likely at the major moments of an investigation, such as the oath-swearing and the compensation-giving, deputies of the sultan and the Hospitallers would have to be present to confirm the raʾis's handling of the case as well as to collect the fees owed to the lords.[121]

The renewed treaty of 1271 worked out in greater detail what would happen should the culprit of a crime not be found. It held that following a twenty-day investigation for a known culprit, the raʾis should designate the nearest neighbor to the thief or killer and the Hospitaller and Mamluk representatives should extract from him after another twenty days a fee of 1,000 Tyrian dinars, to be split evenly between the two parties. It emphasized, however, "the officials shall not be remiss in making search; the search shall be made in concert; there shall be no favour to one before the other."[122] The parties were clearly cognizant that this additional burden would undoubtedly be resented by the unfortunate neighbor and community and were trying to avoid such a situation, if possible, while still ensuring their own receipt of the fees of justice.

Rather than placing the burden on the shoulders of the ordinary peasants, the treaty of 1283 between Qalawun and the Kingdom of Jerusalem seems to have put it on those of the ra'is. Here it used the term *wali* (guardian, manager) and says that each wali of a locality along with three others chosen by the accuser would be placed on oath, should the culprit or goods stolen not come to light. If the wali refused, then three others from the accuser's side would have to be placed on oath and the value of compensation taken from them.[123] The document further provided for cases in which the wali did not fulfill his duty to return the goods or acted unjustly. The accuser would complain to the authorities from both sides who would then perform a forty-day investigation, and the walis from both sides would then be bound by whatever decision they came up with. Furthermore the treaty agreed that a wali who concealed booty or a homicide or failed to take a fee in his *wilaya* (administrative district) would receive summary justice in the form of hanging and seizing his goods from the side that appointed him.[124]

Outlined in the texts of surviving treaties is a clear judicial system integrating Frankish and Islamic law and legal practitioners. Not only did condominia represent a sharing of the produce of the land, but they also constituted a shared authority over the land's inhabitants. Of course, the exercise of justice was also a source of revenue through fees. But it also represented another way in which Muslims exerted power alongside Franks.

## Shared Justice: In Practice

The stipulations of the treaties by themselves do not necessarily mean that this is how justice happened in practice. Fortunately, the narrative sources do provide us with some examples of when the sorts of mechanisms outlined above played out in reality. The more diplomatically resolved conflicts tended to revolve around merchants and ships. For example, we can return to the interactions between Baybars and Isabel, Lady of Beirut, already discussed. In 1265 envoys from Isabel arrived at the sultan's court seeking to extend their truce.[125] At the same time, Baybars had learned that a ship owned by the *atabak* Aqtay al-Mustaʿrib had sought safe harbor on Cyprus to make repairs and had been granted it by the authorities of Hugh II, Isabel's child-husband.[126] The Franks then reneged, seizing the sailors, merchants, and their goods. The sultan made their return and monetary compensation for the ship and merchandise prerequisites for the continuation of the treaty between him and the Lady. In fact we see in the agreement they finally reached in 1269 exactly this kind of provision for the restoration or compensation of merchant goods.[127]

Another such incident occurred in Dhuʾl-Qaʿda 670/May 1272 when a ship carrying Mongol ambassadors of Möngke Temür and their Mamluk negotiator and interpreter was seized by Marseillais sailors and taken in captivity to Acre.[128] At the time, Baybars had a freshly signed treaty with Acre, so he angrily sent to the authorities there demanding their return along with that of their possessions. The authorities in Acre obliged by releasing the interpreter, but refused to release the Mongols, citing that they were not the sultan's subjects and, moreover, that they had been captured on the high seas by subjects of another lord, Charles of Anjou. Baybars had to put financial pressure on the Marseillais by closing all Mamluk-controlled ports to them before they would release the Mongol envoys.[129] It was standard in these treaties to promise not to imprison the subjects of the other party. The interpreter had been seized while on the open sea and not while on Frankish territory, but his status as a Mamluk subject gave the authorities in Acre the right, or at least the impetus, to release him.

These examples notwithstanding, most of the disputes recorded in the narrative sources were resolved via more forceful means. One example followed a Frankish raid into Mamluk territory, reaching as far south as Ascalon in 1264. Ibn ʿAbd al-Zahir reported that when news of this and of the great booty the Franks had seized in men, women, and children, reached the Sultan Baybars, he wrote to his Syrian deputies to resolve the matter. He later received notice from the emir Nasir al-Din al-Qaymari informing him that the emir got them back by negotiating with the Franks. Al-Qaymari pointed out that they were in a truce at the time and the Franks should not have gone raiding into that territory.[130] Ultimately he achieved their release, or at least received compensation, by seizing the Frankish negotiator until the Franks complied.[131]

A decade later, Baybars had to resort to trickery in order to get prisoners released when diplomacy failed.[132] In 1271, a period when there was no truce with the now-joined kingdoms of Cyprus and Jerusalem, he sent a fleet from

Egypt to attack Cyprus. This fleet foundered upon the reefs of Limassol, and the survivors were taken captive. Around the same time, Baybars concluded a treaty with the lordship of Tyre, and so he sent the emir Fakhr al-Din al-Muqri al-Hajib there to work for their release. Al-Muqri was able to buy back everybody but the captains. According to Baybars al-Mansuri, the Franks made them exorbitantly expensive, and the sultan refused to pay.[133] At some point around this time, the captains were transferred to a cell in Acre and were there for three years, despite the conclusion of a treaty between the sultan and the kingdom in 1272. Eventually, the deputy from Safad, Sayf al-Din al-Khatalba, managed to bribe one of the guards to smuggle in tools to the captains, and they were able to escape sometime in September 1274.[134]

This episode highlights the networks treaties created as well as their limitations. The lordship of Tyre enjoyed close relations with King Hugh III, with John of Montfort married to Hugh's sister, Margaret.[135] Baybars, who had just recently concluded, or was in the process of concluding, a treaty with Tyre, must have had this in mind when he chose to send Fakhr al-Din al-Muqri there to negotiate for the sale of the captives. The negotiations were largely successful except for the captains who were probably withheld in part to hurt the chances of Baybars's developing into a naval threat.[136] That the treaty of 1272 with the kingdom did not result in the release of the captains demonstrates the limits of treaty-based diplomacy. Acre did not have to release them, as they released the Mamluk interpreter with the Mongol delegation, because they had been captured prior to the treaty's conclusion. Nor do the narrative sources indicate that the sultan or his agents argued that they should. Rather, the sultan through his agent demonstrated his reach within the Kingdom's political landscape by arranging for them to escape.

We also see the Franks having to resort to more forceful means to ensure treaty stipulations. Decades earlier, shortly after the conclusion of Frederick II's treaty with al-Malik al-Kamil in 1229 which ceded Jerusalem to Frankish control, the people of that city complained to the emperor's *baillis*, Balian of Sidon and Garnier l'Aleman, that they were having trouble exerting control over the area. The Muslims from neighboring towns were attacking the unfortified city.[137] The baillis were able to go to Jerusalem and defend the people who had retreated to the not yet demolished Tower of David. They also, in turn, appealed to the emperor to send reinforcements, which he did in 1231 although more important to him was bolstering his political position vis-à-vis unhappy Frankish barons.[138] Why did they not appeal to al-Malik al-Kamil? Perhaps it was seen as too small an issue to bring to the sultan's attention. Or perhaps they feared being seen as weak. In either case, although the surrounding towns from which these Muslim attackers were coming were part of the sultan's territory, these baillis treated putting them down to defend Jerusalem as an internal matter.

## Conclusion

We know that the notion of the nation-state with fixed political boundaries and circumscribed legal and administrative apparatuses had no place in the medieval world. Ronnie Ellenblum outlined the historiography and problems of this attitude with regard to the Kingdom of Jerusalem.[139] He argued for a central-place model of suzerainty with levels of control decreasing the further from fortified places one got. The analysis of the legal landscape as sculpted by the treaties presented here, though, has shown that even this conception is not quite right. Muslim elites regularly penetrated the kingdom's centers of power, both physically in business conducted at court, as well as politically through their integration in the administration of lands. While the idea that Muslim envoys and ambassadors were regularly visible and active at court should not at first blush be surprising, it is a necessary starting point since Muslims almost exclusively appear in adversarial and military contexts when scholars of the crusader states discuss them. Moreover, in local administrative courts they were engaging in not only diplomacy but also tax collection and the administration of justice. This was not done from a distance but in person, alongside Frankish counterparts or even in their absence.

Without question the pervasiveness of condominia during the thirteenth century meant that on the administrative level, Muslims were very much integrated into the daily business of the kingdom. Up until now Frankish administrative institutions have been explored via an almost exclusive reliance on Frankish sources, which is why condominia, the evidence for which are found primarily in Arabic sources, have yet to make their way into major works on the Latin East.[140] Clearly then, the evidence from the treaties of the joint collection of taxes and joint administration of justice in the form of investigation, prosecution, and eventual punishment of crimes, demonstrates that we need to alter how we think about Frankish institutions.

We have already seen how the legal ideals fostered by the Frankish and Muslim treatises, even theoretically, were unable to create systems entirely closed to out-groups. The analysis here of administration and diplomacy has shown how boundaries between Frank and non-Frank continued to be illusory up to the highest political level of the Latin East. The body of "intersovereign" law created and was created by a set of Frankish and Muslim peers. It forged a regional political and legal network that permitted Muslim elites considerable reach into what has been considered Frankish domain. That the kingdom ended in conquest at the hands of the Mamluks perhaps has made it difficult to see the ways in which Ayyubid and Mamluk sultans were able to enforce their will by working within these systems of diplomacy and administration. This is not to argue naively that military conquest played little role in shaping the political landscape. The fact that the reverse seems not to have been the case and that the Franks were not similarly administering the Mamluk empire, highlights the role of military power. However, it is just as erroneous to envision a Latin Kingdom whose ruling and administrative elite was formed exclusively by Franks. Medieval power came from the right to extract resources from the land, the responsibility for providing justice for the people, and the ability to martial soldiers. This discussion has shown that in various parts of the kingdom, some Muslims were engaging in those first two activities in lands belonging to, at least in part, the Franks, thanks to their ability to do the third. There were some Muslims, therefore, wielding power within the Latin East.

This returns us to the conundrum that scholars have found in the Kingdom of Jerusalem in the thirteenth century. The material discussed here has done nothing to solidify the image of the kingdom, and in fact it has elucidated its very permeability. Although the bulk of the detailed evidence in the form of treaty documents comes from the thirteenth century, there is no reason to think that the penetrability differed in the twelfth. For certain, condominia existed and diplomats and messengers traveled between Syrian, Egyptian, and Frankish courts. Rather, the kingdom in the thirteenth century presents us with an opportunity to see with greater clarity the way power was exercised in the region for the entirety of the crusade period, highlighted as it is by the kingdom's reduced size. It is simply harder to connect dots between centers of power to create imaginary political boundaries, as Ellenblum has argued has been done for the twelfth-century kingdom, when there are fewer of them. The current image of the political landscape and constellation of political power for the twelfth century needs to be reconsidered.

Moreover, given the apparent origin of condominia from Latin Christian European legal systems,[141] this discussion has serious implications for how scholars of medieval Europe more broadly think about the nature of kingdoms, the state, and sovereignty. The example of the Kingdom of Jerusalem demonstrates that kingdoms existed and functioned in the medieval period without having a single set of contiguous, external borders, centralized administrations, or indeed a sole bearer of the right to govern. What would it mean for someone to be sovereign over land where they are not solely responsible for administration or creation of the law and where they do not have sole claim to the land's resources? Medieval Europeanists are used to acknowledging that justice was not the exclusive purview of a sovereign, as this was a sore and long-existing source of conflict between secular lords and the Latin Church. What is perhaps different from examples in Latin Europe is that in the condominia in the Latin East, one religious court did not exist hierarchically over the other, but both operated as equals. But what about resource extraction? In Latin Europe, again, the church complicated matters with tithes, as could perhaps ties of vassalage. Frankish lords could be sovereign but not hold exclusive right to the revenue from land. It was not just partitioned vertically with subordinate vassals, but rather horizontally with equals getting shares. That leaves a claim to the people who live in a territory. Early in the Middle Ages, kings claimed to be kings of a people rather than a land and it was only in the twelfth century that we start to see rulers named by territory instead (e.g., King of the Franks versus King of France). In some areas mobility was severely restricted, but that was not the case everywhere, and certainly not in the Latin East where we have seen rulers competing for residents. Given the various components, I might suggest that a political map for Latin Europe or the Latin East might more accurately look like a pixelated heat map of degrees of sovereignty than anything with lines and borders.

*Chapter 5*

# Shared Webs of Knowledge

It would be fair to say that the Latin East does not hold a reputation among most medievalists of Europe, or the Middle East for that matter, for having been an intellectual "hot spot" in either the twelfth or thirteenth centuries. Although he has moderated his stance since, Benjamin Kedar channeled this unspoken assumption when he wrote that the intellectual interests of the clerics who settled in the Latin East were confined to the Holy Places, and they "were not interested in, or capable of, intellectual give-and-take with Oriental Christian or Muslim scholars."[1] For those who perceive religious difference and holy war to have been the defining features of the region during the central Middle Ages, it might be challenging to see an investigation beyond the political or military as possible or worthwhile. Even so, this chapter will attempt to outline some of the ways that the people of the Latin East and broader region produced, shared, and exchanged information in a way that not only belies the idea of the area being an intellectual backwater, but also demonstrates connectivities that bound the people together across whatever political or religious boundaries there may have been.

Despite this negative association, there has not been a total absence of scholarship on cultural exchange. Scholars have shown that the eastern coast of the Mediterranean was a location of intense cultural contact and interaction. During the period of Frankish presence, there were populations of Latin Christians, Byzantine Greeks, Armenian Christians, Samaritans, Karaite and Rabbanite Jews, Islamized and non-Islamized Turks, and Muslim Arabs among many others all living in relatively close proximity and participating in a shared culture. Historians of medieval art and architecture in particular have been unraveling the influences and production processes of the area's material culture for decades, ever since Kurt Weitzmann identified and examined in-depth the "crusader icons."[2] This is not to say that everyone derived the same meaning from these shared cultural elements. As Scott Redford and Anthony Cutler have outlined, it is likely that there existed an assemblage of shared forms and imagery in art that meant different things to the different communities that consumed them.[3] Material culture and physical remains provide important evidence for shared culture; however, for the purposes of this study the focus will be on evidence from intellectual and literary exchanges.

Fewer scholars working on texts have endeavored to trace the parameters of intellectual exchange in the Latin East. Those few monographs on the subject, in fact, have only come out in recent years. In particular, Jonathan Rubin's monograph on intellectual activity in thirteenth-century Acre has done a great deal to correct the stereotype and advance our knowledge.[4] Rubin amply demonstrates that Acre had a thriving intellectual scene, not only in terms of textual production but also in fostering intellectual discussion and exchange, especially among the different Christian and Jewish communities resident in the city. The focus on manuscripts produced in the city during the thirteenth century, however, leaves a gap in the analysis concerning the contributions Muslims may have made. As Rubin notes, as far as we know, there are no manuscripts attributed to Muslim residents of Acre in the thirteenth century.[5] Brendan Goldman's forthcoming monograph on Jews in the Latin East, however, offers another perspective on Acre (and Tyre) as a hubs of exchange for the entirety of the Frankish presence and draws not only from Frankish sources but from documents in Arabic, Hebrew, and Judeo-Arabic. Bringing these sources together, he shows how knowledge crossed between Syrian and European Jews, Muslims, and Christians.[6]

The present book follows a similar methodology to Goldman's, and takes for granted the overlapping nature of the different political entities of the region, as was demonstrated in the previous chapter. This and the next chapter will take the idea of overlap one step further to show how there existed a cultural landscape defined not by political control but rather by shared knowledge and understanding. This chapter will focus on shared knowledge and systems of knowledge exchange. In particular the investigation centers on intelligence gathering and scientific and medical expertise, two topics that are not entirely unfamiliar to scholars of the period and place. Previous analyses of these kinds of information gathering and exchange have approached their subjects within their particular field. Historians of medicine have explored the creation and exchange of medical knowledge to better understand the evolution of medicine. Scholarship on espionage has approached intelligence gathering as part of military and/or political history. The discussion of these forms of knowledge in this chapter moves from seeing them as only part of a military encounter or medicine and instead approaches them as components of broader knowledge exchange among Christians, Jews, and Muslims during this period. What this discussion adds is integration of these topics into the larger argument about regional interconnection. It demonstrates that both Frankish and Muslim elites valued similar kinds of military intelligence and medical and scientific knowledge, and they viewed similar kinds of people as authorities and purveyors of said knowledge. While the contention on its face is modest, this similarity of values and understanding is important to recognize because it is easily overlooked when the basic assumption is that there was little cultural production of note in the region and that attitudes were largely dictated by religious animosity. Moreover, it is important to highlight because it was not necessary or inevitable that they would share approaches to knowledge. If the Frankish and Muslim elites had truly existed in entirely different cultural worlds, they could easily have emphasized entirely different military and medical practices. Instead, the values were shared, and I posit that this sharing was not exclusive to military intelligence or medical and scientific knowledge. While I do not intend to argue that Frankish culture and Syrian and Egyptian Islamicate culture were identical, I do argue that there was overlap and that this overlapping cultural landscape was held together by shared knowledge.

## Intelligence and Knowledge Exchange

To state the point of this chapter directly, just as the political entities of Syria and Egypt interpenetrated each other in the twelfth and thirteenth centuries, as discussed in the previous chapter, so too were these entities bound by webs of knowledge. People deliberately sought out knowledge from other groups and helped create an economy of knowledge whereby expertise was shared, purchased, or even stolen. The fact that Franks would seek knowledge from people living in Muslim Syria, and vice versa, demonstrates that there was a shared understanding of valuable information, a shared idea of where that information came from, and a shared understanding of how it could be put to use. In other words, there was a shared culture. Muslims, whether inside or outside the Frankish domain, were key players in this knowledge exchange.

This chapter will begin by examining two areas, intelligence or espionage, and scientific and technical knowledge. While exploring how this information came to be shared, it will also investigate contemporary perceptions of how that information came to be transmitted. It will thereby allow us to better understand not only the process by which information was shared, but the contemporary attitudes toward groups seen to have been (un)trustworthy. These attitudes, it turns out, were shared by Franks and regional Muslim elites, further illuminating a shared cultural landscape. These particular topics are not intended as an exhaustive investigation of all the kinds of knowledge that Muslims participated in, but rather as a representation of the importance they held in this exchange.

### *Intelligence*

For people always facing the possibility of battle, whether within their cultural group or against another, intelligence was an important commodity. It thus represents a significant portion of the knowledge created and shared in the region during the crusade period and is one worth examining in a chapter dedicated to exploring how knowledge could bind people together. It seems, however, that at least on the Frankish side, intelligence was not always gathered systematically, and the level of organization involved varied with the Frankish leadership. Susan Edgington has argued that among the leaders of the First Crusade, most relied upon interrogation of prisoners, local informants, and scouts for their information, whereas Bohemond, who came from southern Italy and had access to Arabic speakers, actually employed spies.[7] As Reuven Amitai has shown, early Mamluk sultans carefully built and maintained intelligence networks that included both active secret agents (*qasid*, pl. *qussad*) and more passive informants known as "faithful advisors" (*munasih*, pl. *munasihun*) or sometimes "correspondents" (*mukatib*, pl. *mukatibun*).[8] As will be discussed, contemporaneous masters of the Knights Templar also maintained informants within the Mamluk establishment, and it seems likely that the other military orders would have as well.

To understand the network, we will start with the actors. The landscape of intelligence gathering was occupied by a diverse array of people. From the very beginning, there were those who seem to have occupied more marginal positions within society for whom knowledge was a commodity to be sold. Nomadic groups feature prominently in accounts of intelligence gathering. In both the Arabic and Frankish sources, they are portrayed as simultaneously likely sources of information but also untrustworthy. Ibn al-Athir records how Nur al-Din hired Turcoman agents to follow and capture Count Joscelin II of Edessa in 1150. Joscelin endeavored to pay them more to let him go, which Ibn al-Athir indicates they were willing to do; however, one of the agents remained loyal to Nur al-Din and went to Aleppo to gather more troops and put a stop to that.[9] They were also seen as sources of intelligence as people with deep knowledge of terrain. For example, we are told that Bedouin helped King Louis IX find a ford across a branch of the Nile River during his first crusade to Egypt.[10] Baybars al-Mansuri comments that news reached the sultan Baybars that an entire tribe of Bedouin, the Zubaid, from around Damascus sought out the Franks in 1261 in order to "[inform] them of the Muslims' weaknesses." He sent the emir Jamal al-Din al-Muhammadi to carry out raids and drive them away.[11] As people whose livelihood took them from one territory to the next, Bedouin were well placed to observe the political and military powers around them and provide information as they saw fit.

Even as they were seen as good sources of information, nomadic peoples were also associated with duplicity. Later in the chapter, we will discuss Usama Ibn Munqidh's perception of Bedouin as being as dangerous as the Franks. Ibn al-Athir records an incident involving Turcoman misinformation in 1102 during posturing between Seljuk powers over influence with the caliph in Baghdad. The lord of Hisn Kayfa, Suqman ibn Artuq, sent Turcoman allies into the city of Tikrit in Iraq to spread disinformation about his impending attack. They brought with them cheese, clarified butter, and honey, which they sold at the market and in the process spread the news that Suqman had abandoned the idea of coming into Iraq. The townspeople believed this, letting down their guard, only to be attacked and sacked by Suqman that night.[12] That the *Rothelin* continuation of William of Tyre's history calls them "Saracen Traitors" shows that even though they were seen as useful sources of information, the Franks also held them in contempt.[13]

Syrian Christians were another group of marginal figures who were involved in intelligence and aroused suspicion for untrustworthiness. As Christians whose first language was Arabic, they were useful to the Franks who employed them as translators (*dragomanni*) and scribes.[14] Christopher MacEvitt has argued persuasively that for the twelfth century up until the conquests of Saladin, Christians of all rites practiced "rough tolerance" by which serious investigation of theological difference was avoided and all exercise of power was seen to be local and not motivated against entire religious communities.[15] The term *Syrian* (*surianus*) was therefore a deliberate obfuscation of difference that could include all Arabic-speaking Christians regardless of particular sect.[16] Even so, Susan Edgington has noted the distrust members of the First Crusade had of Armenians and Syrians visiting their camps during the siege of Antioch.[17] The willful ignorance of theological difference, and the unwillingness to paint entire groups with a brush came to an end by the thirteenth century, however. Jacques de Vitry had very little good to say about them in his letter to the Masters of Paris and Ligarde of St. Trond in 1216 or 1217. He wrote, "I discovered, too, Syrian men, who are corrupt and unreliable, for their education among Saracens has marked them with their dissolute morals and some of them have sold the secrets of Christianity to the Saracens."[18] Exactly what he meant by "secrets of Christianity" is open, whether he meant intelligence involving vulnerabilities and the like, or more spiritual secrets. In any case, though, it is clear that for Jacques de Vitry, their perceived closeness with Muslims of the area made them inherently suspect and likely to betray the Franks.

While Jacques de Vitry was arguably an outsider, the Templar of Tyre similarly offers some evidence of distrust for Syrian Christians. In his account of the Mamluk conquest of Safad, the Templar of Tyre relates how a Brother Leo who was sent to the sultan to negotiate because of his Arabic fluency, ended up betraying the defenders. During his discussion with Brother Leo, Baybars informs the Templar that he intends to have a look-alike distribute the safe-conduct to the surrendering Templars of Safad so that the sultan could then attack them in good conscience when they depart. If Brother Leo agreed to keep silent and convince his brothers to go along with the supposed truce, he would be allowed to live and be granted all kinds of gifts, but otherwise he could expect to die cruelly at Mamluk hands. In the story, threatened with death, Leo agrees, Baybars carries out the plot and the Templar defenders of Safad are killed, and Leo then converts to Islam.[19] Although he does not say that Leo was a Syrian, he is indicted by the Templar for his fear of death and lack of steadfastness in his faith.

This suspicion by the Franks of Syrian Christians was so well-known that the Mamluks may have even made use of it. When Baybars was besieging Safad in 1266, he had it announced that all Syrian defenders of the castle would be allowed to go free if they ceased their defensive efforts. As the Templar of Tyre comments, "He did this in order to sow discord between the Franks and the Syrians, so that the Franks would accuse the Syrians of being traitors and there would be conflict between them."[20] Arabic sources do not state specifically that Baybars manipulated the suspicion against Syrians, but they do say that the sultan gave some of the defenders gifts and promises of safety which led to dissension.[21] It is not too much of a stretch to believe that he might have targeted Arabic-speaking Syrian Christians as part of his psychological warfare.

Converts are a third category of people seen as conduits of knowledge and, later, potential threats. An episode of espionage early in the history of the Frankish kingdom centered on a Christian convert Walter Mahomet. As discussed by Edgington, it does not seem like early Frankish kings cultivated networks of spies so much as relied on abilities of courtiers around them and local informants. In a story appended to the earliest versions of Guibert of Nogent's *Dei gesta per Francos*, Walter Mahomet is described as having been captured by Christians as a youth and baptized, and had grown to prominence among the Franks. The citizens of Jerusalem had him go receive a group of supposed merchants from Egypt who were in reality soldiers planning on retaking Jerusalem. The unsuspecting Egyptians spoke freely in Arabic while Walter was around, and so he learned of the plot and was able to warn king Baldwin I who returned and foiled it.[22] Here the story portrays Walter Mahomet, who is attested as the lord of Hebron in 1107/1108, as accidentally falling into the role of counter-spy by virtue of his knowledge of Arabic.

The thirteenth-century sources tend to take a more negative view of converts, however. This impression owes largely to the accounts of a series of assassinations and assassination attempts that were undertaken by people claiming to want to convert. In the accounts given by the Templar of Tyre of the attacks against Philip of Montfort and Prince Edward of England, the Ismaʿili assassins chose to gain access to their target through coming to them asking for baptism. In the story about Philip, the Templar says that the assassins went "straight to the lord of Tyre" asking him for baptism, and "the lord of Tyre, who was not on guard for such things, had them baptized."[23] Thus the Templar indicates immediately that it was prudent to be cautious about Muslims asking to convert under false pretenses. He goes on to explain that Philip "retained them both in his service as turcopoles . . . and trusted them greatly."[24] These were the men, according to the Templar, who in 1270 ended up attacking both Philip and his son, but only managed to kill Philip.

Two years later, the Templar says another assassination attempt took place, this time against Prince Edward of England. The Templar calls this person "a Saracen-men-at-arms" who also came to be baptized. Edward obliged and took the man into his service as a spy. The Templar relates, "This fellow served the Lord Edward in such a capacity that he would go to spy on the

Saracens to find out where one might do them harm" something he did "many times."[25] He was the one who came up with the intelligence that led to the Frankish attacks against St. George and Qaqun, something the Templar seems to hold up as positives, although the scholarship tends to downplay the success of those attacks.[26] The man grew in the prince's esteem to such an extent that he was allowed access to the prince at any time. One night, the man came to the prince's rooms late at night with only the translator with him, was allowed in, and attacked the prince. The prince, though wounded, managed to incapacitate and then kill his assailant.[27] Ibn ʿAbd al-Zahir concurs that there were Ismaʿili assassins who were sent with the promise of providing information, that they stayed with the prince awhile, and that one of them gained access to the prince all alone with only a translator by saying he had something to tell the prince about the sultan. What Ibn ʿAbd al-Zahir does not confirm is the idea that the agent(s) claimed to want to convert.[28]

Thus in trying to understand who the participants of this landscape of knowledge were, we have three categories of people who were viewed in the Frankish and Arabic sources with suspicion as likely conduits of intelligence to the other side. They represented double-edged swords, so to speak, since their linguistic abilities and ability to pass within the two groups undetected made them valuable, and yet their very marginality made them seem more likely to betray the side they were supposed to be on. Syrian Christians and Christian converts were supposed to be on the side of the Franks, their coreligionists. And yet, by the thirteenth century at least, they were viewed more skeptically. Jacques de Vitry does not seem able to overlook their "heretical" ways for example. Instead they are too close to Muslims and, perhaps because of that, associated with selling them secrets. Likewise, converts were not to be taken at face value. Perhaps baptism was a trope necessary to try to explain how assassins were able to get close to their intended victims, and yet the trope's existence suggests that Franks of the time were ready to be skeptical of the sincerity of converts. Certainly, Ibn Munqidh in the previous century was skeptical of the Frankish ability to truly convert to Islam.[29] Transhumant peoples like the Bedouin and Turcomans were perpetual outsiders to Christian and Muslim settled cultures in Syria and Egypt. Neither the Franks nor the Syrian and Egyptian lords seemed to trust them, even as they might turn to them for military aid or intelligence. Indeed, Reuven Aharoni, albeit looking at later Mamluk-Bedouin relations, has argued that this attitude was justified: "[Bedouin] did not hesitate to desert the battlefield the moment they realized that victory would elude their masters. They perceived warfare as a business transaction with no political commitment whatsoever, not even to the shaykh of their fighting unit, through whom they were recruited."[30] We see therefore that these groups were constructed as marginal in both the Frankish and Arabic texts and that their marginality was seen as key to facilitating their ability to gather and transmit information. They served both in the imagined landscape of intelligence as well as probably in reality as the gateways for exchange.

These somewhat marginalized figures were perceived as potential agents for information transmission; however, we have evidence for much more well-placed individuals being actively involved as well. As Amitai noted, many of the munasihun (faithful advisors) were individuals of rank who would send messages containing information they thought would be of interest to the sultan or Franks. How would this have worked? Ibn al-Athir provides several references to high-ranking officials who wrote to others with information. In the Islamic year 495 (1101–1102), an amir in the service of the Seljuk prince Sanjar of Khorasan wrote to Sanjar's rival, Qadir Khan of Samarqand, informing him of Sanjar's poor health and encouraging the latter to strike and make Khorasan his own. Ibn al-Athir notes that the reason for this passing of intelligence came out of jealousy.[31] Another example is when Mujahid al-Din Bahruz, a man of high standing under the former Seljuk sultan Muhammad (d. 1118), wrote in AH 519 (1125–1126) to the caliph al-Mustarshid (d. 1135) informing him of the movement of Dubays ibn Sadaqa, lord of Hilla, and the Seljuk prince Tughril against Baghdad. Thanks to the information, the caliph was able to intercept their forces and foil the plot.[32]

These relationships among elites could be sought or cultivated or even overturned. The story about the attempted assassination of Prince Edward offers some detail. According to Ibn 'Abd al-Zahir, the sultan ordered the governor of Ramla, Ibn Shawar, to approach the Franks offering to become an informant. He writes, "Ibn Shāwar sent messages to try to win favour with [Edward] and to give him to understand that he could provide him with information. He made presents to him, to his wife (Eleanor of Castile) and to his whole entourage" which were brought by the intended assassins.[33] Ibn al-Athir offers insight into how agents could be turned. He mentions how an envoy from the ruler of Kirman sent to Jawuli Saqao, former emir of Mosul and current lord of Fars, in AH 510 (1116–1117) was bribed into turning into a counteragent and transmitting false information to his former master.[34]

The Templar of Tyre also explains how the Templar Master received information about Mamluk operations. He writes in the context of Baybars's planned attack on Tripoli in 1289: "But there was a very old emir, one of the four who governed *Paynimie*; he made my lord the master of the Temple aware of these developments. This emir was called the Emir *Silah*, and he was accustomed to notify the master of the Temple of matter of interest to Christendom, when the sultan wished to injure Christianity in any manner. This contact cost the master fine presents each year, which he sent to him."[35] The *amir al-silah* was a high position in Mamluk organization, in charge of weapons and part of the sultan's guard, and at the time this was the well-respected Badr al-Din Bektash al-Fakhri. Prominent under Baybars, it is believed that he was involved in supporting Qalawun's rise to the sultanate in 1279. Indeed, one source reports that Qalawun bemoaned the fact that Bektash al-Fakhri was the last of the courageous horsemen.[36] He was held in high esteem and it seems trusted by his sultan. And yet it appears that he also passed on information about Mamluk movements to the Master of the Templars in exchange for "presents." If this had been part of the sultan's counterespionage operations, it seems likely that at least one of the sources would have mentioned it as they frequently do when it comes to plots. Since they do not, it seems reasonable to believe that he was indeed providing intelligence to the Templars. Moreover, later on the Templar even refers to the amir al-silah as the Templar Master's friend.[37] This further suggests that his intelligence was welcomed as true and that he was seen as a benefactor for the Franks, at least by the Templars.

Intelligence supplied in this fashion was not always believed. As the Templar of Tyre notes, the Franks were not always willing to believe the intelligence the master supplied them. Not only did the Franks not believe that Qalawun was preparing to attack Tripoli, which he did, but they also dismissed the warning again supplied by Bektash al-Fakhri that the sultan was preparing to attack Acre in the wake of the massacre of Muslim peasants there in 1290. As the Templar soberly notes, "The master of the Temple promptly reported this to all the lords of Acre. But they did not want to believe it."[38] One should hesitate to read too much into the psychology of a historic document, but it appears here that the Templar is not suggesting that the Franks found the source suspicious, but rather preferred to deny the reality of their situation.

The Franks too operated within this system of intelligence and gift exchange. Ibn Wasil reports that a messenger from the Templars came to the court of al-Malik al-Mansur Muhammad of Hama in 1202–1203 (599 AH) offering information about the ongoing Fourth Crusade as well as efforts by the leaders of the Hospitallers and Templars to make peace between Antioch and Armenia.[39] Ibn Wasil reports that the messenger said that there were sixty thousand knights and turcopoles coming and that they were heading toward Jabala and Lattakia. Additionally, the leaders of the military orders and the newly arrived crusaders were all meeting to discuss war against the Muslims. The logic was to frighten the emir into a truce with his neighbors in preparation for the large crusade that had just taken Zara and was now heading, it was presumed, toward Syria. We know in retrospect that no such large contingent ever made it to Syria during the Fourth Crusade, but it seems like the military orders were willing to give up the pretense of a surprise by revealing details in order to secure a peace treaty or that this was an act of counterespionage. In either case, it is an example of the Franks offering information about their own activities (or those of crusaders) to a Muslim leader in exchange for something in return.

Another example of Franks engaging in information transfer seemingly against their own side comes from the period of the Seventh Crusade. It is reported that prior to the arrival of King Louis IX's crusade to Egypt in 1249, an agent from Manfred, or his father Frederick II, came to the Ayyubid Sultan al-Malik al-Salih Najm al-Din Ayyub to inform him of it. He claims to have traveled between the emperor and Egypt disguised as a merchant so no one would "learn that the Emperor had taken the part of the Muslims against them."[40] Decades earlier, in the late 1220s, Frederick had cultivated a good relationship with al-Salih's father, al-Kamil, who was then sultan of Egypt. It is possible that he continued to maintain warm relations with the son and thus sent the message.

We can also parse a little about the locations of such knowledge exchange as well as its gatherers and purveyors. Much of the intelligence seems to have come from persons at more modest social levels sent to major cities and ports. The celebrated eleventh-century Seljuk vizier Nizam al-Mulk's mirror for princes, *Siyasat-nama* (Book of government), has a section dedicated to the importance of cultivating a spy network. He writes, "Spies must constantly go out to the limits of the kingdom in the guise of merchants, travelers, Sufis, peddlers, and mendicants, and bring back reports of everything they, so that no matter of any kind remain concealed."[41] There is substantial evidence that this advice was followed by Seljuk and other leaders in the century that followed. Ibn al-Athir mentions favorably two leaders who cultivated such networks. In his obituary of the Zirid ruler of Ifriqiya, Tamim ibn Mu'izz (d. 1108), he notes, "In his lands he had intelligence agents to whom he paid magnificent pensions that they might inform him of his subordinates' behavior to stop them wronging the populace."[42] In a later obituary of the caliph al-Muqtafi li-Amr Allah (d. 1160), he also notes how the caliph had been the first to act independently of the sultans since the advent of the domineering Buyid dynasty, and as part of that effort, he "used to pay out large sums of money to intelligence agents throughout the land."[43] On its face, the existence of these networks of informants might not seem noteworthy, but analyzing them from the perspective of knowledge more broadly allows us to discern more of what was shared in the region. Informants and spies were prominent operators in the broader field of knowledge production and exchange just like Bedouin and Eastern Christians were. These agents would cross back and forth between the Latin East and the domains of their lord to gather and transmit intelligence. Moreover, we can see how they could generate that knowledge through discussions with other inadvertent informants like merchants, and where they favored, including markets and ports. These were the people and the locations that helped bind the Latin East with its neighbors through the exchange of intelligence.

Rulers similarly cultivated agents in the thirteenth century. As Amitai noted, Qalawun specifically advised his son al-Salih to maintain tabs on the events abroad by gathering information from people at the harbors.[44] Ibn 'Abd al-Zahir at several points throughout his work mentions news coming from ships. Information gathered from such returnees included deaths of prominent Frankish persons like the Lord of Tyre, conflicts between Charles of Anjou and the king of Aragon, and the death of the pope as well as the installation of his successor.[45] The Franks for their part also understood ports to be conduits of information. The Templar of Tyre records that although Philip of Montfort refused to be suspicious of the men who turned out to be his assassins, he nevertheless agreed to make his viscount find and "monitor foreign people who came into Tyre."[46] Baybars seems to have been playing upon this role of information gathering when he orchestrated a bit of political theater for the recently arrived messengers from Charles of Anjou in August 1271, having them meet him at the arsenal.[47] Apparently he wanted it known that he was overseeing the reconstruction of his navy.

There were more active "honest advisors" who seem to have been less high-profile working for the Mamluks in the Frankish port cities as well. Amitai described how an informant named Jawan Khandaq living in Acre, sent a message to Qalawun informing him of the attempt by his emir Kunduk al-Zahiri to ally himself with the Franks. He promised to return much land to the Franks in exchange for their support, during which time al-Zahiri intended to assassinate Qalawun and become sultan himself.[48] There were also such informants in Tripoli who warned the Mamluks that a group of armed Franks were impersonating Mongols in an attempt to cause panic.[49] The advisors seem to have been quite active, especially in Acre in the thirteenth century, which makes sense given the city's important economic and political role. The Templar of Tyre reports that the bloody shirts of the Muslims killed in Acre in August 1290 were taken to Qalawun as evidence.[50] While the Arabic sources do not corroborate that particular detail, they do echo the idea that it took very little time for the information of the murders to reach the sultan.[51]

From this discussion we begin to see a landscape of intelligence that involved figures marginal to mainstream Frankish, Syrian, and Egyptian societies as well as figures at the highest echelons. Both the Latins and the Muslim elites looked upon Bedouin, who were at this point at least nominally Muslim, converts, and Eastern Christians as potential conduits of information. From the Frankish perspective, Bedouin and Christian converts were useful because of their historic, cultural, and linguistic ties to Muslim political leaders. Along with the Eastern Christians, these same ties made them seem a liability to the Franks, as their cultural proximity to Muslims was seen as too close for comfort. Syrian and Egyptian elites from early on had cultivated intelligence networks, relying on similar types of people. Elite Franks would volunteer information for their own purposes, while intelligence could also be gathered from "advisors" resident in the cities, and from transient merchants and sailors in harbors. These networks of knowledge not only involved the transfer of intelligence regarding military movements, geographical information, political events, and so on; they also constituted a shared understanding of authority. Frankish Christian and Syrian and Egyptian Muslim elites were connected by the same understanding of who possessed information, where they could be found, and who was likely to pass it on.

### *Knowledge Exchange*

While regional elites were connected to each other by a shared network of intelligence gathering, the region itself was tied together as well by a shared network of civilian (nonmilitary) information, such as linguistic and medical knowledge. In this section, we will explore how that worked. To begin with, we should start with Arabic as it was largely the medium by which knowledge was shared. While it may have been possible in the eleventh and early twelfth centuries for some of the Franks or their close associates, like Walter Mahomet, to surreptitiously gather information from the Syrian and Egyptian camps through unanticipated knowledge of Arabic, this was almost certainly no longer the case by the thirteenth. The extent to which the Franks knew Arabic has been a matter of debate. Riley-Smith and Kedar have tended to view language knowledge as being largely the purview of Eastern Christians—they were the ones who served as intermediaries between the Franks and the local Arabic-speaking populace.[52] Hussein Attiya, though, has argued that many of the scribes were actually Franks, not Eastern Christians, and that knowledge of Arabic was widespread.[53] An important note, however, has been made by Kevin Lewis, in cautioning that knowledge of spoken Arabic would not necessarily be the same as knowledge of written or literary Arabic. More Franks may have had some spoken rather than reading ability as was certainly the case with literacy in their own languages.[54] By the mid-twelfth century, there are nobles whom sources credit with having knowledge of Arabic and others who spent lengthy captivities in Syria, such as Baldwin II (1104–1108) or Reynaud of Châtillon (1160–1175), can easily be understood as learning some level of the language.[55] The rule of the Templars, which was composed by 1187, indicated that the Master, Seneschal, Commander of the Kingdom of Jerusalem and the Commanders of the cities of Jerusalem, Tripoli and Antioch, should all have a "Saracen scribe"; at the very least this meant someone who knew Arabic, even if they themselves were not Muslim.[56] As Jonathan Rubin has recently noted, Acre in the thirteenth century was a center for language study, especially Arabic.[57] Prince Edward of England had a translator who was responsible for aiding the communications between his spies and himself.[58] Translators by the thirteenth century, and probably toward the end of the so-called first kingdom, were part of the entourage of major nobles and leaders of the military orders. They were therefore relatively plentiful.

The Templar of Tyre provides sufficient reference to Frankish knowledge of Arabic to suggest that it was not unusual. Brother Leo, the Templar casalier of Safed who failed to warn his brethren about Baybars's trick, was "very fluent in the Saracen language."[59] The Templar also signals to the possibility of widespread basic understanding of Arabic among the Franks in the story about the 1267 raid against Acre in which Sir Robert of Crésèques and Oliver of Termès's nephews died. A small Frankish/crusader contingent led by these knights was returning to Acre from raiding the region of Montfort when they came upon the Mamluk army that was trying to provoke the Franks of

Acre into battle. Although they could have made it to Acre, according to the Templar, Robert argued that he came across the sea to fight the Muslims and so attacked. It was a stalemate until "some of the Saracens shouted to the others that they ought to strike at the 'barley storehouses', by which they meant to try to kill the horses. They said this in code so that none of the Franks would understand it."[60] Now, whether this comment was based on fact or rather intended to liven up the story, it is hard to say. However, it does at the very least suggest that it would have been plausible to his audience that the Mamluks would speak in code due to the Franks' knowledge of Arabic. The Templar also provides the names of Franks who knew Arabic from the Frankish delegation sent to Qalawun in 1290, including Sir Philip Mainebeuf, "a knight of Acre who knew the Saracen language very well," a Templar brother named Bartholomew Pisan who the Templar notes was born in Cyprus as if that were significant, and a scribe, George, who almost certainly would have had to know Arabic to do his job.[61] Although the precise percentage or numbers of Franks who knew Arabic is impossible to determine, this discussion has shown that that number was not zero. I would go further and argue that by the late twelfth and thirteenth centuries, some knowledge of Arabic by Franks was not unusual. Living in the midst of Arabic speakers made it necessary for some set of Franks to learn Arabic in order for basic communication and knowledge exchange to occur. Recognizing this is again necessary because it forces us to confront a level of shared knowledge and connectivity between the Franks and their neighbors that denying this skill would conceal.

Another set of knowledge that can offer insight into how the peoples of the region were connected is scientific and medical knowledge. Like espionage, this topic has largely been approached in the context of a specific branch of history, in this case history of science and medicine. This next part of the chapter will trace how medical and scientific knowledge circulated and thus illuminate another thread connecting Franks and Muslims.

Piers Mitchell in his book on the impact of the Crusades on medieval medicine notes that early on medieval scholars traveled to Antioch and Tripoli as centers of translation of medical texts. For example, Adelard of Bath went to Antioch around 1114 to find manuscripts. Stephen of Pisa also lived in Antioch between 1126 and 1130 working on his own translation of al-Majusi's *Kitab kamil al-sina'a al-tibbiyya* (Complete book of the medical art).[62] Rubin describes an understudied Arabic-French pharmaceutical glossary that may have been produced in Acre during the thirteenth century.[63] Authored by Willame, a poulain and knight, and Jacques Sarasin, a "new Christian" and apothecary, this text highlights the interest Franks had in gathering medical knowledge from the Islamic world.[64] The glossary consists of 565 entries with the names of plants, minerals, and animals with the Arabic and French names written in Latin characters. The goal would have been to help both merchants and apothecaries with basic Arabic terminology. The transfer of knowledge thus was achieved through the interfacing of a (likely Muslim given his new French name "Sarasin") convert to Christianity and a Levantine-born Frank both located in the major port where medical stuffs were traded and sent to Europe.

In the Arabic sources, the exchange of medical knowledge seems to have come mainly via Eastern Christians, however. Several of the biographies in Ibn Abi Usaybiʿa's voluminous compendium of biographies of people connected to medicine are doctors with connection to Jerusalem during the crusader period. Muwaffaq al-Din b. al-Mutran (d. 587/1191) was a Christian who converted to Islam and traveled to Byzantium (Bilad al-Rum) in order to learn science.[65] He spent much of his career in the employ of Saladin during his campaigns against the Franks, and upon his conquest of Jerusalem, Muwaffaq al-Din went there on pilgrimage. He eventually settled in Damascus where other students would seek him out. One such was another Christian named Muwaffaq al-Din Yaqub b. Siqlab (d. 624/1227). Apparently Yaqub went to Damascus as a youth seeking to serve Muwaffaq al-Din b. al-Mutran. He came wearing the clothes of a Frankish doctor, described as a blue cloth gown with sleeves and a head covering with a small scarf. The older doctor eventually told Yaqub that such clothes would not work for him if he wanted to practice medicine among the Muslims and advised that he change into those normally worn in the country.[66] Although neither this entry nor that of Yaqub's explain why he might have been wearing the Frankish outfit, it seems likely it was because he came from one of the Frankish states. It does state in Yaqub's biography that he also met another Christian doctor, Shaykh Abu Mansur al-Nasrani al-Tabib in Jerusalem. However Yaqub ended up settling in Damascus where he died on Easter 1228.[67] Between these two men we see a transfer of knowledge and expertise from among Eastern Christians and Byzantium to the Frankish and Syrian Muslim spheres.

There are also doctors recorded as having worked with high-ranking Franks as well as Syrian or Egyptian lords. Another Christian doctor, named Abu Sulayman Daʾud b. Abi al-Muna ibn Abi Faris, was born in Jerusalem but then moved to Egypt to serve the last Fatimid caliphs.[68] He is said to have excelled in medical theory as well as astrology, and even predicted when Saladin would conquer Jerusalem. His biography states that when King Amaury was in Egypt, he impressed the king with this skill and the king requested that he enter his service. The sultan agreed and so Abu Sulayman moved to Jerusalem with his five sons. It does not indicate the exact date of this encounter, so it is not certain which of Amaury's invasions of Egypt—1163, 1164, or 1167—this could have been, but given the caliph's involvement in the treaty negotiated in 1167, perhaps that is the most likely occasion. In any event, after his move to Jerusalem, Abu Sulayman worked for the king for a while, even treating his son Baldwin's leprosy, before he retired to a monastic life. His biography also notes that four of his sons went into medicine as well, but one became a knight and grew up with Amaury's leprous son who taught him horse-riding. When Baldwin IV became king, this son al-Faris Abu al-Khair entered Baldwin's service as a knight. The other sons went on to have prosperous careers under the Ayyubids in Egypt and in Syria. This Eastern Christian family thus knit together different political and religious groups of the region by bringing their medical expertise to serve both the Franks and the Ayyubids.

Another such doctor who crossed between Frankish and Ayyubid domains, and who was probably a Muslim given his title, was Rashid al-Din Ibn al-Suri (d. 639/1242).[69] He was born and raised in the Frankish city of Tyre in 1177. He then moved to study medicine with experts in the Ayyubid sphere, including the renowned polymath Abd al-Latif al-Baghdadi (d. 1231). After his studies, he went to Jerusalem where he worked in the hospital for two years. Unfortunately we do not know the exact dates of his residence in Jerusalem, but it was likely during its Ayyubid governance. He then went to work for al-Malik al-'Adil in Egypt until the sultan's death and then served his son al-Mu'azzam 'Isa until his death in 1227 in Damascus. Rashid al-Din remained there until his own death in 639/1242. The biography ends with a comment that Rashid al-Din was a master illustrator and worked on books depicting plants, especially those from the Mount Lebanon area. This may mean that he traveled through the region that would have been part of the County of Tripoli.

A final doctor, who was a Muslim and who found employ among the Franks, was Abu al-Fawaris Hamdan b. 'Abd al-Rahim al-Atharibi (d. 543/1148).[70] According to Ibn al-'Adim, he was born in a village known as Ma'aratha al-Atharib in the vicinity of Aleppo, before he and his father moved to Atharib itself. He spent most of his childhood in a village called al-Jazr, which we are told went back and forth between the hands of the Franks and the Muslims. He eventually came to govern it under the Franks. During this period while he was under Frankish lordship, the lord of Atharib, who is called Sir Manuel in the text, fell ill. Abu Fawaris went to the lord and took care of him until he recovered. Sir Manuel told Abu Fawaris to ask for something, to which he replied that he wanted a village. Sir Manuel obliged, giving him Maʿarbuniyya in 1127 where he lived for thirty years.[71] In addition to being a man of medicine, Abu al-Fawaris was also an *adib* who had studied under a shaykh named ʿAli Abu'l-Hasan Ibn Abi Jaradah. This former tutor was angry enough to learn about Abu Fawaris's living under Frankish lordship that he wrote him a letter of rebuke and censure including a poem.[72] Thus with Abu Fawaris, we have a Muslim landholder, adib, and doctor who came into the service of a Frankish lord for part of his life. Manuel seemingly had no problem using the medical skills of a Muslim, and repaid him with a village.

The preceding discussion has shown two patterns that illuminate the regional cultural landscape. The first is how Arabic biographies of men connected to medicine seem to indicate a general flow outward of expertise—that Christians and Muslims (converts or not) tended to flow away from the Latin East to enter the service of Syrian or Egyptian lords. But this was not universally the case. As we saw with the family of Abu Sulayman b. Daʾud, doctors would go from patron to patron, in this case, from service to the Fatimids to King Amaury and then into service of the Ayyubids. Likewise, the adib and doctor Abu al-Fawaris lived and held lands under Latins and Muslims, seemingly preferring to stay where he was rather than move to remain under Muslim lordship. He likewise was willing to use his medical expertise and minister to his Frankish lord, Manuel, as necessary. The second pattern is that it seems that in the realm of medical knowledge from the Islamicate world and perhaps scientific knowledge more broadly, Eastern Christians were the main, immediate source for the Franks. However, again there were exceptions with Muslims and converts from Islam to Christianity also providing some information and expertise. The overall point, though, is that rather than there being an unbridged chasm between Frankish and Islamicate approaches to medicine, there was in fact a shared medical culture in the region. This shared culture was certainly contested among the Franks by other practices and expectations brought from Europe, as illuminated by William of Tyre's complaint about Franks using local doctors.[73] Even so, having access to multiple medical cultures in the region did not preclude the forging of a shared one.

## Conclusion

The analysis presented here has shown some of the contours of the shared cultural landscape in which the Franks, Seljuks, Abbasids, Fatimids, Ayyubids, and Mamluks participated. Knowledge was an important component in the shared culture of the region. Frankish and Muslim elites sought the same kinds of knowledge from each other. Muslims were important participants in the circulation of knowledge, whether military or political intelligence, or more academic topics like medicine. Although in the twelfth century, especially earlier on, it is likely that the Abbasids, Fatimids, and Seljuks had more developed intelligence systems in place, by the thirteenth century both the Franks and the Mamluks had networks of informants and spies working for them. All parties suspected converts, Eastern Christians, and especially nomadic peoples when it came to the transmission of illicit intelligence. In reality, the circulation of knowledge did not come down to only marginal figures but elites as well. High-placed individuals like the Master of the Templars and the Mamluk amir al-silah engaged in information exchanges in return for gifts and favors. Coastal cities and ports were hotspots for information gathering as well, with the Mamluks seeking news about potential new crusades or other important political events in Europe from recently arrived sailors. Likewise, Latin merchants and travelers returning from Egyptian ports or other trading hubs were similarly questioned for information or observations.

There existed a common culture of medicine as well. Islamicate medical science was valued by some Franks and was sought after through Eastern Christian intermediaries. Both Egyptian and Frankish rulers vied for the medical services of the family of Abu Sulayman. The overlap was not perfect, and indeed among the Franks one can say that there existed multiple medical cultures at work. Frankish doctors continued to practice Frankish medicine born out of the knowledge brought from Europe. This situation, however, does not preclude one of those being a culture shared across the region.

Although certain kinds of factual knowledge, like geography or topography, might be thought of as something someone of any culture might value, there was nothing automatic or necessary about common understandings this chapter has outlined. The Franks and the Syrian and Egyptian Muslim leaders did not have to share intelligence networks. They did not have to approach gathering information in the same way. They did not have to share the same stereotypes about who was trustworthy. But they did. They also shared an appreciation for the expertise of doctors trained in the hospitals of Damascus and Baghdad, often Eastern Christians. It is important to not lose sight of the fact that even in areas where we might think of things as naturally desirable, there is very little that is naturally or obviously occurring in culture.[74] We therefore should pay attention when the same kinds of knowledge and expertise are valued in similar ways and see that as indicative of a shared culture.

*Chapter 6*

# Literary Intersections

Shortly after the devastation of the city of Jerusalem by the Khwarazmian Turks in 1244, a poet and one-time imam of the Dome of the Rock, Isma'il al-Maghrebi, wrote a poem directly on the walls of the Church of Mount Zion. With the line "Let it not distress you even though they be bare of ornament," Isma'il described the abandoned and destroyed buildings of the city that had been his home, waxing nostalgic over the city's lost grandeur. A visiting Damascene poet saw the poem and added his own lines, "It has been obliterated. But there has not been effaced from my heart its admiring love for their original inhabitants. They are the basis of my torment."[1] Both poets drew attention to the ruined walls of the abbey church of St. Mary of Sion by using them to display their comments on the city's destruction. But why the church? At the time, the church of St. Mary of Sion was a distinctly Frankish building, having been rebuilt in the Romanesque style by the Franks in the mid-twelfth century.[2] It could not have been mistaken for anything other than what it was. Any attempt to parse these lines and address the questions that they raise necessarily prompts one to see a cultural and literary landscape that was shared in some way among the inhabitants of the various polities in the region, Christian or Muslim. The vignette provides an example of how Syrian-Muslim poets, and litterateurs more broadly, adapted to and incorporated the Franks into their works. In this case, the poets very concretely manifested their work in such a way, written on a Frankish building, that directly acknowledged the Franks, and indeed could be consumed in some fashion by them as well.

While shared conceptions of and approaches to kinds of knowledge as discussed in the previous chapter might not be an intuitive component of culture for many, shared literary genres should be more familiar. The idea of a shared literary culture between Latin Christians, Muslims, and Jews is not new by any means.[3] Samuel England has recently directed our attention to a shared literary culture of competition in Mediterranean courts that lends a particularly useful model for this study. Although medieval Franks and Muslims are so often studied together in the context of violent competition over territory, England examines how competition played out in the courts in the far less violent field of poetry and belles lettres. Tracing how courtly elites used poetic competition and competitive imagery, particularly of the Crusades, from Abbasid-period Baghdad to Alfonso X's Castile and León and late medieval Italy, he argues that "competition gave a sense of order—both temporal and spatial—that enhanced the court's oftentimes coercive power over its subjects."[4] Through competition, courts were able to (re)assert unity and harmony, when challenged or potentially disturbed from within or without. Rulers such as Saladin used Abbasid models to promote their position during moments of political strife, while Alfonso X articulated himself as a troubadour who battled his Islamic foes in the field of poetry while unable to expand territorially.[5]

A key point to England's analysis is that the medieval world did not Other in the same binary way identified in Edward Said's study of Orientalism. Highlighting Suzanne Conklin Akbari's critique, he notes that not only did medieval people **not** conceive of the world as divided between East and West, but they rarely ever conceived of the world as bipartite, favoring tri- or quadripartite models.[6] When trying to represent foreigners, the courts of Islamic and Christian rulers did so not by focusing on difference between their ideal vision of themselves and the Other, but rather by focusing on the vision of the ideal *courtly* subject and "those of questionable credentials seeking admission to the court."[7] These may have been individuals from afar, belonging to another religion, but most important, England argues, was whether they qualified for a position at court through their morals, comportment, and eloquence.[8] The question of national or religious identity was secondary to the question of whether someone belonged at court. In what follows, England's idea of competition will be pushed further to shed light on the specifics of Muslim-Frankish literary culture in the Levant.

In this second chapter engaging with components of the cultural landscape of the eastern Mediterranean, we explore shared components of literary expression and medieval Muslim responses to the cultural proximity of the Franks. We will do so through an analysis of works from three different genres: letters, poetry, and anthology. The progression operates thematically and goes somewhat against chronology, as the letters primarily date from the thirteenth century while the specific anthology under discussion, Usama Ibn Munqidh's *Book of Contemplation*, dates from the late twelfth century. As intelligence was often transferred through the medium of letters, discussing them serves as a transition from the area of knowledge production and circulation discussed in Chapter 5, to literary production. The poetry dates from both centuries and testifies to the Islamic response to the Frankish presence as well as their acceptance of the Franks into their cultural production. We end with Usama's work as it offers the keenest insight into how an individual member of the Muslim elite conceptualized his own culture's relationship with the Franks, and displayed both deep cultural familiarity and empathy, as well as unease with that familiarity.

This chapter does something new in the field of Crusades studies. It first brings together texts not often discussed together. It second adopts a new methodology, in applying and expanding on Samuel England's approach to courtly competition to the literary production of the eastern Mediterranean. For example, while well-known to crusades scholars, Usama Ibn Munqidh's text is normally used as a historical rather than a literary source.[9] In this chapter I will be discussing his text as a literary artifact in conversation with other literary artifacts. Similarly, letters fall into multiple genres and can be used in different ways by scholars. In this chapter, I argue that they existed and were seen as examples of literature, just as the poetic literature that was more recognizable to modern readers was. I build from Samuel England's theoretical framework by applying the conception of literary competition to the polities of the eastern Mediterranean and argue that we can see a shared literary culture at work that bound the Frankish polities to their Arabophone neighbors. Going even further, we can see in the Arabic literary production not only a recognition of this cultural proximity but a response, which is one of profound ambivalence. By taking this novel approach, we can see that the modern idea of bordered polities with neatly contained and separated cultures just was not the case in twelfth- and thirteenth-century Syria and Palestine, as argued in the previous chapters with political power and knowledge.

## Competition in the Epistolary Field

Perhaps the largest body of direct evidence for a shared literary culture during the crusader period comes from letters. Although it is certain that many letters were exchanged in the twelfth century, the majority of the letters that survive date to the thirteenth and were exchanged between the Mamluk Sultan Baybars and various Frankish leaders. An analysis of these letters exemplifies Samuel England's conception of the "literature of contest."[10] We see from the Mamluks a clear bravado in the letters taunting the Frankish recipient in a poetic fashion. The evidence of Frankish responses, albeit coming largely from Arabic sources, likewise indicates that the Franks engaged in similar styles and endeavored to compete with the Mamluks through this literary genre. These letters thus are indicative of a literary culture that tied the polities of the eastern Mediterranean together.

Before progressing to the letters themselves, some background into the genre is useful in order to understand how they can and should be read as literary productions. As Adrian Gully notes, letter-writing was the dominant Arabic prose literary form for centuries during the Middle Ages and was considered an independent genre.[11] The genre was particularly important to the secretarial class who crafted and could become famous for their ability to write letters. Contemporary theories about proper letter-writing between the medieval Latin and Arabic traditions were comparable, both inheriting a lot from Greek and Roman tradition, and sharing similar structural format requirements. Theorists in both traditions were reading Aristotle. An important difference, however, was in the purpose. While medieval Latin letter-writing inherited the idea that the purpose was to persuade, Gully argues, "Arabic epistolary style was driven much more by stylistic and aesthetic consideration and appreciation."[12] The letter should demonstrate the power of the writer or the sender's position in terms of the hierarchical relationship between the sender and addressee rather than persuade.[13] For some, the ideal letter would be unified, focused on a single theme, and with an introduction that could be placed at the conclusion without impacting the meaning of the text.

The superiority of prose or poetry was hotly debated by such literary critics as Abu Hilal al-'Askari (d. 1005) and Diya' al-Din Ibn al-Athir (d. 1239), the brother of the historian whose *Kamil fi'l-ta'rikh* is a staple source for Crusades scholars.[14] There was a great deal in common between letters and poetry. Formal letters were usually written in a form of rhymed prose called *saj* and were supposed to engage in a single theme (*ma'na*), set by the author in the salutation and developed over the course of the letter.[15] The key difference as literary critics understood it was that while poetry was bound by rigid rules of form, prose was much less so.

Letters were divided into formal and informal, with different sets of expectations but not strictly speaking governed by rules. For our purposes, we will assume that the surviving letters to Franks were considered to be of the formal variety by their authors as they all touch upon diplomatic or military issues. Those who wrote about epistolary formulas tended to focus much more on the introduction and body than on the conclusion, but the general format of a letter to a sovereign would go as follows: an introduction that would start with the royal insignia, the titles of the sender and appropriate prayers to God on his behalf, the identity of the addressee including his titles, and ending with the salutation that establishes the subject of the letter; the body, which first outlines the reasons for the letter and then proposes a solution; the end, which would include the date and final greetings and prayers for the recipient.[16] As outlined by Gully, Ibn al-Athir proposed that formal letters were supposed to have five essential characteristics:[17]

1. The opening part of the letter should be elegant and original
2. The salutation and invocation (*du'a'*), also at the beginning, should be derived from the theme of the letter
3. The author should move from one idea to another in a way that connects them together
4. Expression in the letter should not be common[18]
5. The letter should contain at least one rhetorical concept from either the Qur'an or the Hadith

In the Ayyubid period, informal letters would draw more from poetry, while formal letters would involve Qur'anic citation.[19] As we will see, extant letters from the Mamluk court to the Franks included many if not all of these characteristics.

Letters were to reflect the status of the sender and the recipient, which in some respects shaped the format as well as language. Al-Qalqashandi (d. 821/1418), who preserved a number of treaties between the Mamluks and the Franks in his treatise on bureaucratic procedure and writing, *Subh al-A'sha fi Sina'at al-Insha*, also covered letters. He noted that the layout of letters should differ for letters addressed to non-Muslim groups, such as Byzantines, Georgians, Jews, and of course, Franks. The letters should not begin with the official royal insignia but with a note written from the secretary. As we shall see, the letters that survive tend to begin abruptly but do involve the usual invocation of God's help or blessing for the recipient.[20] The rank of the recipient would also determine whether the letter was written in saj'. Great kings who would be able to appreciate literary eloquence, merited saj', whereas lesser kings and rulers did not.[21] This consideration of the recipient went beyond just his political status, to an estimation of his ability to comprehend and recognize eloquence. If the recipient (or his secretary) were judged to be well-versed in principles of communication, the letter-writer would fill his letter with eloquence. If, however, this was not the case, then the letter-writer should write in a manner that those listening would be able to understand and appreciate.[22] The Franks, it turns out, were considered to be worthy.

The theory behind letter-writing was not inflexible, however, and there is evidence that chanceries would adapt when engaging in transcultural communications. In her analysis of official letters sent by the Mamluks to the khan of the Golden Horde from the later thirteenth through fifteenth centuries, Marie Favereau notes how frequently it seems that Mamluk court secretaries opted to emulate the style of the letter they received and were responding to rather than adhere to strict epistolary formulas dating to previous centuries.[23] For example, chancellery practice held that different kinds and sizes of paper were appropriate for letters depending on the recipient. A large format paper known as "Baghdadi" was appropriate for letters to other sovereigns, and yet letters of a much less prestigious size were sometimes used in communications with the khan of the Golden Horde. This was not out of disrespect, Favereau argues, but rather because it was mimicking the size of paper they had used to communicate with Cairo.[24] In the evolution of diplomatic letters that she traces through changes such as this, Favereau argues that there was an exchange in epistolary culture and knowledge between the diplomatic offices of the two sultans of the Mamluks and the Mongols of the Golden Horde.[25] Although the Franks did not maintain diplomatic relations with any single Muslim power for as long as the Mamluks did with the Golden Horde, each dynasty being around for decades as opposed to centuries, I argue that one is able to recognize some adaptation in the culture in a similar fashion to that identified by Favereau. Thus, letters were not only a practical means of exchanging information but also examples of literary culture that can shape and adapt and be shared in ways specific to parties participating in the exchanges.

For the rest of this section, we will analyze letters recorded, and in at least two cases written, by the same secretary, Ibn ʿAbd al-Zahir, on behalf of the Sultan Baybars to the Franks. This analysis will show the ways in which Franks were folded into epistolary culture and were participants in a literary contest of letters. Unfortunately, we do not have letters from the Franks to the Ayyubids or Mamluks, but we do have a few indications of what they said, which do suggest an effort to engage in a literary contest as well as a military one.

The four letters under consideration here were written between 1268 and 1271 and informed Frankish leaders of losses inflicted upon them by Baybars. Ibn ʿAbd al-Zahir tells us that he wrote two of these himself: a letter sent to Bohemond VI about the conquest of Antioch in 1268[26] and a letter sent to King Hugh of Cyprus and Jerusalem in 1271 about the capture of Montfort castle.[27] The other two are both from 1271: one sent to Hugh Revel, Master of the Hospitallers, regarding the conquest of Crac des Chevaliers,[28] and the other sent to Bohemond VI about the conquest of Gibelacar (Hisn ʿAkkar).[29] The letters are preserved in the narrative history of Ibn ʿAbd al-Zahir, and appear also in the later histories of Baybars al-Mansuri and Ibn al-Furat who both copied him. Although he himself wrote at least two of these, it seems likely that Ibn ʿAbd al-Zahir left portions of the letters out as there is no dating or signature for example. It is further possible that much of the body of certain letters was left out given the disparity in length among them, with the Antioch letter running for several pages in the edition, and the Crac des Chevaliers letter a mere paragraph. Still, they all appear to have parts of their openings and we can get a sense of the language used.

By far the longest, at about four pages in the current edition, is the letter to Bohemond VI informing him in detail about the capture of Antioch. In compliance with the rules for letters to non-Muslims, the opening address is brief and without the sultan's insignia. It does, however, provide expansive titles for Bohemond, who is addressed as "his majesty the count, the revered, the illustrious, the gallant, the courageous lion, pride of the Christian nation, chief of the crusader sect, great of the nation of Jesus, Bohemond."[30] The address in the letter Ibn ʿAbd al-Zahir composed to King Hugh was far briefer, calling him merely "king Hugh de Lusignan."[31] Although of differing lengths, the latter being one long paragraph, both are written in sajʿ and exemplify high literary skill. In the letter regarding the capture of Antioch, after the list of titles, Bohemond is informed that his titles have changed from that of a prince to a count (*min al-brinsiyya ila al-qumisiyya*) due to the conquest of Antioch. Baybars and his staff secretaries were clearly aware that the title of prince was tied to the lordship of Antioch, whereas the lordship of Tripoli was merely a county, despite these titles being foreign imports from Europe. This clever turn of phrase relishing Bohemond's reduced status exemplifies the desired need for originality and unity in epistles. As part of the address, it immediately identifies the theme of the letter (conquest/loss), the events and sequence of which the body of the letter explains in detail. It is thus following the elements of high epistolary form.

The opening section, in addition to being rhymed, is written in a poetically stylized manner, further showing its literary value. Following the titles and the comment about his loss of status, the letter goes on to make a series of statements meant to underline the magnitude of Bohemond's loss and Baybars's victory. For example, he writes, "[The Count] knows what he saw after we left . . . how the churches were swept from the face of the earth, and calamities befell each house; how butchered corpses were set like islands on the sea-shore; how the men were killed, the children enslaved and the freeborn women taken as slaves."[32] Sentiments such as these continue for lines. The letter progresses to the body, which gives a more narrative retelling of the siege and subsequent conquest and sack of Antioch, and which wraps up with a set of conditional phrases emphasizing the magnitude of the devastation and loss: "If you had seen your churches with their crosses broken and rent, the pages from the false Testament scattered, . . . If you had seen the fires burning in your castles and the slain being consumed by the fire of this world . . . had you seen these things, you would have said: 'Would that I were dust.'"[33] The conditional statement rejoices in the humiliation of the Count through the destruction of churches and Bibles that represent the Frankish presence in Antioch. The second part of the clause, "would that I were dust," is a quote from the Qur'an's Sura al-Naba verse 40, which an unbeliever at the end of days cries out upon confronting his punishment.[34] He thus connects Bohemond directly with an unbeliever in the Qur'an and the destruction of Antioch with God's judgment and the destruction of the end of days.

The final section of the letter explains why the sultan wrote. In doing so, it offers a kind of moral:

> This letter, then, gives you good news of the safety and prolongation of life that God has granted to you because you were not staying at Antioch at this time and you did not happen to be there. For (otherwise) you would have been killed or captured, wounded or broken. The living rejoice in the preservation of their own lives when they see the dead. Perhaps God has granted you a delay only that you may make up for your past lack of obedience and service. Since no one escaped to tell you of what has happened, we have told you ourselves, and as there is no one who can give you the good tiding of your own safety and of the loss of the lives of the others, we have given you this account and sent you the news so that you may be sure of what has happened.[35]

The letter concludes by simultaneously taunting Bohemond with the sarcastic good news of his escape while offering the implied moral of the necessity of obeying God and the inevitability of His will. The paragraphs detailing the destruction of Antioch and enslavement of its populace are hardly good news, and yet the letter is framed as such: Behold, you are still alive and could be dead! For both Baybars and Bohemond as members of the military elite, the failure to participate in a battle, either won or lost, could hardly have been seen as a good thing. Baybars almost offers consolation by framing the loss as God's will, and yet it is Bohemond's failure to be obedient and serve that he attributes the loss to. He ends by returning to the idea of the totality of devastation, that only he, the sultan, could inform Bohemond of exactly how the conquest happened "since no one escaped." This returns the letter to a wish expressed at its very beginning in the invocation of God following the address: "May God inspire him to follow the right course, turn his purpose to good and cause him to remember His admonition."[36] The letter as a whole, then, represents the ideal epistolary form as discussed by literary critics and shows how the Franks were fully incorporated into the system. As Gully discussed, not all letters produced by the chancery merited literary eloquence. This one to Bohemond, however, included sajʿ, smooth connections of parts, a Qurʾanic quotation, and a stylized, unified idea. Thus we have evidence that Frankish rulers, such as Bohemond, were seen as worthy recipients of epistles in their highest form. As such recipients, they are also being marked as worthy members of literary competition described by England. These letters as a whole can be taken as a venue of that literary contest, and this particular letter as an example of one side's volley against the other.

A second letter to Bohemond VI that Ibn ʿAbd al-Zahir includes in his narrative but does not claim to have written continues the condescending tone. After Baybars's conquest of the castle of ʿAkkar in May 1271, he once again sent a letter to "count Bohemond" about the loss. He invokes God, asking that Bohemond be made "one who takes thought for himself and considers his future fate in the light of what had passed" perhaps hinting at not only the most recent loss but also those further in the past like Antioch.[37] It too is written in sajʿ and contains a number of poetic images. For example, in describing the ordeals of the Muslim troops as they prepared to besiege the castle in rain and mud, he notes, "how we erected [the mangonels] in places where ants would slip were they to walk there." The second part of the letter describing the outcome of the victory goes even further in its evocative imagery. He writes, "This letter of ours announces to you that our yellow standard has been raised in place of your red one; and that the sound of bells has been replaced by the cry 'Allah Akbar'."[38] Here the letter-writer is using *tibaq* or antithesis, placing two opposing things together for the point. The sound of the bell was directly associated with the Franks as it was only with the coming of Latin Christians that bells became widespread in the region.[39] The replacement of bells by the *adhan* or call to prayer that begins with "Allah Akbar" represents the military victory of the Mamluks over the Franks, just as the change in standards does. The letter goes on to make the literary threat of continued Mamluk military victory with the statement "We tell the bodies of your horsemen that our swords say they will be coming for hospitality as the people of 'Akkar did not satisfy their hunger."[40] The swords are personified as possessing hunger that only being thrust into the bodies of Frankish knights can sate. The letter as given ends with, "Let the Count take note of the thread of this discourse and act on it, or let him prepare his ships and those of his companions, for otherwise we have prepared shackles for them and for him."[41] The letter circles back around to the concept of obeying God's fate—in this case, preparing to leave the country, taking their ships back to Europe, or to suffer death and captivity. This second letter represents another volley in the literary battle. In this case, the exchange, rather than sublimating or substituting for military competition, actually mirrors it. For someone of lesser cultural status, the sultan's chancery could have chosen to forgo writing anything and not have bothered with the epistolary coup de grâce. Bohemond is clearly someone who they felt the need to compete with not only militarily but also literarily.

Another letter sent upon the capture of Crac des Chevaliers from the Hospitallers earlier that year in April adopts a similar tone.[42] Addressed to "Ifrir Awk," "Brother Hugh," meaning Hugh Revel (d. 1277), the Master of the Knights Hospitaller, we see the use of the Frankish title the Hospitaller brother would have used. Similar to the theme of the letter about the fall of 'Akkar, this letter asks God to "make him [Hugh] one of those who do not oppose destiny nor rebel against Him who has made victory and conquest the servants of his army."[43] It likewise asks God to make Hugh one who does not think precautions or walls can stave off His will. The Hospitallers, like the other military orders, were the main holders of big fortresses in the thirteenth century and were long used to defending themselves behind massive walls, weathering invasion and siege as best they could. The invocation here alludes to that fact and likens it to denying the will of God who favored the Mamluk enterprise. The letter goes on to state: "You relied on your brothers to preserve [Crac des Chevaliers], but they were of no avail to you. You lost them by making them stay there, as they lost it and caused your ruin."[44] The theme of inevitability continues with the added layer of guilt that the letter lays on the Master for the loss of his men. If only he had not fought, if only he had not thought walls could protect them. From this letter we glean that leaders of military orders were considered to be of a similar status of kings and other rulers and also merited letters of a high literary quality.

Ibn ʿAbd al-Zahir's other letter sent on behalf of sultan Baybars to King Hugh has an almost sarcastic style and represents a specific model for the epistolary response (*jawab*). Within Arabic literary criticism and in the discussion about epistolary form, there was some debate about whether the initial letter or the response was more important. According to Gully, "the majority of secretaries held that the letters of response were more demanding and more challenging intellectually than the original letters (Ar. *Kutub ibtidāʾiyya*)."[45] Whereas the initiator of the exchange was free to decide what the theme was and how to approach it, the respondent was constrained to respond in the manner set by the initiator. As recorded by Ibn ʿAbd al-Zahir, this is just the situation in which the letter concerning Montfort was written. In the month of Shawwal 669 in the Islamic calendar (May 13–June 10, 1271), Baybars sent a fleet from Egypt to attack Cyprus. This fleet never made it, having been largely destroyed upon the reefs outside Limassol with nearly all the survivors being taken captive.[46] According to Ibn ʿAbd al-Zahir, King Hugh of Cyprus and Jerusalem (r. 1267/8–1284) sent a letter to Baybars "reproaching him, 'the fleet of Egypt was sent to Cyprus then the wind destroyed it, and I seized it, which comprised eleven ships, and I imprisoned all those who were in it.'"[47] As presented, it appears that King Hugh was engaging in epistolary competition, and composed a letter that would have resembled in some fashion those that Baybars sent.

It was only after the capture of Montfort on June 12, 1271, that the sultan decided to reply. It starts abruptly, "This letter is to his majesty king Hugh de Lusignan," and dives immediately into an exhortation to God that signals the triumphant nature of this epistolary response: "May God make him one who gives men their dues [sic], and who does not boast of a victory unless he can precede or follow it by a better or an equal."[48] He nods to the king's initial letter and returns with a request that God help him understand that one should only brag about something if he can back it up with other victories. The letter continues: "We tell him that when God wishes to favour a man, He uses the minor calamites of Fate to ward off the major ones from him, and He directs him well in the paths of destiny. You told us how the wind destroyed a number of our ships, and you rejoiced and were glad at this. Now it is our turn to give the King news of the capture of al-Qurain [Montfort]."[49] The letter seamlessly transitions from the exhortation to directly replying to the failure of the Mamluk fleet by turning it back to God's will. Baybars was content with a "minor calamity" so long as it deflected anything major, like losing a castle. His response is to acknowledge the loss of the fleet and respond with the news that he has captured the Teutonic castle. The letter continues to upbraid the king for boasting prematurely. Moreover, the letter explains how a sea victory is paltry compared to a land victory: "It is not victory given by the wind that is fine, but victory by the sword. In one day we can build a number of ships, while you cannot build one section of one fortress: and we can equip one hundred sailing ships, whereas not in one hundred years can you prepare a single fort. Anyone, given an oar, can row, but it is not everyone who, given a sword, can strike properly with it or cut."[50] The sultan, through his secretary, belittles the Frankish victory by attributing it not to skill but to an accident of nature, "the wind," and saying the ships and their crew can easily be replaced. He heightens his own success by attributing it to the real skill with weaponry possessed by his soldiers and exaggerating the length of time it would take to rebuild a castle. As the letter approaches its finale, the sultan's anger or at least indignation becomes more palpable: "How can those who pierce the breast of the ocean with their oars bear comparison with those who plunge their spears into the breasts of men in the battle ranks? Your steeds are ships, our ships are steeds. What a difference there is between the one who gallops his (horses) like the sea waves and one (whose ship) strands him on the mud; between one who hunts with falcons from Arab horses and one who, when he boasts, says: 'I have hunted with a crow'."[51] The comparison of the images of an oar piercing waves and spear piercing a chest augments Baybars's contention that the latter is more of a challenge. In typical Mamluk fashion, as horse-warriors, he glorifies the soldier on horseback as more impressive than Franks sailing around the sea on ships.[52] Invoking the shared culture of hunting, he disparages the Franks by suggesting they hunt with inferior birds. The word used in the final line of the quote above, *ghurab*, means both crow and a kind of warship, thus tying sailing to poor hunting. The final line of the letter acts as a virtual slammed door in the face of the Frankish king: "Had the King been a man of calmness he should have remained quiet and not spoken."[53] With this comment, the letter is brought back to the initial invocation to God that He make the king someone who knows when and when not to boast.

Baybars's letter to Hugh in 1271 stands as an example of high literary epistolary response. While it does not contain a Qur'anic quotation, unlike the letter to Bohemond, it is written in saj' and contains vivid poetic imagery and wordplay. It begins with an exhortation to God that establishes its theme of conquest as rebuke, as set by the initial letter from the king, and continues to follow it throughout the body. Clearly, the Franks were seen as not only regional political players but ones who could appreciate a good letter and were thus equal competitors in a shared literary field. Of course this is entirely mediated through the secretarial staff, but it does suggest that Mamluk secretaries like Ibn 'Abd al-Zahir judged the secretaries and translators who received the Arabic compositions and rendered them into "Frankish" as capable of appreciating the art and presumably rendering it appropriately to the intended recipient. Since Ibn 'Abd al-Zahir also recorded these and other letters to the Franks in his histories, he clearly thought that his Muslim audience would appreciate his work and see it as worthy. While other powers elsewhere in the world also would have received such letters, not all did. Remembering that a prevailing attitude toward the cultural competency of the Latin East has long been dim, it is a valuable corrective to see that the secretaries for Muslim powers did not write to the Franks as they would to some bumpkins. Moreover, these letters can be seen as part of a courtly field of competition in the vein outlined by England. The letters sent between the Franks and their Muslim peers generated and contributed to a culture of epistolary competition that both mirrored and perhaps provided an outlet for military and political competition.

Due to a lack of surviving letters sent by the Franks to their Syrian and Egyptian peers, there is little direct evidence for the Frankish side of this culture of literary competition. Indirect evidence includes references such as that above to letters sent to Syrian or Egyptian courts that elicited responses or references to previous missives in the surviving Arabic letters themselves. A rare piece of evidence from a Frank about his understanding of Arabic literary letters comes from the Templar of Tyre. Near the end of his history, in the build-up to the conquest of Acre in 1291, he quotes from the beginning of a letter sent by the sultan al-Malik al-Ashraf Khalil (r. 1290–1293), Qalawun's son. Upon his ascension, the Franks sent a delegation intended to smooth things over with the new Mamluk sultan in an effort to make up for the massacre of Muslim merchants that had occurred in August 1290. The previous sultan Qalawun had taken this event as a breaking of the truce between him and the Franks and had begun preparations for war that were interrupted upon his demise. Al-Ashraf was not appeased and refused to read the letters and imprisoned the delegation. He had sent a letter to the Franks beforehand that the Templar of Tyre says he translated into French himself and then brought before the Templar master and other lords of Acre.[54] His account gives us an idea of the process of correspondence, with a secretary like the Templar of Tyre, writing out a translation and then presenting it to court to be read.

The Templar himself indicates an understanding of the nuance of these letters when he draws the reader's attention to al-Ashraf's opening. He states, "Now let me show you the tenor of the letter which the sultan sent to the master of the Temple. Notice the sort of salutation which the sultan sent in his letter." He then presents the letter:

> The Sultan of Sultans, King of Kings, Lord of Lords, al-Malik al-Ashraf, the Powerful, the Dreadful, the Scourge of Rebels, the Hunter of Franks and Tartars and Armenians, Snatcher of Castles from the Hands of Miscreants, Lord of the Two Seas, Guardian of the Two Pilgrim Sites, Khalil al-Salihi,
> To the noble master of the Temple, the true and wise:
> Greetings and our good will! Because you have been a true man, so we send you advance notice of our intentions, and give you to understand that we are coming into your parts to right the wrongs that have been done. Therefore we do not want the community of Acre to send us any letters or presents [regarding this matter], for we will by no means receive them.[55]

Unlike in the letters preserved in Arabic narrative sources, the Templar of Tyre has included the sultan's titles at the beginning. They certainly emphasize the point that al-Ashraf posed a serious threat to the Franks, and perhaps were used to help bolster the idea that it was folly for the Frankish leadership to not treat with him (and the local Muslims of Acre) correctly. He points it out to the reader, at any rate, as a sign of the sultan's wrath: Scourge of Rebels, Hunter of Franks, Snatcher of Castles from the Hands of Miscreants. These were hardly the names of someone who was willing to make peace and forgive.

Although the Arabic original does not survive for comparison, the Old French does not appear to have been rendered into verse resembling sajʿ; rather, it seems to have been made for the purpose of comprehension alone. The courtesy comes across as between two men who respect each other, but none of any of the eloquence, apart from perhaps the titles, survives. Still, the Templar's commentary does present an inkling that Frankish secretaries did understand the Arabic epistolary conventions, and that they could indeed appreciate a high-quality letter when sent their way.

Given the evidence and analysis just presented, we see that secretaries like Ibn ʿAbd al-Zahir clearly understood the Franks to be worthy recipients of eloquent letters and full participants in the epistolary version of literary competition. Although the Mamluk chancery produced many diplomatic letters intended for a wide array of recipients, we know that the level of eloquence used in each depended upon the recipient as well as the subject matter. As Gully discussed, premodern theorists of epistolography like Ibn Khalaf, Ibn al-Athir, and al-Qalqashandi all believed that rank and origin should guide secretaries in what kinds of eloquence (balaga) they used in letters from the ruler to others. He notes that "[Ibn Khalaf] clearly distinguished between the levels and complexity of speech required to address each group, stating that when writing to the masses and non-Arabs, for instance, the lowest degrees of *balāġa* should be used, namely, those that reach their levels of understanding."[56] Sajʿ was one of these elements of eloquence that would not be used with "lesser Kings and Rulers."[57] That Ibn ʿAbd al-Zahir included several letters in his narrative history, indicates that he was not concerned that his peers would question the way these letters to the Franks were written. His audience would have recognized not only his skill in the art form, but that it was not wasted on the Franks even though several of the correspondents were not in fact kings. The Franks were a fair outlet for literary expression and represented an opportunity for secretaries to display their talents. If the comments about letters received from the Franks and the Templar of Tyre's comments themselves are anything to go by, the Franks likewise recognized and actively participated in the competition by letters even as the correspondence mirrored in many cases military competition as well.

This discussion of the letters exchanged between the Franks and the Mamluks has illuminated two ideas. First, it has demonstrated how the concept of literary contest in the court setting could and in fact did extend beyond individual courts to encompass a larger regional literary sphere. Frankish and Mamluk elites used their letters to advance their own position. As Samuel England notes, courtly competition was most vibrant in moments of uncertainty, which was certainly the case for both the Mamluks and the Franks in the thirteenth century. This was a time when the former endeavored to consolidate itself and legitimize its rulers, and the latter navigated a series of regents and absentee kings. Second, and related to the first, is how the discussion furthers Marie Favereau's argument that diplomatic correspondence prompted adaptation and change in the respective parties' epistolary culture.[58] As discussed in Chapter 4, Arabic secretaries seem to have easily accommodated Frankish titular practice into their own formulas. They also adapted and evolved symbolic rhetoric like the conquest of the adhan over the bell in their epistolary rhetoric. Likewise, for the Franks, although coming from a similar but distinct epistolary theoretical background, they too seemed to have adapted their letters to participate in a literary contest with their Syrian and Egyptian neighbors. They were able to recognize some, if not all, of the subtleties that theoreticians like Ibn al-Athir expected in letters and respond in kind. In prose there was forged a shared literary culture even as Franks and their Muslim counterparts also engaged in literary production distinct from and unrelated to each other. The next section explores how Muslims responded to the Franks through poetry and how the Franks, in turn, may have become consumers of such poetry themselves.

## The Impact on the Poetic World

Poetry was the preeminent form of classical Arabic literature from antiquity. Although by the time of the Crusades, Arabic literature comprised an array of other genres, it continued to hold a position of prestige. It thus represents an appropriate vantage point from which to explore the possibility of a shared culture among the peoples living in the Latin East and neighboring states. A number of excellent studies on the impact of the crusades on the Arabic literary world have recently been published, and the long-standing notion that the Muslim world was slow to respond to the Franks has been dispelled.[59] Indeed, although the political leaders may have not been able to respond to the Frankish presence militarily until the time of 'Imad al-Din Zengi, the region's litterateurs reacted quickly, generating a significant amount of poetry on related themes. This falls into England's conception of literary competition, wherein poetry filled the gap when military conquest was not forthcoming. What follows is an analysis providing an overview of the changing attitudes toward the Franks as well as local Muslim leadership crafted in Crusades-era Arabic poetry. It demonstrates how such poetry both engaged in stereotypes of the Franks but also presented a close familiarity with them. Over time, the Franks ceased representing the ultimate evil, and instead came to be a more mundane foe, from whom local leaders either failed or succeeded in their duty to protect their cities. Indeed, by the thirteenth century there is evidence that Muslim poets used their poetry to comment on internal Frankish politics, independent of any desire to see them driven out of the land. Although scant, there are also some glimpses into how the Franks themselves were exposed to and even participated in this Arabic poetic culture. The poetry indicates another way that the Latin East became incorporated into the cultural fabric of the eastern Mediterranean and the *bilad al-Sham*. Far from being culturally impermeable to one another, the Franks and their Arab-Muslim neighbors responded to each other, and perhaps even communicated with each other, using poetry.

Arguably the most shocking event of the First Crusade to regional observers was the capture of Jerusalem, and this manifested early in Arabic poetry. Jerusalem had already for centuries been perceived as a sacred space and locus of veneration. In literature, this fact is best demonstrated by the existence of the *fada'il al-Quds* (merits of Jerusalem) genre, in which the various references to Jerusalem from the Qur'an and other texts were assembled into anthologies. These excerpted passages could come from hadiths, prose histories, biographies of people connected to the city, and poetry about it. After the city of Jerusalem was captured by the Franks, the genre came to expand to include the larger region of Syria (al-Sham) and Damascus in particular.[60] In fact, toward the mid-twelfth century there was an increase in the production of fada'il literature, as Latiff argues, because, "*jihād* leaders such as Nūr al-Dīn and Ṣalāḥ al-Dīn made use of existing material that had the emotional capacity to inspire a Muslim population to fight in the *jihād* and to liberate the cities (especially Jerusalem) that carry deep religious symbolism in Muslim religious imagination."[61] Fada'il al-Quds literature not only included poetry about Jerusalem and the region of Syria, but also fed into poetic conceptions of Jerusalem as sacred space. With the coming of the Franks, these poems included depictions of the sacred space defiled by invaders as well as exhortations for Muslims to retake it. Nizar Hermes in his analysis of Arabic literary conceptions of the European Other from the ninth to twelfth centuries CE sees the poetry that engaged with the Crusades as having developed out of the earlier genre of works about battle with the Byzantines along the frontier, known as *al-Rumiyyat* (poems about the Byzantines or *al-Rum*). The forms these poems could take included panegyrics (*madih*) or praise (*fakhr*) for Muslims participating or dying in the jihad, and invective (*hija'*) that could take a humorous stance against the enemy or those the poet wished to criticize.[62] One example of the latter with a nonhumorous approach, written by the Syrian poet Ibn al-Khayyat (d. 1120) and translated by Hermes, goes as follows:

> For how long will you stay unmoved!
> While the infidels are streaming as a tide.
> As massive as an ocean wide!
> Huge armies, like collapsing mountains
> Are moving from the Frankish side.
> For how long will you accept oppression?
> Overlooking those whose currency is war!
> You sleep in comfort, ignore the foe,
> In times of sorrow and tinged with woe!
> The infidels do not forbid vice,
> Nor do they set a limit to what is wrong.
> When killing, they do not spare a soul.
> Nor do they show mercy at all.[63]

Here we see the poet criticizing his audience, the political leaders of Syria, for their inaction against the Franks, and shaming them in the face of Frankish barbarity and vice. Another example, excerpted from a poem that was written in the wake of the Third Crusade by ʿAbd al-Munʿim al-Jilyani (d. 602/1207), praises Saladin ("the son of Ayyub") while criticizing the Franks:

1. O rescuer of Jerusalem from the hands of tyrants, the Franks swore that with their Lord's support they would enter it [a second time]
2. So they spoke their lies in their description of their Lord, and the promise of God has instead been delivered in favour of the Muslims.
3. Have you not seen the son of Ayyub who, by himself, did what the era and its people could not do?
4. The Franks became infuriated and cowardice afflicted them, and they became frightened and terrified.
5. When Ṣalāḥ al-Dīn took Jerusalem, they said, "how can we leave it while our Lord is buried there?"

6. Consider how many kings sailed there by sea to give support to the grave, but destiny was not on the side of those kings.
7. Consider how many huge armies travelled to reach there, yet their destiny was to meet hyenas on the way.
8. They cried out for help, spreading infection that divided them, and they gathered, for the war, much money which became booty [for us].[64]

As Latiff commented in his analysis, the poem praises the individual achievement of Saladin, while advancing, with the comment about "the son of Ayyub," the idea of his founding and being part of a dynasty that has justly taken over from the Zengids. Al-Jilyani also demonstrates a knowledge of the religious devotion of the Franks to Jerusalem, while simultaneously denouncing their misguided beliefs by referencing "their lies in their description of their Lord."

The poems witness how poets of the twelfth century grappled with Franks in their work and the shifting conception of them as time provided greater experience and exposure to them. Separated by a number of decades, these poems present a change in the depiction of the Franks. Ibn al-Khayyat, at the very beginning of the Frankish presence, depicts them as vice-ridden and violent. Likened to an ocean, they are more of a force of nature than humans. As such, they are bringers of woe, whom the Syrian lords sadly ignore. Decades later, al-Jilyani depicts them in far more human terms and shows a greater understanding of what they do. He invokes their sailing long distances and bringing great treasure. He understands that the Franks are on a religious mission and that they believe that God's favor is theirs. Rather than harbingers of unrelenting death, they are instead fearful and cowardly. In a matter of decades then, we can see a development in the depiction of the Franks, a humanization, and also an incorporation of knowledge about them in Arabic poetry. Although arguably still in the realm of caricature, the poets are undoubtedly influenced by their ongoing exposure to and interactions with the Franks, which by itself shows how interactions that seem to have nothing to do with cultural production can impact cultural products.

Most of the early poetic responses to the Franks come from outside observers rather than poets who directly encountered or even lived under Frankish rule, so it is difficult to assess how they may have felt or written about the Franks. Just as the Muslim legal experts and jurists of the area likely fled to other Syrian and Egyptian cities upon the crusader conquest,[65] so too, it seems, did most of the poets and other litterateurs (sing. *adib*, pl. *udaba'*). The dearth of known Muslim poets in the Latin East is largely what leads to this conclusion. We do, though, know of at least one poet who was such a refugee who might provide a bit of an insider's perspective. Ahmad Ibn Munir al-Tarablusi was born in Tripoli in 493/1099–1100 and left the city at some point afterward, perhaps with his family after the Frankish conquest in 1109. He spent much time in Zengid Aleppo and died there in 1153. He wrote the following in praise of Zengi's conquest of Edessa:

> The victory of Edessa had outshone all victories
> By the deeds of Zengi, Islam awakened
> If justice is done, he should be called the caliph
> Tomorrow he will invade Jerusalem.[66]

He portrays Zengi as a true Muslim leader, who "awakened" his fellows to participate in battle against the Franks. It also presents the hope of the imminent reconquest of Jerusalem. As someone who came from a city currently ruled by the Franks, one can imagine that despite his immediate goal of supporting his patron, he did also hope for a complete Frankish withdrawal with the potential for returning to his ancestral home.

After Zengi's death, Ibn Munir continued to write poems in honor of Zengi's son Nur al-Din. In honor of Nur al-Din's victory at the battle of Inab/al-Ruj in 1149, which crushed the army of Antioch and resulted in the death of Prince Raymond, he composed the following:

> The cross was struck against his relentlessness
> its timbers were scattered
> While the Prince wore the robe of humiliation
> [Nur al-Din] made the Prince drink the results of his perfidy
> The spear passed through his head while he was the one
> whose spear used to adjust the orbits and the time[67]

We have here the invocation of the cross as a stand-in for the Franks. It was broken symbolically against the relentlessness of Nur al-Din's Muslim army, just as the Frankish army had been. The poem also plays on the image of the spear, the one killing the Prince and the other referencing his former power to rule. Although we do not know the exact manner of Raymond's death, we do know that his head and right hand or arm were taken and sent to the caliph in Baghdad.[68] From Ibn Munir we get the perspective of the encounter between Frank and Muslim as being one inherently about opposed religions. The leaders are defined by their commitment to their religion and that to fight the Franks is to fight for Islam. Ibn Munir was not the first or only person to depict the encounter in these terms, but what we know of his own biography might help us contextualize this imagery at a more personal level. His family were driven away from their home by invaders not motivated by wealth or power but by religion, and those whom he came to serve were likewise motivated to expel them. The literary as well as physical competition as defined by Ibn Munir's poetry at least was one of religious truth rather than military might.

Another poet with connections to the Kingdom of Jerusalem, and who may have even worked there, was al-Rashid b. Nabulsi [sic], a poet from Nablus, which was part of the kingdom in the twelfth century. One of his poems recorded in Abu Shama's *Kitab al-Rawdatayn* was written in praise of Saladin's conquest of Jerusalem.[69] Latiff translated it as follows:

1. O the happiness of Jerusalem which woke with the unfurling of the flag of Islam, after it has been folded.
2. O the light of al-Aqṣā, how it now rises with verses and chapters [of the Qur'ān] after having the cross inside it.[70]

Unlike other poets who portrayed the Qur'an and cross in explicitly antagonistic or violent terms, Nabulsi instead focuses on the return to Jerusalem of the recitation of the verses of the Qur'an after the implied exit of the cross. Al-Aqsa mosque had been the headquarters of the Knights Templar and portions had been converted into a church, as indeed was the Dome of the Rock. The return of Islamic worship to these places is described in gentle almost pastoral terms, likened to the dawning of a new day in which people woke up to the renewed presence of the call to prayer. Perhaps as someone who had lived under the Franks and with Frankish Christians, Nabulsi was less inclined to violent triumphalism than more quiet rejoicing in the return of Muslim rule over the Islamic holy places.

Victory against the Franks continued to be an important element of poetry praising leaders in the thirteenth century. Indeed, the reign of Baybars provided ample opportunity for poets to write poems of praise as he systematically whittled away at the Frankish states and Cilician Armenia. The poet

Zayn al-Din Muhammad al-Katib al-Misri (d. 674/1275) wrote the following in honor of Baybars's conquest of Hisn 'Akkar (Gibelacar) in 1271:

> Oh the Sultan of Humankind
> may God increase his happiness
> The enemy was so terrified that he slayed them with terror
> victory is just his usual habit
> The fortress of 'Akkar is conquered
> and Acre will be in addition.[71]

The poem is a straightforward device of praise. Whereas in the twelfth-century praise poetry for the Zengids or Saladin poets looked toward the anticipated capture of Jerusalem, in the thirteenth century, especially in the second half, the focus was on Acre, now the seat of Frankish government. While the goal of praising leadership in military encounters against the Franks remained the same, the goal had shifted from reclaiming the holy city of Jerusalem, to reclaiming the coastal region that the poetry itself was playing a role in sanctifying. So we continue to see how the fact of the geographical location of Frankish political power prompted a development in an Arabic literary genre.

Interactions with the Franks stimulated not only poetry in praise of Muslim rulers but also critique. The response to the initial crusader victories of the late eleventh and twelfth centuries has been documented. Similar to Latins later responding to the failure of the Second Crusade, Muslim writers blamed the Frankish victories on a failure of spiritual resolve among the Muslims. The Ibn al-Khayyat poem discussed at the beginning of this section provides a good example of this. The Franks won because God was punishing them, just as was the case with the Byzantines before them.[72]

In the thirteenth century, the Ayyubid actions around Jerusalem invited further rebuke. Latiff has drawn our attention to the special sense of loss evinced by Muslim poets upon al-Mu'azzam 'Isa's decision to destroy Jerusalem's walls in 1219. The difficult decision was made in the course of the Fifth Crusade as an attempt to discourage the Franks from returning to the city and to hinder their ability to defend themselves should they do so.[73] The outpouring of sorrow, as Latiff argues, was aimed not so much at the Ayyubid prince as at the seeming inevitability of the loss of Jerusalem once more.[74] For example, Abu Shama presents a poem composed by the *qadi* of al-Tur, perhaps the village on the Mount of Olives, Majd al-Din Muhammad b. 'Abdallah al-Hanafi:

1. The rest of my tears overflow because of what is set to occur in the coming time
2. If it [Jerusalem] could be ransomed with souls, I would ransom it and this is the thought of every Muslim.[75]

These lines indicate Majd al-Din's fear that due to the loss of its walls, Jerusalem will surely succumb once more to Frankish control ("what is set to occur"). The poet voices the sentiment that if the sacrifice of his life could preserve the city, he would. In the framework of literary competition between Frank and Muslim, Majd al-Din's poem seems to present both sides as losers. The Frankish return is inevitable, but rather than being human, they again are only obliquely referenced as if they were a force of nature as they were presented in the earliest poetry about them. But the Muslims, and arguably the power behind the dismantlement of the walls most of all, have also lost even before the fact of Jerusalem's seizure became reality.

After the Khwarazmians sacked Jerusalem in 1244, a similar outpouring of grief occurred, although this time the blame was more pointed and the Franks occupied a different position than before. From Ibn al-'Adim's biographical dictionary we learn about Isma'il b. Muhammad al-Maghrebi, mentioned in the introduction to this chapter, who was the author's friend and served as the imam at the Dome of the Rock until 1244 when the post was given to someone else.[76] From this biography we learn about some interesting behaviors in the face of the political change. Isma'il seems to have stayed in the city throughout the period of shifting control, eventually dying there in 1258. When the Khwarazmian Turks took Jerusalem in 1244, driving the Franks out for good, there followed a massive destruction of the city.[77] In his sadness, Isma'il wrote the following verses displayed publicly on the walls of the Church of Mount Zion:

They are the dwelling-places. So stop in their empty space. Let it not distress you, even though they be bare of ornament.

Ask the rain-drops to water it, and kiss a mound over the earth of which the Lady of the Mole had dragged her skirts.[78]

This poem commenting on loss and the passage of time remained written on the walls of the church until later a Damascene poet named Najm al-Din al-Shaybani (1206–78) saw them and added another line: "It has been obliterated.

But there has not been effaced from my heart its admiring love for their original inhabitants. They are the basis of my torment."[79] The poems together place the Franks in an entirely new position vis-à-vis Jerusalem and the poets themselves. Although the date of al-Shaybani's visit to Jerusalem is unknown, his couplets along with those of Isma'il suggest a regret for the Khwarazmian destruction and longing for a time prior to it. Rather than rejoicing at the restoration of complete Muslim control of the city, they instead focus on the destroyed state. The Franks and their now-broken monuments are part of this nostalgia. Isma'il's verses have him resigning himself to its current aesthetic. The references to empty space and lack of adornment point perhaps to the razing of walls and buildings and the destruction of architectural elements. We know that the Khwarazmians destroyed the tombs of the Frankish kings in the Church of the Holy Sepulchre, so it is not unimaginable that other Frankish or Christian monuments suffered similar fates. The reference to the Lady of the Mole is obscure to me, but it could be likening how a facial mole can emphasize facial beauty in the same way a mound of detritus could emphasize the barren beauty of the city. Al-Shaybani restates the obliterated condition of the city, and then shifts audience to thinking about the city's former residents whom he mourns and whose memory actually torments him. Again, rather than anger or triumph, these poems display a mournfulness and at least ambivalence toward the fate of Jerusalem in its return to Muslim control.

The nostalgia of these couplets along with their placement on the walls of the Church of Mt. Zion place the Franks on the inside of the self-conception of the poets. They are part of the mourned-for citizenry. The lines through their placement directly connect the ideas with the former Frankish presence. The new enemy is surely the one responsible for the destruction, the Khwarazmians. Not only do we have the Frankish present incorporated into the realm of the Arabic literary, but here we seem them being incorporated into the poet's sense of self and explicitly not being othered.

Anger does appear in a different poem Ibn al-'Adim presents in Isma'il's biography. This one Isma'il said he had heard from a pious pauper in Jerusalem who said he had heard some righteous people of the city proclaim:

If support for me has been little in Syria,
and I am subsequently destroyed and my ruined state had persisted;
Then my ruined state has become,
in the forenoon, the brand of shame upon the brow of kings.[80]

Here we have a poem taking the perspective of the city itself, blaming the Syrian powers for its decline. It suggests that the unhappiness of the Muslims of Jerusalem was directed not at the Franks but at the Ayyubids. Moreover, this anger was not specifically because they exchanged control of the city for a political alliance with the Franks, but rather at their inviting into the country and then allowing the Khwarazmian Turks, their coreligionists, to destroy the city. After all, it was the Ayyubid al-Salih Ayyub who had invited the Khwarazmians into the region in hopes of toppling his uncle al-Salih Isma'il of Damascus. Al-Salih Isma'il and his supporter al-Nasir Da'ud lord of Kerak, another Ayyubid, withdrew behind the walls of their fortified cities and did not oppose the Khwarazmians as they proceeded toward Jerusalem. After the city's destruction, the Ayyubids were too busy with their own internal fighting to do much to help the city until the final defeat of the Khwarazmians in 1246.[81] These are the kings the poet refers to, whose preoccupation has caused the destruction of the city to persist, and who now wear a "brand of shame." In this poem we can see Isma'il going even further in his reconceptualization of identities in his work. He even more explicitly shifts the idea of the other onto members of his own group, that is to say, the Muslim Ayyubid leadership. Jerusalem does not complain about the Franks or any other member of her populace, but rather the "lack of support" from Syria. The Franks again are part of the in group, rather than the outgroup. For a poet to take this stance is significant in that it reveals the extent to which our idea of a permanent us/them dichotomy between Syrian Muslims and Franks is erroneous. While that binary did exist in poetry, it did not always, and Arabic poets could and did shift their self-conceptualization depending on the given context.

Muslim litterateurs not only reflected on how the Franks impacted their lives; they also commented directly about Frankish matters. They were close observers of the Franks and over time even internal Frankish politics found their way into Arabic poetry. For example, there is an incident from the late thirteenth century involving the somewhat mysterious figure of Bartholomew of Maraclea, the lord of Maraclea castle located between Tortosa and Banyas on the coast.[82] Some background is necessary in order to appreciate the poetic reference, however. We know that the castle and town of Maraclea were taken by Baybars in 1271, and its lord, Bartholomew, fled to the Mongols to seek aid. According to some sources, Baybars dispatched members of the Nizaris to assassinate him.[83] Sometime afterward a new castle or fortification was built, probably with the Hospitallers' aid, and according to the Arabic sources, it was reoccupied by Bartholomew. This posed a problem for the Mamluks as they could not attack it easily. In 1285 things came to a head and Qalawun convinced the count of Tripoli, Bohemond VII, to agree to demolish the tower in return for the promise that the Mamluks would not attack Tripoli.[84] Multiple sources mention these events and so the narrative thus far is on relatively solid ground.

The incident stemming from this sequence of events that inspired Ibn ʿAbd al-Zahir to compose a poem about it is less secure. According to Ibn ʿAbd al-Zahir, Bartholomew of Maraclea's son went to the sultan Qalawun and attempted unsuccessfully to negotiate with him. He then tried to hide in Acre, where his father found him and killed him publicly.[85] Ibn ʿAbd al-Zahir composed a poem about Prince Bohemond's seizure of Maraclea and the incident of the murder:

> How much the Prince argued for Maraclea
> with its lord to convince him to give it up and to leave
> Your [the sultan's] sword manifested behind and in front of him
>    [Prince Bohemond]
> and swords of your ruse are on the throats [of the Franks]
> He killed his son in the middle of Acre intentionally
> and he came to the fortified tower and destroyed it.[86]

Beginning with the sultan's "ruse," that is his demand that Bohemond destroy one fortification, Maraclea, in order to save his city, Tripoli, Ibn ʿAbd al-Zahir weaves in this poem praise for Qalawun with commentary on Frankish domestic matters. Indeed, the poem even suggests that the lord of Maraclea murdered his son because of the sultan's ruse, thereby amplifying its success. Not only did the sultan's machinations result in weakening the defensive infrastructure of the Franks, but they also threatened Frankish internal cohesion, breaking the bonds between father and son.

The poem and Ibn ʿAbd al-Zahir's relation of the story may indicate the general level of interest by the Mamluks and their administrators in the internal politics of the Franks. One must take the veracity of this story with a grain of salt since the Frankish sources do not mention this murder at all, and one might expect that such a public display by a member of the nobility would have made a splash and found its way into some Frankish record. It could, however, provide some insight into the kinds of rumors that spread among the communities. A few years earlier, in 1282, Bohemond VII did capture and gruesomely kill members of the Embriaco family of Jubail who rebelled against his over-lordship.[87] Perhaps in the wake of such events, the idea of a disgruntled Frank killing his own son for betraying him to the Mamluks would not seem far-fetched? In any event, such internal politics were clearly acceptable fodder for poetic commentary. Referencing them in such a way indicates again the familiarity Muslim writers felt with Frankish society and how intertwined it seemed to them to be with their own.

So far, the discussion has focused on the impact of the Frankish presence on Arabic poetry. But what about the impact of Arabic poetry on the Franks? The evidence is very sparse, but there is some that indicates the Franks might have consumed Arabic poetry and even patronized its creation. The two poems written on a wall of the Church of Mount Zion are intriguing in this regard. Arabic literature, verse as well as prose, was very much a performative thing. Even as it was written down, one of the most important ways it was consumed was through literary salons, either private, informal gatherings or more formal ones in the presence of patrons or political elites.[88] If, however, writing poetry on public façades was a common practice, perhaps this continued even under Frankish rule. There is a very small, late, but tantalizing reference to one Frankish lord who patronized an Arabic poet. In his sixteenth-century history of Jerusalem and Hebron, Mujir al-Din records that Raymond of St. Gilles, the First Crusade leader, hired a poet to compose a poem in honor of the count's victory at the battle of Ascalon against the forces of al-Afdal of Egypt.[89] The note does not state the religion of this poet, so he could have been Christian, but it does indicate that at least one Frank saw the advantage of having his reputation amplified through the composition of Arabic poetry.

We have at least one reference to a Frank with knowledge of Arabic poetry not composed for him. Ibn al-ʿAdim relates a poem that one of his sources, Ahmad b. Masʿud b. Shaddad al-Mawsili (545–613/1150–1216) claims to have heard recited by a "knight of the Franks" in Antioch.[90] The poem this Antiochene knight recited is as follows:

> By God, your Lord, stop at my abode
> And reprove him so that perhaps reproving would make him
>     become compassionate
> And allude to me and say in your speech
> "What is it about your servant [that] through severing [ties] you
>     destroyed him?"
> . . .
> [But] if anger from the lord becomes manifest to you
> then blame me and say "We don't know him."[91]

Not much in the way of context is provided for this exchange, we only know that Ibn al-ʿAdim considered Ahmad al-Mawsili to be a *shaykh* and that his nickname was *al-dhaki* (the sharp-witted). He visited Aleppo many times and lived there at the end of his life. It is possible that he spent enough time visiting Antioch that he could become friends with a Frank and exchange couplets with him. The poem itself appears to be part of one composed by the tenth-century Damascene poet Abu'l-Faraj al-Waʾwaʾ al-Dimashqi who was at the court of Sayf al-Dawla, amir of Aleppo. Missing is the original third line: "If he smiles, then say with civility 'It wouldn't harm if you connect him, as a connection with you will rescue him.'"[92] This poem asking the favor of two people, perhaps friends, to intercede on the poet's behalf with an unnamed fourth person has no apparent particular significance or implication when put in the mouth of a Frank. At the very least, it demonstrates the possibility in the mind of an adib that a Frank could have learned Arabic poetry, and it does not seem unreasonable that such a thing could and did happen.

To conclude this section, we can see that an examination of poetry by regional Muslim observers of the Franks furthers the work of others demonstrating that Muslims were far from indifferent to their presence or uninterested in who they were. Arab poets not only took note of the Frankish presence in the region, but responded to it in their works, thus incorporating them. In this way the Franks can be seen as impacting Arabic poetry. The poetry itself adapted over time to suit different needs and contexts, shifting from portraying the Franks as a force of nature to very human and flawed opponents, to even being part of the poet's own group. The poets used their works to lampoon and criticize not only the Franks but also regional Muslim leaders. Over time, the Franks even came to be viewed not as the all-encompassing adversary, but as accepted residents in the region, preferable to newer immigrants like the Khwarazmians. The poetry does not support the idea that Muslim poets embraced the Franks completely, but they certainly accepted them as a fact.

The Franks for their part, may also have been impacted by local poetic culture. Frankish lords desiring to promote themselves among their largely Arabic-speaking populace may well have patronized Arabic poets, as perhaps Raymond of St. Gilles did. It is even possible that some learned Arabic poetry, having learned sufficient spoken Arabic. By the thirteenth century, the idea was at least not so absurd as to be unimaginable for such litterateurs as Ibn al-ʿAdim.

## The Franks in Usama Ibn Munqidh's Cultural Landscape

This chapter ends with a discussion of Usama Ibn Munqidh's *Book of Contemplation* as the author and work encompass many of the strands discussed throughout the chapter.[93] This is also a work much used by scholars of the Latin East and those who teach the crusades. However, it has not often used by historians as literature in conversation with other literature. Instead, it tends to be mined for factual data about life in the Latin East. In this final section of the chapter, we will explore the ways that Usama grappled with the fact of the Frankish presence in the *Book of Contemplation*, and the ways in which he found to place and understand them as part of God's creation. We will see that this incorporation was complex and at time ambivalent and marked out his own discomfort with how similar they were to his own milieu. Usama had ample opportunity to observe the Franks, and indeed he claimed to have counted Franks among his friends. He shared elite cultural pursuits like hunting. As we will see, both in life and in his work, the Franks made a huge impact. Moreover, his work reflects the cultural proximity and discomfort that proximity caused in him.

Born in 1095 and dying in 1188, Usama's life spanned the "first Kingdom of Jerusalem." Moreover, from the beginning, his education was directly shaped by the Franks, as his childhood tutors, Abu Abdallah al-Tulaytuli, former director of the library called House of Learning in Tripoli, and Yanis, a calligrapher and copyist, were refugees from the Frankish invasions.[94] He belonged to the noble Munqidh family (or *Banu Munqidh*), who ruled the Syrian fortress town of Shayzar and its environs, and spent cycles alternately raiding and being raided by their Frankish neighbors of Antioch and Apamea. In 1124 the family even hosted the captured King Baldwin II during his ransom negotiations.[95] As an adult, Usama led a varied career in the service of Syrian and Egyptian leaders, and in the process became a well-known and respected adib (man of letters). People of his time read and valued his many literary productions.[96] Saladin, Usama's patron at the end of his life, is said to have carried around Usama's *diwan* (collection of poetry).[97] Usama was a keen observer of his surroundings and neighbors, and his *Book of Contemplation* is a favorite among those who teach the Crusades due to its humorous, accessible, and sometimes ghastly stories, many involving the Franks. Composed in 1171 or 1172, toward the end of the author's long life, the work was meant to induce the reader into contemplating the ineffability and mysteriousness of God through the consideration of many small tales, often placed in seeming opposition to each other.[98] The Franks provided Usama with a great deal of fodder.

Samuel England touches briefly on Usama's account of the Franks and cautions against reading the inclusion of stories about the Franks as an example of a simple binary us/them, Muslims/Franks. He discusses in depth the story "Franks That Are Acclimatized are Better."[99] In this story, a friend of Usama's related how he once dined at the Antiochene home of a Frank who arrived with the earliest crusaders. The friend was afraid at first to eat, but the Frank assured him that it was prepared by Egyptian women and that he never eats pork. After eating, the friend left, only to be accosted by a Frankish woman claiming that he had murdered her brother. The friend was only saved from the mob that developed by the intervention of the same Frank who had been his host, who quickly claimed that the friend was no soldier, but rather a merchant, and dispersed the crowd. England notes how Usama does not linger on whether the Frank got the finer points of Islamic culture absolutely correct. Rather he draws attention to the many roles the Frank was able to adopt and how these enabled him to successfully navigate between courtly hospitality to foreign, deceptive speech when saving his Muslim friend from the mob. The Frank in the story, according to England's reading, is not simply an Other but several individuals, simultaneously familiar to courtly Muslims and able to mediate between that world and that of violent Christian Antioch.

A strength and attraction of the work is that it vividly portrays in detail the world according to Usama. As Paul Cobb notes in his introduction, "[*The Book of Contemplation*] is, by any token, a remarkable record of one man's vision of his times."[100] This is a vision that does not simply ignore the Franks, or uniformly condemn them. Rather, it embraces them, however reluctantly, and endeavors to elucidate how they fit into the larger mystery of God's creation. As any cursory glance at the stories involving the Franks reveals, Usama does engage in the routine invocation of God confounding or cursing individuals, and despite his knowledge of and friendship with Franks, he incorporates the usual assortment of (negative) stereotypes of the Franks—that they are dirty, uncultured, immodest, and so forth. Even so, he rarely invokes jihad or frames his encounters, however violent, with the Franks in terms of jihad. Cobb, in his analysis of this fact, understands this as stemming from the uneasy positioning of Franks within the category of "human." According to his analysis of Usama's perspective, although human, their failings make them closer to beasts, and so Usama presents battle with them in much the same light as another favorite topic, hunting.[101] Usama comments that they have only the virtue of courage, which beasts also possess, and no sense of social precedence, reason, or jealousy, all virtues belonging to humans alone.[102] Thus, the routine raiding and skirmishes that marked life on the frontier with the Franks was something he conceived of as wholly part of the noble lifestyle and played a similar function to the other routine violence such nobles sought out, hunting.

While it is clear that Usama does not present his interactions with the Franks in terms of jihad, how we understand Usama's vision of the Franks and where they fit should be modified somewhat. I argue that the way Usama presents the Franks is quite like how he presents the Bedouin, or Arabs as he calls them and which usage I adopt here. The routine of peace punctuated by violence is also very much paralleled by his discussion of relationships with other Muslim Syrian leaders. The Franks, as I will show, are not fundamentally different from other groups Usama could identify with and who shared his world. The Franks so depicted are part of a shared cultural landscape and are depicted in that way, even as Usama may have wished otherwise.

An important similarity is how Usama presents the threat of violence posed by Bedouin in a parallel fashion to that of the Franks. For instance, during the coup against the Fatimid vizier 'Abbas, Bedouin tribes who had at one point been in his service, turned on him and Usama's family as they tried to flee Cairo.[103] Usama was severely wounded when his horse stumbled and as a result he hit his head falling on rocks. One of the Bedouin then came up to him and "struck me twice with his sword" wanting his money, eventually taking his horse and sword after Usama proved unable to speak. After escaping this group, Usama and his party came under further threat from other Bedouin groups in the area of Wadi Musa (in modern-day southern Jordan). He writes, "Under conditions worse than death—without provisions for the men or fodder for the horses—we continued on through Frankish territory until we reached the mountains of the Banu Fuhayd (may God curse them), in Wadi Musa. . . . The Banu Fuhayd killed anyone who got separated from the main party straight away."[104] There happened to be some men from another group of Arabs, the Banu Rabi'a, whose amir, Mansur ibn Ghidfal, Usama was friends with. Usama asked someone to get him while the group spent a terror-filled night awaiting Mansur's arrival. The next morning, Usama reports that the Banu Fuhayd would not allow them to get water from the well hoping to provoke a fight that would allow them to kidnap Usama's party.[105] Finally, Usama's friend arrived and was able to disperse the Banu

Fuhayd threatening Usama's group by "scream[ing] at the Arab tribesmen and curs[ing] them." After being led to safety, Usama collected one thousand Egyptian dinars to give to Mansur, and then he left.[106]

The parallel between Franks and Arabs in this sequence of events is striking. Bedouins here represent a grave threat, both in terms of material predation and physical harm and death. Franks throughout the book are often shown as opportunistic raiders, as are the Bedouin. In this story Bedouin pose the threat of either killing or kidnapping Usama and his group, similar to the Franks who would either kill warriors on raids or take people to be sold into bondage or ransom. As with the Franks, there are exceptions and Usama has a friend among the Arabs who he can call upon for help. Mansur does not engage in reasoned dialogue, in fact we are not told what was said, instead all Usama reports is that Mansur had to yell and curse at the Banu Fuhayd. Despite the bond of friendship, Usama must still pay for the services Mansur rendered for extricating them from their dire situation. In this series of events, therefore, we can see how Usama's depiction of nomadic Arabs in the region bears striking similarity to that of the Franks. His opinion is similarly low.

Usama depicts the uncouthness of Arabs in speech as well. At al-Jafr, when interrogating one of the Banu Ubayy asking who they are, Usama switches into colloquial Arabic (e.g., *aysh antum*).[107] Another example comes earlier in the story of Usama's flight from Cairo during the coup before he encountered the Arabs around Wadi Musa discussed above. Early in his flight, Usama is injured by Arabs hired by ʿAbbas. Laying on the ground, stunned from a wound to the head, one of his attackers comes to him and demands that he "hand over the dosh!" (*hat al-wazn*) again reflecting a different, slangy register of language.[108] A potential source of irony here is that at an earlier stage, Arabic grammarians and litterateurs once sought out Arab tribes in order to study what was considered a purer form of the language.[109] Rural Arabs in the second-century AH/eighth-century CE were renowned for eloquence of speech and continued to be associated with that quality through the twelfth century. Even so, Usama characterized some at least by the opposite.

Another parallel to the depiction of the Franks is how Arabs in the stories defy expectations. The story of the prison escape of the son of the governor of Mount Sinai (*wali al-tur*) highlights how one Bedouin defies the negative stereotypes of the storyteller.[110] This man was captured by the Franks and put into prison until such as time as his family ransomed him. He remained there for over a year without a word, until one day a Bedouin man was put into the pit with him. Time passed and the Bedouin offered to rescue the man if the man would rescue him first. The man did not believe that the Bedouin could do any such thing, thinking to himself, "This is a man who, having fallen into misfortune, desperately wants to escape" and did not bother answering him.[111] More days passed, and the Bedouin tried again, and this time the man agreed, not because he actually believed that the Bedouin would help him, but out of the idea that perhaps by doing a good deed for someone else God would rescue him. The man called to his Frankish guards and had them add the Bedouin's ransom to his own in exchange for allowing the Bedouin to leave and tell the man's family about his situation. The Franks agreed and released the Bedouin man. The man continued to wait in prison and after two months without a word "despaired of him" and gave up hope. One night several months later, the Bedouin arrived in the pit through a tunnel he had dug. The two escaped through the tunnel leading to a nearby abandoned village where the Bedouin broke the man's chains and took him home. The man ends his story, "I don't know what should surprise me more—his integrity, or his sense of direction being so good that his burrow ended right at the side of the pit!"[112]

The Bedouin man's defiance of expectations is the crux of this story. The storyteller is clearly of noble background since his father is the governor of Mount Sinai. He makes his low opinion of the Bedouin clear from the beginning, when he will not consider his offer even after already spending over a year in prison waiting for his family to ransom him, refusing even to speak to the Bedouin. Even after he agrees to the Bedouin's plan, he does not hope that the Bedouin will be able to free him, but rather hopes that God will. He gives up on the Bedouin after only two months, whereas he still had not given up on his family after twelve. His final remarks about the surprising integrity of the man finally articulate what was lying in the background in terms of his prejudice.

Not only does Usama's treatment of Bedouin resemble his treatment of the Franks, but so does his depiction of violence against Franks resemble that of violence against other Muslims. If the idea that fighting Franks was seen to be as routine as hunting is true, it must have also been the case for raids against other Syrians and nomadic Arabs. Numerous tales in *The Book of Contemplation* stem from military encounters against fellow Muslims. The ongoing nature of these violent episodes was such that Usama even begins a story, "One day we were engaged in some war or another that had broken out between us and the lord of Hama."[113] In fact, the numerous sequences of stories that feature first battle against the Franks, then battle against Muslim lords or the Bedouin, demonstrate how Usama saw these encounters as paralleling each other. For example, there are back-to-back stories involving Jumʿa and his son Mahmud, two knights in the Banu Munqidh army.[114] In the first, the Antiochene army attacks Shayzar and Usama and his comrades repel them, but not before Mahmud flees. In the next story, Jumʿa apologizes for his son to Usama, to which Usama replies that one day, Jumʿa will also flee. The story goes on to say that a few days later, "the cavalry of Hama made a raid on us" and took a herd of cattle. In this instance Jumʿa turns his horse away from the raiders, rather than attacking with Usama, thereby fulfilling Usama's prediction. One of the ways these stories work is to make a comment about courage in the face of the enemy, and the Franks and army of Hama are used interchangeably. As for the Arabs, Usama remarks that in his father's day, most of the battles were with the Arabs.[115] Again, battles are expected and ongoing, and it does not really matter whether they are against Franks, the forces of Syrian-Muslim lords, or Bedouin.

Raiding against the Franks may have been portrayed as the same as raiding against other Syrian border lords, but does he actually see Frankish lords as similar to Syrian lords? No, but the Franks are not so bestial, I would argue, as Cobb suggests. Although there are not many examples of the Franks performing well in the finer aspects of civilization in Usama's account, there are a few. Usama readily acknowledges the courage of the Franks, and the story of the hospitable Frank of Antioch who rescues a Muslim guest has already been discussed.[116] He famously notes that Franks who have lived among the Muslims longer are better than those who have recently arrived from Europe.[117] Usama believed, at a minimum, that Franks could gain polish after time spent in civilized Levantine society. Animals could never accomplish the same. Another area of civilized, elite life that Usama shows the Franks excelling at, without particular comment, is the hunt. He relates how on one occasion when he and his patron the amir Muʿin al-Din traveled to Acre to visit King Fulk, they encountered a Genoese man with a goshawk skilled at hunting with a hound.[118] Muʿin al-Din was so impressed by the pair that he asked Fulk to make the Genoese give them to him, and he did. At another point, Usama relates how "the most sharp-set and cleverest of my father's birds of prey" was a goshawk that had escaped from the Franks and was captured by one of his father's austringers.[119] In fact, Usama's father even cultivated a friendship with the Armenian Rupenids, close allies of the Franks, in order to facilitate an exchange of hunting animals.[120] Given the importance of hunting to elite culture, it is not insignificant for Usama to acknowledge that Franks (and their associates) were skilled in that area.

From this discussion we can see that the Franks formed an inextricable part of Usama's world, not just militarily but in his conception of the cultural landscape. Within years of his birth, the Franks upended the political and cultural fields of Syria. Usama grew up with the expectation that as part of his life as a noble, he would engage in routine battles against rival Syrian lords, bandits, Bedouin, and, yes, the Franks. These battles presented Usama and his peers with opportunities to demonstrate their martial skills, a critical aspect of elite culture. In other words, in order for Usama to perform his elite identity, he needed the Franks, and Bedouin, and other Syrian lords who surrounded him. They likewise formed an important component of Usama's written work and offered fodder for the reader to contemplate God's ineffable nature. They do so by being confoundingly strange but also recognizable. They raid, fight, and hunt just like Usama. They could learn etiquette and appreciate fine food when given time. They do not exist as beast men or barely humans, but rather bad humans. In sum, by virtue of being part of the political reality of twelfth-century Syria, we see them likewise being incorporated into the cultural landscape as well.

\* \* \*

The investigation of literature reveals some of the ways Arabic-Muslim literature responded and adapted to the Frankish presence. Rather than being ignored or relegated to unchanging stereotype, this literature inserted the Franks into existing tropes from the Byzantine wars and then over time came to develop new ways to describe and present them depending on the needs of the poet or the given historical context. The cultural impact was not unidirectional, but rather there seems to have been a shared literary culture of competition, as particularly evidenced in the exchange of letters between Mamluk and Frankish elites. Secretaries like Ibn ʿAbd al-Zahir were able to flex their literary muscle in composing letters to Frankish kings and lords, and it appears likely that the Franks responded in kind. The Templar of Tyre certainly was aware of conventions of Arabic letter-writing and it does not seem unreasonable to suppose that the Frankish secretarial pool would have reciprocated in the letters they drafted.

While stereotyping did certainly take place, it was at odds with the specificity and detail Muslim litterateurs evinced in their work. Franks in poetry were cowardly but motivated by a familiar devotion to God and convinced of His support for their endeavors. Franks in Usama's world were confounding in their foreignness yet unrelenting similarity. Even if Muslim litterateurs wanted to portray the Franks as the absolute antithesis to themselves, as monsters, they simply could not. They did not have a single way of depicting the Franks, which signals an ambivalence that breaks down any attempt to render the relationship in a simple good/evil binary.

The cultural landscape of the region was not one demarcated by political or religious boundaries. What might seem to be the component of society most likely to be segregated by identity group was not so. As this discussion has shown, the various Frankish and Muslim residents of the region, inside the kingdom and without, forged a shared cultural landscape.

# Conclusion

Over the course of the last chapters, the discussion has progressed in focus from more to less concrete components of society. It begins with an attempt to delineate the geographic distribution of Muslims within areas under Frankish control. Following and based on this analysis, it explored the economic contributions that Muslims within and without the kingdom made to its economy. Shifting to a more theoretical topic, it examined the legal traditions Muslims in the kingdom had recourse to as well as how those traditions endeavored to impact and control Muslims in the kingdom. Continuing from this, the discussion turned to evidence of actual political power wielded by Muslims within the kingdom, revealing that the kingdom was porous with supposedly external Muslims frequently wielding or sharing administrative power with Franks. Finally, it ends by moving to look at how Muslims operated in and responded to intellectual and cultural landscapes shared across the Levantine polities.

Although there were real disadvantages that Muslims living in the kingdom endured, the discussion has demonstrated that the idea of them being fully separated from the Christian segments of the population is inaccurate. Muslims were visible components of society. They made important contributions to the economy and could hold power over other inhabitants. Within the admittedly vast arena of culture and knowledge, they also were acknowledged as important participants in the generation and exchange of knowledge. They helped craft a local shared cultural landscape through participation in literary exchanges, whether through poetry or letters.

None of these conclusions would have been possible without approaching the study of society in an interdisciplinary way. In the introduction I have already discussed how art historians studied the cultural interactions manifested in Levantine art in the twelfth and thirteenth centuries long before historians accepted that Franks were not entirely segregated from local populations. While historians like Joshua Prawer called Frankish society apartheid, art historians like Carl Weitzmann, Jaroslav Folda, and Annemarie Weyl Carr were exploring the adoption of Eastern and Western artistic elements in Levantine pictorial arts. They were showing that there must have been contact at some level, long before the historical geographer Ronnie Ellenblum convinced historians, using archaeological evidence in connection with surviving texts, that Franks settled in the hinterland among existing populations of Eastern Christians.

Limiting the study of the Latin East to texts produced by Latins has generated a necessarily limited and flawed view. Bringing in archaeological evidence, as Ellenblum did, revolutionized the mainstream understanding of Frankish settlement by demonstrating that they lived not just in the cities and fortified outposts but also in the hinterland. It showed that the Franks lived in areas that continued to have populations of Eastern Christians. Drawing from the archaeology, this book has similarly shown that Muslims were part of the mix. They were not relegated to the margins of the Latin East, but lived, worked, and traveled in and around major Frankish towns. This book also provides valuable information about economic activity that could only be guessed at through textual sources. We have a better understanding of the extent and location of such industries as sugar and ceramic production thanks to the study of ceramics and archaeological sites by archaeologists like Edna Stern. When put into conversation with each other, archaeological and textual data have helped create a fuller and more concrete image of the economics in the entire region.

Bringing in the textual sources seen as belonging to different areas of historical study has had similarly revolutionary results. Approaching the Latin East as if it were solely an outgrowth of medieval Europe and capable of being studied exclusively from European sources resulted in the flawed models of Frankish society. Christopher MacEvitt brought the tools stemming from Middle Eastern studies into his analysis of Frankish society. Through incorporating Melkite, Jacobite, and Armenian sources into the discussion with Frankish ones, and treating them not merely as supports to the latter but as equal partners in historical study, he was able to make the convincing argument for "rough tolerance" being the model of interaction between Latin and Eastern Christians.

In this book I have attempted to build upon this work to incorporate Arabic sources into the earlier discussions. It has enhanced the picture of where Muslims lived, just as using archaeology has. It has enhanced our understanding of the areas where there was active Islamic worship. Using Arabic sources as equal partners with the Frankish has critically revised the idea that

## Conclusion

Muslims held no power and were universally disenfranchised in the Latin East. Comparing the evidence from the Arabic chronicles with the Latin legal texts reveals how the latter were attempts to construct an ideal legal status for all within the kingdom, and did not reflect the political or administrative reality. Moreover the treaties preserved only in Arabic greatly enhance the picture of how justice was to be administered in the kingdom and elsewhere.

Furthermore, bringing the Arabic and Frankish sources together further bolsters the argument made by Ellenblum and MacEvitt that the Levantine states cannot be studied independently of one another. Neither can they be studied without reference to their geographical context or their neighbors. The economic and political landscapes were regional. Muslim lords played a role in the administration of Frankish states. Muslim and Frankish litterateurs participated in a shared cultural landscape, responding to and influencing each other.

Bringing in different disciplinary approaches and sources, and giving them equal weight, further illuminates the integrated nature of Levantine polities during the twelfth and thirteenth centuries. Although crusades scholars have had access to some of the eastern sources in translation for over a century, they have not been used on equal terms. Privileging the Frankish sources in this way has permitted the idea that the Latin East was an extension of Europe. It was self-reinforcing in a way; scholars of medieval Europe studied the crusades and the Latin East, using only European sources, and therefore found the Latin East to be fundamentally European. It is not coincidental that when scholars trained in Middle East studies investigate the Latin East, they have found it to be something else. An interdisciplinary approach has shown that indeed none of the Levantine polities can really be studied without reference to their neighbors.

Just as the interdisciplinary approach gives us a different and more accurate conception of the place of the Kingdom of Jerusalem in the Levantine regions, so too does it give us a better understanding of the Muslims within it. Drawing only from Frankish sources left a great deal unknown. The (legal) sources that did mention Muslims were endeavoring to craft a system that preserved elite Frankish privilege. Drawing in Arabic sources permitted a fresh examination of the Frankish legal texts and offered additional detail on the lives of Muslims in the kingdom and engaging with it in some way. Although the discussion here began with the idea of the kingdom as a container, as an entity with boundaries of some sort, it arrives at the idea that those boundaries were largely irrelevant. Although we can investigate the lives of Muslims most subject to the Franks given where they lived, we can likewise see that Muslims living elsewhere likewise had an impact on Frankish society. It is not tenable to hold that Muslims were unimportant, outsiders to the Latin East.

It is of course unrealistic to expect any single scholar wishing to work on the Latin East to become an expert in all the fields that provide insight into its past. What scholars can and should do, however, is embrace the notion that the Latin East was not just an extension of Europe but a part of its regional environment. They should also acknowledge and fully incorporate the information provided by art, archaeology, and literature and not just pay lip-service to their importance. None of these fields is the handmaiden to (European) history, but rather are equal contributors to the study of the past. With individual as well as collaborative interdisciplinary efforts, our understanding of the Latin East will grow to be more inclusive, accurate, and vivid.

# Notes

## INTRODUCTION

1. Recent books on the First Crusade include Thomas Asbridge, *The First Crusade: A New History* (New York: Oxford University Press, 2004); Peter Frankopan, *The First Crusade: The Call from the East* (Cambridge, MA: Belknap Press, 2011); Jay Rubenstein, *Armies of Heaven: The First Crusade and the Quest for the Apocalypse* (New York: Basic Books, 2011); and Conor Kostick, *The Siege of Jerusalem: Crusade and Conquest in 1099* (London: Continuum, 2009).

2. There are a number of works covering the Latin East in the twelfth century. Some of the more recent contributions include Nicholas Morton, *The Crusader States & Their Neighbours: A Military History, 1099–1187* (Oxford: Oxford University Press, 2020); Andrew D. Buck, *The Principality of Antioch and Its Frontiers in the Twelfth Century* (Woodbridge: Boydell and Brewer, 2017); Malcolm Barber, *The Crusader States* (New Haven, CT: Yale University Press, 2012); Peter M. Holt, *The Crusader States and Their Neighbours, 1098–1291* (Harlow: Pearson Longman, 2004); Andrew Jotischky, *Crusading and the Crusader States* (Harlow: Pearson Longman, 2004).

3. Ronnie Ellenblum, *Crusader Castles and Modern Histories* (Cambridge: Cambridge University Press, 2007), 149–51 and *passim*. See also Morton, *The Crusader States & Their Neighbours*.

4. Jonathan Phillips, *The Second Crusade: Extending the Frontiers of Christendom* (New Haven, CT: Yale University Press, 2007).

5. For a recent biography, see Anne-Marie Eddé, *Saladin* (Cambridge, MA: Belknap Press, 2011).

6. For an overview of the politics leading up to the Battle of Hattin, see Peter W. Edbury, "Propaganda and Faction in the Kingdom of Jerusalem: the Background to Hattin," in *Crusaders and Muslims in Twelfth-Century Syria*, ed. M. Shatzmiller (Leiden: Brill, 1993), 173–89.

7. Although traditionally interpreted as a blunder on the part of Guy de Lusignan, Morton has argued convincingly that the decision to relieve Tiberias was a logical one and that the only special aspect was Saladin's ability to stop the Frankish fighting march. Morton, *The Crusader States & Their Neighbours*, 184–98.

8. Jonathan Riley-Smith, *The Crusades: A History*, 2nd ed. (New Haven, CT: Yale Nota Bene, 2005), 137–47; Jean Richard, *The Crusades, c.1071–c.1291* (Cambridge: Cambridge University Press, 1999), 217–31.

9. For a history of the Kingdom of Cyprus under the Lusignans, see Peter W. Edbury, *The Kingdom of Cyprus and the Crusades, 1191–1374* (Cambridge: Cambridge University Press, 1991).

10. For an overview of this period, see R. Stephen Humphreys, *From Saladin to the Mongols: The Ayyubids of Damascus, 1193–1260* (Albany: SUNY Press, 1977); Claude Cahen, "Ayyubids," in Encyclopaedia of Islam, 2nd ed., Brill Reference Online, accessed March 15, 2023; Paul A. Blaum, "Eagles in the Sun: The Ayyubids after Saladin," *The International Journal of Kurdish Studies* 13 (1999): 105–80.

11. Richard, *The Crusades*, 307–18.

12. Richard, 386–93.

13. See Michael Lower, *The Barons' Crusade: A Call to Arms and Its Consequences* (Philadelphia: University of Pennsylvania Press, 2005).

14. Paul Cobb gives a succinct overview of these maneuverings from the Ayyubid perspective in *The Race for Paradise* (Oxford: Oxford University Press, 2014), 212–15.

15. Reuven Amitai, *Mongols and Mamluks: the Mamluk-Īlkhānid War, 1260–1281* (Cambridge: Cambridge University Press, 1995); David Ayalon, *Le phénomène mamelouk dans l'Orient islamique* (Paris: Presses Universitaires de France, 1996); Julien Loiseau, *Les Mamelouks XIIIe–XVIe siècle: une experience du pouvoir dans l'islam medieval* (Paris: Seuil, 2014).

16. Peter Thorau, *The Lion of Egypt: Sultan Baybars I and the Near East in the Thirteenth Century* (London: Longman, 1992); Linda Northrup, *From Slave to Sultan: The Career of Al-Manṣūr Qalāwūn and the Consolidation of Mamluk Rule in Egypt and Syria (678–689 A.H./1279–1290 A.D.)* (Stuttgart: Franz Steiner Verlag, 1998).

17. Richard, *The Crusades*, 464; Northrup, *From Slave to Sultan*, 157.

18. Ellenblum, *Crusader Castles and Modern Histories*; Christopher MacEvitt, *The Crusades and the Christian World of the East: Rough Tolerance* (Philadelphia: University of Pennsylvania Press, 2008), 13–20; and "What Was Crusader about the Crusader States?" *al-Masaq* 30, no. 3 (2018): 317–30; Paul M. Cobb, *The Race for Paradise: An Islamic History of the Crusades* (Oxford: Oxford University Press, 2014), 3–8.

19. Nicholas Morton makes the same point with regard to military history of the crusader states in his recent monograph on the topic. Nicholas Morton, *The Crusader States & Their Neighbours*, 1–3.

20. Happily, women and gender are starting to receive long-overdue attention. See *Crusading and Masculinities*, ed. Natasha R. Hodgson, Katherine J. Lew, and Matthew M. Mesley (Abingdon: Routledge, 2019); Sabine Geldsetzer, *Frauen auf Kreuzzügen, 1096–1291* (Darmstadt: Wissenschaftliche Buchgesellschaft, 2003); Natasha Hodgson, *Women, Crusading and the Holy Land in Historical Narrative* (Woodbridge: Boydell & Brewer, 2007); and *Gendering the Crusades*, ed. Susan B. Edgington and Sarah Lambert (New York: Columbia University Press, 2002).

21. Heinrich Hagenmayer ed., *Die Kreuzzugsbriefe aus den Jahren 1088–1100* (Innsbruck: Wagner'sche universitäts-buchhandlung, 1901); Reinhold Röhricht, *Regesta regni Hierosolymitani, 1097–1291* (Oeniponti: Wagner, 1893–1904).

22. Emmanuel Rey, *Les colonies franques de Syrie aux XIIe et XIIIe siècles* (Paris: Alphonse Picard, 1883).

23. René Grousset, *Histoire des croisades et du royaume franc de Jerusalem*, 3 vols. (Paris: Perrin, 1934–36).

24. And continues its influence through the work of Jean Richard, *Le Royaume Latin de Jérusalem* (Paris: Presses Universitaires de France, 1953) [English translation published as *The Latin Kingdom of Jerusalem*, trans. Janet Shirley, 2 vols. (New York: North-Holland Publishing Company, 1979)]. Richard subsequently wrote several books related to the Crusades, and published another textbook *The Crusades, c. 1071–c.1291* (Cambridge: Cambridge University Press, 1999), which does not stray substantively from the narrative he wrote fifty years previously.

25. R. C. Smail, *Crusading Warfare (1097–1193)* (Cambridge: Cambridge University Press, 1956). I have consulted the second edition published by the same press in 1995.

26. Joshua Prawer, *The Crusaders' Kingdom: European Colonialism in the Middle Ages* (New York: Praeger, 1972). In England, this book was published as *The Latin Kingdom of Jerusalem: European Colonialism in the Middle Ages* (London: Weidenfeld and Nicolson, 1973).

27. Jonathan Riley-Smith, *The Feudal Nobility and the Kingdom of Jerusalem, 1174–1277* (London: Macmillan, 1973).

28. Peter W. Edbury, *John of Ibelin and the Kingdom of Jerusalem* (Woodbridge: Boydell Press, 1997); "Reading John of Jaffa," in *The Experience of Crusading 2*, eds. Peter Edbury and Jonathan Philips (Cambridge: Cambridge University Press, 2003), 135–57; John of Ibelin, *Le Livre des Assises*, ed. Peter W. Edbury (Leiden: Brill, 2003).

29. *Le Livre au Roi*, ed. Myriam Greilsammer (Paris: Académie des Inscriptions et Belles-Lettres, 1995).

30. Myriam Greilsammer, "Anatomie d'un mensonge: le *Livre au Roi* et la révision de l'histoire du Royaume Latin par les juristes du XIIIe siècle," *Tijdschrift voor rechtgeschiedenis, Revue d'Histoire du Droit* 67 (1999): 239–54; Graham A. Loud, "The *Assise sur la Ligece* and Ralph of Tiberias," in *Crusade and Settlement*, ed. Peter W. Edbury (Cardiff: University College Cardiff Press, 1985), 204–12.

31. Jean Richard, "La culture juridique de la noblesse aux XIe, XIIe et XIIIe siecles," in *Nobilitas. Funktion und Repräsentation des Adels in Alteuropa (Veröffentlichungen des Max-Planck Institut für Geschichte, 133)*, ed. Otto Gerhard Oexle and Werner Paravicini (Göttingen: Vandenhoeck & Ruprecht, 1997), 53–66.

32. David Jacoby, "Knightly Values and Class Consciousness in the Crusader States of the Eastern Mediterranean," *Mediterranean Historical Review* 1 (1986): 158–86. See also David Jacoby, "La littérature française dans les états latins de la Méditerranée orientale à l'époque des Croisades: diffusion et création," in *Essor et fortune de la chanson de geste dans l'Europe et l'Orient latin. Actes du IXe Congrès International de la Société Rencevals pour l'Étude des Épopées Romanes (Padoue-Venise, 1982)* (Modena: Mucchi Editore, 1984), 617–46. Art historian Bianca Kühnel has done some interesting work tying together illuminations created in Acre at the end of the thirteenth century with attempts at self-justification by the Frankish patrons in the face of political decline. "The Perception of History in Thirteenth-Century Crusader Art," in *France and the Holy Land: Frankish Culture at the End of the Crusades*, ed. Daniel H. Weiss and Lisa Mahoney (Baltimore: Johns Hopkins University Press, 2004), 161–86.

33. Conor Kostick, "William of Tyre, Livy, and the Vocabulary of Class," *Journal of the History of Ideas* 65 (2004): 353–69; "The Terms *milites*, *equites* and *equestres* in the Early Crusading Histories," *Nottingham Medieval Studies* 50 (2006): 1–21; *The Social Structure of the First Crusade* (Boston: Brill, 2008).

34. Alan Murray, "Ethnic Identity in the Crusader States: The Frankish Race and the Settlement of Outremer," in *Concepts of National Identity in the Middle Ages*, eds. Simon Forde, Lesley Johnson and Alan V. Murray (Leeds: University of Leeds, 1995), 59–73.

35. Murray, "Ethnic Identity," 61.

36. There were a few notable exceptions, most prominently the French historian Claude Cahen and more recently Carole Hillenbrand whose *Crusades: Islamic Perspectives* (Edinburgh: University of Edinburgh Press, 1999) has been a very important resource. However, none of the most prominent crusades historians of the second half of the twentieth century noted above work with primary sources in non-Western languages. When they do incorporate Arabic chronicles, for instance, they rely upon translations, many of which were edited and translated

by nineteenth-century French Orientalists interested in promoting French colonial policy as already discussed.

37. See Jaroslav Folda, *Crusader Manuscript Illumination at Saint-Jean d'Acre: 1275–1291* (Princeton, NJ: Princeton University Press, 1976); *The Art of the Crusaders in the Holy Land 1098–1187* (Cambridge: Cambridge University Press, 1995); "Crusader Art, A Multicultural Phenomenon: Historiographical Reflections," in *Autour de la Première Croisade*, ed. Michel Balard (Paris: Publications de la Sorbonne, 1996), 609–15; *Crusader Art in the Holy Land: From the Third Crusade to the Fall of Acre, 1187–1291* (Cambridge: Cambridge University Press, 2005).

38. Annemarie Weyl Carr, "Perspectives on Visual Culture in Early Lusignan Cyprus: Balancing Art and Archaeology," in *Archaeology of the Crusades*, ed. Peter Edbury and Sophia Kalopissi-Verti (Athens: Pieridies Foundation, 2007), 83–110.

39. Anthony Cutler, "Everywhere and Nowhere: The Invisible Muslim and Christian Self-Fashioning in the Culture of Outremer," in *France and the Holy Land: Frankish Culture at the End of the Crusades*, ed. Daniel H. Weiss and Lisa Mahoney (Baltimore: Johns Hopkins University Press, 2004), 253–81.

40. Scott Redford and Tasha Vorderstrasse have conducted research in Anatolia and Lebanon. See Scott Redford, "On *Sâqîs* and Ceramics: Systems of Representation in the Northeast Mediterranean," in *France and the Holy Land: Frankish Culture at the End of the Crusades*, ed. Daniel H. Weiss and Lisa Mahoney (Baltimore: Johns Hopkins University Press, 2004), 282–312; Tasha Vorderstrasse, "A Port of Antioch under Byzantium, Islam, and the Crusades: Acculturation and Differentiation at Al-Mina, AD 350–1268" (Dissertation, University of Chicago, 2004); "A Port Without a Harbour: Reconstructing Medieval al-Mina," in *Studies in Archaeology of the Medieval Mediterranean*, ed. James G. Schryver (Leiden: Brill, 2010), 15–39; "Archaeology of Medieval Lebanon: An Overview," *Chronos: Revue d'Histoire d l'Université de Balamand* 20 (2009): 103–28.

41. See Denys Pringle, *Fortification and Settlement in Crusader Palestine* (Aldershot: Variorum, 2000) for a collection of his works on rural fortified sites. See also Denys Pringle, *The Churches of the Crusader Kingdom of Jerusalem: A Corpus*, 4 vols. (Cambridge: Cambridge University Press, 1993–2009).

42. For example, Denys Pringle, *The Red Tower* (London: The British School of Archaeology, 1986); "Magna Mahumeria (al-Bira): The Archeology of a Frankish New Town in Palestine," in *Crusade and Settlement*, ed. Peter W. Edbury (Cardiff: University College Cardiff Press, 1985), 147–68; "Two Medieval Villages North of Jerusalem: Archaeological Investigations in al-Jib and ar-Ram," *Levant* 13 (1983): 141–77.

43. Andrew Petersen, *A Gazetteer of Buildings in Muslim Palestine* (Oxford: Oxford University Press, 2001); *The Towns of Palestine under Muslim Rule: AD 600–1600* (Oxford: Archaeopress, 2005).

44. I will discuss this further in Chapter 1. Bogdan Smarandache, "A Reassessment of Frankish Settlement Patterns in the Latin Kingdom of Jerusalem, 493–583 AH/1099-1187 AD," in *Minorites in Contact in the Medieval Mediterranean*, ed. Clara Almagro Vidal, Jessica Tearney-Pearce, and Luke Yarbrough (Turnhout: Brepols, 2020), 285–335.

45. Adrian Boas, "Domestic Architecture in the Frankish Kingdom of Jerusalem" (Dissertation, Hebrew University, 1995); "Three Stages in the Evolution of Rural Settlement in the Kingdom of Jerusalem during the Twelfth Century," in *In Laudem Hierosolymitani: Studies in Crusades and Medieval Culture in Honour of Benjamin Z. Kedar*, ed. Iris Shagrir, Ronnie Ellenblum, and Jonathan Riley-Smith (Aldershot: Ashgate, 2007), 77–92. Ronnie Ellenblum,

"Construction Methods in Frankish Rural Settlement," in *The Horns of Hattin*, ed. Benjamin Z. Kedar (London: Variorum, 1992), 168–92.

46. Adrian Boas, "Domestic Architecture," 301; "Archaeological Sources for the History of Palestine: The Frankish Period: A Unique Medieval Society Emerges," *Near Eastern Archaeology* 61 (1998): 138–73.

47. *Frankish Rural Settlement in the Latin Kingdom of Jerusalem* (Cambridge: Cambridge University Press, 1998). For a summary of his argument, see also "Settlement and Society in Crusader Palestine," in *Knights of the Holy Land: The Crusader Kingdom of Jerusalem*, ed. Silvia Rozenberg (Jerusalem: The Israel Museum, 1999), 34–41.

48. This against a prevailing idea that the majority of the population of Syria-Palestine had converted to Islam by the tenth century—for example, Philip K. Hitti, *History of the Arabs*, 10th ed. (London: Macmillan, 1970); Francesco Gabrieli, *Muhammad and the Conquests of Islam*, trans. Virginia Lulin and Rosamund Linell (New York: McGraw-Hill Book Company, 1968); Richard W. Bulliet, *Conversion to Islam in the Medieval Period: An Essay in Quantitative History* (Cambridge, MA: Harvard University Press, 1979).

49. Jonathan Riley-Smith, "Government and the Indigenous in the Latin Kingdom of Jerusalem," in *Medieval Frontiers: Concepts and Practices*, ed. David Abulafia and Nora Berend (Aldershot: Ashgate, 2002), 125–26.

50. Michel Balard's survey of crusade history also presents a fine example of acknowledging Ellenblum as having altered the field without actually changing the narrative presented. Cf. Michel Balard, *Les Latins en Orient, XIe-XVe siècle* (Paris: Presses Universitaires de France, 2006), 97 and 162. Riley-Smith himself was one of these: *The Crusades: A History* (New Haven, CT: Yale Nota Bene, 2005), 82–86.

51. Joshua Prawer, *The History of the Jews in the Latin Kingdom of Jerusalem* (New York: Clarendon Press, 1988).

52. Brendan Goldman, *Those Who Remained Among the Slaughtered: Regime Changes and Everyday Jewish Life in the Ports of Latin Syria (1098–1291)* (University of Pennsylvania Press, forthcoming).

53. Although a recent doctoral dissertation considers the role of diplomacy in impacting the conditions of minorities, including Muslims in the Latin Kingdom of Jerusalem. Bogdan Smarandache, "Frankish-Muslim Diplomatic Relations and the Shared Minority Discourse in the Eastern Mediterranean, 517-692 AH/1123-1292 AD" (PhD dissertation, University of Toronto, 2019).

54. In opposition to what Hans Eberhard Mayer argued in "Latins, Muslims and Greeks in the Latin Kingdom of Jerusalem," *History* 63 (1978): 175–92.

55. Benjamin Z. Kedar, "The Subjected Muslims of the Frankish Levant," in *Muslims Under Latin Rule, 1100–1300*, ed. James M. Powell (Princeton, NJ: Princeton University Press, 1990), 174.

56. Benjamin Z. Kedar and Muhammad al-Hajjuj, "Muslim Villagers of the Frankish Kingdom of Jerusalem: Some Demographic and Onomastic Data," *Itinéraires d'Orient: Hommages à Claude Cahen. Res Orientales* 1 (1994): 151.

57. Benjamin Z. Kedar, "On the Origins of the Earliest Laws of Frankish Jerusalem: The Canons of the Council of Nablus, 1120," *Speculum* 74 (1999): 310–35. See also Benjamin Z. Kedar and Etan Kohlberg, "The Intercultural Career of Theodore of Antioch," in *Intercultural Contacts in the Medieval Mediterranean: Studies in Honour of David Jacoby*, ed. Benjamin Arbel (London: Frank Cass, 1995), 164–76; "A Twelfth-Century Description of the Jerusalem

Hospital," in *The Military Orders, 2: Welfare and Warfare*, ed. Helen Nicholson (Aldershot: Ashgate, 1998), 3–26.

58. Not discussed here but of interest and importance are Thomas E. Burman, *Reading the Qur'an in Latin Christendom, 1140–1560* (Philadelphia: University of Pennsylvania Press, 2007); Olivia Remie Constable, *Housing the Stranger in the Mediterranean World: Lodging, Trade, and Travel in Late Antiquity and the Middle Ages* (Cambridge: Cambridge University Press, 2003); and Maria Rosa Menocal, *The Ornament of the World: How Muslims, Jews, and Christians Created a Culture of Tolerance in Medieval Spain* (Boston: Little, Brown and Co., 2002).

59. David Nirenberg, *Communities of Violence: Persecution of Minorities in the Middle Ages* (Princeton, NJ: Princeton University Press, 1996).

60. Brian Catlos, *The Victors and the Vanquished: Christians and Muslims of Catalonia and Aragon, 1050–1300* (Cambridge: Cambridge University Press, 2004), esp. 397–408.

61. Catlos, *Victors and Vanquished*, 398.

62. Brian Catlos, *Muslims of Medieval Latin Christendom c. 1050–1614* (Cambridge: Cambridge University Press, 2014), 128–62.

63. Catlos tends to take a negative view of the Crusades and the Franks in their interactions with Muslims. He is not wrong to cite incredible violence during the First Crusade; however, he characterizes it as indiscriminate, which the scholarship suggests it was not. He likewise starts his section on the Muslims of Frankish Syria with a rather polemical quote from Diya' al-Din and leaves to a footnote a comment that perhaps things were not as bad as the quote suggests. He similarly characterizes in scare quotes the Treaty of Jaffa of 1229 as conquest and misidentifies al-Salih of Damascus as the Sultan who concluded it with Frederick II when it was al-Kamil of Egypt. Catlos, *Muslims of Medieval Latin Christendom*, 137, 144, 160.

64. Christopher MacEvitt, *The Crusades and the Christian World of the East: Rough Tolerance* (Philadelphia: University of Pennsylvania Press, 2008). See also Richard B. Rose, "The Native Christians of Jerusalem, 1187-1260," in *The Horns of Hattin*, ed. Benjamin Z. Kedar (Jerusalem: Yad Izhak Ben-Zvi, 1992), 239–49. Cf. R. C. Smail's take on Frankish assimilation in *The Crusaders in Syria and the Holy Land* (Southampton: Thames and Hudson Ltd., 1973), 182–87.

65. Johannes Pahlitzsch, "The Melkites between Byzantium, Muslims and Crusaders," in *Religious Plurality and Interreligious Contacts in the Middle Ages*, ed. Ana Echevarría and Dorothea Weltecke (Wiesbaden: Harrassowitz Verlag, 2020), 157–70; "People of the Book," in *Ayyubid Jerusalem: The Holy City in Context, 1187–1250*, eds. Robert Hillenbrand and Sylvia Auld (London: Altajir Trust, 2009), 435–40.

66. Johannes Pahlitzsch and Daniel Baraz, "Christian Communities in the Latin Kingdom of Jerusalem (1099-1187)," in *Christians and Christianity in the Holy Land: From the Origins to the Latin Kingdoms*, ed. Ora Limor and Guy G. Stroumsa (Turnhout: Brepols, 2006), 232.

67. As argued by recent scholars including MacEvitt, "What Was Crusader about the Crusader States?" and Goldman, *Those Who Remained Among the Slaughtered*.

68. For an examination of Muslim non-elite responses to the Crusades, see Alex Mallett, *Popular Muslim Reactions to the Franks in the Levant, 1097–1291* (Farnham, Surrey: Ashgate, 2014).

69. Foucher de Chartres, *Fulcheri Carnotensis Historia Hierosolymitana (1095–1127)*, ed. Heinrich Hagenmeyer (Heidelberg: Carl Winters Universitätsbuchhandlung, 1913); William of Tyre, *Willelmus Tyrensis, Archiepiscopus, Chronicon*, ed. R.B.C. Huygens (Turnhout: Brepols, 1986).

70. *Cronaca del Templare di Tiro (1243–1314): la caduta degli Stati Crociati nel racconto di un testimone oculare*, ed. and trans. Laura Minervini (Naples: Liguori, 2000).

71. For more on the author, see Paul Crawford's discussion prior to his English translation of the text in *The "Templar of Tyre" Part III of the "Deeds of the Cypriots"* (Aldershot: Ashgate, 2003), 2–7.

72. 'Izz al-Din Ibn al-Athir, *The Chronicle of Ibn al-Athīr for the Crusading Period from al-Kāmil fi'l-ta'rīkh*, ed. D. S. Richards, 3 vols. (Aldershot: Ashgate, 2006–2008); Usama Ibn Munqidh, *The Book of Contemplation: Islam and the Crusades*, trans. Paul M Cobb (London: Penguin, 2008).

73. Jamal al-Din ibn Salim Ibn Wasil, *Mufarrij al-kurub fi akhbar bani Ayyub*, 5 vols., ed. Jamal al-Din al-Shayyal (Cairo: Matba'at Dar al-Kutub, 1953–55). There is a recent edition of the later volumes that I have not consulted: Ibn Wasil, *Mufarrij al-kurub fi akhbar bani Ayyub*, ed. Mohamed Rahim, *Die Chronik des ibn Wāṣil. . . . Kritische Edition des letzten Teils (646/1248-659/1261) mit Kommentar*, Arabische Studien 6 (Wiesbaden: Harrassowitz, 2010).

74. 'Izz al-Din Muhammad Ibn Shaddad, *Ta'rikh al-malik al-zahir*, ed. Ahmad Hutait (Weisbaden: Franz Steiner Verlag, 1983).

75. Rukn al-Din Baybars al-Mansuri, *Mukhtar al-akhbar: ta'rikh al-dawla al-Ayyubiyya wa-dawla al-mamalik al-bahriyya hatta sanat 703AH*, ed. 'Abd al-Hamid Salih Hamdan (Cairo: al-Dar al-Misriyya al-Lubnaniyya, 1993); *Kitab al-tuhfa al-mulukiyya fi al-dawla al-turkiyya*, ed. 'Abd al-Hamid Salih Hamdan (Cairo: al-Dar al-Misriyya al-Lubnaniyya, 1987); *Zubdat al-fikra fi ta'rikh al-hijra*, ed. D. S. Richards (Berlin: Das Arabische Buch, 1998).

76. Muhyi al-Din Ibn 'Abd al-Zahir, *al-Rawd al-zahir fi sirat al-malik al-zahir*, ed. 'Abd al-'Aziz al-Khuwaytir (Riyadh: al-Khuwaytir, 1976).

77. This work exists in two known manuscripts, both of which I have consulted: Vienna 814, now cataloged as O.N.B. Cod. A.F. 117–125 at the Austrian National Library in Vienna, and Vatican Ar. 720 housed at the Vatican library. Parts of the history have been published: vol. 4, ed. Al-Shamma' (Basra: Dar al-Tiba'ah al-Hadithah, 1967); vol. 7, ed. Zuraiq (Beirut: al-Matba'ah al-Amirkaniyah, 1942); vol. 8, ed. Zuraiq and 'Izz al-Din (Beirut: al-Matba'ah al-Amirkaniyah, 1939); vol. 9, pt. 1, ed. Zuraiq (Beirut: al-Matba'ah al-Amirkaniyah, 1936); pt. 2, ed. 'Izz al-Din (Beirut: al-Matba'ah al-Amirkaniyah, 1938). Parts of interest to crusades historians coming from volumes 5–7 have been published in Arabic and English translation in *Ayyubids, Mamlukes and Crusaders: Selections from the Tarikh al-duwal wal-Muluk of Ibn al Furat*, 2 vols., ed. and trans. U. and M. C. Lyons (Cambridge: W. Heffer and Sons, 1971).

78. Ibn Wasil, *Mufarrij al-kurub fi akhbar Bani Ayyub*, 1: 4.

79. Ibn Shaddad, *Ta'rikh*, 1:10.

80. Ibn 'Abd al-Zahir, *Tashrif*, 9.

81. Baybars al-Mansuri, *Zubdat al-fikra*, xv-xvi.

82. See a very helpful discussion of thirteenth- and fourteenth-century Mamluk sources in Reuven Amitai, *Mongols and Mamluks: The Mamluk-Ilkhanid War, 1260–1281* (Cambridge: Cambridge University Press, 1995), 3–6.

83. Ibn al-Furat, *Ayyubids*, 1: vii.

84. Kamal al-Din Ibn al-'Adim, *Bughyat al-talab fi ta'rikh Halab*, ed. Suhayl Zakkar, 12 vols. (Damascus: [s.n.] 1988–89); selected entries have been published in English in David Morray, *An Ayyubid Notable and His World: Ibn al-'Adim and Aleppo as Portrayed in his Biographical Dictionary of People Associated with the City* (Leiden: Brill, 1994).

85. For more on Ibn al-'Adim and this work in particular, see Anne-Marie Eddé, "Kamal al-Din 'Umar Ibn al- 'Adim" in *Medieval Muslim Historians and the Franks in the Levant*, ed. Alex Mattlett (Boston: Brill, 2014), 109–35.

86. Diya' al-Din al-Maqdisi, *Al-Hikayat al-muqtabasa fi karamat mashayikh al-ard al-muqaddasa*, in Daniella Talmon-Heller, "'The Cited Tales of the Wonderous Doings of the Shaykhs of the Holy Land' by Diya' al-Din Abi 'Abd Allah Muhammad b. 'Abd al-Wahid al-Maqdisi (569/1173-643/1245): text, translation and commentary," *Crusades* 1 (2002): 111–54.

87. 'Ali ibn Abi Bakr al-Harawi, *A Lonely Wayfarer's Guide to Pilgrimage*, trans. Josef W. Meri (Princeton, NJ: Darwin Press, 2004).

88. *Livre des Assises de la Cour des Bourgeois*, in *Recueil des Historians des Croisades: Les Assises de Jérusalem*, vol. 2 (Paris: Académie des Inscriptions et Belles-Lettres, 1843); John of Ibelin, *Le livre des Assises*, ed. Peter W. Edbury (Leiden: Brill, 2003).

89. Maurice Grandclaude, *Étude critique sur les livres des assises de Jérusalem* (Paris: Jouve, 1923), 66-68. Marwan Nadar, *Burgesses*, 48-57.

90. *Livre au Roi*, ed. Myriam Greilsammer (Paris: Academie des Inscriptions et Belles-Lettres, 1995). This book of customary law concerns the practice of feudal legislation and justice of the Kingdom of Jerusalem and was written by or at the command of King Aimery de Lusignan around 1200.

91. For vassals, see Philip of Novara, "Le Livre de Forme de Plait," in *Recueil des Historians des Croisades: Les Assises de Jérusalem* vol. 1 (Paris: Académie des Inscriptions et Belles-Lettres, 1841), ch. 58; for captured kings, see John of Ibelin, *Le livre des Assises*, ch. 216.

92. The fatwas I used come from 'Ala al-Din Ibn al-'Attar al-Nawawi, *Fatawa al-imam al-nawawi al-musamma al-masa'il al-manthurah* (Beirut: Dar al-Kutub al-'Ilmiyah, 1982). Ahmad ibn 'Ali al-Qalqashandi, *Kitab subh al-a'sha fi sina'at al-insha*, vol. 13–14 (Cairo: Al-Matba'ah al-Kubra al-Amiriyah, 1964).

93. J. Delaville le Roulx, ed., *Cartulaire générale de l'Ordre des Hospitaliers de Saint-Jean de Jérusalem (1100-1310)* 4 vols (Paris: E. Leroux, 1894); *Tabulae Ordinis Theutonici ex Tabularii Regii Berolinensis Codice Postissimum*, ed. Ernest Strehke (Berolini: [s.n.], 1869); *Codex Diplomaticus Ordinis S. Mariae Theutonicorum* 2 vols, ed. H. Hennes (Mainz: Kirchheim, Schott und Theilmann, 1845-1861); *Le Cartulaire du Chapitre du Saint-Sépulchre de Jérusalem*, ed. Genviève Bresc-Bautier (Paris: Paul Geuthner, 1984).

94. *Regesta Regni Hierosolymitani (1097–1291)*, 2 vols., ed. Reinhold Röhricht (New York [Oeniponti]: Burt Franklin [Libraria Academica Wagneriana], 1960 [1893–1904]); Hans Eberhard Mayer ed., *Die Urkunden der lateinischen Könige von Jerusalem*, 4 vols. (Hannover: Hahnsche Buchhandlung, 2010).

95. *Urkunden zur älteren Handels- un Staatsgeschichte der Republik Venedig mit besonderer Beiziehung auf Byzanz und die Levante*, eds. G.L.F. Tafel and G. M. Thomas (Vienna: Hof- und Staatsdruckerei, 1856), 351–416.

96. For an overview of crusade-period ceramics, see Edna J. Stern, "Ceramic Ware from the Crusader Period in the Holy Land," in *Knights in the Holy Land: The Crusader Kingdom of Jerusalem* (Jerusalem: Israel Museum, 1999), 259–65. Also Edna J. Stern, "The Crusader, Mamluk and Early Ottoman-Period Pottery from Khirbat Din'ila: Typology, Chronology, Production and Consumption Trends," *'Atiqot* 78 (2014): 71–104.

97. For example, Benjamin Kedar and Muhammad al-Hajjuj published an article concerning the demography and naming practices of Muslim communities during the crusader period comparing the twelfth-century text of the flight of the Nablus Hanbali community by Diya' al-Din al-Maqdisi with an Ottoman register of births from 1905 and another by the British Mandate from the 1920s. Benjamin Z. Kedar and Muhammad al-Hajjuj, "Muslim Villagers of the Frankish Kingdom of Jerusalem: Some Demographic and Onomastic Data," in *Itinéraires d'Orient: Hommages à Claude Cahen*, ed. Claude Cahen, Raoul Curiel, and Rika

Gyselen (Bures-sur-Yvette: Group pour l'étude de la civilization du Moyen-Orient, 1994), 145–56.

98. The scholarship on the process of Islamization is discussed in greater depth in Chapter 1.

99. Ellenblum himself made use of chronologically diverse evidence to build his argument for which areas continued to have high Christian populations. He compared maps of churches and synagogues from the sixth century, and Samaritan sites from the fifth century, with his own map of Frankish buildings from the eleventh and twelfth centuries. Ellenblum, *Frankish Rural Settlement*, 225–27.

100. For example, see Jonathan Riley-Smith on *dragomans* and scribes. "Some Lesser Officials in Latin Syria," *The English Historical Review* 87 (1972): 1–26; and reinforced and amplified as to the role of specifically Eastern Christians Ellenblum, *Frankish Rural Settlement*, 194–204.

101. Catlos, *Victors and the Vanquished*, 398.

102. Marshall Hodgson, *The Venture of Islam: Conscience and History in a World Civilization* (Chicago: University of Chicago Press, 1974).

CHAPTER 1

1. Ronnie Ellenblum, *Frankish Rural Settlement in the Latin Kingdom of Jerusalem* (Cambridge: Cambridge University Press, 1998), 284.

2. In his excellent study of the Eastern Christian experience of Frankish rule in the twelfth century, Christopher MacEvitt did set out to interrogate the assumption that Eastern Christians were treated better than Jews or Muslims. His model of "rough tolerance," though, is based on a careful analysis of Eastern Christian sources in conversation with the Frankish ones, arguing that a similar reflection on Muslim communities was not possible because sources speaking to their attitudes were "written from the perspective of those living outside the Frankish principalities, and therefore cannot represent those who experienced Frankish authority directly." The present study is an argument that we are able to understand, to a certain extent, the Muslim experience despite the challenges of the sources. Christopher MacEvitt, *The Crusades and the Christian World of the East: Rough Tolerance* (Philadelphia: University of Pennsylvania Press, 2008), 12.

3. Bogdan C. Smarandache, "A Reassessment of Frankish Settlement Patterns in the Latin Kingdom of Jerusalem, 493-583/1099-1187 AD," in *Minorities in Contact in the Medieval Mediterranean*, ed. Clara Almagro Vidal, Jessica Tearney-Pearce, and Luke Yarbrough (Turnhout: Brepols, 2020), 285–335.

4. Ronnie Ellenblum wrote a succinct and helpful discussion of this debate in the context of his own contribution to it in *Frankish Rural Settlement*, 3–38.

5. Archaeologist Robert Schick took a materialist approach, studying evidence for mosques in the early Islamic period and also posits that the greatest period of conversion to Islam occurred during the Abbasid caliphate from 750 CE. *The Christian Communities of Palestine from Byzantine to Islamic Rule* (Princeton, NJ: The Darwin Press, 1995), esp. 139–58.

6. Those in the first camp included Philip K. Hitti, *History of the Arabs*, 10th ed. (London: Macmillan, 1970), 360; Moshe Gil, *A History of Palestine, 634–1099* (Cambridge: Cambridge University Press, 1992), 169–71; Claude Cahen, "An Introduction to the First Crusade," *Past and Present* 6 (1954): 6–7; while those in the opposite camp included Michael Brett, "The Spread of Islam in Egypt and North Africa," in *Northern Africa: Islam and Modernization*, ed. Michael Brett (London: Cass, 1973), 1–12; Ira Lapidus, "The Conversion of Egypt to Islam," *Israel Oriental Studies* 2 (1972): 256–57; R. C. Smail, *Crusading Warfare (1097–1193). A Contribution to*

*Medieval Military History* (Cambridge: Cambridge University Press, 1956), 204; Joshua Prawer, *The Crusaders' Kingdom: European Colonialism in the Middle Ages* (New York: Praeger, 1972), 48–52.

7. Richard W. Bulliet, *Conversion to Islam in the Medieval Period: An Essay in Quantitative History* (Cambridge, MA: Harvard University Press, 1979), 64–79.

8. Bulliet, *Conversion to Islam*, Graph 18, 104 and 110.

9. Nehemia Levtzion, "Toward a Comparative Study of Islamization," in *Conversion to Islam*, ed. Nehemia Levtzion (New York: Holmes & Meier Publishers Inc., 1979), 7; "Conversion to Islam in Syria and Palestine, and the Survival of Christian Communities," in *Conversion and Continuity: Indigenous Christian Communities in Medieval Islamic Lands, Eighth to Eighteenth Century*, ed. M. Gervers and R. J. Bikhazi (Toronto: Pontifical Institute of Mediaeval Studies, 1990), 289–311; Thomas Carlson, "Contours of Conversion: The Geography of Islamization in Syria, 600–1500," *Journal of American Oriental Society* 135, no. 4 (2015): 791–816.

10. Here and throughout, Syria is a regional name equivalent to the Arabic *bilad al-Sham*, not to the modern country. Levtzion, "Conversion to Islam in Syria and Palestine," 290.

11. Benjamin Z. Kedar, "The Subjected Muslims of the Frankish Levant," in *Muslims Under Latin Rule, 1100–1300*, ed. James M. Powell (Princeton, NJ: Princeton University Press, 1990), 135–74.

12. Ellenblum, *Frankish Rural Settlement*, 224–25, 270, Map 8.

13. Levtzion, "Toward a Comparative Study of Islamization," 1–23; Speros Vryonis, *The Decline of Medieval Hellenism in Asia Minor and the Process of Islamization from the Eleventh through the Fifteenth Century* (Berkeley: 1971); it should be noted that Arabization, Turkicization, and Islamization are elided in Ellenblum's account of their work, *Frankish Rural Settlement*, 254–55.

14. Milka Levy-Rubin has offered a gentle critique of Ellenblum's reading in "New Evidence Relating to the Process of Islamization in Palestine in the Early Muslim Period: The Case of Samaria," *Journal of the Economic and Social History of the Orient* 34 (2000): 257–76.

15. Ellenblum, *Frankish Rural Settlement*, 262, 266–69.

16. Ellenblum, *Frankish Rural Settlement*, Map 1, xviii, 232.

17. Gideon Avni, *The Byzantine-Islamic Transition in Palestine: An Archaeological Approach* (Oxford: Oxford University Press, 2014).

18. Avni, *Byzantine-Islamic Transition*, 9.

19. Avni, 38.

20. Avni, 158.

21. Regarding Ramla and its surroundings, see Avni, 183–87.

22. Avni, 246.

23. Avni, 249–52.

24. Avni, 254.

25. Avni, 255.

26. Avni, 284–85.

27. Avni, 336.

28. Smarandache, "Reassessment of Frankish Settlement Patterns," 299–89.

29. Smarandache, 290.

30. Smarandache, 302.

31. Indeed he concluded "The Franks did not refer to the Muslim population because they did not settle among them." Ellenblum, *Frankish Rural Settlement*, 233.

32. Kedar, "Subjected Muslims," 143–44.

33. Daniella Talmon-Heller, "'The Cited Tales of the Wonderous Doings of the Shaykhs of the Holy Land' by Diya' al-Din Abi 'Abd Allah Muhammad b. 'Abd al-Wahid al-Maqdisi (569/1173-643/1245): text, translation and commentary," *Crusades* 1 (2002): 111–54; *Urkunden zur älteren Handels- und Staatsgeschichte der Republik Venedig mit besonderer Beziehung auf Byzanz und die Levante*, ed. G.L.F. Tafel and G. M. Thomas (Vienna: Hof- und Staatsdruckerei, 1956), no. 299, pp. 351–89 and no. 300, pp. 389–416.

34. Daniella-Talmon Heller, "Muslims and Eastern Christians under Frankish Rule in the Land of Israel," in *Knights in the Holy Land: The Crusader Kingdom of Jerusalem*, ed. Silvia Rozenberg (Jerusalem: The Israel Museum, 1999), 43; Jonathan Riley-Smith, "Government and the Indigenous in the Latin Kingdom of Jerusalem," in *Medieval Frontiers: Concepts and Practices*, ed. David Abulafia and Nora Berend (Burlington, VT: Ashgate, 2002), 123. Riley-Smith does acknowledge that Muslims were able to visit as pilgrims, however.

35. I have relied heavily upon Andrew Petersen, *A Gazetteer of Buildings in Muslim Palestine (Part I)* (Oxford: Council for British Research in the Levant, 2001). All buildings identified on the map have entries in this book.

36. Matthew Bradley, "Preliminary Assessment of the Medieval Christian Burials from Tel Jezreel," *Levant* 26 (1994): 63–65. Archaeological excavation has demonstrated, however, that Christian/Frankish burials were not always so neatly organized; see, for example, Hassan Salamé-Sarkis, *Contribution à l'histoire de Tripoli et de sa région à l'époque des croisades: problèmes d'histoire, d'architecture et de céramique* (Paris: P. Geuthner, 1980).

37. James A. Sauer, "Syro-Palestinian Archeology, History, and Biblical Studies," *The Biblical Archaeologist* 45 (1982): 201; Uza Baram, "The Development of Historical Archaeology in Israel: An Overview and Prospects," *Historical Archaeology* 36 (2002): 12–29.

38. For example, the 1997 excavation published in Howard Smithline et al., "A Crusader-Period Bathhouse in 'Akko (Acre)," *'Atiqot* 73 (2013): 71–108.

39. As cited in Petersen, *Gazetteer of Buildings*, 131.

40. See entry for "Damun" in Petersen, *Gazetteer of Buildings*, 131. Indeed many villages and sites have been destroyed since the creation of the State of Israel. See Raz Kletter, *Just Past? The Making of Israeli Archaeology* (London: Routledge, 2006) for a look into the archival material concerning the early Israeli government's and military's relationship with archaeology and archaeological remains.

41. "Kabul" in Petersen, *Gazetteer of Buildings*, 192–93.

42. References gathered from Guy LeStrange, *Palestine Under the Moslems: A Description of Syria and the Holy Land from A.D. 650 to 1500* (London: Alexander P. Watt, 1890).

43. Ali ibn Abi Bakr al-Harawi, *Lonely Wayfarer's Guide to Pilgrimage*, ed. Josef Meri (Princeton, NJ: Darwin Press, 2005).

44. al-Harawi, *Lonely Wayfarer's Guide*, xx–xxii.

45. al-Harawi, 78–79.

46. al-Harawi, xxiv.

47. al-Harawi, xxviii.

48. al-Harawi, 40, 70.

49. al-Harawi, 42–43.

50. al-Harawi, 42–44.

51. My thanks to the anonymous reviewer who drew my attention to this.

52. MacEvitt, *The Crusades and Christian World of the East*, 22–24.

53. Smarandache, "Reassessment of Frankish Settlement Patterns," 302.

54. Ellenblum, *Frankish Rural Settlement*, 233.

55. David Jacoby echoes this view with regards to Acre, holding that they passed through the city, staying perhaps for a few days, but "no Muslims resided permanently in Acre." David Jacoby, "Migration, Trade and Banking in Crusader Acre," in *The Balkans and the Eastern Mediterranean, 12th-17th Centuries* [Greek], ed. L. Mavroutis (Athens: The National Hellenic Research Foundation), 107–8.

56. Usama Ibn Munqidh, *The Book of Contemplation: Islam and the Crusades*, trans. Paul M. Cobb (New York: Penguin, 2008), 147. An exception can be seen in Jonathan Riley-Smith, "Government and the Indigenous," 122-23.

57. Smarandache, "Reassessment of Frankish Settlement Patterns," 290.

58. al-Harawi, *Lonely Wayfarer's Guide*, 70–71.

59. al-Harawi, 70–71.

60. al-Harawi, 74–75, with some slight modification by the present author.

61. Cf. James G. Schryver, "Identities in the Crusader East," in *Mediterranean Identities in the Premodern Era*, ed. John Watkins and Kathryn Reyerson (Farnham: Ashgate, 2014), 173–89.

62. Ibn al-'Adim, *Bughyat al-talab fi tarikh Halab*, ed. Suhayl Zakkar, 12 vols. (Damascus: [s.n.], 1988–89), 3593.

63. Ibn al-'Adim, *Bughyat al-talab*, 2284–88; English translation of the entry in David Morray, *An Ayyubid Notable and His World: Ibn al-'Adim and Aleppo as Portrayed in His Biographical Dictionary of People Associated with the City* (Leiden: Brill, 1994), 75–77.

64. Ibn al-'Adim, *Bughyat al-talab*, 2285.

65. Jamal al-Din Muhammad ibn Salim Ibn Wasil, *Mufarrij al-kurub fi Akhbar Bani Ayyub*, ed. Jamal al-Din al-Shayyal, 5 vols. (Cairo: Matba'at Dar al-Kutub, 1953), 4:32.

66. Ibn al-'Adim, *Bughyat al-talab*, 1820–21; English translation in Morray, *An Ayyubid Notable and His World*, 62–63.

67. Ibn al-'Adim, *Bughyat al-talab*, 1820; Morray, *An Ayyubid Notable*, 63.

68. For example, see Jill Claster, *Sacred Violence: The European Crusades to the Middle East, 1095–1396* (Toronto: University of Toronto Press, 2009), 88–89; Jonathan Riley-Smith, *The Crusades: A History* (New Haven, CT: Yale Nota Bene, 2005), 61–62; and Kedar, "Subjected Muslims," 143–44. The Frankish sources of the First Crusade do emphasize the violence of the capture and sack of Jerusalem and undoubtedly have influenced historians in this regard. Cf. Thomas Madden, "Rivers of Blood: An Analysis of One Aspect of the Crusader Conquest of Jerusalem in 1099," *Revista Chilena de Estudios Medievales* 1 (2012): 25–37.

69. It is also the location of the depopulated Arab village of al-Haram.

70. See "Haram Sidna 'Ali," in Petersen, *Gazetteer of Buildings*, 146–47 for the dating of the structure. For a discussion of the development and meaning of the site, see Hana Taragan, "The Tomb of Sayyidna 'Ali in Arsuf: The Story of a Holy Place," *Journal of the Royal Asiatic Society*, 3rd series, 14 (2004): 83–102.

71. The most detailed account was written by Mujir al-Din al-Hanbali in his *al-Uns al-jalil bi-tarikh al-quds wa'l-khalil* written in the late fifteenth century. The complete English translation can be found in Taragan, "Tomb of Sayyidna 'Ali," 83–84.

72. Taragan, 86.

73. Muhyi al-Din Ibn 'Abd al-Zahir, *Al-Rawd al-zahir fi sirat al-malik al-zahir*, ed 'Abd al-'Aziz al-Khuwaytir (Riyadh: al-Khuwaytir: 1976), 239–41; English translation in Taragan, "Tomb of Sayyidna 'Ali," 88.

74. Tarragan, 91.

75. Ellenblum, *Frankish Rural Settlement*, 194–98.

76. al-Harawi, *Lonely Wayfarer's Guide*, 42.

Notes to Pages 43–46

77. Smarandache, "Reassessment of Frankish Settlement Patterns," 288–89.
78. Paul Crawford, *The "Templar of Tyre" Part III of the "Deeds of the Cypriots"* (Aldershot: Ashgate, 2003), 101–2; Laura Minvervini ed. and trans., *Cronaca del Templare di Tiro (1243–1314): la caduta degli stati crociati nel racconto di un testimone oculare* (Naples: Liguori, 2000), 349.
79. Petersen, *Gazetteer of Buildings*, 131; LeStrange, *Palestine*, 435–36.
80. Another village nearby is that of modern Sha'ab, which contains a maqam to Shaykh 'Alami and which Petersen identified as possibly medieval. Petersen, *Gazetteer of Buildings*, 276.
81. Petersen, 282.
82. Ibn 'Abd al-Zahir, *Al-Rawd*, 267; also in Ibn al-Furat, *Ayyubids, Mamlukes and Crusaders: Selections from the Tarikh al-duwal wal-Muluk of Ibn al Furat*, trans. U. and M. C. Lyons, 2 vols. (Cambridge: W. Heffer and Sons, 1971), 1:125; 2:99.
83. Burchard of Mt. Sion highlights the great productivity of the area, and it being in Muslim hands when he visited in 1283. "Burchard of Mt Sion A.D. 1280," in *Library of the Palestine Pilgrims Text Society*, ed. and trans. Angus Stewart, 12:26; Burchardus de Monte Sion, *Descriptio Terrae Sanctae, Peregrinatores Medii Aevi Quatuor: Brochardus de Monte Sion, Ricoldus de Monte Crucis, Odoricus de Foro Julii, Willebrandus de Oldenburg*, ed. J.C.M. Laurent, 2nd ed. (Leipzig: J.C. Hinrichs, 1873), 34.
84. H. E. Mayer, *Die Urkunden der lateinischen Könige von Jerusalem* (Hannover: Hahnsche Buchhandlung, 2010), 1350.
85. "James of Vitry letter to Parisian masters and to Ligarde of St. Trond and the convent of Aywières (1216 or 1217)," in *Letters from the East: Crusaders, Pilgrims and Settlers in the 12th–13th Centuries*, ed. Malcolm Barber and Keith Bate (Burlington, VT: Ashgate, 2010), 103.
86. As well as according to Frankish law in the Kingdom of Jerusalem, see also the discussion of slaves in Chapter 3.
87. Benjamin Z. Kedar, ed., "Urban IV on Saracens and Jews Asking to Convert at Acre, Orvieto, July 26, 1264," in *Crusade and Mission: European Approaches Toward the Muslims* (Princeton, NJ: Princeton University Press, 1984), 215.
88. Crawford, *Templar of Tyre*, 479; Minvervini, *Cronaca*, 198; Ibn 'Abd al-Zahir, *Tashrif al-ayyam wa al- 'usur fi sirat al-malik al-mansur*, ed. Murad Kamil (Cairo: al-Sharika al-'arabiyya lil-țibaʿa wa-al-nashr, 1961), 177–78; Shafiʿ ibn 'Ali Ibn 'Asakir, *Kitab al-fadl al-ma'thur min sirat al-sultan al-malik al-mansur*, ed. Umar Tadmuri (Beirut: al-Maktabah al-'Asiriyah, 1998), 173–74.
89. Crawford, *Templar of Tyre*, 479.
90. Shafiʿ ibn 'Ali, *Kitab al-Fadl*, 173.
91. Shafiʿ ibn 'Ali, 162; translation somewhat modified from P. M. Holt, *Early Mamluk Diplomacy*, 73.
92. The entry from Ibn Taghribirdi is short and focuses on those from whom he studied hadiths and those to whom he transmitted them. Abu al-Mahasin Yusuf Ibn Taghribirdi, *Al-Manhal al-safi wa'l-mustawfa ba'da al-wafi*, ed. Nabil Muhammad Abd al-Aziz, 13 vols. (Cairo: Markaz Tahqiq al-Turath, 1985), 10:112.
93. Yvonne Friedman, *Encounter Between Enemies: Captivity and Ransom in the Latin Kingdom of Jerusalem* (Leiden: Brill, 2002), especially Chapter 5 "Life in Captivity," 104–129.
94. Crawford, *Templar of Tyre*, 40; Minvervini, *Cronaca*, 90.
95. Ibn 'Abd al-Zahir, *Al-Rawd*, 151–62; reproduced in Ibn al-Furat, *Ayyubids*, 2:53–59; Crawford, *Templar of Tyre*, 318; Minvervini, *Cronaca*, 90.
96. Crawford, *Templar of Tyre*, 318; Minvervini, *Cronaca*, 90.
97. Ibn al-Furat, *Ayyubids*, 1:112; 2:88–89.

98. The primary accounts of the escape come from Muhammad Ibn Shaddad, *Ta'rikh al-malik al-zahir*, ed. Ahmad Hutait (Wiesbaden: Franz Steiner Verlag, 1983), 102–103; Ibn 'Abd al-Zahir, *Al-Rawd*, 430–31; and Baybars al-Mansuri, *Mukhtar al-Akhbar: Ta'rikh al-Dawla al-Ayyubiyya wa-Dawlat al-Mamalik al-Bahriyya Hatta sanat 702 hijri* (Cairo: al-Dar al-Misriyah al-Lubnaniyah, 1993), 52–53.

99. Ibn Shaddad, *Ta'rikh*, 103. He also provides the names for those who died at sea or while imprisoned, which itself can probably be taken as evidence of poor conditions: al-Ra'is Sayf al-Din Muhammad b. al-Mujahid, al-Ra'is Sayf al-Din b. Abi Sulama, al-Ra'is Sharif al-Dawla 'Alawi, al-Ra'is Najm al-Din Najm b. al-Ra'is Sayf al-Dawla Ibn al-Hajj al-Jabali, al-Ra'is Sayf al-Din Abu Bakr b. al-Ra'is al-Mukhlis b. Tamim b. Ishaq, al-Ra'is Jamal al-Dawla Yusuf b. Mukhlis, al-Ra'is Sayf al-Din Muhammad b. al-Ra'is Nur al-Dawla 'Ali b. al-Mukhlis, al-Ra'is Muwwafaq known as Ibn al-Ra'is al-Mukhlis b. Ishaq.

100. Marsilio Zorzi, *Urkunden zur älteren Handels- und Staatsgeschichte der Republik Venedig mit besonderer Beiziehung auf Byzanz und die Levante*, ed. G.L.F. Tafel and G. M. Thomas (Wien: Hof- und Staatsdruckerei, 1856), no. 299, 370.

101. Jonathan Riley-Smith, "Some Lesser Officials in Latin Syria," *The English Historical Review* 87 (1972): 20n11.

102. Marsilio Zorzi, *Urkunden*, no. 299, 374, 376, 384.

103. Marsilio Zorzi, no. 299, 374.

104. Crawford, *Templar of Tyre*, 52; Minervini, *Cronaca*, 112.

105. Ibn 'Abd al-Zahir, *Al-Rawd*, 282.

106. See examples in P. M. Holt, *Early Mamluk Diplomacy, 1260–1290: Treaties of Baybars and Qalawun with Christian Rulers* (Leiden: Brill, 1995); also Chapter 3 of the present work.

107. Ibn 'Abd al-Zahir, *Al-Rawd*, 282.

108. Ibn 'Abd al-Zahir, 347. For the English translation see Ibn al-Furat, *Ayyubids*, 2:133.

109. Slaves and slavery as a component of the economic landscape are discussed in Chapter 2 of the present work.

110. Recorded in Ibn 'Abd al-Zahir, *Tashrif*, 103–10; for English see Holt, *Early Mamluk Diplomacy*, 109–17.

111. Maurice H. Chéhab, *Tyr à l'époque des croisades*, 2 vols. (Paris: A. Maisonneuve, 1979), *passim*.

112. Another parallel topic of courts is discussed in Chapter 3.

113. Ibn 'Abd al-Zahir, *Al-Rawd*, 282.

114. James of Vitry, *Letters from the East*, 105.

115. Riley-Smith, *The Crusades*, 119, 147, 151.

116. James of Vitry, *Letters from the East*, 105.

117. "Lettre à Charles d'Anjou sur les affaires de Terre Sainte (Acre, 22 avril 1260)," in *Bibliothèque de l'école des chartes* LXXXVII (Paris: 1917), 489.

118. *Letters from the East*, no. 71, 155.

119. Kamal al-Din 'Umar ibn Ahmad Ibn al-'Adim, *Bughyat al-talab fi tarikh Halab*, ed. Suhayl Zakkar, 11 vols. (Damascus: [s.n.], 1988–1989), 3547.

120. Ibn al-Adim, *Bughyat al-talab*, 1270.

121. Ahmad Ibn Abi Usaybi'ah, *'Uyun al-anba' fi tabaqat al-atibba'* (Beirut: Dar Maktabat al-Hayah, 1965), 682.

122. Muhammad Ibn Shaddad, *Tarikh*, 143–44.

123. Ibn Taghribirdi, *Al-Manhal*, 9:191.

124. Ibn al-'Adim, *Bughyat al-talab*, 4356–57.

125. Ibn ʿAbd al-Zahir, *Al-Rawd*, 346.
126. Smarandache, "Reassessment of Frankish Settlement Patterns," 290.
127. Smarandache, 289.
128. Al-Harawi, *Lonely Wayfarer's Guide*, 44; Jaroslav Folda, *Crusader Art in the Holy Land from the Third Crusade to the Fall of Acre* (Cambridge: Cambridge University Press, 2005), 274.

CHAPTER 2

1. Paul Crawford, *The "Templar of Tyre" Part III of the "Deeds of the Cypriots"* (Aldershot: Ashgate, 2003), 101–2.
2. Muhyi al-Din Ibn ʿAbd al-Zahir, *Tashrif al-ayyam wa al-ʿusur fi sirat al-malik al-mansur*, ed. Murad Kamil (Cairo: al-Sharika al-ʿarabiyya lil-tibaʿa wa-al-nashr, 1961), 177.
3. David Jacoby wrote an article presenting an overview of the kingdom's economy but a more detailed monograph remains a desideratum: David Jacoby, "The Economic Function of the Crusader States of the Levant: A New Approach," in *Relazioni economiche tra Europa e mondo islamico. Secc. XIII–XVIII (Instituto Internazionale di Storia Economica "F. Datini," Atti delle Settimane di Studi e altri convegni, vol. 38)*, ed. Simonetta Cavaciocchi (Grassina, Italy: Le Monnier, 2007), 159–91. For a recent collection of Michel Balard's work, see *La Méditerranée médiévale. Espace, itinéraires, comptoirs* (Paris: Picard, 2006); also "L'empire génois au Moyen Age," in *Les Empires. Antiquité et Moyen Ages. Analyse comparée*, ed. Frédéric Hurlet (Rennes: Presses universitaires de Rennes, 2008), 181–97. For David Jacoby, see *Commercial Exchange Across the Mediterranean: Byzantium, the Crusader Levant, Egypt and Italy* (Aldershot: Variorum, 2005); *Byzantium, Latin Romania and the Mediterranean* (Aldershot: Variorum, 2001); and *Trade, Commodities and Shipping in the Medieval Mediterranean* (Aldershot: Variorum, 1997).
4. Benjamin Z. Kedar, "The Crusading Kingdom of Jerusalem—The First European Colonial Society? A Symposium," in *The Horns of Hattin*, ed. Benjamin Z. Kedar (London: Variorum, 1992), 358.
5. Judith Bronstein, *The Hospitallers and the Holy Land: Financing the Latin East 1187–1274* (Woodbridge: Boydell Press, 2005); Rabei G. Khamisy, "The Templar Estates in the Territory of Acre," *Ordines Militares—Colloquia Torunensia Historica* 18 (2013): 267–85; Denys Pringle, "A Rental of Hospitaller Properties from Twelfth-Century Jerusalem," in *Deeds Done Beyond the Sea: Essays on William of Tyre, Cyprus and the Military Orders Presented to Peter Edbury*, ed. Susan B. Edgington and Helen J. Nicholson (Farnham: Ashgate, 2014), 181–96; "The Military Orders in the Cities of the Holy Land," in *Les Ordres militaires dans la ville médiévale (1100–1350): Actes du colloque international de Clermont-Ferrand 26–28 mai 2010*, ed. Damien Carraz (Clermont-Ferrand: Presses Universitaires Blaises Pascal, 2013), 79–95; Karl Borchardt, "Zucker und Mohren: zur Krise der Johanniter auf Zypern im 15. Jahrhundert," *Ordines Militares—Colloquia Torunensia Historica* 16 (2011): 191–212; Shlomo Lotan, "Empowering and Struggling in an Era of Uncertainty and Crisis—The Teutonic Military Order in the Latin East, 1250–1291," *Ordines Militares—Colloquia Torunensia Historica* 16 (2011): 19–28.
6. More on this later. See also Mohamed Ouerfelli, *Le Sucre: Production, commercialisation et usages dans la Méditerranée médiévale* (Leiden: Brill, 2008); Jong-Kuk Nam, *Le commerce du coton en Méditerranée à la fin du Moyen Age* (Leiden: Brill, 2007).
7. Jacoby, "Economic Function," esp. 163, 169–77.
8. Nicholas Morton, *The Crusader States & Their Neighbours: A Military History, 1099–1187* (Oxford: Oxford University Press, 2020), 154.

9. Jean Richard, *The Crusades, c.1071–c.1291* (Cambridge: Cambridge University Press, 1999), 386–93.

10. P. M. Holt, *Early Mamluk Diplomacy, 1260–1290: Treaties of Baybars and Qalawun with Christian Rulers* (Leiden: Brill, 1995), 40; Ahmad ibn ʿAli al-Qalqashandi, *Kitab subh al-aʾsha fi sinaʾat al-inshaʾ*, 14 vols. (Cairo: Al-Matbaʿah al-Kubra al-Amriyah; 1964), 14:31–39.

11. Holt, *Early Mamluk Diplomacy*, 46; al-Qalqashandi, *Subh*, 14:40–42.

12. Rukn al-Din Baybars al-Mansuri, *Zubdat al-fikra fi taʾrikh al-hijra*, ed. Donald S. Richards (Beirut: Dar al-Nashr al-Kitab al-ʿArabi, 1998), 67; Nasir al-Din Muhammad Ibn al-Furat, *Ayyubids, Mamlukes and Crusaders: Selections from the Tarikh al-duwal wal-Muluk of Ibn al-Furat*, trans. U. and M. C. Lyons, 2 vols. (Cambridge: W. Heffer and Sons, 1971), 1:53; 2:44.

13. Holt, *Early Mamluk Diplomacy*, 52–53; al-Qalqashandi, *Subh*, 14:42–51.

14. Holt, *Early Mamluk Diplomacy*, 68.

15. Holt, 65; Baybars al-Mansuri, *Zubdat al-fikra*, 212.

16. The Arabic source does not name the atabek, but Peter Thorau indicates that it was ʿIzz al-Din. Peter Thorau, *The Lion of Egypt: Sultan Baybars I and the Near East in the Thirteenth Century* (London: Longman, 1992), 168, 172, 178.

17. As Jonathan Riley-Smith has pointed out in his note from the Ibn al-Furat translation of this story, Isabel did not have a brother, so this probably should read "her husband" who was the child King Hugh of Cyprus. Ibn al-Furat, *Ayyubids*, 2: 4n4.

18. Muhyi al-Din Ibn ʿAbd al-Zahir, *Al-Rawd al-zahir fi sirat al-malik al-zahir*, ed. ʿAbd al-ʿAziz al-Khuwaytir (Riyadh: al-Khuwaytir, 1976), 283–84, 299; Baybars al-Mansuri, *Zubdat al-fikra*, 107–8; for the English translation, see Ibn al-Furat, *Ayyubids*, 2: 104–5, 113.

19. Thorau, *Lion of Egypt*, 221; ʿIzz al-Din Muhammad Ibn Shaddad, *Taʾrikh al-malik al-zahir*, ed. Ahmad Hutait (Weisbaden: Franz Steiner Verlag, 1983), 36; Ibn ʿAbd al-Zahir, *Al-Rawd*, 399–400; Ibn al-Furat, *Ayyubids*, 2:158.

20. Shafiʿ bin ʿAli Ibn ʿAsakir, *Kitab al-fadl al-maʾthur min sirat al-sultan al-malik al-mansur*, ed. Umar Tadmuri (Beirut: Al-Maktabah al-ʿAsriyah, 1998), 162.

21. Linda Northrup, *From Slave to Sultan: The Career of Al-Mansur Qalāwūn and the Consolidation of Mamluk Rule in Egypt and Syria (678–689 A.H./1279–1290 A.D.)* (Stuttgart: Franz Steiner Verlag, 1998), 299.

22. I am grateful to professor Mahmood Ibrahim for bringing this to my attention and sharing his draft edition of Shams al-Din Muhammad ibn Ibrahim al-Jazari's *Taʾrikh al-Jazari*, Gotha, Forschungsbibliothek Gotha, MS Orient A 1561, fols. 28b, 29a.

23. Jacoby, "Economic Function," 165; Adrian J. Boas, *Crusader Archaeology: The Material Culture of the Latin East* (London: Routledge, 1999), 150–51.

24. Fred Aldsworth, George Haggarty, Sarah Jennings, and David Whitehouse, "Medieval Glassmaking at Tyre, Lebanon," *Journal of Glass Studies* 44 (2002): 49–66.

25. Gladys Davidson Weinberg, "A Glass Factory of Crusader Times in Northern Israel," in *Annales du 10e Congrès de l'Association internationale pour l'histoire du verre: Madrid-Segovie, 23–28 septembre 1985* (Amsterdam: 1987), 305–16.

26. See Boas, *Crusader Archaeology*, 150–51; Benjamin of Tudela, *The Itinerary of Benjamin of Tudela*, ed. and trans. Marcus N. Adler (New York: P. Feldheim, 1907), 18.

27. Maya Shatzmiller briefly discussed pottery production in her larger work on labor in the Islamic world, concluding that while her sources indicated that ceramics comprised a small percentage of the labor force, the material remains of pottery indicate that ceramics production was much more important than her textual sources would suggest. *Labour in the Medieval Islamic World* (Leiden: Brill, 1994), 238–40.

28. Edna J. Stern, S. Y. Waksman, and A. Shapiro, "The Impact of the Crusades on Ceramic Production and Use in the Southern Levant: Continuity or Change?" in S. Y. Waksman, ed., *Multidisciplinary Approaches to Food and Foodways in the Medieval Eastern Mediterranean* (Lyon: MOM Éditions, 2020), 113–46.

29. Véronique François, Andreas Nicolaïdes, Lucy Vallauri, and Yona Waksman, "Premiers éléments d'une caractérisation des productions de céremique de Beyrouth entre domination franque et mamelouke," in *VIIe Congrès Internationale de la Céramique médiévale en Méditterranée, Thessaloniki, 11–16 Octobre 1999* (Athens: Caisse des Recettes Archéologiques, 2003), 325–40; Sami el-Masri, "Medieval Pottery from Beirut's Downtown Excavations: The First Results," *Aram* 9–10 (1997–1998): 103–19.

30. el-Masri, "Medieval Pottery," 105.

31. el-Masri, 108.

32. François et al., "Premiers éléments," 325–27.

33. François et al., 327–29.

34. François et al., 329.

35. François et al., 337–39.

36. Edna J. Stern, "Ceramic Ware from the Crusader Era in the Holy Land," in *Knights in the Holy Land: The Crusader Kingdom of Jerusalem* (Jerusalem: Israel Museum, 1999), 259–65; "Excavation of the Courthouse Site at ʿAkko: The Pottery of the Crusader and Ottoman Periods," *ʿAtiqot* 39 (1997): 35–70; "The Crusader, Mamluk and Early Ottoman-Period Pottery from Khirbat Dinʿila: Typology, Chronology, Production and Consumption Trends," *ʿAtiqot* 78 (2014): 71–104; Nimrod Getzov, Dina Avshalom-Gorni, Yael Gorin-Rosen, Edna J. Stern, Danny Syon, and Ayelet Tatcher, *Horbat Uza: The 1991 Excavations Volume II: The Late Periods* (Jerusalem: Israel Antiquities Authority, 2009); Danny Syon and Edna J. Stern, "Excavations at the Dar el-Gharbiya Neighborhood of Kafr Yasif: A Crusader Estate in the Territory of ʿAkko," *ʿAtiqot* 79 (2014): 233–61.

37. Yona Waksman, Edna J. Stern, Irina Segal, Naomi Porat, and Joseph Yellin, "Elemental and Petrographic Analyses of Local and Imported Ceramics from Crusader Acre," *ʿAtiqot* 59 (2008): 159.

38. Edna Stern and Ayelet Tatcher, "The Early Islamic, Crusader, and Mamluk Pottery," in Nimrod Getzov, Dina Avshalom-Gorni, Yael Gorin-Rosen, Edna J. Stern, Danny Syon, and Ayelet Tatcher, *Horbat ʿUza the 1991 Excavations Volume II: The Late Periods* (Jerusalem: Israel Antiquities Authority, 2009), 133–34.

39. Stern and Tatcher, "Early Islamic, Crusader and Mamluk Pottery," 134; Edna J. Stern, "The Excavations at Lower Horbat Manot: A Medieval Sugar-Production Site," *ʿAtiqot* 42 (2001): 277–308.

40. Waksman, et al., "Elemental and Petrographic Analyses," 178–79.

41. Edna J. Stern, "The Last Years of Crusader Acre (ʿAkko) and Resettlement in the Ottoman Period: Archaeological Evidence from the *Boverel* Quarter," *ʿAtiqot* 103 (2021): 148; Syon and Stern, "Excavations at the Dar el-Gharbiya," 247.

42. *Livre des Assises de la Cour des Bourgeois*, in *Recueil des Historiens des Croisades*, vol. 2 (Paris: Académie des Inscriptions et Belles-Lettres, 1843), 179.

43. Stern, Waksman, and Shapiro, "The Impact of the Crusades," 113–46.

44. David Jacoby, "The Trade of Crusader Acre in the Levantine Context: An Overview," *Archivio Storico del Sannio*, n.s. 3 (1998): 114; Jacoby, "Economic Function," 180. For the Venetian participation in Levantine trade, though now dated, Frederic Chapin Lane's *Venice, A Maritime Republic* (Baltimore: Johns Hopkins University Press, 1973) is still important.

45. Yvonne Friedman, *Encounter Between Enemies: Captivity and Ransom in the Latin Kingdom of Jerusalem* (Leiden: Brill, 2002), 76–77, 82. See also James Wilson, "The Ransom of High-Ranking Captives, Tributary Relationships and the Practice of Diplomacy in Northern Syria 442-522/1050-1128," *Journal of the Royal Asiatic Society* 32, no. 3 (2022): 635–69.

46. Usama Ibn Munqidh, *The Book of Contemplation: Islam and the Crusades*, trans. Paul M. Cobb (New York: Penguin, 2008), 94.

47. For Hama: Jamal al-Din Ibn Wasil, *Mufarrij al-kurub fi akhbar bani ayyub*, ed. Jamal al-Din al-Shayyal, 5 vols. (Cairo: Matba'at Dar al-Kutub, 1953–55), 3:162–63; Ibn al-Furat, Vienna, Österreichische Nationalbibliothek, MS A.F. 121, fols. 11v-12r. For Homs: Ibn Wasil, *Mufarrij*, 3:168; Ibn al-Furat, MS A.F. 121, fol. 12r.

48. Ibn al-Furat, *Ayyubids*, 1:50; 2:41.

49. Ibn Wasil, *Mufarrij*, 3:223.

50. Ibn 'Abd al-Zahir, *Al-Rawd*, 151–58; for an English account, see Ibn al-Furat, *Ayyubids*, 2:53–56.

51. Baybars al-Mansuri, *Zubdat al-fikra*, 145. Baybars al-Mansuri actually reports twenty prisoners, but this must be a mistake, as suggested by Peter Thorau in *Lion of Egypt*, 234.

52. Baybars al-Mansuri, *Zubdat al-fikra*, 191.

53. A similar movement occurred in Europe from the twelfth century on, with the development of the Trinitarian and other religious orders devoted to securing the release of Christian captives. See Friedman, *Encounter Between Enemies*, 187–211.

54. Kamal al-Din 'Umar ibn Ahmad Ibn al-'Adim, *Bughyat al-talab fi ta'rikh halab*, ed. Suhayl Zakkar, 12 vols. (Damascus: [s.n.] 1988), 4356; D. W. Morray, *An Ayyubid Notable and His World: Ibn Al-'Adim and Aleppo as Portrayed in His Biographical Dictionary of People Associated with the City* (Leiden: Brill, 1994), 116–18.

55. Ibn 'Abd al-Zahir, *Al-Rawd*, 245.

56. Ibn Shaddad, *Ta'rikh*, 80.

57. Ibn Shaddad, 113.

58. Ibn Wasil, *Mufarrij*, 5:51.

59. Ibn al-Furat, *Ayyubids*, 1:120; 2:95.

60. Ibn al-Furat, 2:133.

61. Such agents were known as al-fakkak or alfaqueques. Jarbel Rodriguez, *Captives and Their Saviors in the Medieval Crown of Aragon* (Washington, DC: Catholic University of America Press, 2007).

62. Friedman, *Encounter Between Enemies*, 114.

63. Crawford, *Templar of Tyre*, 318; Minervini, *Cronaca*, 90. See also Peter W. Edbury, "A New Text of the *Annales de Terre Sainte*," in *In Laudem Hierosolymitani*, ed. Iris Shagrir, Ronnie Ellenblum, Jonathan Riley-Smith (Aldershot: Ashgate, 2007), 157–58.

64. Ibn al-Furat, *Ayyubids*, 1:66; 2:55.

65. Ibn al-Furat, 1:135; 2:108.

66. Ibn al-Furat, 2:88–89.

67. Christopher MacEvitt, *The Crusades and the Christian World of the East* (Philadelphia: University of Pennsylvania Press, 2008), 147–49.

68. Ibn Jubayr, *Rihlat Ibn Jubayr* (Beirut: Dar Sadr li-l-Tiba'ah wa-l-Nashr, 1964), 274–75; *The Travels of Ibn Jubayr*, trans. R.J.C. Broadhurst (London: Jonathan Cape, 1952), 316.

69. The taxes detailed in Marsilio Zorzi's documents appear to be much less, for instance.

70. Joshua Prawer wrote several analyses deriving from data from Tyre, the most recent of which was his chapter "Palestinian Agriculture and the Crusader Rural System," in *Crusader Institutions* (Oxford: Clarendon Press, 1980), 143–200.

71. MacEvitt, *The Crusades and the Christian World*, 145.

72. The same as the Arabic *faddan*, approximately 3–4 hectares or 7.4–9.8 acres. The exact size has been debated but Ellenblum seems to have had the last word on this issue. Ronnie Ellenblum, *Frankish Rural Settlement in the Latin Kingdom of Jerusalem* (Cambridge: Cambridge University Press, 1998), 98–99. For larger estimates see Joshua Prawer, *Crusader Institutions* (Oxford: Clarendon Press, 1980), 121; and Meron Benvenisti, *The Crusaders in the Holy Land* (Jerusalem: Israel Universities Press, 1976), 216.

73. Prawer, *Crusader Institutions*, 146-148.

74. Jacoby, "Economic Function," 161, 169.

75. Jacoby, 169. Jonathan Riley-Smith has argued along similar lines, although he focuses on the administrative apparatus. See Jonathan Riley-Smith, *Crusades: A History*, 2nd ed. (New Haven, CT: Yale Nota Bene, 2005), 85–86. Paul Sidelko has convincingly argued against Riley-Smith and others' readings that the Franks simply adopted the same tax structure, featuring the *kharaj* and *jizya* taxes. See Paul Sidelko, "Muslim Taxation under Crusader Rule," in *Tolerance and Intolerance: Social Conflict in the Ages of the Crusades*, eds. Michael Gervers and James M. Powell (Syracuse: Syracuse University Press, 2001), 65–74.

76. Jacoby, "Economic Function," 163, 170.

77. J. Delaville le Roulx, ed., *Cartulaire générale de l'Ordre des Hospitaliers de Saint Jean de Jérusalem, 1100–1310*, 4 vols. (Paris: E. Leroux, 1894–1906), no.1144, 1:96–97; no. 2120, 2:489; also Bronstein, *Hospitallers and the Holy Land*, 114.

78. Bogdan Smarandache, "A Reassessment of Frankish Settlement Patterns in the Latin Kingdom of Jerusalem, 493-583 AH/1099-1187 AD," in *Minorities in Contact in the Medieval Mediterranean*, ed. Clara Almagro Vidal, Jessica Tearney-Pearce, and Luke Yarbrough (Turnhout: Brepols, 2020), 289.

79. Made famous by the flight to Damascus of a group of the Hanbali residents in the 1150s. Joseph Drory, "Hanbalis of the Nablus Region in the Eleventh and Twelfth Centuries," *Asian and African Studies* 22 (1988): 93–112; Daniella Talmon-Heller ed. and trans., "'The Cited Tales of the Wondrous Doings of the Shaykhs of the Holy Land' by Diya' al-Din Abu 'Abd Allah Muhammad b. 'Abd al-Wahid al-Maqdisi (569/1173-643/1245): Text, Translation and Commentary," *Crusades* 1 (2002): 111–54.

80. Benvenisti, *Crusaders in the Holy Land*, 163.

81. Jochen G. Schenk, "Nomadic Violence in the First Latin Kingdom of Jerusalem and the Military Orders," *Reading Medieval Studies* 36 (2010): 39–55.

82. *Livre des Assises de la Cour des Bourgeois*, 177.

83. ÖNB A.F. 121, fol. 13v.

84. Ibn Wasil, *Mufarrij*, 5:131–32.

85. Janet Shirley, trans., *Crusader Syria in the Thirteenth Century: The Rothelin Continuation of the History of William of Tyre with Part of the Eracles or Acre Text* (Aldershot: Ashgate, 1999), 42–44.

86. Peter W. Edbury, "A New Text of the *Annales de Terre Sainte*," in *In Laudem Hierosolymitani*, ed. Iris Shagrir, Ronnie Ellenblum, and Jonathan Riley-Smith (Aldershot: Ashgate, 2007), 160.

87. Crawford, *Templar of Tyre*, 403; Minervini, *Cronaca*, 167.

88. Ibn 'Abd al-Zahir, *Al-Rawd*, 267.

89. Rabei G. Khamisy, "Frankish Viticulture, Wine Presses, and Wine Production in the Levant: New Evidence from Castellum Regis (Mi'ilyā)," *Palestine Exploration Quarterly* 153, no. 3 (2021): 191–221.

90. *Livre des Assises de la Cour des Bourgeois*, 177.

91. *Livre des Assises de la Cour des Bourgeois*, 179.

92. For example in al-Andalus, see: Vincent Lagardère, "Cépages, raisin et vin en al-Andalus (X-XVe siècle)," *Médiévales* 33 (1997): 81–90; Pauline Lewicka, "Alcohol and Its Consumption in Medieval Cairo. The story of a habit," *Studie Arabistyczne* 12 (2006): 55–97.

93. Lewicka, "Alcohol and Its Consumption," 74–75.

94. Lewicka, 67.

95. Lewicka, 70.

96. That is, the European institution of the *ban*. Prawer, *Crusader Institutions*, 134.

97. Khamisy, "Frankish Viticulture," 214–15.

98. Talmon-Heller, "*Cited Tales*," 135; Jean Richard, "Agricultural Conditions in the Crusader States," in *A History of the Crusades*, ed. Kenneth Setton, Norman Zacour, Harry Hazard, vol. 5 (Madison: University of Madison Press, 1985), 260.

99. Richard, "Agricultural Conditions," 264.

100. Rafael Frankel, Nimrod Getzov, Mordechai Aviam, and Avi Degani, *Settlement Dynamics and Regional Diversity in Ancient Upper Galilee: Archaeological Survey of Upper Galilee*, IAA Reports 14 (Jerusalem: Israel Antiquities Authority 2001), 129–30; Richard, "Agricultural Conditions," 264.

101. The Levantine coast actually comprises at least three different named entities. The furthest south is the Sharon Plain, which runs from the Yarkon River (Nahr al-ʿAuja) just north of Jaffa to the Taninim river (Wadi az-Zarqa) 50km north. Then comes Mt. Carmel where Haifa is located, followed by the Western Galilee and the Plain of Acre, which is then followed by the very narrow Lebanese coastal strip or *sahl* up to Beirut. For a thorough discussion of the geography, geology, and settlement patterns of the Sharon Plain, see Denys Pringle, *The Red Tower (al-Burj al-Ahmar)* (London: British School of Archaeology, 1986), esp. 5–12.

102. Victor Guérin, *Description géographique, historique et archéologique de la Palestine* (Paris: Imprimerie impériale, 1880), 44–45; Ellenblum, *Frankish Rural Settlement*, 143–44; Ernst Strehlke, *Tabulae Ordinis Theutonici, ex Tabularii Regii Berolinenesis Codice Potissimum* (Berolini: [s.n.] 1869), 20.

103. Gustav Beyer, "Die Kreuzfahrergebiete Akko und Galileae," *Zeitschrift des deutschen Palästina-Vereins* 67 (1945), 207.

104. Ibn al-Furat, *Ayyubids*, 2:157 quoting Ibn ʿAbd al-Zahir, *Al-Rawd*, 398; Benvenisti, *Crusaders in the Holy Land*, 253; Petersen, *A Gazetteer of Buildings in Muslim Palestine (Part I)* (Oxford: Council for British Research in the Levant, 2001), 192–93.

105. Strehlke, *Tabulae Ordinis Theutonici*, 84–85; *Cartulaire générale de l'Ordre des Hospitaliers*, 2:141; Benvenisti, *Crusaders in the Holy Land*, 229–30; Stern, "Lower Horbat Manot," 277–308.

106. Jacoby, "Economic Function," 163.

107. David Jacoby, "Migration, Trade and Banking in Crusader Acre," in *The Balkans and the Eastern Mediterranean, 12th-17th Centuries* [Greek], ed. L Mavromatis (Athens: The National Hellenic Research Foundation, 1998), 105.

108. *Urkunden zur älteren Handels- und Staatsgeschichte der Republik Venedig mit besonderer Beizeihung auf Byzanz und die Levante*, ed. G.L.F. Tafel and G. M. Thomas (Vienna: Hof- und Staatssruckerei, 1856), 368; Jacoby, "Economic Function," 172.

109. Edna J. Stern, "The Excavations at Lower Horbot Manot: A Medieval Sugar-Production Site," *ʿAtiqot* 42 (2001): 277–308," 279–80. See also Ouerfelli, *Le Sucre*, passim.

110. Rafael Frankel and Edna J. Stern, "A Crusader Screw Press from Western Galilee—The Manot Press," *Techniques & Culture* 27 (1996): 89–122.

## Notes to Pages 73–77

111. Stern, "Lower Horbot Manot," 277–308.
112. P. M. Holt, *Early Mamluk Diplomacy (1260–1290): Treaties of Baybars and Qalawun with Christian Rulers* (Leiden: Brill, 1995), 78.
113. Stern, "Lower Horbot Manot," 282.
114. Stern, 302–303.
115. Stern, 300.
116. S. D. Goitein, *Letters of Medieval Jewish Traders* (Princeton, NJ: Princeton University Press, 1973), 89–95.
117. Richard, "Agricultural Conditions," 259.
118. Peter W, Edbury, ed., "A New Text of the *Annales de Terre Sainte*," in *In Laudem Hierosolymitani*, ed. I. Shagrir, R. Ellenblum, J. Riley-Smith (Aldershot: Ashgate, 2007, 145–62), 159; Crawford, *Templar of Tyre*, 353; Minervini, *Cronaca*, 116–18; Ibn ʿAbd al-Zahir, *Al-Rawd*, 158–62; 280–82; Baybars al-Mansuri, *Zubdat al-fikra*, 107–8.
119. *Urkunden zur älteren Handels-*, 351–416.
120. *Urkunden zur älteren Handels-*, 374.
121. *Urkunden zur älteren Handels-*, 382.
122. *Urkunden zur älteren Handels-*, 382–83.
123. *Urkunden zur älteren Handels-*, 379–80.
124. *Urkunden zur älteren Handels-*, 379–80. I am grateful for the anonymous reviewer's suggestion of this name.
125. *Urkunden zur älteren Handels-*, 381.
126. Ibn ʿAbd al-Zahir, *Al-Rawd*, 387.
127. Peter Thorau, *Lion of Egypt*, 206.
128. Ibn al-Furat, *Ayyubids*, 2:154. Quoting from Ibn ʿAbd al-Zahir's *Al-Rawd*.
129. David Ayalon, "The Mamluks and Naval Power: A Phase of the Struggle between Islam and Christian Europe," in *Medieval Ships and Warfare*, ed. Susan Rose (Aldershot: Ashgate, 2008), 223–34.
130. Marino Sanudo Torsello, *The Book of the Secret of the Faithful of the Cross*, trans. Peter Lock (Farnham: Ashgate, 2011), 327.
131. Sanudo Torsello, *Book of the Secret*, 351.
132. ʿAla al-Din Ibn al-ʿAttar al-Nawawi, *Fatawa al-Imam al-Nawawi al-musamma al-masaʾil al-manthurah* (Beirut: Dar al-Kutub al-ʿIlmiyah, 1982), 159. This concerned the giving of *khums* or the traditional fifth of loot or profit taken and given as charity, often to the local qadi or other charitable institution.
133. See Peter Edbury's comments in his edition: Philip of Novara, *Le Livre de Forme de Plait*, ed. Peter W. Edbury (Nicosia: Hetaireia Kypriakon Spoudon, 2009), 322.
134. Myriam Greilsammer, *Le Livre au roi* (Paris: Académie des Inscriptions et Belles-Lettres, 1995), 214.
135. Hugh Kennedy, *Crusader Castles* (Cambridge: Cambridge University Press, 1994), 148–49.
136. J. Delaville Le Roulx, ed., *Cartulaire générale de l'Ordre des Hospitaliers de Saint Jean de Jérusalem, 1100–1310*, 4 vols. (Paris: E. Leroux, 1894–1906): 4:291–92.
137. *Cartulaire générale de l'Ordre des Hospitaliers*, 4:292.
138. Musa ibn Muhammad al-Yunini, *Dhayl mirʾat al-zaman*, 3 vols. (Hyderabad: Daʾirat al-Maʿarif al- ʿUthmaniyah, 1954), 2:444.
139. Holt, *Early Mamluk Diplomacy*, 38.
140. Holt, 35.

141. Holt, 36 and fn. 11.
142. Holt, 39.
143. Holt, 54. The word *mamluk* means *property* or *slave*; however, it also came to mean the very particular kind of slave soldier. See al-Qalqashandi, *Subh*, 14:48.
144. Holt, *Early Mamluk Diplomacy*, 54.
145. Holt, 54.
146. Jean Richard notes that the Hospitallers of 'Akkar had made raids from the castle into the neighboring Orontes valley, so it is perhaps peasants of the Orontes valley who came and complained to Baybars. Richard, *The Crusades*, 419.
147. Ibn Jubayr, *Rihlat*, 233.
148. Baybars al-Mansuri, *Zubdat al-fikra*, 106.
149. *Cartulaire générale de l'Ordre des Hospitaliers*, 4:292.
150. This claim is also supported by the treaty concluded between the Armenian king Leo III and the Sultan Qalawun in 1285, which contained provisions that neither party would keep the peasants of the other. Holt, *Early Mamluk Diplomacy*, 102.
151. Al-Yunini, *Dhayl mir'at al-zaman*, 2:450.
152. That is, *mansio Platanus* or today's Mahalibeh Castle sixteen miles north of Latakia.
153. Ibn 'Abd al-Zahir, *Al-Rawd*, 446.
154. Crawford, *Templar of Tyre*, 52.
155. Crawford, 55.
156. Ibn 'Abd al-Zahir, *Al-Rawd*, 281; for the English translation see Ibn al-Furat, *Ayyubids*, 2:102–3. Jonathan Riley-Smith suggests that he was referring to the raid on Mashghara east of Sidon. See Ibn al-Furat, *Ayyubids*, 2:218n3.
157. The English translation is from Ibn al-Furat, *Ayyubids*, 2:103, which is lifted directly from Ibn 'Abd al-Zahir, *Al-Rawd*, 282.
158. Crawford, *Templar of Tyre*, 59.
159. In the Islamic month of Rajab, which lasted between February 2 and March 2, 1272.
160. Ibn al-Furat, *Ayyubids*, 2:157, quoting Ibn 'Abd al-Zahir, *Al-Rawd*, 398.
161. Baybars al-Mansuri also records this episode and the return of the peasants to their villages but dates it to Shaban 669/March 14–April 12, 1271. Rukn al-Din Baybars al-Mansuri, *Mukhtar al-akhbar: tar'ikh al-Dawlah al-Ayyubiyah wa-Dawlat al-Mamalik al-Bahriyah hattá sanat 702 H*, ed. Abd al-Hamid Salih Hamdan (Cairo: al-Dar al-Misriyah al-Lubnaniyah, 1993), 48.
162. Holt, *Early Mamluk Diplomacy*, 86.
163. Holt, 102.
164. Modern Rosh ha-Nikra on the border between Israel and Lebanon.
165. Ibn 'Abd al-Zahir, *Al-Rawd*, 347; English: Ibn al-Furat, *Ayyubids*, 2:133. Jean Richard was skeptical that these events occurred, rather laying the blame for the broken truce on Baybars. *The Crusades*, 443.
166. Ibn Wasil, *Mufarrij*, 5:309.
167. Shirley, *Crusader Syria*, 136–37.
168. Helen Nicholson, *Medieval Warfare* (New York: Palgrave Macmillan, 2004), 129–30.

CHAPTER 3

1. For Jews in Europe, see Leonard B. Glick, *Abraham's Heirs: Jews and Christians in Medieval Europe* (Syracuse: Syracuse University Press, 1999); David Nirenberg, "Conversion, Sex,

and Segregation: Jews and Christians in Medieval Spain," *The American Historical Review* 107 (2002): 1065–93; Jonathan Elukin, *Living Together, Living Apart: Rethinking Jewish-Christian Relations in the Middle Ages* (Princeton, NJ: Princeton University Press, 2007). For Muslims in Europe, see Brian Catlos, *The Victors and the Vanquished: Christians and Muslims of Catalonia and Aragon, 1050–1300* (Cambridge: Cambridge University Press, 2004); Brian Catlos, *Muslims of Medieval Latin Christendom, c.1050–1614* (Cambridge: Cambridge University Press, 2014); Alex Metcalfe, *The Muslims of Medieval Italy* (Edinburgh: Edinburgh University Press, 2009). Also see Nora Berend, *At the Gate of Christendom: Jews, Muslims and "Pagans" in Medieval Hungary, c. 1000–c.1300* (Cambridge: Cambridge University Press, 2001).

2. See Wael B. Hallaq, *A History of Islamic Legal Theories* (Cambridge: Cambridge University Press, 1999) for a good introduction to Islamic law and its theories. See also Muhammad Khalid Masud, Brinkley Messick, and David Powers, eds., *Islamic Legal Interpretation: Muftis and Their Fatwas* (Cambridge, MA: Harvard University Press, 1996); Noel J. Coulson, *A History of Islamic Law* (New Brunswick, NJ: Aldine Transaction, 2011).

3. Joshua Prawer, *Crusader Institutions* (Oxford: Oxford University Press, 1980); Jonathan Riley-Smith, *The Feudal Nobility and the Kingdom of Jerusalem, 1174–1277* (London: Macmillan, 1973), esp. 121–84; idem., "Government and the Indigenous in the Latin Kingdom of Jerusalem," in *Medieval Frontiers: Concepts and Practices*, eds. David Abulafia and Nora Berend (Burlington, VT: Ashgate, 2002), 121–31; Peter W. Edbury, "Law and Custom in the Latin East: Les letres dou sepulcre," *Crusades* 10, no. 1 (1995): 71–79; Peter W. Edbury, "Cultural Encounters in the Latin East. John of Jaffa and Philip of Novara," in *Cultural Encounters During the Crusades*, ed. Kurt Villads Jensen, Kirsi Salonen, and Helle Vogt (Odense: University Press of Southern Denmark, 2013), 229–326.

4. For example, Benjamin Z. Kedar, "The Subjected Muslims of the Frankish Levant," in *Muslims Under Latin Rule, 1100–1300*, ed. James M. Powell (Princeton, NJ: Princeton University Press, 1990), esp. 164–66.

5. The dhimmi system developed under Islam in which non-Muslim communities were granted autonomy in exchange for the payment of an annual *jizya* (head tax) and recognition of their inferior status vis-à-vis Muslims. Each community would be represented by a leader, often a religious leader like a bishop, who would report to the Islamic authorities. For a discussion of this system and how it differed from what the Franks established, see Christopher MacEvitt, *Crusades and the Christian World of the East: Rough Tolerance* (Philadelphia: University of Pennsylvania Press, 2005), 24–25.

6. MacEvitt, *Crusades and the Christian World of the East*, 142–49. Catlos echoing Jean Richard asserts that serfdom was imposed on Muslims in the Latin East: *Muslims of the Medieval Latin Christendom*, 146; Richard, "La seignuerie franque en Syrie et à Chypre: modèle oriental ou modèle occidental?" in *117e Congrès national des sociétés savantes, Clermont-Ferrand, 1992. Histoire medieval* (Paris: CTHS, 1994): 155–66. See also discussion of peasantry in previous chapter.

7. Benjamin Z. Kedar, "On the Origins of the Earliest Laws of Frankish Jerusalem: The Canons of the Council of Nablus, 1120," *Speculum* 74 (1999): 310–35; *Recueil des Historiens des Croisades: Les Assises de Jérusalem*, vol. 2 (Paris: Académie des Inscriptions et Belles-Lettres, 1843); Smbat, *Assises d'Antioche: réproduites en français et publiées au sixième centenaire de la mort de Sempad le connétable, leur ancien traducteur arménien: dédiées à l'Académie des inscriptions et belles-lettres de France par la Société mekhithariste de Saint-Lazare* (Venise: Impr. arménien médaillée, 1876); Myriam Greilsammer, *Le Livre au Roi* (Paris: Académie des Inscriptions et Belles-Lettres, 1995); Philip of Novara, "Le Livre de Forme de Plait," in *Recueil des Historians*

*des Croisades: Les Assises de Jérusalem*, vol. 1 (Paris: Académie des Inscriptions et Belles-Lettres, 1841); John of Ibelin, *Le livre des Assises*, ed. Peter W. Edbury (Leiden: Brill, 2003).

8. Edbury, "Law and Custom," 72, 78.

9. John of Ibelin, *Livre des Assises*, ch. IV, 26.

10. Jonathan Riley-Smith has argued that the *Cour des Suriens* had jurisdiction over all non-Franks; however, more recent treatments of the non-Frankish populations tend to hold that each community had judicial competence in cases involving only members of their own community. Jonathan Riley-Smith, "Some Lesser Officials in Latin Syria," *The English Historical Review* 87, 342 (1972): esp. 2–9; vis-à-vis Christopher MacEvitt, *Crusades and the Christian World of the East*, esp. 151–52.

11. In fact J. J. LaMonte in his translation of Philip of Novara's history actually lists an Islamic Court as an item in the treaty based on the fact that in his letter to Pope Gregory IX, Gerold of Lausanne, the Patriarch of Jerusalem explained that the Saracens "should maintain the Temple of the Lord as previously." Philip of Novara, *The Wars of Frederick II Against the Ibelins in Syria and Cyprus*, trans. John L. LaMonte (New York: Columbia University Press, 1936), 36; *Letters from the East: Crusaders, Pilgrims and Settlers in the 12th-13th Centuries*, trans. Malcolm Barber and Keith Bates (Burlington, VT: Ashgate, 2010), 129–30.

12. Kedar, who discusses him, cautions against taking the one reference to mean that qadis were rare in the kingdom, preferring to interpret this as just another example of our sources failing to be interested enough in the lives of the Muslims under Frankish rule to record information about it. "Subjected Muslims," 141–43.

13. Yaqut Ibn ʿAbd Allah al-Hamawi, *Muʿjam al-udabaʾ: Irshad al-arib ila maʿrifat al-adib*, ed. Ihsan ʿAbbas (Beirut: Dar al-Gharb al-Islami, 1993), 2022–36.

14. Abu al-Mahasin Yusuf Ibn Taghribirdi, *Al-Manhal al-safi waʾl-mustawfa baʿda al-wafi*, ed. Nabil Muhammad Abd al-Aziz, 13 vols. (Cairo: Markaz Tahqiq al-Turath, 1985), 10:41–42.

15. Ibn Taghribirdi, *Al-Manhal*, 10:42.

16. Jamal al-Din Muhammad Ibn Wasil, *Mufarrij al-kurub fi akhbar Bani Ayyub*, ed. Jamal al-Din al-Shayyal, 5 vols. (Cairo: Matbaʿat Dar al-Kutub, 1953–55), 4:241–42.

17. For example, see Kedar, "Subjected Muslims," 173–74; and Richard W. Bulliet, *Conversion to Islam in the Medieval Period: An Essay in Quantitative History* (Cambridge, MA: Harvard University Press, 1979), 135.

18. Anthony Cutler, "Everywhere and Nowhere: The Invisible Muslim and Christian Self-Fashioning in the Culture of Outremer," in *France and the Holy Land: Frankish Culture at the End of the Crusades*, ed. Daniel H. Weiss and Lisa Mahoney (Baltimore: Johns Hopkins University Press, 2004), 253–81; Jaroslav Folda, *Crusader Art in the Holy Land: From the Third Crusade to the Fall of Acre, 1187–1291* (Cambridge: Cambridge University Press, 2005); Annemarie Weyl Carr, "Perspectives on Visual Culture in Early Lusignan Cyprus: Balancing Art and Archaeology," in *Archaeology of the Crusades*, ed. Peter Edbury and Sophia Kalopissi-Verti (Athens: Pieridies Foundation, 2007), 83–110; Jesse W. Izzo, "The Frankish Nobility and the Fall of Acre: Diplomacy, Society, and War in the Latin Kingdom of Jerusalem, c.1240-1291" (PhD dissertation, University of Minnesota, 2016).

19. For a discussion of Mamluk endowment practices in the Levant, see Yehoshua Frenkel, "*Awqaf* in Mamluk Bilad al-Sham," *Mamluk Studies Review* 13 (2009): 149–66.

20. Benjamin Kedar, "Some New Sources on Palestinian Muslims before and during the Crusades," in *Die Kreuzfahrerstaaten als multikulturelle Gesellschaft*, ed. H. E. Mayer (Munich: Oldenbourg, 1997), 130–31. In Sunni Islam, there are four legal "schools" of Islamic interpretation: the Shafiʿi, Hanbali, Hanafi, and Maliki. They are each recognized as authoritative despite

often having quite differing views on issues. In general, what distinguishes them has to do with what sources they prioritize as well as the emphasis they give to analogy in ruling on issues. In the twelfth and thirteenth centuries, the Shafi'i school generally dominated, but members of all four lived in the region.

21. Although we have no named qadis for them, an exception for where Muslim lords were involved in administering justice in Frankish territory was for jointly administered lands known as *condominia* or *munasafat*, which will be discussed in the next chapter.

22. Daniella Talmon-Heller, "'The Cited Tales of the Wondrous Doings of the Shaykhs of the Holy Land' by Diya' al-Din Abu 'Abd Allah Muhammad b. 'Abd al-Wahid al-Maqdisi (569/1173-643/1245): Text, Translation and Commentary," *Crusades* 1 (2002): 111–54.

23. The city of Nablus which served as the administrative center of the region, is located approximately 30 miles north of Jerusalem in what is today the West Bank.

24. For her introduction to the text see Talmon-Heller, "*The Cited Tales*," 111–17.

25. Talmon-Heller, 136.

26. Talmon-Heller, 137–38.

27. Talmon-Heller, 146.

28. Kedar, "Subjected Muslims," 143–45.

29. Joseph Drory, "Hanbalis of the Nablus Region in the Eleventh and Twelfth Centuries," *Asian and African Studies* 22 (1988): 95–96.

30. For overviews of this topic, see Khaled Abou El Fadl, "Islamic Law and Muslim Minorities: The Juristic Discourse on Muslim Minorities from the Second/Eighth to the Eleventh/Seventeenth Centuries," *Islamic Law and Society* 1 (1994): 141–87; Michael Brett, "Muslim Justice under Infidel Rule: The Normans in Ifriqiya 517-555H/1123-1160 AD," *Cahiers de Tunisie* 43 (1995): 325–68; Jean-Pierre Molénat, "Le problème de la permanence des musulmans dans les territoires conquis par les chrétiens, du point de vue de la loi islamique," *Arabica* 48 (2001): 392–400; Sarah Davis-Secord, "Muslims in Norman Sicily: The Evidence of Imam al-Mazari's Fatwas," *Mediterranean Studies* 16 (2007): 46–66.

31. Abou El Fadl, "Islamic Law and Muslim Minorities," 150–51.

32. Abou El Fadl, 162.

33. Abou El Fadl, 152.

34. Abou El Fadl, 157.

35. For the English translation of this account, see Drory, "Hanbalis of the Nablus Region," 96.

36. Imad al-Din al-Isfahani writes that at the time of Saladin's conquest, the majority of the population was Muslim. See Milka Levy-Rubin, "New Evidence Relating to the Process of Islamization in the Palestine in the Early Muslim Period: The Case of Samaria," *Journal of the Economic and Social History of the Orient* 43 (2000): 257–76; and Ronnie Ellenblum, *Frankish Rural Settlement in the Latin Kingdom of Jerusalem* (Cambridge: Cambridge University Press, 1998): esp. 222–33.

37. Ibn Taghribirdi, *Al-Manhal*, 9:273–74. The text reads "before the battle of Hülagü," which I understand to mean the Battle of 'Ayn Jalut, where the Mongol leader Hülagü's army was defeated by the Mamluks of Egypt.

38. Ibn Taghribirdi, 11:48.

39. Ibn Taghribirdi, 9:219–20.

40. Michael Chamberlain tackles this issue in his book *Knowledge and Social Practice in Medieval Damascus, 1190–1350* (Cambridge: Cambridge University Press, 1994), in which he argues that framing the medieval Middle East as lacking formal institutions that resulted in a

scarcity of documents of practice artificially compares the region with Europe. Power, he argues, was held by houses, not institutions, which maintained and gained prestige through practices associated with knowledge production and dissemination. The enormous corpus of literary sources that do survive are evidence for this, and it is through them that society can be better and more accurately accessed.

41. For an overview of fatwas and the law, see Wael B. Hallaq, "From Fatwas to Furuʿ: Growth and Change in Islamic Substantive Law," *Islamic Law and Society* 1 (1994): esp. 28–38.

42. The hadith are sayings attributed to the Prophet Muhammad that were collected by his followers and passed down orally. They play an important role in Islamic jurisprudence.

43. ʿAla al-Din Ibn al-ʿAttar al-Nawawi, *Fatawa al-imam al-nawawi al-musamma al-masaʾil al-manthurah* (Beirut: Dar al-Kutub al-ʿIlmiyah, 1982).

44. al-Nawawi, *Fatawa*, 43.

45. al-Nawawi, 43.

46. Ibn al-Furat, *Ayyubids, Mamlukes and Crusaders: Selections from the Tarikh al-Duwal wa'l-Muluk*, trans. U and M. C. Lyons, 2 vols. (Cambridge: W. Heffer and Sons Ltd., 1971), 1:193; 2:152; Qaratay al-Khazindari, *Tarikh majmuʿ al-nawadir mimma jara lil-awaʾil wa-al-awakhir*, ed. Horst Hein and Muhammad al-Hujairi (Beirut: Klaus Schwarz Verlag, 2005), 145.

47. al-Nawawi, *Fatawa*, 127.

48. Adrian Boas, "Archaeological Sources for the History of Palestine: The Frankish Period: A Unique Medieval Society Emerges," *Near Eastern Archaeology* 61 (1998): 149, 155.

49. Ibn Munqidh tells the story of a Frank who sees that a Muslim bath attendant in Maʿarra shaved his pubic hair off and is so impressed that the Frank has him do it to himself and then his wife. Usama ibn Munqidh, *The Book of Contemplation: Islam and the Crusades*, ed. Paul M. Cobb (London: Penguin, 2008), 149.

50. Al-Nawawi, *Fatawa*, 58.

51. Al-Nawawi, 141–42. The reply is lengthy and involved, but the first action counseled is simply to wait a while to see if as the boys age, they take on obviously distinguishing features.

52. Al-Nawawi, 161.

53. Al-Nawawi, 161.

54. Al-Nawawi, 159.

55. Al-Nawawi, 143.

56. There are five canons directly dealing with relations between different religious groups—in this case between the Franks and "Saracens." Canons 12–15 define the punishments for sexual relations, and Canon 16 forbids Muslims from wearing Frankish clothing. Benjamin Z. Kedar, "On the Origins of the Earliest Laws of Frankish Jerusalem: The Canons of the Council of Nablus, 1120," *Speculum* 74 (1999): 310–35.

57. Kedar, "Canons," 324.

58. With the exception of the *Assises d'Antioche* dating from 1201 to 1219, which survives only as an Armenian translation of the Old French made between 1254 and 1265 in a manuscript dating from 1330 to 1331. They do not have anything to say about Muslims. Smbat, *Assises d'Antioche*.

59. Greilsammer, *Livre au Roi*, ch. 1, 42, 45.

60. See also Greilsammer's comment on the difference in *Livre au Roi*, 195–96, n93.

61. Peter Edbury compared the texts of Philip of Novara and John of Ibelin and emphasized both authors' priority of keeping the High Court an elite space with limited access to Muslims and others. He points to the instances I discuss later in the chapter. "Cultural Encounters in the Latin East. John of Jaffa and Philip of Novara," in *Cultural Encounters During the*

*Crusades*, ed. Kurt Villads Jense, Kirsi Salonen, and Helle Vogt (Odense: University Press of Southern Denmark, 2013), 229–36.

62. John of Ibelin, *Livre des Assises*, ch. 58, 167.

63. *Cour de Bourgeois*, ch. 296; John of Ibelin, *Livre des Assises*, ch. 101, 265.

64. John of Ibelin, ch. 101, 265.

65. John of Ibelin, ch. 48, 149.

66. John of Ibelin, ch. 48, 149.

67. Edbury discusses the additions to the text in the introduction to his edition, John of Ibelin, *Livre des Assises*, 11–15; also *passim*. Peter Edbury, "Reading John of Jaffa," *The Experience of Crusading* 2, ed. Peter Edbury and Jonathan Philips (Cambridge: Cambridge University Press, 2003), 135–57.

68. Philip of Novara, "Livre de Forme de Plait," ch. 62, 533; also John of Ibelin, *Livre des Assises*, ch. 3, 11, 671.

69. For similar legal administration in Aragon, see Brian Catlos, *The Victors and the Vanquished* (Cambridge: Cambridge University Press, 2004), 158–77.

70. The most recent, thorough discussion of this court is Marwan Nader, *Burgess Law in the Latin Kingdoms of Jerusalem and Cyprus (1099–1325)* (Aldershot: Ashgate, 2006).

71. Prawer, *Crusader Institutions*, 284; J. Delaville Le Roulx, *Cartulaire générale*, no. 1167, 2:8–9; no. 2212, 2:536; Reinhold Röhricht, ed., *Regesta Regni Hierosolymitani (1097-1291)* (Oeniponti, 1893–1904), no. 784; no. 1084a.

72. *Cour des Bourgeois*, ch. 65, 54–56.

73. *Cour des Bourgeois*, ch. 65, 55–56.

74. *Cour des Bourgeois*, ch. 241, 172. This kind of oath-taking procedure took place elsewhere in Europe as well.

75. *Cour des Bourgeois*, ch. 241, 171. David Jacoby outlines the office and operation of the court in "The Fonde of Crusader Acre and Its Tariff: Some New Considerations," in *Dei gesta per Francos: Etudes sur les croisades dédiées à Jean Richard*, ed. Michel Balard, Benjamin Z. Kedar, and Jonathan Riley-Smith (Aldershot: Ashgate, 2001), 280.

76. *Cour des Bourgeois*, ch. 241, 171.

77. "Et est tenus, par dreit, de mener auci par raison, si com est establi, le Sarasin come le Surien, et le Surien come le Jude, et le Jude come le Samaritan, et toutes autres manieres de gens, auci come les Crestiens, car ce est dreit et raison par l'asise." *Cour des Bourgeois*, ch. 241, 171; "Car encore seient il Suriens et Grifons, ou Judes, ou Samaritans, ou Nestourins, ou Sarasins, si sont il auci homes come les Frans, et sont tenus de paier et de rendre ce que jugé leur sera, tout auci come est establi en la Cort des Borgeis, en ce livre où est establie toutes raison et toutes droitures por toutes gens." *Cour des Bourgeois*, ch. 241, 172.

78. *Cour des Bourgeois*, ch. 47, 45.

79. *Cour des Bourgeois*, ch. 180, 121. See also Marwan Nader, "Urban Muslims, Latin Laws, and Legal Institutions in the Kingdom of Jerusalem," in *Medieval Encounters* 13 (2007): 260.

80. *Cour des Bourgeois*, ch. 255, 191.

81. *Cour des Bourgeois*, ch. 209, 141–42.

82. Nader, "Urban Muslims," 262–65.

83. In his book on the Jews of the Kingdom of Jerusalem, Prawer indicates that most of the Jews captured in the wake of the First Crusade were sent to Apulia, while the rest were ransomed by the quickly mobilized communities of Egypt and Syria. Yvonne Friedman also indicates that Jews probably ended up ransomed more often than enslaved due to the organized and prompt expenditures of ransom money. Joshua Prawer, *The History of the Jews in the Latin*

*Kingdom of Jerusalem* (Oxford: Clarendon Press, 1988), 26–31, 46; Yvonne Friedman, *Encounter Between Enemies: Captivity and Ransom in the Latin Kingdom of Jerusalem* (Leiden: Brill, 2002), 155n43.

84. *Cour des Bourgeois*, ch. 243, 178. The word used is "Mosserins," which is an unusual way to say "Muslims"; Jean Richard has suggested that it means "merchants from Mosul." Jean Richard, "La confrérie des Mosserins d'Acre et les marchands de Mossoul au XIIIe siècle," *L'Orient syrien* 11 (1966): 254–58.

85. Joshua Prawer, "Social Classes in the Crusader States: The Minorities," in *A History of the Crusades*, ed. Kenneth Setton, Norman P. Zacour, and Harry W. Hazard, 2nd ed., vol. 5 (Madison: University of Wisconsin Press, 1985), 113–14; Prawer, *History of the Jews*, 259–63.

86. Jacoby, "The Fonde of Crusader Acre," 277–93.

87. MacEvitt, *The Crusades and the Christian World of the East*, 137–39.

CHAPTER 4

1. Examples of recent discussions that focus on the twelfth century include Paul M. Cobb, *The Race for Paradise: An Islamic History of the Crusades* (Oxford: Oxford University Press, 2014); S. J. Allen, "The Crusades—A Brief History," in *An Introduction to the Crusades* (Toronto: University of Toronto Press, 2017), 1–60; Jill N. Claster, *Sacred Violence: The European Crusades to the Middle East, 1095–1396* (Toronto: University of Toronto Press, 2009); Christopher Tyerman, *God's War: A New History of the Crusades* (Cambridge: Belknap Press, 2006).

2. Ronnie Ellenblum, *Crusader Castles and Modern Histories* (Cambridge: Cambridge University Press, 2007) *passim*; Rees Davies, "The Medieval State: The Tyranny of a Concept?" *Journal of Historical Sociology* 16 (2003): 280–300; Susan Reynolds, "The Historiography of the Medieval State," in *Companion to Historiography*, ed. Michael Bentley (Abingdon Oxon: Routledge, 1997), 117–38.

3. Ronnie Ellenblum, "Were There Borders and Borderlines in the Middle Ages? The Example of the Latin Kingdom of Jerusalem," in *Medieval Frontiers: Concepts and Practices*, ed. David Abulafia and Nora Berend (Burlington, VT: Ashgate, 2002), 108.

4. Carole Hillenbrand, *The Crusades: Islamic Perspectives* (Edinburgh: Edinburgh University Press, 1999).

5. Cobb, *The Race for Paradise*.

6. The standard work on the topic of the institutions within the Kingdom of Jerusalem is still Joshua Prawer's *Crusader Institutions* (Oxford: Oxford University Press, 1980), which relies primarily on European sources. See also Benjamin Z. Kedar, "The Subjected Muslims of the Frankish Levant," in *Muslims Under Latin Rule, 1100–1300*, ed. James M. Powell (Princeton, NJ: Princeton University Press, 1990), 135–74.

7. Michael Köhler, *Alliances and Treaties Between Frankish and Muslim Rulers in the Middle East: Cross-Cultural Diplomacy in the Period of the Crusades*, trans. Peter M. Holt, revised, edited, and introduced by Konrad Hirschler (Leiden: Brill, 2013); orig. *Allianzen und Verträge zwischen fränkischen und islamischen Herrschern im Vorderen Orient: Eine Studie über das zwischenstaatliche Zusammenleben vom 12. bis ins 13. Jahrhundert* (Berlin: Walter de Gruyter, 1991). See also Yvonne Friedman, "Gestures of Conciliation: Peacemaking Endeavors in the Latin East," in *In Laudem Hierosolymitani. Studies in Crusades and Medieval Culture in Honour of Benjamin Z. Kedar*, ed. Iris Shagrir, Ronnie Ellenblum, and Jonathan Riley-Smith (Aldershot: Ashgate, 2007), 31–48.

8. On the origin of this term, see Köhler, *Alliances and Treaties*, 66.
9. Köhler, *Alliances and Treaties*, 245.
10. See especially Köhler, 267–70.
11. For example, see Jean Richard, *The Crusades, c. 1071–c. 1291* (Cambridge: Cambridge University Press, 1999); Jonathan Riley-Smith, *The Crusades: A Short History* (New Haven, CT: Yale University Press, 1987); Ronnie Ellenblum, *Frankish Rural Settlement in the Latin Kingdom of Jerusalem* (Cambridge: Cambridge University Press, 1998), esp. 37–38.
12. For Norman Sicily, see Alex Metcalfe, *Muslims and Christians in Norman Sicily* (London: Routledge, 2003), 26, 32–34. For Iberia, see Brian Catlos, *The Victors and the Vanquished* (Oxford: Oxford University Press, 2004), 71–120.
13. Köhler, *Alliances and Treaties*, 283–85.
14. John of Ibelin, *Le Livre des Assises*, ed. Peter W. Edbury (Leiden: Brill, 2003).
15. See P. M. Holt's discussion of these sources in his introduction to *Early Mamluk Diplomacy (1260–1290)* (Leiden: Brill, 1995), 1–3; also Frédéric Bauden, "Mamluk Diplomatics: The Present State of Research," in *Mamluk Cairo: A Crossroads for Embassies*, ed. Frédéric Bauden and Malika Dekkiche (Leiden: Brill, 2019), esp. pp. 26–35.
16. Rabei G. Khamisy and Denys Pringle, "Richard of Cornwall's Treaty with Egypt, 1241," in *Crusading and Trading Between West and East: Studies in Honour of David Jacoby*, ed. Sophia Menache, Benjamin Z. Kedar, and Michel Balard (Abingdon: Routledge, 2019), 54–57 and *passim*; Köhler, *Alliances and Treaties*, 269; Stephen Humphreys, "Ayyubids, Mamluks, and the Latin East in the Thirteenth Century," *Mamluk Studies Review* 2 (1998): 8; Paul A. Blaum, "Eagles in the Sun: The Ayyubids after Saladin," *The International Journal of Kurdish Studies* 13 (1999): 122; Jamal al-Din Muhammad Ibn Wasil, *Mufarrij al-kurub fi akhbar bani ayyub*, ed. Jamal al-Din al-Shayyal, 5 vols. (Cairo: Matbaʿat Dar al-Kutub, 1953–55), 3:162.
17. Phillip of Novara, *The Wars of Frederick II Against the Ibelins in Syria and Cyprus*, trans. John L. La Monte (New York: Columbia University Press, 1936), 36.
18. Köhler, *Alliances and Treaties*, 272. Also see Richard, *The Crusades*, 314–17.
19. Ibn Wasil, *Mufarrij*, 4:244.
20. Frederick did act as regent for the kingdom on behalf of his son Conrad, but experienced considerable resistance to attempts to enforce his suzerainty. Nevertheless, the treaty was treated in the same manner as those concluded by elites from the kingdom.
21. Michael Lower, *The Barons' Crusade* (Philadelphia: University of Pennsylvania Press, 2005), 171–75.
22. Richard, *The Crusades*, 329–30.
23. Ann E. Zimo, "Baybars, Naval Power and Mamlūk Psychological Warfare against the Franks," *al-Masāq: Journal of the Medieval Mediterranean* 30, no. 3 (2018): 305.
24. Muhyi al-Din Ibn ʿAbd al-Zahir, *Al-Rawd al-zahir fi sirat al-malik al-zahir*, ed. Abdul-Aziz al-Khuwaytir (Riyadh: al-Khuwaytir, 1976), 398; Ibn al-Furat, *Ayyubids, Mamlukes and Crusaders: Selections from the Tarikh al-duwal wal-Muluk of Ibn al Furat*, trans. U. and M. C. Lyons 2 vols. (Cambridge: W. Heffer and Sons, 1971), 2:157–58; Baybars al-Mansuri, *Zubdat al-fikra fi taʾrikh al-hijra*, ed. D. S. Richards (Beirut: Dar al-Nashr al-Kitab al-ʿArabi, 1998), 134; Peter W. Edbury, "A New Text of the Annales de Terre Sainte," in *In Laudem Hierosolymitani*, ed. Iris Shagrir, Ronnie Ellenblum, and Jonathan Riley-Smith (Aldershot: Ashgate, 2007), 160.
25. Peter Thorau, *The Lion of Egypt*, trans. P. M. Holt (London: Longman, 1992), 167–73; P. M. Holt, *Early Mamluk Diplomacy, 1260–1290: Treaties of Baybars and Qalawun with Christian Rulers* (Leiden: Brill, 1995), 32–33; Ibn ʿAbd al-Zahir, *Al-Rawd*, 182–83.

26. Holt, *Early Mamluk Diplomacy*, 61–62.

27. The issue of the identity of contracting parties is muddied by sources since we only have surviving treaties from the thirteenth century, and information we have for twelfth-century treaties comes from narrative sources. See Yvonne Friedman, "Peacemaking: Perception and practices in the medieval Latin East," in *The Crusades and the Near East: Cultural Histories*, ed. Conor Kostick (London: Routledge, 2011), 229–57; Nakamura Taeko, "The Concepts of Territory in Islamic Law and Thought," in *Territorial Disputes Between Syrian Cities and the Early Crusaders*, ed. Yanagihashi Hiroyuki (London: Kegan Paul International, 2000), 101–24.

28. For example, 1269 with Lady Isabel of Beirut; 1285 with Lady Margaret of Tyre; 1267 and 1271 with the Hospitallers; 1282 with the Templars. The texts in English are in Holt, *Early Mamluk Diplomacy*.

29. Ahmad ibn ʿAli al-Qalqashandi, *Kitab subh al-aʿsha fi sinaʾat al-inshaʾ*, 14 vols. (Cairo: Al-Matbaʿah al-Kubra al-Amiriyah, 1964); Holt, *Early Mamluk Diplomacy*, 1:3–4.

30. al-Qalqashandi, *Subh*, 14:3.

31. Brian Catlos, *Muslims of Medieval Latin Christendom, c. 1050–1614* (Cambridge: Cambridge University Press, 2014), twelfth-century Castile and León: 21; twelfth-century Aragon: 32–33; thirteenth century: 54, 56–57.

32. al-Qalqalshandi, *Subh*, 14: 7; Holt, *Early Mamluk Diplomacy*, 4.

33. Ibn al-Furat, *Ayyubids*, 1:164; 2:129; Baybars al-Mansuri in his two short accounts of the treaty rather less respectfully calls him "Hugh son of Henri lord (*sahib*) of Cyprus and Akka." Baybars al-Mansuri, *Zubdat*, 115–16; Baybars al-Mansuri, *Mukhtar al-akhbar: tarikh al-dawla al-ayyubiyya wa-dawla al-mamalik al-bahriyya hatta sanat 702 AH*, ed. Abd al-Hamid Salih Hamdan (Cairo: al-Dar al-Misriyya al-Lubnaniyya, 1993), 37–38.

34. Holt, *Early Mamluk Diplomacy*, 97; Ibn ʿAbd al-Zahir, *Tashrif al-Ayyam wa al-ʿusur fi sirat al-Malik al-Mansur*, ed. Murad Kamil (Cairo: al-Sharika al-ʿarabiyya lil-ṭibaʿa wa-al-nashr, 1961), 95.

35. Holt translates *jalila* here as *exalted*, however I have chosen to keep *majesty*, which he used for King Leo's treaty for consistency's sake. Holt, *Early Mamluk Diplomacy*, 109; Ibn ʿAbd al-Zahir, *Tashrif*, 104.

36. al-Qalqashandi does not give the name, so this quotation is a combination of Holt's translation of the formula with my insertion of the actual names. Holt, *Early Mamluk Diplomacy*, 44; Arabic in al-Qalqashandi, *Subh*, 14:39–42.

37. Ibn ʿAbd al-Zahir, *Al-Rawd*, 383.

38. Baybars al-Mansuri, *Zubdat al-fikra*, 210; Holt, *Early Mamluk Diplomacy*, 62.

39. Ibn ʿAbd al-Zahir, *Al-Rawd*, 313.

40. Holt, *Early Mamluk Diplomacy*, 62.

41. "al-muqaddam al-kabir al-humam fulan muqaddam bayt al-isbitar al-fulani bi Akka, wa-l-bilad al-sahiliyya." Holt translates this less literally. Holt, *Early Mamluk Diplomacy*, 34; al-Qalqashandi, *Subh*, 14:31.

42. "al-mubashir al-muqaddam al-jalil ifrir auldkal muqaddam jamiʿ bayt isbitar sirjuan bi-l-bilad al-sahiliyya." The Arabic "al-mubashir" in al-Qalqashandi is a word for a Mamluk bureaucrat instead of the more usual transliteration *al-mastar* for *master*. See Holt, *Early Mamluk Diplomacy*, 49; al-Qalqashandi, *Subh*, 14:42.

43. Ibn ʿAbd al-Zahir, *Tashrif*, 20. See also Holt, *Early Mamluk Diplomacy*, 66.

44. Holt, 74; Ibn ʿAbd al-Zahir, *Tashrif*, 34–35.

45. Letter 73 in Malcolm Barber and Keith Bate, trans., *Letters from the East* (Farnham: Ashgate, 2010), 160–61.

46. Ibn al-Furat, *Ayyubids*, 2:43; Baybars al-Mansuri, *Zubdat al-fikra*, 67; See also Thorau, *Lion of Egypt*, 143.

47. Paul Crawford, *The "Templar of Tyre" Part III of the "Deeds of the Cypriots"* (Aldershot: Ashgate, 2003), 37; Laura Minervini, ed. and trans., *Cronaca del Templare di Tiro (1243–1314): la caduta degli stati crociati nel racconto di un testimone oculare* (Naples: Liguori, 2000), 86.

48. Janet Shirley, *Crusader Syria in the Thirteenth Century: The* Rothelin *Continuation of the History of William of Tyre with Part of the Eracles or Acre Text* (Aldershot: Ashgate, 1999), 118–19.

49. Ibn al-Furat, *Ayyubids*, 2:42.

50. Ibn ʿAbd al-Zahir, *Al-Rawd*, 63–64.

51. Crawford, *Templar of Tyre*, 37; Minervini, *Cronaca*, 86.

52. Blaum, "Eagles in the Sun," 128.

53. Jean de Joinville, "Life of Saint Louis," in *Chronicles of the Crusades*, trans. Caroline Smith (Penguin Classics, 2009), 254–55.

54. Shirley, *Crusader Syria*, 109; Joinville, "Life of Saint Louis," 256–59.

55. Shirley, 53.

56. Shirley, 55–57.

57. Kamal al-Din Ibn al-ʿAdim, *Bughyat al-talab fi tarikh Halab*, ed. S. Zakkar, 11 vols. (Damascus [s.n.], 1988–89), 4356–57. See also, David Morray, *An Ayyubid Notable and His World: Ibn al-ʿAdim and Aleppo as Portrayed in His Biographical Dictionary of People Associated with the City* (Leiden: Brill, 1994), 116–18.

58. See Stephen Humphreys, *From Saladin to the Mongols: The Ayyubids of Damascus, 1193–1260* (Albany: State University of New York Press, 1977), 301.

59. Ibn Wasil, *Mufarrij*, 4:242.

60. Muhammad Ibn Shaddad, *Ta'rikh al-Malik al-Zahir* (Weisbaden: Franz Steiner Verlag, 1983), 113.

61. Thorau, *Lion of Egypt*, 53. According to Joinville, a "Faracataye" or Faris al-Din Aqtay, was responsible for the killing of the Sultan Turanshah at the Egyptian encampment at Fariskur on 2 May 1250. Joinville, "Life of Saint Louis," 233.

62. Ibn al-Furat, *Ayyubids*, 2:43; Baybars al-Mansuri, *Zubdat al-fikra*, 67.

63. Yvonne Friedmann, *Encounter Between Enemies: Captivity and Ransom in the Latin Kingdom of Jerusalem* (Leiden: Brill, 2002), *passim*.

64. See also Holt, *Early Mamluk Diplomacy*, 6–8.

65. Holt, 8; al-Qalqashandi, *Subh*, 14:71.

66. *Letters from the East*, no. 63, 130. He also declares that it was customary for there to be a third-party guarantor, but this was done without in order to avoid having the contents of the sealed treaty read aloud and explained. The necessity of a third party, however, is not upheld by the Arabic sources.

67. Ibn al-Furat, *Ayyubids*, 1:131; 2:104. This also happened with the 659/1261 treaty with Acre: Ibn al-Furat, 1:53; 2:44.

68. Ibn al-Furat, 1:199–200; 2:157–58.

69. Ibn ʿAbd al-Zahir, *Al-Rawd*, 333. For the English translation, see Ibn al-Furat, *Ayyubids*, 2:130.

70. Ibn ʿAbd al-Zahir calls this Frank "the wazir" and Riley-Smith suggests this might have been the seneschal who would have been Geoffrey of Sergines at the time. Ibn al-Furat, *Ayyubids*, 2:233 note 2.

71. Ibn ʿAbd al-Zahir, *Al-Rawd*, 447; Ibn al-Furat, *Ayyubids*, 1:209; 2:164.

72. Prince Edward of England arrived in the Levant in 1271 as part of the crusading contingent who continued on from Tunis after the death of Louis IX there in August 1270.

73. Holt, *Early Mamluk Diplomacy*, 44; Ibn al-Furat, *Ayyubids*, 2:164. Ibn ʿAbd al-Zahir's Arabic is ambiguous as to whether the treaty was formed by Hamo giving Isabel to Baybars's care, or whether that act was subsequent to (presumably) the treaty of 1269.

74. Holt, *Early Mamluk Diplomacy*, 44.

75. Among other things, there was a land dispute over the village of La Fauconnerie. Richard, *The Crusades*, 448.

76. Thorau, *Lion of Egypt*, 234.

77. Ibn ʿAbd al-Zahir, *Al-Rawd*, 443–45; Ibn al-Furat, *Ayyubids*, 2:164–65.

78. Ibn ʿAbd al-Zahir, *Al-Rawd*, 443–45; Ibn al-Furat, *Ayyubids*, 2:164–65. Citing the same sources, Thorau relates it as two hundred Muslim prisoners and 2,000 dinars: *Lion of Egypt*, 234.

79. Köhler, *Alliances and Treaties*, 319.

80. For a discussion of the Frankish evidence, see Köhler, 312–13.

81. For example, ʿImad al-Din al-Isfahani and Ibn al-Athir. Köhler, *Alliances and Treaties*, 315–16.

82. Köhler, 317–18.

83. Ronnie Ellenblum, *Crusader Castles and Modern Histories* (Cambridge: Cambridge University Press, 2007), 129n28.

84. Ibn Wasil, *Mufarrij*, 4:233–35. The treaty of 682/1283 between Qalawun and the Kingdom specifies that while Sidon, the citadel, town and surrounding territory was Frankish property "the whole of the mountain settlements" belonged to the sultan and his son. Holt, *Early Mamluk Diplomacy*, 88–89.

85. Jonathan Riley-Smith, who provided the notes to the partial English translation of Ibn al-Furat, suggests that this was Peter of Avelon, lord of Adelo and Constable of Tiberias. Ibn al-Furat, *Ayyubids*, 45-46, en. 5.

86. Ibn al-Furat, 2:97–98.

87. Ibn ʿAbd al-Zahir, *Al-Rawd*, 389; Baybars al-Mansuri, *Zubdat*, 130–31; Ibn al-Furat, *Ayyubids*, 2:154.

88. Ibn ʿAbd al-Zahir, *Al-Rawd*, 398; Ibn al-Furat, *Ayyubids*, 2:157–58. Baybars al-Mansuri gives a brief notice in *Zubdat*, 134. This is the same treaty referenced in the previous section in which the sultan sent the emir Fakhr al-Din Ayaz al-Muqri and al-Sadr Fath al-Din Ibn al-Qaysarani to administer to oath to the king.

89. Ibn al-Furat, *Ayyubids*, 2:66; Baybars al-Mansuri, *Zubdat*, 87.

90. Ibn al-Furat, *Ayyubids*, 2:166.

91. Holt, *Early Mamluk Diplomacy*, 34; al-Qalqashandi, *Subh*, 14:31–39.

92. Holt, *Early Mamluk Diplomacy*, 35.

93. Holt, 36.

94. Holt, 50.

95. Holt, 50.

96. Holt, 51, 56.

97. Holt, 64; Baybars al-Mansuri, *Zubdat*, 211.

98. Holt, *Early Mamluk Diplomacy*, 64.

99. Translation my own. Ibn Wasil, *Mufarrij*, 3:233.

100. Jonathan Riley-Smith, *The Crusades: A Short History* (New Haven, CT: Yale University Press, 1987), 192.

101. Ibn Wasil, *Mufarrij*, 5:67–68.

Notes to Pages 132–138

102. Ibn Wasil, 5:67.
103. Baybars al-Mansuri, *Zubdat*, 266. For a briefer notice that mentions complaints from the sultan's deputies in Syria, see Baybars al-Mansuri, *Mukhtar al-Akhbar*, 87.
104. Crawford, *Templar of Tyre*, 96.
105. Riley-Smith, *The Crusades*, 204.
106. al-Qalqashandi, *Subh*, 14:34. See also, Holt, *Early Mamluk Diplomacy*, 36.
107. Holt, 113–14.
108. Holt, 36–37.
109. The treaty goes on to provide for the situation in which no pledge was taken. If the person owing the tax goes into Hospitaller territory, it is their responsibility to collect the entire tax and return half to the sultan and vice versa.
110. Holt, *Early Mamluk Diplomacy*, 39–40; al-Qalqashandi, *Subh*, 14:35. Another ra'is named Abd al-Masih (Abdelmessie), presumably an ancestor, is referenced in an 1174 Hospitaller document as having three parts of the village, J. Delaville le Roulx, *Cartulaire générale*, no. 457, 1: 313–14; Joshua Prawer, *Crusader Institutions* (Oxford: Clarendon Press, 1980), 207–8.
111. Holt, *Early Mamluk Diplomacy*, 37; al-Qalqashandi, *Subh*, 14:39.
112. Holt, *Early Mamluk Diplomacy*, 56.
113. Holt, 35.
114. Holt, 52.
115. Holt, 115.
116. Holt, 39; al-Qalqashandi, *Subh*, 14:35.
117. Holt, *Early Mamluk Diplomacy*, 40; al-Qalqashandi, *Subh*, 14:37.
118. al-Qalqashandi, 14:38n1.
119. Holt, *Early Mamluk Diplomacy*, 41. The same held in the 682/1283 treaty between Qalawun and the Latin Kingdom; compensation would be according to the rank of the slain, and there would be a forty-day period of investigation. Holt, 82.
120. Holt suspects this should probably be a hundred dirhams as the approximate exchange was 20 dirhams for the dinar. Although given the value placed on peasants and how fiercely elites competed for them, it is tempting to read it as is. Holt, 115.
121. This set-up seems to have been standard as it was provided for in the 1269/677 treaty between Baybars and Lady Isabel of Beirut. Holt, 46.
122. Holt, 53–54.
123. The Arabic and the English translation are very vague. The idea is that those placed on oath are accordingly made responsible for compensation that would be extracted by the *wali*. See al-Qalqashandi, *Subh*, 14:58.
124. Holt, *Early Mamluk Diplomacy*, 83. The document also goes on to provide for when the accuser claims more was stolen than actually was.
125. Ibn ʿAbd al-Zahir, *Al-Rawd*, 283–84; Ibn al-Furat, *Ayyubids*, 2:104–5.
126. Thorau, *Lion of Egypt*, 178; Holt, *Early Mamluk Diplomacy*, 42–43.
127. Holt, 46.
128. This incident was mentioned in Chapter 2. Thorau, *Lion of Egypt*, 221; Baybars al-Mansuri, *Zubdat*, 134.
129. Ibn ʿAbd al-Zahir, *Al-Rawd*, 399–400; Ibn al-Furat, *Ayyubids*, 2:158.
130. It is unclear to which treaty he might have been referring. There was the temporary truce to plant and harvest the land from 1263. There was also a truce with Jaffa from 1261. The Franks from Acre had attempted to make a truce at the same time as Jaffa, but that fell through when they refused to return their Muslim prisoners. See Thorau, *Lion of Egypt*, 144–46.

131. Ibn ʿAbd al-Zahir, *Al-Rawd*, 201; also Ibn al-Furat, *Ayyubids*, 2:67.
132. Zimo, "Baybars, Naval Power and Mamlūk Psychological Warfare," 304–16. This incident is referenced briefly toward the beginning of the chapter as well.
133. Baybars al-Mansuri, *Mukhtar al-Akhbar*, 52–53. Also, Ibn ʿAbd al-Zahir, *Al-Rawd*, 430–31.
134. Baybars al-Mansuri, *Mukhtar al-Akhbar*, 53.
135. Peter W. Edbury, *The Kingdom of Cyprus and the Crusades, 1191–1374* (Cambridge: Cambridge University Press, 1991), 91.
136. Zimo, "Baybars, Naval Power, and Mamlūk Psychological," 310–12.
137. Philip of Novara, *The Wars of Frederick II Against the Ibelins in Syria and Cyprus*, trans. John LaMonte (New York: Columbia University Press, 1936), 118; *Guerra di Federico II in Oriente (1223–1242)*, ed. Silvio Melani (Naples: Liguori, 1994), 146 and 148; Shirley, *Crusader Syria*, 13.
138. Richard, *The Crusades*, 319.
139. Ellenblum, "Were There Borders and Borderlines in the Middle Ages?," 105–19.
140. For example, Joshua Prawer, *Crusader Institutions* (Oxford: Oxford University Press, 1980).
141. Köhler, *Alliances and Treaties*, 316–18.

CHAPTER 5

1. Benjamin Z. Kedar, "The Subjected Muslims of the Frankish Levant," in *Muslims Under Latin Rule, 1100–1300*, ed. James M. Powell (Princeton, NJ: Princeton University Press, 1990), 174.
2. Kurt Weitzmann, "Thirteenth Century Crusader Icon on Mount Sinai," *The Art Bulletin* 45, no. 3 (1963): 179–203; "Icon Painting in the Crusader Kingdom," *Dumbarton Oaks Papers* 20 (1966): 49–83.
3. Anthony Cutler, "Everywhere and Nowhere: The Invisible Muslim and Christian Self-Fashioning in the Culture of Outremer," in *France and the Holy Land: Frankish Culture at the End of the Crusades*, ed. Daniel H. Weiss and Lisa Mahoney (Baltimore: Johns Hopkins University Press, 2004), 253–81; Scott Redford, "On Sâqîs and Ceramics: Systems of Representation in the Northeast Mediterranean," in *France and the Holy Land*, 282–312.
4. Jonathan Rubin, *Learning in a Crusader City: Intellectual Activity and Intercultural Exchanges in Acre, 1191–1291* (Cambridge: Cambridge University Press, 2018).
5. Rubin, *Learning in a Crusader City*, 4.
6. Brendan Goldman, *Camps of the Uncircumcised: The Cairo Geniza and Jewish Life in the Latin Kingdom of Jerusalem* (Philadelphia: University of Pennsylvania Press, forthcoming).
7. Susan B. Edgington, "Espionage and Military Intelligence During the First Crusade, 1095–99," in *Crusading and Warfare in the Middle Ages: Realities and Representations. Essays in Honour of John France*, ed. Simon John and Nicholas Morton (Farnham: Ashgate, 2014), 75–85.
8. Reuven Amitai, "Mamlūk Espionage among Mongols and Franks," *Asian and African Studies* 22 (1988): 173–81.
9. ʿIzz al-Din Ibn al-Athir, *The Chronicle of Ibn al-Athir for the Crusading Period from al-Kamil fi'l-taʾrikh. Part 2 The Age of Nur al-Din and Saladin*, trans. D. S. Richards (Aldershot: Ashgate, 2007), 39.

10. Jean de Joinville, "Life of Saint Louis," in *Chronicles of the Crusades*, trans. Caroline Smith (New York: Penguin Classics, 2009), 198–99; Marino Sanudo Torsello, *The Book of the Secret of the Faithful of the Cross*, trans. Peter Lock (Farnham: Ashgate, 2011), 346.

11. Baybars al-Mansuri, *Mukhtar al-akhbar: Tar'ikh al-dawla al-ayyubiyya wa al-dawla al-mamalik al-bahriyya hatta sanat 703 AH*, ed. ʿAbd al-Hamid Salih Hamdan (Cairo: Dar al-Misriyya al-Lubnaniyya, 1993), 20.

12. ʿIzz al-Din Ibn al-Athir, *The Chronicle of Ibn al-Athir for the Crusading Period from al-Kamil fi'l-ta'rikh. Part 1 The Coming of the Franks and the Muslim Response*, trans. D. S. Richards (Aldershot: Ashgate, 2006), 67.

13. Janet Shirley, trans., *Crusader Syria in the Thirteenth Century: The* Rothelin *Continuation of the History of William of Tyre with Part of the Eracles or Acre Text* (Aldershot: Ashgate, 1999), 94–95.

14. Jonathan Riley-Smith, "Some Lesser Officials in Latin Syria," *English Historical Review* 87:342 (1972): 16–19, 20–25.

15. Christopher MacEvitt, *The Crusades and the Christian World of the East: Rough Tolerance* (Philadelphia: University of Pennsylvania Press, 2008), 22–24, 101, 104.

16. MacEvitt, *The Crusades*, 102–4.

17. Edgington, "Espionage and Military Intelligence," 78.

18. Malcolm Barber and Keith Bate, eds., *Letters to the East, Pilgrims and Settlers in the 12th–13th Centuries* (Burlington, VT: Ashgate, 2010), 101.

19. Paul Crawford, trans., *The "Templar of Tyre" Part III of the "Deeds of the Cypriots"* (Aldershot: Ashgate, 2003), 51.

20. Crawford, *Templar of Tyre*, 50; Laura Minervini ed. and trans., *Cronaca del Templare di Tiro (1243–1314): La caduta degli stati crociati nel racconto di un testimone oculare* (Naples: Liguori, 2000), 108.

21. Ibn ʿAbd al-Zahir, *Al-Rawd*, 260; Nasir al-Din Muhammad Ibn al-Furat, *Ayyubids, Mamlukes and Crusaders: Selections from the Tarikh al-Duwal wa'l-Muluk*, trans. U. and M. C. Lyons, 2 vols. (Cambridge: W. Heffer and Sons, 1971), 2:94.

22. Edgington, "Espionage and Military Intelligence," 164–65.

23. Crawford, *Templar of Tyre*, 63; Minervini, *Cronaca*, 132.

24. Crawford, *Templar of Tyre*, 63–64.

25. Crawford, *Templar of Tyre*, 68; Minervini, *Cronaca*, 140.

26. Michael Lower, *The Tunis Crusade of 1270: A Mediterranean History* (Oxford: Oxford University Press, 2018), 182.

27. Crawford, *Templar of Tyre*, 69.

28. Ibn ʿAbd al-Zahir, *Al-Rawd*, 401; Ibn al-Furat, *Ayyubids*, 2:159.

29. Usama Ibn Munqidh, *The Book of Contemplation: Islam and the Crusades*, trans. Paul M. Cobb (New York: Penguin, 2008), 142–43.

30. Reuven Aharoni, "Bedouin and Mamluks in Egypt—Co-existence in a State of Duality," in *Mamluks in Egyptian and Syrian Politics and Society*, ed. Michael Winter and Amalia Levanoni (Leiden: Brill, 2004), 412. For the Franks, see Jochen G. Schenk, "Nomadic Violence in the First Latin Kingdom of Jerusalem and the Military Orders," *Reading Medieval Studies* 36 (2010): 39–55.

31. Ibn al-Athir, *The Chronicle Part 1*, 62.

32. Ibn al-Athir, 256–58.

33. English from Ibn al-Furat, *Ayyubids*, 2:159; Ibn ʿAbd al-Zahir, *Al-Rawd*, 401.

34. Ibn al-Athir, *The Chronicle Part 1*, 179.

35. Crawford, *Templar of Tyre*, 98–99; Minervini, *Cronaca*, 194.

36. Linda Northrup, *From Slave to Sultan: The Career of Al-Manṣūr Qalāwūn and the Consolidation of Mamluk Rule in Egypt and Syria (678–689 A.H./1279–1290 A.D.)* (Stuttgart: Franz Steiner Verlag, 1998), 187, 208.

37. Crawford, *Templar of Tyre*, 102; Minervini, *Cronaca*, 200.

38. Crawford, *Templar of Tyre*, 103; Minervini, *Cronaca*, 200.

39. Jamal al-Din Muhammad Ibn Wasil, *Mufarrij al-kurub fi akhbar bani ayyub*, ed. Jamal al-Din al-Shayyal, 5 vols. (Cairo: Matba'at Dar al-Kutub, 1953–55), 3:145–46.

40. Ibn al-Furat, *Ayyubids*, 1:15, 2:13.

41. Hubert Darke, trans., *The Book of Government or Rules for Kings: The Siyar al-Muluk or Siyasat-nama of Nizam Al-Mulk* (London: Routledge, 2002), 74–75.

42. Ibn al-Athir, *Chronicle Part 1*, 131.

43. Ibn al-Athir, *Chronicle Part 2*, 113.

44. Amitai, "Mamluk Espionage," 177.

45. Muhyi al-Din Ibn 'Abd al-Zahir, *Tashrif al-ayyam wa al-'usur fi sirat al-malik al-mansur*, ed. Murad Kamil (Cairo: Al-Sharika al-'arabiyya lil-tiba'a wa-al-nashr, 1961), 59, 114.

46. Crawford, *Templar of Tyre*, 64; Minervini, *Cronaca*, 132.

47. Ibn 'Abd al-Zahir, *Al-Rawd*, 397.

48. Amitai, "Mamluk Espionage," 178.

49. Amitai, 178–79.

50. Crawford, *Templar of Tyre*, 102; Minervini, *Cronaca*, 200.

51. Rukn al-Din Baybars al-Mansuri, *Zubdat al-fikra fi ta'rikh al-hijra*, ed. D. S. Richards (Berlin: Dar al-Nashr al-Kitab al-'Arabi, 1998), 270; Baybars al-Mansuri, *Kitab al-tuhfa al-mulukiyya fi al-dawla al-turkiyya*, ed. 'Abd al-Hamid Salih Hamdan (Cairo: Dar al-Misriyya al-Lubnaniyya, 1987), 122; Shafi' bin 'Ali Ibn Asakir, *Kitab al-fadl al-ma'thur min sirat al-sultan al-malik al-mansur*, ed. Umar Tadmuri (Beirut: al-Maktabah al-'Asriyah, 1998), 174; Northrup, *From Slave to Sultan*, 156–57.

52. Kedar, "The Subjected Muslims the Frankish Levant," 157–58; Riley-Smith, "Some Lesser Officials in Latin Syria," 22–23.

53. Hussein M. Attiya, "Knowledge of Arabic in the Crusader States in the Twelfth and Thirteenth Centuries," *Journal of Medieval History* 25, no. 3 (1999): 203–13.

54. I believe that the evidence supports a wider knowledge of spoken Arabic by the Franks than Lewis envisions. Kevin James Lewis, "Medieval Diglossia: The Diversity of the Latin Christian Encounter with Written and Spoken Arabic in the 'Crusader' County of Tripoli, with a Hitherto Unpublished Arabic Notes from the Principality of Antioch (MS, AOM 3, Valletta: National Library of Malta, no. 51v)," *al-Masaq* 27, no. 2 (2015): 119–52. See also Charles F. Briggs, "Literacy, Reading, and Writing in the Medieval West," *Journal of Medieval History* 26, no. 4 (2000): 397–420; Alan Forey, "Literacy and Learning in the Military Orders during the Twelfth and Thirteenth Centuries," in *The Military Orders, Volume 2 Welfare and Warfare*, ed. Helen Nicholson, 185–206 (Aldershot: Ashgate, 1998).

55. Attiya, "Knowledge of Arabic," 206.

56. Judith M. Upton-Ward, *The Rule of the Templars: The French Text of the Rule of the Order of the Knights Templar* (Rochester, NY: Boydell Press, 2008), 39, 44, 47, 49, 50; Henri de Curzon, *La règle du Temple* (Paris: Librairie Renouard, H. Laurens, successeur, 1886), 75, 86–87, 94, 100, 102–3.

57. Rubin, *Learning in a Crusader City*, 62–70.

58. Crawford, *Templar of Tyre*, 68; Ibn ʿAbd al-Zahir, *Al-Rawd*, 401; Ibn al-Furat, *Ayyubids*, 2:159.

59. Crawford, *Templar of Tyre*, 50; Minervini, *Cronaca*, 108.

60. Crawford, *Templar of Tyre*, 54; Minervini, *Cronaca*, 116.

61. Crawford, *Templar of Tyre*, 104; Minervini, *Cronaca*, 204.

62. Piers D. Mitchell, *Medicine in the Crusades: Warfare, Wounds and the Medieval Surgeon* (Cambridge: Cambridge University Press, 2004), 206–8.

63. Rubin, *Learning in a Crusader City*, 66–67; see also Gustav Ineichen, "Il glossario arabo-francese di messer Guglielmo e maestro Giacomo," *Atti dell'Instituto Veneto di Scienze, Lettere ed Arti* 130 (1971–72), 353–407.

64. Ineichen, "Il glossario," 363.

65. Ahmad ibn al-Qasim Ibn Abi Usaybiʿah, *ʿUyun al-anbaʾ fi tabaqat al-atibba*' (Beirut: Dar Maktabat al-Hayah, 1965), 651–59.

66. Ibn Abi Usaybiʿah, *ʿUyun al-anba*', 654.

67. Ibn Abi Usaybiʿah, *ʿUyun al-anba*', 697–99.

68. Ibn Abi Usaybiʿah, *ʿUyun al-anba*', 587–89.

69. Ibn Abi Usaybiʿah, *ʿUyun al-anba*', 699–703.

70. Ibn al-ʿAdim, *Bughyat al-talab*, 2926–32; a shorter biography is also in Yaqut Ibn ʿAbd Allah al-Hamawi, *Muʿjam al-ʿudabaʾ: Irshad al-arib ila maʿrifat al-adib*, ed. Ihsan ʿAbbas, 7 vols. (Beirut: Dar al-Gharb al-Islami, 1993), 5:1208–10.

71. Ibn al-ʿAdim, *Bughyat al-talab*, 2928.

72. Ibn al-ʿAdim, *Bughyat al-talab*, 2928–29.

73. William of Tyre, *Chronicon*, ed. R.B.C. Huygens (Turnhout: Brepols, 1986), 2: 859–60. See also Piers D. Mitchell's commentary in *Medicine in the Crusades*, 212–16.

74. As I write, a significant portion of my country's population doubts that experts from the CDC or WHO are best placed to help us manage the COVID-19 pandemic.

CHAPTER 6

1. Kamal al-Din ʿUmar Ibn Ahmad Ibn al-ʿAdim, *Bughyat al-talab fi taʾrikh Halab*, ed. Suhayl Zakkar 11 vols. (Damascus: [s.n.] 1988–89), 1821. English translation by David Morray, *An Ayyubid Notable and His World* (Leiden: Brill, 1994), 63.

2. Denys Pringle, *The Churches of the Crusader Kingdom of Jerusalem: A Corpus*, vol. 3 (Cambridge: Cambridge University Press, 2007), 265.

3. Perhaps most famously encapsulated by Maria Rosa Menocal's *The Ornament of the World: How Muslims, Jews, and Christians Created a Culture of Tolerance in Medieval Spain* (Boston: Little, Brown and Co., 2002).

4. Samuel England, *Medieval Empires and the Culture of Competition: Literary Duels at Islamic and Christian Courts* (Edinburgh: Edinburgh University Press, 2019), 4–5.

5. England, *Medieval Empires*, 5–6.

6. He quotes Akbari, "the binary opposition of East and West, fundamental to Said's theory, cannot be projected back onto a Middle Ages which seldom conceived the world as bipartite." England, 8. For an important contribution to the discussion that England does not engage with, perhaps due it having been published shortly before his own book, and which in some ways disagrees or at least complicates the matter, see Geraldine Heng, *The Invention of Race in the European Middle Ages* (Cambridge: Cambridge University Press, 2018), in particular

Heng's discussion of the continental European construction of the "Saracen" in her third chapter "War/Empire" pp.110–80.

7. England, 9.

8. England, 9–10.

9. Cobb's introduction to Usama Ibn Munqidh, *The Book of Contemplation: Islam and the Crusades*, trans. Paul. M. Cobb (New York: Penguin 2008), xxxi–xxxvi. For example, Nicholas Morton, *The Crusader States & Their Neighbours: A Military History, 1099–1187* (Oxford: Oxford University Press, 2020); Benjamin Z. Kedar, "The Subjected Muslims of the Frankish Levant," in *Muslims under Latin Rule, 1100–1300*, ed. James M. Powell (Princeton, NJ: Princeton University Press, 1990), 135–74.

10. England, *Medieval Empires*, 4–5, 10–11.

11. Adrian Gully, *The Culture of Letter-Writing in Premodern Islamic Society* (Edinburgh: Edinburgh University Press, 2008), 5.

12. Gully, *Culture of Letter-Writing*, 7.

13. Gully, 10.

14. Gully, 29–49.

15. Gully, 8.

16. Marie Favereau, "Comment le sultan mamlouk s'adressait au khan de la Horde d'Or. Formulaire des lettres et règles d'usage d'après trois manuels de chancellerie (1262–v. 1430)," *Annales Islamologiques* 41 (2007): 85–88.

17. Gully, *Culture of Letter-Writing*, 133.

18. Meaning the letter should be written in the elevated, literary register of Arabic, not the vernacular as spoken in daily life.

19. Gully, *Culture of Letter-Writing*, 32.

20. Gully, 17.

21. Gully, 18.

22. Gully, 19.

23. Favereau, "Comment le sultan mamlouk," 73–74.

24. Favereau, 73.

25. Favereau, 89–92.

26. Muhyi al-Din Ibn ʿAbd al-Zahir, *Al-Rawd al-zahir fi sirat al-malik al-zahir*, ed ʿAbd al-ʿAziz al-Khuwaytir, 309–13 (Riyadh: al-Khuwaytir, 1976). See also Baybars al-Mansuri, *Zubdat*, 112–14; Ibn al-Furat, *Ayyubids*, 1:155–59; 2:122–25.

27. Ibn ʿAbd al-Zahir, *Al-Rawd*, 387–88. See also Baybars al-Mansuri, *Zubdat*, 130; Ibn al-Furat, *Ayyubids*, 1:188–89; 2:152–53.

28. Ibn ʿAbd al-Zahir, *Al-Rawd*, 376. See also, Baybars al-Mansuri, *Zubdat*, 127–28.

29. Ibn ʿAbd al-Zahir, *Al-Rawd*, 380–81. See also Ibn al-Furat, *Ayyubids*, 1:188–88; 2:148–49.

30. "Al-qumis al-jalil, al-mubajjal, al-muʿazzaz, al-humam, al-asad al-dirgham, fakhr al-umma al-masihiyya, raʾis al-taʾifa al-salibiyya, kabir al-umma al-ʿIsawiyya bimand," Ibn ʿAbd al-Zahir, *Al-Rawd*, 309. Translation my own. See also Chapter 4 for discussion of titles and the political landscape.

31. "al-malik awak dalzinial," Ibn ʿAbd al-Zahir, *Al-Rawd*, 387.

32. Ibn ʿAbd al-Zahir, 309. Translation adapted from Ibn al-Furat, *Ayyubids*, 2:122.

33. Ibn ʿAbd al-Zahir, *Al-Rawd*, 312; Ibn al-Furat, *Ayyubids*, 2:124.

34. 78:40 trans. Abdullah Yusuf Ali.

35. Ibn al-Furat, *Ayyubids*, 2:124–25.

36. Ibn al-Furat, 2:122.

37. Ibn ʿAbd al-Zahir, *Al-Rawd*, 380; Ibn al-Furat, *Ayyubids*, 2:148–49.
38. Ibn al-Furat, 2:148–49.
39. Iris Shagrir, "Urban Soundscape: Defining Space and Community in Twelfth Century of Jerusalem," in *Communicating the Middle Ages. Essays in Honour of Sophia Menache*, ed. Iris Shagrir, Benjamin Kedar, and Michel Balard (London: Routledge, 2018), 108.
40. Ibn al-Furat, *Ayyubids*, 2:149.
41. Ibn al-Furat, 2:149.
42. Ibn ʿAbd al-Zahir, *Al-Rawd*, 376; Baybars al-Mansuri, *Zubdat*, 127–28; Ibn al-Furat, *Ayyubids*, 2:146.
43. Ibn al-Furat, 2:146.
44. Ibn al-Furat, 2:146.
45. Gully, *Culture of Letter-Writing*, 155.
46. Ann E. Zimo, "Baybars, Naval Power and Mamlūk Psychological Warfare against the Franks," *al-Masāq* 30, no. 3 (2018): 304–16.
47. Ibn ʿAbd al-Zahir, *Al-Rawd*, 387. Translation my own.
48. English translation from Ibn al-Furat, *Ayyubids*, 2:153.
49. Ibn al-Furat, 2:153.
50. Ibn al-Furat, 2:153.
51. Ibn al-Furat, 2:154.
52. David Ayalon, "The Mamluks and Naval Power: A Phase of the Struggle between Islam and Christian Europe," in *Medieval Ships and Warfare*, ed. Susan Rose (Aldershot: Ashgate, 2008), 227–28; Albrecht Fuess, *Verbranntes Ufer: Auswirkungen mamlukischer Seepolitik auf Beirut und die syro-palästinensiche Küste (1250–1517)* (Leiden: Brill, 2001); idem, "Rotting Ships and Razed Harbors: The Naval Policy of the Mamluks," *Mamluk Studies Review* 5 (2001): 45–71.
53. Ibn al-Furat, *Ayyubids*, 2:154.
54. Crawford, *Templar of Tyre*, 104; Minervini, *Cronaca*, 204.
55. Crawford, *Templar of Tyre*, 104–5.
56. Gully, *Culture of Letter-Writing*, 149.
57. Gully, 18.
58. For how a similar process of acculturation worked in peacemaking diplomacy, see Yvonne Friedman, "Peacemaking Perceptions and practices in the medieval Latin East," in *The Crusades and the Near East: Cultural Histories*, ed. Conor Kostick (London: Routledge, 2011), 229–57.
59. A few of the important recent and earlier studies include Osman Latiff, *The Cutting Edge of the Poet's Sword: Muslim Poetic Responses to the Crusades* (Leiden: Brill, 2017); Nizar F. Hermes, *The [European] Other in Medieval Arabic Literature and Culture, Ninth-Twelfth Century AD* (New York: Palgrave-Macmillan, 2012); Carole Hillenbrand, "Jihad Propaganda in Syria from the Time of the First Crusade until the Death of Zengi: The Evidence of Monumental Inscriptions," in *The Frankish Wars and Their Influence on Palestine*, ed. Khalil Athamina and Roger Heacock (Birzeit: Birzeit University Publications, 1994), 60–69; Hadia Dajani-Shakeel, "*Jihad* in Twelfth-Century Arabic Poetry: A Moral and Religious Force to Counter the Crusades," *Muslim World* 66 (1976): 96–113.
60. Latiff, *Cutting Edge*, 30–33, 93–97.
61. Latiff, 32.
62. Hermes, *[European] Other*, 138.
63. Hermes, 159–60.
64. Latiff, *Cutting Edge*, 135–36.

65. See Chapter 3.

66. Taef El-Azhari, *Zengi and the Muslim Response to the Crusades: The Politics of Jihad* (Abingdon: Routledge, 2016), 1.

67. Ibn al-ʿAdim, *Bughyat al-talab*, 1159. Translation my own.

68. Steven Runciman, *A History of the Crusades*, vol. 2 (Harmondsworth UK: Penguin, 1972), 326; William of Tyre, *Chronicon* (Turnhout: Brepols, 1986), vol. 2, 772.

69. Another in the same source was written in defiance of the Third Crusade. Latiff, *Cutting Edge*, 91–93, 108.

70. Latiff, 108.

71. Yusuf Ibn Taghribirdi, *Al-Manhal al-safi wa'l-mustawfa baʿda al-wafi*, ed. Nabil Muhammad Abd al-Aziz (Cairo: Markaz Tahqiq al-Turath), vol. 10, 163.

72. Hermes, *[European] Other*, 152.

73. Latiff, *Cutting Edge*, 214.

74. Latiff, 215.

75. Latiff translates line 5 as "If souls could ransom themselves then I would surely ransom myself and this is the thought of every Muslim," but I agree with the anonymous reviewer that the verb should instead be read as passive as it makes more sense grammatically and I thank them for bringing this reading to my attention. Latiff, 215.

76. Ibn al-ʿAdim, *Bughyat al-talab*, 1820–21. See also David Morray, *An Ayyubid Notable and His World* (Leiden: Brill, 1994), 62–63, under al-Ruhān al-Maghribī.

77. Ibn al-Furat, *Ayyubids*, 1:3–4; 2:3.

78. English translation by Morray, *An Ayyubid Notable*, 63.

79. Ibn al-ʿAdim, *Bughyat al-talab*, 1821. English translation by Morray, *An Ayyubid Notable*, 63.

80. Ibn al-ʿAdim, *Bughyat al-talab*, 1821. English translation by Morray, *An Ayyubid Notable*, 63.

81. They had switched sides and had been supporting al-Salih Ismaʿil. Paul A. Blaum, "Eagles in the Sun: The Ayyubids after Saladin," *The International Journal of Kurdish Studies* 13, no. 1 (1999): 160.

82. For what is known about Bartholomew, see Robert Irwin, "The Mamluk Conquest of the County of Tripoli," in *Crusade and Settlement: Papers Read at the First Conference of the Society for the Study of the Crusades and the Latin East and Presented to R.C. Smail*, ed. Peter W. Edbury (Cardiff: University College Cardiff Press, 1985), 248–49.

83. Thorau, *Lion of Egypt*, 208; Runciman, *History of the Crusades*, vol. 3, 334.

84. Northrup, *From Slave to Sultan*, 131–32.

85. Muhyi al-Din Ibn ʿAbd al-Zahir, *Tashrif al-ayyam wa al-ʿusur fi sirat al-malik al-mansur*, ed. Murad Kamil (Cairo: al-Sharika al-ʿarabiyya lil-ṭibaʿa wa-al-nashr, 1961), 88–90.

86. Ibn ʿAbd al-Zahir, *Tashrif al-ayyam*, 90. Translation my own.

87. Jesse W. Izzo, "The Revolts of the Embriaco and the Fall of the County of Tripoli," *The Haskins Society Journal* 27 (2015): 149–60. For al-Yunini's account in his obituary of Guy II Embriaco, see Irwin, "County of Tripoli," 247. Crawford, *Templar of Tyre*, 78–79.

88. Samer M. Ali, *Arabic Literary Salons in the Islamic Middle Ages: Poetry, Public Performance, and the Presentation of the Past* (Notre Dame: University of Notre Dame Press, 2010), 15–59.

89. Discussed and translated in Lewis, "Medieval Diglossia," 136.

90. Ibn al-ʿAdim, *Bughyat al-talab*, 1140–41.

91. Ibn al-ʿAdim, 1141. Translation my own.

92. Carl Brockelmann, *History of the Arabic Written Tradition Supplement*, vol. 1 (Leiden: Brill, 1996), 135.

93. Usama Ibn Munqidh, *The Book of Contemplation: Islam and the Crusades*, trans. Paul M. Cobb (New York: Penguin, 2008).

94. Ibn Munqidh, *Book of Contemplation*, 217.

95. Ibn Munqidh, xxv.

96. Ibn Munqidh, xxix–xxx.

97. Latiff, *Cutting Edge*, 40.

98. See Paul Cobb's discussion in Ibn Munqidh, *Book of Contemplation*, xxxi–xxxvi.

99. England, *Medieval Empires and the Culture of Competition*, 10. For the full story, see Ibn Munqidh, "Franks That Are Acclimatized Are Better," in *Book of Contemplation*, 153–54.

100. Ibn Munqidh, xvi.

101. Paul M. Cobb, "Infidel Dogs: Hunting Crusaders with Usama ibn Munqidh," *Crusades* 6 (2007): 57–68.

102. Cobb, "Infidel Dogs," 64. "The Franks (may God confound them) have none of the human virtues except for courage"; Ibn Munqidh, *Book of Contemplation*, 76.

103. Ibn Munqidh, 34–35.

104. Ibn Munqidh, 36.

105. Ibn Munqidh, 36.

106. Ibn Munqidh, 37.

107. Ibn Munqidh, 20, 279n42. See Usama ibn Munqidh, *Kitab al-I'tibar*, ed. Philip K. Hitti (Princeton, NJ: Princeton University Press, 1930), 12.

108. Ibn Munqidh, *Book of Contemplation*, 35; *Kitab al-I'tibar*, 26.

109. Monica Balda, "Le Bédouin face au citadin dans la "Rihla" d'Ibn Gubayr: portrait d'une civilisation urbaine," *Bulletin d'études orientales* 55 (2003), 14.

110. Ibn Munqidh, *Book of Contemplation*, 92–93; *Kitab al-I'tibar*, 80. The father is also called "lord" or *sahib*.

111. Ibn Munqidh, *Book of Contemplation*, 93.

112. Ibn Munqidh, 93.

113. Ibn Munqidh, 114.

114. Ibn Munqidh, 72–74.

115. Ibn Munqidh, 62.

116. Ibn Munqidh, 76, 144.

117. Ibn Munqidh, 147.

118. Ibn Munqidh, 205–6.

119. Ibn Munqidh, 219.

120. Ibn Munqidh, 211.

# Bibliography

PRIMARY SOURCES

Barber, Malcolm, and Keith Bate, eds. *Letters from the East: Crusaders, Pilgrims and Settlers in the 12th-13th Centuries.* Burlington, VT: Ashgate, 2010.
Baybars al-Mansuri, Rukn al-Din. *Kitab al-tuhfa al-mulukiyya fi al-dawla al-turkiyya*, ed. 'Abd al-Hamid Salih Hamdan. Cairo: Al-Dar al-Misriyya al-Lubnaniyya, 1987.
———. *Mukhtar al-akhbar: ta'rikh al-dawla al-ayyubiyya wa dawla al-mamalik al-bahriyya hatta sanat 702 AH*, ed. 'Abd al-Hamid Salih Hamdan. Cairo: Al-Dar al-Misriyya al-Lubnaniyya, 1993.
———. *Zubdat al-fikra fi ta'rikh al-hijra*, ed. D. S. Richards. Berlin: Dar al-Nashr al-Kitab al-'Arabi, 1998.
Benjamin of Tudela. *The Itinerary of Benjamin of Tudela*, ed. and trans. Marcus N. Adler. New York: P. Feldheim, 1907.
Bresc-Bautier, Genviève, ed. *Le Cartulaire du Chapitre du Saint-Sépulchre de Jérusalem.* Paris: Paul Geuthner, 1984.
Burchardus de Monte Sion. *Descriptio Terrae Sanctae, Peregrinatores Medii Aevi Quatuor: Brochardus de Monte Sion, Ricoldus de Monte Crucis, Odoricus de Foro Julii, Willebrandus de Oldenburg*, ed. J.C.M. Laurent. 2nd ed. Leipzig: J. C. Hinrichs, 1873.
Crawford, Paul, trans. *The "Templar of Tyre" Part III of the "Deeds of the Cypriots."* Aldershot: Ashgate, 2003.
Darke, Hubert, trans. *The Book of Government or Rules for Kings: The Siyar al-Muluk or Siyasatnama of Nizam Al-Mulk.* London: Routledge, 2002.
Delaville Le Roulx, J., ed. *Cartulaire générale de l'Ordre des Hospitaliers de Saint Jean de Jérusalem, 1100-1310.* 4 vols. Paris: E. Leroux, 1894–1906.
Edbury, Peter W., ed. "A New Text of the *Annales de Terre Sainte.*" In *In Laudem Hierosolymitani*, ed. I. Shagrir, R. Ellenblum, J. Riley-Smith, 145–62. Aldershot: Ashgate, 2007.
Goitein, S. D. *Letters of Medieval Jewish Traders.* Princeton, NJ: Princeton University Press, 1973.
Greilsammer, Myriam, ed. *Le Livre au Roi.* Paris: Académie des Inscriptions et Belles-Lettres, 1995.
Al-Hamawi, Yaqut Ibn 'Abd Allah. *Mu'jam al-udaba': Irshad al-arib ila ma'rifat al-adib*, ed. Ihsan 'Abbas. 7 vols. Beirut: Dar al-Gharb al-Islami, 1993.
Al-Harawi, Ali ibn Abi Bakr. *Lonely Wayfarer's Guide to Pilgrimage*, ed. Josef Meri. Princeton, NJ: Darwin Press, 2005.
Hennes, Johann Heinrich, ed. *Codex Diplomaticus Ordinis S. Mariae Theutonicorum.* 2 vols. Mainz: Kirchheim, Schott und Theilmann, 1845–61.
Henri de Curzon. *La règle du Temple.* Paris: Librairie Renouard, H. Laurens, successeur, 1886.

Holt, P. M., trans. *Early Mamluk Diplomacy, 1260–1290: Treaties of Baybars and Qalawun with Christian Rulers*. Leiden: Brill, 1995.

Ibn ʿAbd al-Zahir, Muhyi al-Din. *Al-Rawd al-zahir fi sirat al-malik al-zahir*, ed. ʿAbd al-ʿAziz al-Khuwaytir. Riyadh: al-Khuwaytir, 1976.

———. *Tashrif al-ayyam wa al-ʿusur fi sirat al-malik al-mansur*, ed. Murad Kamil. Cairo: al-Sharika al- ʿarabiyya lil-tibaʿa wa-al-nashr, 1961.

Ibn Abi Usaybiʿah, Ahmad ibn al-Qasim. *ʿUyun al-anba' fi tabaqat al-atibba'*. Beirut: Dar Maktabat al-Hayah, 1965.

Ibn al-ʿAdim, Kamal al-Din ʿUmar Ibn Ahmad. *Bughyat al-talab fi tar'ikh Halab*, ed. Suhayl Zakkar, 11 vols. Damascus: [s.n.], 1988–89.

Ibn al-Athir, ʿIzz al-Din. *The Chronicle of Ibn al-Athir for the Crusading Period from al-Kamil fi'l-ta'rikh*. 3 vols. Trans. D. S. Richards. Aldershot: Ashgate, 2006–2008.

Ibn al-Furat, Nasir al-Din Muhammad. *Ayyubids, Mamlukes and Crusaders: Selections from the Tarikh al-duwal wal-Muluk of Ibn al Furat*, trans. U. and M. C. Lyons. 2 vols. Cambridge: W. Heffer and Sons, 1971.

———. *Ta'rikh al-duwal wa'l-muluk*. Vol. 4, ed. Al-Shamma. Basra: Dar al-Tibaʿah al-Hadithah, 1967; Vol. 7, ed. Zuraiq. Beirut: al-Matbaʿah al-Amirkaniyah, 1942; Vol. 8, ed. Zuraiq and ʿIzz al-Din. Beirut: Al-Matbaʿah al-Amirkaniyah, 1939; Vol. 9, pt. 1, ed. Zuraiq. Beirut: al-Matbaʿah al-Amirkaniyah, 1936; Vol. 9, pt. 2, ed. ʿIzz al-Din. Beirut: Al-Matbaʿah al-Amirkaniyah, 1938.

———. *Ta'rikh al-duwal wa'l-muluk*. Vienna, Österreichische Nationalbibliothek. MS A.F. 117–25; Vatican, Vatican Library. MS Vat. Ar. 720.

Ibn ʿAsakir, Shafiʿ bin ʿAli. *Kitab al-fadl al-ma'thur min sirat al-sultan al-malik al-mansur*, ed. Umar Tadmuri. Beirut: Al-Maktabah al-ʿAsriyah, 1998.

Ibn Jubayr, Muhammad bin Ahmad. *Rihlat Ibn Jubayr*. Beirut: Dar Sadir lil-Tibaʿah wa-al-Nashr, 1964.

———. *The Travels of Ibn Jubayr*, trans. R.J.C. Broadhurst. London: Jonathan Cape, 1952.

Ibn Munqidh, Usama. *The Book of Contemplation: Islam and the Crusades*, trans. Paul M. Cobb. New York: Penguin, 2008.

———. *Kitab al-I'tibar*, ed. Philip K. Hitti. Princeton, NJ: Princeton University Press, 1930.

Ibn Shaddad, ʿIzz al-Din Muhammad. *Ta'rikh al-malik al-zahir*, ed. Ahmad Hutait. Wiesbaden, Franz Steiner Verlag, 1983.

Ibn Taghribirdi, Abu al-Mahasin Yusuf. *Al-Manhal al-safi wa'l-mustawfa baʿda al-wafi*, ed. Nabil Muhammad Abd al-Aziz. 13 vols. Cairo: Markaz Tahqiq al-Turath, 1985.

Ibn Wasil, Jamal al-Din Muhammad. *Mufarrij al-kurab fi akhbar bani Ayyub*, ed. Mohamed Rahim, *Die Chronik des ibn Wāṣil Kritische Edition des letzten Teils (646/1248–659/1261) mit Kommentar*. Arabische Studien 6 Wiesbaden: Harrassowitz, 2010.

———. *Mufarrij al-kurub fi akhbar bani ayyub*, ed. Jamal al-Din al-Shayyal. 5 vols. Cairo: Matbaʿat Dar al-Kutub, 1953–55.

The Institute for Ismaili Studies. "The Safar-nama of Nasir Khusraw." The Institute for Ismaili Studies. http://nasirkhusraw.iis.ac.uk.

Jean de Joinville. "Life of Saint Louis." In *Chronicles of the Crusades*, trans. Caroline Smith. New York: Penguin Classics, 2009.

John of Ibelin. *Le Livre des Assises*, ed. Peter W. Edbury. Leiden: Brill, 2003.

Kedar, Benjamin Z., ed. "Urban IV on Saracens and Jews Asking to Convert at Acre, Orvieto, July 26, 1264." In *Crusade and Mission: European Approaches Toward the Muslims*, ed. Benjamin Z. Kedar, 215. Princeton, NJ: Princeton University Press, 1984.

Al-Khazindari, Qirtay. *Tarikh majmu' al-nawadir mimma jara lil-awa'il wa-al-awakhir*, ed. Horst Hein and Muhammad al-Hujairi. Beirut: Klaus Schwarz Verlag, 2005.

LeStrange, Guy. *Palestine Under the Moslems: A Description of Syria and the Holy Land from A.D. 650 to 1500*. London: Alexander P. Watt, 1890.

"Lettre à Charles d'Anjou sur les affaires de Terre Sainte (Acre, 22 avril 1260)." In *Bibliothèque de l'école des chartes*. LXXXVII Paris: 1917, 489.

*Livre des Assises de la Cour des Bourgeois*. In *Recueil des Historiens des Croisades*. Vol. 2. Paris: Académie des Inscriptions et Belles-Lettres, 1843.

Marino Sanudo Torsello. *The Book of the Secret of the Faithful of the Cross*, trans. Peter Lock. Farnham: Ashgate, 2011.

Mayer, Hans E. *Die Urkunden der lateinischen Könige von Jerusalem*. Hannover: Hahnsche Buchhandlung, 2010.

Minervini, Laura, ed. and trans. *Cronaca del Templare di Tiro (1243–1314): La caduta degli stati crociati nel racconto di un testimone oculare*. Naples: Liguori, 2000.

Morray, David, trans. *An Ayyubid Notable and His World: Ibn al-'Adim and Aleppo as Portrayed in his Biographical Dictionary of People Associated with the City*. Leiden: Brill, 1994.

Al-Nawawi, 'Ala al-Din Ibn al-'Attar. *Fatawa al-imam al-nawawi al-musamma al-masa'il al-manthurah*. Beirut: Dar al-Kutub al-'Ilmiyah, 1982.

Philip of Novara. *Le Livre de Forme de Plait*, ed. Peter W. Edbury. Nicosia: Cyprus Research Centre, 2009.

———. "Le Livre de Forme de Plait." In *Recueil des Historians des Croisades: Les Assises de Jérusalem*. Vol. 1. Paris: Académie des Inscriptions et Belles-Lettres, 1841.

———. *The Wars of Frederick II Against the Ibelins in Syria and Cyprus*, trans. John L. LaMonte. New York: Columbia University Press, 1936.

Al-Qalqashandi, Ahmad ibn 'Ali. *Kitab subh al-a'sha fi sina'at al-insha'*. 14 vols. Cairo: Al-Matba'ah al-Kubra al-Amiriyah, 1964.

Röhricht, Reinhold, ed. *Regesta Regni Hierosolymitani (1097–1291)*. 2 vols. Oeniponti, 1893–1904.

Shirley, Janet, trans. *Crusader Syria in the Thirteenth Century: The Rothelin Continuation of the History of William of Tyre with Part of the Eracles or Acre Text*. Aldershot: Ashgate, 1999.

Smbat. *Assises d'Antioche: réproduites en français et publiées au sixième centenaire de la mort de Sempad le connétable, leur ancien traducteur arménien: dédiées à l'Académie des inscriptions et belles-lettres de France par la Société mekhithariste de Saint-Lazare*. Venice: Imprimerie arménien médaillée, 1876.

Stewart, Aubrey, ed. and trans. "Burchard of Mount Sion A.D. 1280." In *Library of the Palestine Pilgrims Text Society*. Vol. 12. London, 1896.

Strehlke, Ernst, ed. *Tabulae Ordinis Theutonici, ex Tabularii Regii Berolinenesis Codice Potissimum*. Berolini: [s.n.], 1869.

Tafel, G.L.F., and G. M. Thomas, eds. *Urkunden zur älteren Handels- und Staatsgeschichte der Republik Venedig mit besonderer Beziehung auf Byzanz und die Levante*. Vienna: Hof- und Staatsdruckerei, 1956.

Talmon-Heller, Daniella, ed. and trans. "'The Cited Tales of the Wonderous Doings of the Shaykhs of the Holy Land' by Diya' al-Din Abi 'Abd Allah Muhammad b. 'Abd al-Wahid al-Maqdisi (569/1173-643/1245): Text, Translation and Commentary." *Crusades* 1 (2002): 111–54.

Upton-Ward, Judith M. *The Rule of the Templars: The French Text of the Rule of the Order of the Knights Templar*. Rochester, NY: Boydell Press, 2008.

William of Tyre. *Chronicon*, ed. R.B.C. Huygens. Turnholt: Brepols, 1986.

———. *A History of Deeds Done Beyond the Sea*, trans. Emily A. Babcock and August C. Krey. 2 vols. New York: Columbia University Press, 1943.

Al-Yunini, Musa ibn Muhammad. *Dhayl mir'at al-zaman*. 3 vols. Hyderabad: Da'irat al-Ma'arif al-'Urthmaniyah,1954.

SECONDARY SOURCES

Abou El Fadl, Khaled. "Islamic Law and Muslim Minorities: The Juristic Discourse on Muslim Minorities from the Second/Eighth to the Eleventh/Seventeenth Centuries." *Islamic Law and Society* 1 (1994): 141–87.

Aharoni, Reuven. "Bedouin and Mamluks in Egypt—Co-existence in a State of Duality." In *Mamluks in Egyptian and Syrian Politics and Society*, ed. Michael Winter and Amalia Levanoni, 407–34. Leiden: Brill, 2004.

Aldsworth, Fred, George Haggarty, Sarah Jennings, and David Whitehouse. "Medieval Glassmaking at Tyre, Lebanon." *Journal of Glass Studies* 44 (2002): 49–66.

Ali, Samer M. *Arabic Literary Salons in the Islamic Middle Ages: Poetry, Public Performance, and the Presentation of the Past*. Notre Dame: University of Notre Dame Press, 2010.

Amitai, Reuven. "Mamlūk Espionage Among Mongols and Franks." *Asian and African Studies* 22 (1988): 173–81.

———. *Mongols and Mamluks: The Mamluk-Īlkhānid War, 1260–1281*. Cambridge: Cambridge University Press, 1995.

Asbridge, Thomas. *The First Crusade: A New History*. New York: Oxford University Press, 2004.

Attiya, Hussein M. "Knowledge of Arabic in the Crusader States in the Twelfth and Thirteenth Centuries." *Journal of Medieval History* 25, no. 3 (1999): 203–13.

Avni, Gideon. *The Byzantine-Islamic Transition in Palestine: An Archaeological Approach*. Oxford: Oxford University Press, 2014.

Ayalon, David. "The Mamluks and Naval Power: A Phase of the Struggle between Islam and Christian Europe." In *Medieval Ships and Warfare*, ed. Susan Rose, 223–34. Aldershot: Ashgate, 2008.

———. *Le phénomène mamelouk dans l'Orient islamique*. Paris: Presses Universitaires de France, 1996.

Bachrach, David. "Review of *The Social Structure of the First Crusade*." *Speculum* 84 (2009): 739–40.

Balard, Michel. "L'empire génois au Moyen Age." In *Les Empires. Antiquité et Moyen Ages. Analyse comparée*, ed. F. Hurlet, 181–97. Rennes: Presses universitaires de Rennes, 2008.

———. *La Méditerranée médiévale. Espace, itinéraires, comptoirs*. Paris: Picard, 2006.

———. *Les Latins en Orient, XIe–XVe Siècle*. Paris: Presses Universitaires de France, 2006.

Balda, Monica. "Le Bédouin face au citadin dans la 'Rihla' d'Ibn Gubayr: Portrait d'une civilisation urbaine." *Bulletin d'études orientales* 55 (2003): 11–26.

Baram, Uza. "The Development of Historical Archaeology in Israel: An Overview and Prospects." *Historical Archaeology* 36 (2002): 12–29.

Berend, Nora. *At the Gate of Christendom: Jews, Muslims and "Pagans" in Medieval Hungary, c. 1000–c.1300*. Cambridge: Cambridge University Press, 2001.

Beyer, Gustav. "Die Kreuzfahrergebiete Akko und Galileae." *Zeitschrift des deutschen Palästina-Vereins* 67 (1945): 183–260.

Benvenisti, Meron. *The Crusaders in the Holy Land*. Jerusalem: Israel Universities Press, 1976.

Blaum, Paul A. "Eagles in the Sun: The Ayyubids after Saladin," *The International Journal of Kurdish Studies* 13 (1999): 105–80.
Boas, Adrian J. "Archaeological Sources for the History of Palestine: The Frankish Period: A Unique Medieval Society Emerges." *Near Eastern Archaeology* 61 (1998): 138–73.
———. *Crusader Archaeology: The Material Culture of the Latin East*. London: Routledge, 1999.
———. "Domestic Architecture in the Frankish Kingdom of Jerusalem." PhD dissertation, Hebrew University, 1995.
———. "Three Stages in the Evolution of Rural Settlement in the Kingdom of Jerusalem During the Twelfth Century." In *In Laudem Hierosolymitani: Studies in Crusades and Medieval Culture in Honour of Benjamin Z. Kedar*, ed. Iris Shagrir, Ronnie Ellenblum, and Jonathan Riley-Smith, 77–92. Aldershot: Ashgate, 2007.
Blumenkranz, Bernhard. *Juifs et Chrétiens dans le Monde Occidental, 430-1096*. Paris: Mouton & Co., 1960.
Borchardt, Karl. "Zucker und Mohren: zur Krise der Johanniter auf Zypern im 15. Jahrhundert." *Ordines Militares—Colloquia Torunensia Historica* 16 (2011): 191–212.
Bradley, Matthew. "Preliminary Assessment of the Medieval Christian Burials from Tel Jezreel." *Levant* 26 (1994): 63–65.
Brett, Michael. "Muslim Justice under Infidel Rule: The Normans in Ifriqiya 517–555H/1123–1160 AD." *Cahiers de Tunisie* 43 (1995): 325–68.
———. "The Spread of Islam in Egypt and North Africa." In *Northern Africa: Islam and Modernization*, ed. M. Brett, 1–2. London: Frank Cass, 1973.
Briggs, Charles F. "Literacy, Reading, and Writing in the Medieval West." *Journal of Medieval History* 26, no. 4 (2000): 397–420.
Brockelmann, Carl. *History of the Arabic Written Tradition Supplement*. Vol. 1. Leiden: Brill, 1996.
Bronstein, Judith. *The Hospitallers and the Holy Land: Financing the Latin East 1187–1274*. Woodbridge: Boydell Press, 2005.
Brundage, James A. "Intermarriage between Christians and Jews in Medieval Canon Law." *Jewish History* 3 (1988): 25–40.
Buck, Andrew D. *The Principality of Antioch and Its Frontiers in the Twelfth Century*. Woodbridge: Boydell and Brewer, 2017.
Bulliet, Richard W. *Conversion to Islam in the Medieval Period: An Essay in Quantitative History*. Cambridge, MA: Harvard University Press, 1979.
Burman, Thomas E. *Reading the Qur'an in Latin Christendom, 1140-1560*. Philadelphia: University of Pennsylvania Press, 2007.
Cahen, Claude. "Ayyubids." In *Encyclopaedia of Islam*, 2nd ed. Brill Reference Online. Accessed March 15, 2023.
———. "An Introduction to the First Crusade." *Past and Present* 6 (1954): 6–30.
Carlson, Thomas. "Contours of Conversion: The Geography of Islamization in Syria, 600–1500." *Journal of American Oriental Society* 135, no. 4 (2015): 791–816.
Carr, Annemarie Weyl. "Perspectives on Visual Culture in Early Lusignan Cyprus: Balancing Art and Archaeology." In *Archaeology of the Crusades*, ed. Peter Edbury and Sophia Kalopissi-Verti, 83–110. Athens: Pierides Foundation, 2007.
Catlos, Brian. *Muslims of Medieval Latin Christendom, c.1050–1614*. Cambridge: Cambridge University Press, 2014.
———. *The Victors and the Vanquished: Christians and Muslims of Catalonia and Aragon, 1050–1300*. Cambridge: Cambridge University Press, 2004.

Chamberlain, Michael. *Knowledge and Social Practice in Medieval Damascus, 1190–1350.* Cambridge: Cambridge University Press, 1994.
Chéhab, Maurice H. *Tyr à l'époque des croisades*, 2 vols. Paris: A. Maisonneuve, 1979.
Claster, Jill. *Sacred Violence: The European Crusades to the Middle East, 1095–1396.* Toronto: University of Toronto Press, 2009.
Cobb, Paul. "Infidel Dogs: Hunting Crusaders with Usama ibn Munqidh." *Crusades* 6 (2007): 57–68.
———. *The Race for Paradise: An Islamic History of the Crusades.* Oxford: Oxford University Press, 2014.
Constable, Olivia Remie. *Housing the Stranger in the Mediterranean World: Lodging, Trade, and Travel in Late Antiquity and the Middle Ages.* Cambridge: Cambridge University Press, 2003.
Coulson, Noel J. *A History of Islamic Law.* New Brunswick, NJ: Aldine Transaction, 2011.
Cutler, Anthony. "Everywhere and Nowhere: The Invisible Muslim and Christian Self-Fashioning in the Culture of Outremer." In *France and the Holy Land: Frankish Culture at the End of the Crusades*, ed. Daniel H. Weiss and Lisa Mahoney, 253–81. Baltimore: Johns Hopkins University Press, 2004.
Dajani-Shakeel, Hadia. "*Jihad* in Twelfth-Century Arabic Poetry: A Moral and Religious Force to Counter the Crusades." *Muslim World* 66 (1976): 96–13.
Davies, Rees. "The Medieval State: The Tyranny of a Concept?" *Journal of Historical Sociology* 16 (2003): 280–300.
Davis-Secord, Sarah. "Muslims in Norman Sicily: The Evidence of Imam al-Mazari's Fatwas." *Mediterranean Studies* 16 (2007): 46–66.
Drory, Joseph. "Hanbalis of the Nablus Region in the Eleventh and Twelfth Centuries." *Asian and African Studies* 22 (1988): 93–112.
Edbury, Peter W. "Cultural Encounters in the Latin East. John of Jaffa and Philip of Novara." In *Cultural Encounters During the Crusades*, ed. Kurt Villads Jensen, Kirsi Salonen, and Helle Vogt, 229–36. Odense: University Press of Southern Denmark, 2013.
———. *John of Ibelin and the Kingdom of Jerusalem.* Woodbridge: Boydell Press, 1997.
———. "Law and Custom in the Latin East: Les letres dou sepulcre." *Crusades* 10, no. 1 (1995): 71–79.
———. *The Kingdom of Cyprus and the Crusades, 1191–1374.* Cambridge: Cambridge University Press, 1991.
———. "Philip of Novara and the Livre de Forme de Plait." In *Praktika tou Tritou Diethnous Kypriologikou Synedriou: Leukosia, 16–20 Aprilou 1996*, ed. Georgios Ioannides, 3:555–65. 3 vols. Nicosia: Hetaireia Kypriakon Spoudon, 2001.
———. "Reading John of Jaffa." In *The Experience of Crusading 2*, ed. Peter Edbury and Jonathan Philips, 135–57. Cambridge: Cambridge University Press, 2003.
Eddé, Anne-Marie. "Kamal al-Din 'Umar Ibn al-'Adim." In *Medieval Muslim Historians and the Franks in the Levant*, ed. Alex Mattlett, 109–35. Boston: Brill, 2014.
———. *Saladin.* Cambridge, MA: Belknap Press, 2011.
Edgington, Susan B. "Espionage and Military Intelligence During the First Crusade, 1095-99." In *Crusading and Warfare in the Middle Ages: Realities and Representations. Essays in Honour of John France*, ed. Simon John and Nicholas Morton, 75–85. Farnham: Ashgate, 2014.
Edgington, Susan B., and Sarah Lambert, eds. *Gendering the Crusades.* New York: Columbia University Press, 2002.
El-Azhari, Taef. *Zengi and the Muslim Response to the Crusades: The Politics of Jihad.* Abingdon: Routledge, 2016.

Ellenblum, Ronnie. "Construction Methods in Frankish Rural Settlement." In *The Horns of Hattin*, ed. B. Z. Kedar, 168–92. London: Variorum, 1992.

———. *Crusader Castles and Modern Histories*. Cambridge: Cambridge University Press, 2007.

———. *Frankish Rural Settlement in the Latin Kingdom of Jerusalem*. Cambridge, Cambridge University Press, 1998.

———. "Settlement and Society in Crusader Palestine." In *Knights of the Holy Land: The Crusader Kingdom of Jerusalem*, ed. Silvia Rozenberg. Jerusalem: The Israel Museum, 1999, 34–41.

———. "Were There Borders and Borderlines in the Middle Ages? The Example of the Latin Kingdom of Jerusalem." In *Medieval Frontiers: Concepts and Practices*, ed. David Abulafia and Nora Berend, 105–19. Burlington, VT: Ashgate, 2002.

Elukin, Jonathan. *Living Together, Living Apart: Rethinking Jewish-Christian Relations in the Middle Ages*. Princeton, NJ: Princeton University Press, 2007.

England, Samuel. *Medieval Empires and the Culture of Competition: Literary Duels at Islamic and Christian Courts*. Edinburgh: Edinburgh University Press, 2019.

Epstein, Steven A. *Purity Lost: Transgressing Boundaries in the Eastern Mediterranean 1000–1400*. Baltimore: Johns Hopkins University Press, 2006.

Favereau, Marie. "Comment le sultan mamlouk d'adressait au khan de la Horde d'Or. Formulaire des lettres et règles d'usage trois manuels de chancellerie (1262-v. 1430)." *Annales Islamologiques* 41 (2007): 59–95.

Folda, Jaroslav. *The Art of the Crusaders in the Holy Land 1098–1187*. Cambridge: Cambridge University Press, 1995.

———. "Crusader Art, A Multicultural Phenomenon: Historiographical Reflections." In *Autour de la Première Croisade*, ed. M. Balard, 609–15. Paris: Publications de la Sorbonne, 1996.

———. *Crusader Art in the Holy Land from the Third Crusade to the Fall of Acre, 1187–1291*. Cambridge: Cambridge University Press, 2005.

———. *Crusader Manuscript Illumination at Saint-Jean d'Acre, 1272–1291*. Princeton, NJ: Princeton University Press, 1976.

Forey, Alan. "Literacy and Learning in the Military Orders During the Twelfth and Thirteenth Centuries." In *The Military Orders, Volume 2 Welfare and Warfare*, ed. Helen Nicholson, 185–206. Aldershot: Ashgate, 1998.

François, Véronique, Andreas Nicolaïdes, Lucy Vallauri, and Yona Waksman. "Premiers éléments d'une caractérisation des productions de céremique de Beyrouth entre domination franque et mamelouke." In *VIIe Congrès Internationale de la Céramique médiévale en Méditerranée, Thessaloniki, 11–16 Octobre 1999*, 325–40. Athènes: Caisse des Recettes Archéologiques, 2003.

Frankel, Rafael, Nimrod Getzov, Mordechai Aviam, and Avi Degani. *Settlement Dynamics and Regional Diversity in Ancient Upper Galilee: Archaeological Survey of Upper Galilee*. IAA Reports 14. Jerusalem: Israel Antiquities Authority, 2001.

Frankel, Rafael, and Edna J. Stern. "A Crusader Screw Press from Western Galilee—The Manot Press." *Techniques & Culture* 27 (1996): 89–22.

Frankopan, Peter. *The First Crusade: The Call from the East*. Cambridge, MA: Belknap Press, 2011.

Frenkel, Yehoshua. "*Awqaf* in Mamluk Bilad al-Sham." *Mamluk Studies Review* 13 (2009): 149–66.

Friedman, Yvonne. *Encounter Between Enemies: Captivity and Ransom in the Latin Kingdom of Jerusalem*. Leiden: Brill, 2002.

———. "Peacemaking Perceptions and Practices in the Medieval Latin East." In *The Crusades and the Near East: Cultural Histories*, ed. Conor Kostick, 229–57. London: Routledge, 2011.

Fuess, Albrecht. "Rotting Ships and Razed Harbors: The Naval Policy of the Mamluks." *Mamluk Studies Review* 5 (2001): 45–71.

———. *Verbranntes Ufer: Auswirkungen mamlukischer Seepolitik auf Beirut und die syropalästinensiche Küste (1250–1517)*. Leiden: Brill, 2001.

Gabrieli, Francesco. *Muhammad and the Conquests of Islam*, trans. Virginia Lulin and Rosamund Linell. New York: McGraw-Hill Book Company, 1968.

Geldsetzer, Sabine. *Frauen auf Kreuzzügen, 1096–1291*. Darmstadt: Wissenschaftliche Buchgesellschaft, 2003.

Getzov, Nimrod, Dina Avshalom-Gorni, Yael Gorein-Rosen, Edna J. Stern, Danny Syon, and Ayelet Tatcher. *Horbat Uza: The 1991 Excavations—Volume II: The Late Periods*. Jerusalem: Israel Antiquities Authority, 2009.

Gil, Moshe. *A History of Palestine, 634–1099*. Cambridge: Cambridge University Press, 1992.

Glick, Leonard B. *Abraham's Heirs: Jews and Christians in Medieval Europe*. Syracuse: Syracuse University Press, 1999.

Glick, Thomas. *Islamic and Christian Spain in the Early Middle Ages*. Princeton, NJ: Princeton University Press, 1979.

Goldman, Brendan. *Camps of the Uncircumcised: The Cairo Geniza and Jewish Life in the Latin Kingdom of Jerusalem*. Philadelphia: University of Pennsylvania Press, forthcoming.

Grandclaude, Maurice. *Etude Critique sur les livres des assises de Jérusalem*. Paris: Jouve, 1923.

Greilsammer, Myriam. "Anatomie d'un mensonge: le *Livre au Roi* et la révision de l'histoire du Royaume Latin par les juristes du XIIIe siècle." *Tijdschrift voor rechtgeschiedenis. Revue d'Histoire du Droit* 67 (1999): 239–54.

Grousset, René. *Histoire des croisades et du royaume franc de Jerusalem*. 3 vols. Paris: Perrin, 1934–36.

Guérin, Victor. *Description géographique, historique et archéologique de la Palestine*. Paris, 1880.

Gully, Adrian. *The Culture of Letter-Writing in Premodern Islamic Society*. Edinburgh: Edinburgh University Press, 2008.

Hallaq, Wael B. "From Fatwās to Furū': Growth and Change in Islamic Substantive Law." *Islamic Law and Society* 1 (1994): 29–65.

———. *A History of Islamic Legal Theories*. Cambridge: Cambridge University Press, 1999.

Heng, Geraldine. *The Invention of Race in the European Middle Ages*. Cambridge: Cambridge University Press, 2018.

Hermes, Nizar F. *The [European] Other in Medieval Arabic Literature and Culture, Ninth-Twelfth Century AD*. New York: Palgrave-Macmillan, 2012.

Hillenbrand, Carole. *The Crusades: Islamic Perspectives*. Edinburgh: Edinburgh University Press, 1999.

———. "Jihad Propaganda in Syria from the Time of the First Crusade until the Death of Zengi: The Evidence of Monumental Inscriptions." In *The Frankish Wars and Their Influence on Palestine*, ed. Khalil Athamina and Roger Heacock, 60–69. Birzeit: Birzeit University Publications, 1994.

Hitti, Philip K. *History of the Arabs*, 10th ed. London: Macmillan, 1970.

Hodgson, Marshall G. S. *The Venture of Islam: Conscience and History in a World Civilization*. Chicago: University of Chicago Press, 1974.

Hodgson, Natasha. *Women, Crusading and the Holy Land in Historical Narrative*. Woodbridge: Boydell & Brewer, 2007.

Holt, Peter M. *The Crusader States and Their Neighbours, 1098–1291.* Harlow: Pearson Longman, 2004.
Housely, Norman. *Contesting the Crusades.* Malden, MA: Blackwell Publishing, 2006.
Humphreys, Stephen. "Ayyubids, Mamluks, and the Latin East in the Thirteenth Century." *Mamluk Studies Review* 2 (1998): 1–7.
———. *From Saladin to the Mongols: The Ayyubids of Damascus, 1193–1260.* Albany: SUNY Press, 1977.
Ineichen, Gustav. "Il glossario arabo-francese di messer Guglielmo e maestro Giacomo." *Atti dell'Instituto Veneto di Scienze, Lettere ed Arti* 130 (1971–72): 353–407.
Irwin, Robert. "The Mamluk Conquest of the County of Tripoli." In *Crusade and Settlement: Papers read at the First Conference of the Society for the Study of the Crusades and the Latin East and Presented to R. C. Smail*, ed. Peter W. Edbury, 246–50. Cardiff: University College Cardiff Press, 1985.
Izzo, Jesse W. "The Frankish Nobility and the Fall of Acre: Diplomacy, Society, and War in the Latin Kingdom of Jerusalem, c.1240-1291." PhD dissertation, University of Minnesota, 2016.
———. "The Revolts of the Embriaco and the Fall of the County of Tripoli." *The Haskins Society Journal* 27 (2015): 149–60.
Jacoby, David. *Byzantium, Latin Romania and the Mediterranean.* Aldershot: Variorum, 2001.
———. *Commercial Exchange Across the Mediterranean: Byzantium, the Crusader Levant, Egypt and Italy.* Aldershot: Variorum, 2005.
———. "The Economic Function of the Crusader States of the Levant: A New Approach." In *Relazioni economiche tra Europa e mondo islamico. Secc. XIII-XVIII (Instituto Internazionale di Storia Economica 'F. Datini', Atti delle Settimane di Studi e altri convegni, vol. 38)*, ed. S. Cavaciocchi, 159–91. Florence: 2007.
———. "The Fonde of Crusader Acre and Its Tariff: Some New Considerations." In *Dei gesta per Francos: Etudes sur les croisades dédiées à Jean Richard*, ed. Michel Balard, Benjamin Z. Kedar, and Jonathan Riley-Smith, 277–93. Aldershot: Ashgate, 2001.
———. "Knightly Values and Class Consciousness in the Crusader States of the Eastern Mediterranean." *Mediterranean Historical Review* 1 (1986): 158–86.
———. "La littérature Française dans les états latins de la Méditerranée orientale à l'époque des croisades: diffusion et création." In *Essor et fortune de la Chanson de Geste dans l'Europe et l'Orient latin. Actes du IXe Congrès International de la Société Rencevals pour l'Étude des Épopées Romanes (Padoue-Venise, 1982)*, 617–46. Modena: Mucchi Editore, 1984.
———. "Migration, Trade and Banking in Crusader Acre." In *The Balkans and the Eastern Mediterranean, 12th-17th Centuries* [Greek], ed. L. Mavroutis, 105–19. Athens: The National Hellenic Research Foundation, 1998.
———. *Trade, Commodities and Shipping in the Medieval Mediterranean.* Aldershot: Variorum, 1997.
———. "The Trade of Crusader Acre in the Levantine Context: An Overview." *Archivio Storico del Sannio*, n.s. 3 (1998): 103–20.
Jotischky, Andrew. *Crusading and the Crusader States.* Harlow: Pearson Longman, 2004.
Kedar, Benjamin Z. "The Crusading Kingdom of Jerusalem—The First European Colonial Society? A Symposium." In *The Horns of Hattin*, ed. Benjamin Z. Kedar, 341–66. London: Variorum, 1992.
———. "On the Origins of the Earliest Laws of Frankish Jerusalem: The Canons of the Council of Nablus, 1120." *Speculum* 74, no. 2 (1999): 310–35.

---. "Some New Sources on Palestinian Muslims Before and During the Crusade." In *Die Kreuzfahrerstaaten als multikulturelle Gesellschaft*, ed. H. E. Mayer, 129–40. Munich: Oldenbourg, 1997.

---. "The Subjected Muslims of the Frankish Levant." In *Muslims under Latin Rule, 1100–1300*, ed. James M. Powell, 135–74. Princeton, NJ: Princeton University Press, 1990.

---. "A Twelfth-Century Description of the Jerusalem Hospital." In *The Military Orders, 2: Welfare and Warfare*, ed. Helen Nicholson, 3–26. Aldershot: Ashgate, 1998.

Kedar, Benjamin Z., and Etan Kohlberg. "The Intercultural Career of Theodore of Antioch." In *Intercultural Contacts in the Medieval Mediterranean: Studies in Honour of David Jacoby*, ed. B. Arbel, 164–76. London: Frank Cass, 1995.

Kedar, Benjamin Z., and Muhammad al-Hajjuj. "Muslim Villagers of the Frankish Kingdom of Jerusalem: Some Demographic and Onomastic Data." *Itinéraires d'Orient: Hommages à Claude Cahen. Res Orientales* 1 (1994): 145–56.

Kennedy, Hugh. *Crusader Castles*. Cambridge: Cambridge University Press, 1994.

Khamisy, Rabei G. "Frankish Viticulture, Wine Presses, and wine production in the Levant: New Evidence from Castellum Regis (Miʿilyā)." *Palestine Exploration Quarterly* 153, no. 3 (2021): 191–221.

---. "The Templar Estates in the Territory of Acre." *Ordines Militares—Colloquia Torunensia Historica* 18 (2013): 267–85.

Kletter, Raz. *Just Past? The Making of Israeli Archaeology*. London: Routledge, 2006.

Köhler, Michael. *Alliances and Treaties between Frankish and Muslim Rulers in the Middle East: Cross-Cultural Diplomacy in the Period of the Crusades*, trans. Peter M. Holt, ed. Konrad Hirschler. Leiden: Brill, 2013.

---. *Allianzen und Verträge zwischen fränkischen und islamischen Herrschern im Vorderen Orient: Eine Studie über das zwischenstaatliche Zusammenleben vom 12. bis ins 13. Jahrhundert*. Berlin: Walter de Gruyter, 1991.

Kostick, Conor. *The Siege of Jerusalem: Crusade and Conquest in 1099*. London: Continuum, 2009.

---. *The Social Structure of the First Crusade*. Boston: Brill, 2008.

---. "The Terms *milites*, *equites* and *equestres* in the Early Crusading Histories." *Nottingham Medieval Studies* 50 (2006): 1–21.

---. "William of Tyre, Livy, and the Vocabulary of Class." *Journal of the History of Ideas* 65 (2004): 353–69.

Kühnel, Bianca. "The Perception of History in Thirteenth-Century Crusader Art." In *France and the Holy Land: Frankish Culture at the End of the Crusades*, ed. Daniel H. Weiss and Lisa Mahoney, 161–86. Baltimore: Johns Hopkins University Press, 2004.

Lagardère, Vincent. "Cépages, raisin et vin en al-Andalus (X-XVe siècle)." *Médiévales* 33 (1997): 81–90.

Lane, Frederic Chapin. *Venice, A Maritime Republic*. Baltimore: Johns Hopkins University Press, 1973.

Lapidus, Ira. "The Conversion of Egypt to Islam." *Israel Oriental Studies* 2 (1972): 248–62.

Latiff, Osman. *The Cutting Edge of the Poet's Sword: Muslim Poetic Responses to the Crusades*. Leiden: Brill, 2017.

Levtzion, Nehemia. "Conversion to Islam in Syria and Palestine, and the Survival of Christian Communities." In *Conversion and Continuity: Indigenous Christian Communities in Medieval Islamic Lands, Eighth to Eighteenth Century*, ed. Michael Gervers and Ramzi J. Bikhazi, 289–311. Toronto: Pontifical Institute of Mediaeval Studies, 1990.

———. "Toward a Comparative Study of Islamization." In *Conversion to Islam*, ed. Nehemia Levtzion, 1–23. New York: Holmes & Meier Publishers, 1979.

Levy-Rubin, Milka. "New Evidence Relating to the Process of Islamization in Palestine in the Early Muslim Period: The Case of Samaria." *Journal of the Economic and Social History of the Orient* 34 (2000): 257–76.

Lewicka, Pauline. "Alcohol and Its Consumption in Medieval Cairo. The Story of a Habit." *Studie Arabistyczne* 12 (2006): 55–97.

Lewis, Bernard. *Islam and the West*. Oxford: Oxford University Press, 1993.

———. *The Muslim Discovery of Europe*. New York: W. W. Norton, 1982.

Lewis, Kevin James. "Medieval Diglossia: The Diversity of the Latin Christian Encounter with Written and Spoken Arabic in the 'Crusader' County of Tripoli, with a Hitherto Unpublished Arabic Notes from the Principality of Antioch (MS, AOM 3, Valletta: National Library of Malta, no. 51v." *al-Masaq* 27, no. 2 (2015): 119–52.

Loiseau, Julien. *Les Mamelouks XIIIe-XVIe siècle: une experience du pouvoir dans l'islam medieval*. Paris: Seuil, 2014.

Lotan, Shlomo. "Empowering and Struggling in an Era of Uncertainty and Crisis—The Teutonic Military Order in the Latin East, 1250-1291." *Ordines Militares—Colloquia Torunensia Historica* 16 (2011): 19–28.

Loud, G. A. "The *Assise sur la Ligece* and Ralph of Tiberias." In *Crusade and Settlement*, ed. Peter W. Edbury, 204–12. Cardiff: University College Cardiff Press, 1985.

Lower, Michael. *The Barons' Crusade*. Philadelphia: University of Pennsylvania Press, 2005.

———. *The Tunis Crusade of 1270: A Mediterranean History*. Oxford: Oxford University Press, 2018.

MacEvitt, Christopher. *The Crusades and the Christian World of the East: Rough Tolerance*. Philadelphia: University of Pennsylvania Press, 2008.

Madden, Thomas F. *The New Concise History of the Crusades*, Updated Student edition. Lanham: Rowman & Littlefield Publishers, Inc., 2006.

Mallett, Alex. *Popular Muslim Reactions to the Franks in the Levant, 1097–1291*. Farnham, Surrey: Ashgate, 2014.

El-Masri, Sami. "Medieval Pottery from Beirut's Downtown Excavations: The First Results." *Aram* 9–0 (1997–98): 103–19.

Masud, Muhammad Khalid, Brinkley Messick, and David Powers, eds. *Islamic Legal Interpretation: Muftis and Their Fatwas*. Cambridge, MA: Harvard University Press, 1996.

Mayer, Hans E. "Latins, Muslims and Greeks in the Latin Kingdom of Jerusalem." *History* 63 (1978): 175–92.

Menocal, Maria Rosa. *The Ornament of the World: How Muslims, Jews, and Christians Created a Culture of Tolerance in Medieval Spain*. Boston: Little, Brown and Co., 2002.

Metcalfe, Alex. *Muslims and Christians in Norman Sicily*. London: Routledge, 2003.

———. *The Muslims of Medieval Italy*. Edinburgh: Edinburgh University Press, 2009.

Mitchell, Piers D. *Medicine in the Crusades: Warfare, Wounds and the Medieval Surgeon*. Cambridge: Cambridge University Press, 2004.

Molénat, Jean-Pierre. "Le problème de la permanence des musulmans dans les territoires conquis par les chrétiens, du point de vue de la loi islamique." *Arabica* 48 (2001): 392–400.

Morton, Nicholas. *The Crusader States & Their Neighbours: A Military History, 1099–1187*. Oxford: Oxford University Press, 2020.

Murray, Alan. "Ethnic Identity in the Crusader States: The Frankish Race and the Settlement of Outremer." In *Concepts of National Identity in the Middle Ages*, ed. Simon Forde, Lesley Johnson, and Alan V. Murray, 59–73. Leeds: University of Leeds, 1995.

Nader, Marwan. *Burgess Law in the Latin Kingdoms of Jerusalem and Cyprus (1099–1325)*. Aldershot: Ashgate, 2006.

———. "Urban Muslims, Latin Laws, and Legal Institutions in the Kingdom of Jerusalem." In *Medieval Encounters* 13 (2007): 260.

Nam, Jong-Kuk. *Le commerce du coton en Méditerranée à la fin du Moyen Age*. Leiden: Brill, 2007.

Nicholson, Helen. *Medieval Warfare*. New York: Palgrave Macmillan, 2004.

Nirenberg, David. *Communities of Violence: Persecution of Minorities in the Middle Ages*. Princeton, NJ: Princeton University Press, 1996.

———. "Conversion, Sex, and Segregation: Jews and Christians in Medieval Spain." *The American Historical Review* 107 (2002): 1065–93.

Northrup, Linda. *From Slave to Sultan: The Career of Al-Manṣūr Qalāwūn and the Consolidation of Mamluk Rule in Egypt and Syria (678–689 A.H./1279–1290 A.D.)*. Stuttgart: Franz Steiner Verlag, 1998.

Ouerfelli, Mohamed. *Le Sucre: Production, commercialisation et usages dans la Méditerranée médiévale*. Leiden: Brill, 2008.

Pahlitzsch, Johannes. "The Melkites between Byzantium, Muslims and Crusaders." In *Religious Plurality and Interreligious Contacts in the Middle Ages*, ed. Ana Echevarría and Dorothea Weltecke, 157–70. Wiesbaden: Harrassowitz Verlag, 2020.

———. "People of the Book." In *Ayyubid Jerusalem: The Holy City in Context, 1187–1250*, eds. Robert Hillenbrand and Sylvia Auld, 435–40. London: Altajir Trust, 2009.

Pahlitzsch Johannes, and Daniel Baraz. "Christian Communities in the Latin Kingdom of Jerusalem (1099-1187)." In *Christians and Christianity in the Holy Land: From the Origins to the Latin Kingdoms*, ed. Ora Limor and Guy G. Stroumsa, 205–35. Turnout: Brepols, 2006.

Petersen, Andrew. *A Gazetteer of Buildings in Muslim Palestine (Part I)*. Oxford: Council for British Research in the Levant, 2001.

———. *The Towns of Palestine under Muslim Rule: AD 600–1600*. Oxford: Archaeopress, 2005.

Phillips, Jonathan. *The Second Crusade: Extending the Frontiers of Christendom*. New Haven, CT: Yale University Press, 2007.

Powell, James, ed., *Muslims Under Latin Rule, 1100–1300*. Princeton, NJ: Princeton University Press, 1990.

Prawer, Joshua. *Crusader Institutions*. Oxford: Oxford University Press, 1980.

———. *The Crusaders' Kingdom: European Colonialism in the Middle Ages*. New York: Praeger, 1972.

———. *The History of the Jews in the Latin Kingdom of Jerusalem*. Oxford: Clarendon Press, 1988.

———. "Social Classes in the Crusader States: The Minorities." In *A History of the Crusades* gen. ed., Kenneth Setton, 59–115. 2nd ed. Vol. 5 Madison: University of Wisconsin Press, 1985.

Pringle, Denys. *The Churches of the Crusader Kingdom of Jerusalem: A Corpus*. 4 vols. Cambridge: Cambridge University Press, 1993–2009.

———. *Fortification and Settlement in Crusader Palestine*. Aldershot: Variorum, 2000.

———. "Magna Mahumeria (al-Bira); The Archeology of a Frankish New Town in Palestine." In *Crusade and Settlement*, ed. Peter W. Edbury, 147–68. Cardiff: University College Cardiff Press, 1985.

———. "The Military Orders in the Cities of the Holy Land." In *Les Ordres militaires dans la ville médiévale (1100–1350): Actes du colloque international de Clermont-Ferrand 26-28 mai 2010*, ed. Damien Carraz, 79–95. Clermont-Ferrand: Presses Universitaires Blaises Pascal, 2013.

———. *The Red Tower (al-Burj al-Ahmar)*. London: British School of Archaeology, 1986.

———. "A Rental of Hospitaller Properties from Twelfth-Century Jerusalem." In *Deeds Done Beyond the Sea: Essays on William of Tyre, Cyprus and the Military Orders presented to Peter Edbury*, ed. Susan B. Edgington and Helen J. Nicholson, 181–96. Farnham: Ashgate, 2014.

———. "Two Medieval Villages North of Jerusalem: Archaeological Investigations in al-Jib and ar-Ram." *Levant* 13 (1983): 141–77.

Redford, Scott. "On *Sâqîs* and Ceramics: Systems of Representation in the Northeast Mediterranean." In *France and the Holy Land: Frankish Culture at the End of the Crusades*, ed. Daniel H. Weiss and Lisa Mahoney, 282–312. Baltimore: Johns Hopkins University Press, 2004.

Re'em, Amit, Jon Seligman, Zubair 'Adawi, and Refeh Abu Raya. "Crusader Remains in the Muristan, Old City of Jerusalem: A Decade of Archaeological Gleanings." *'Atiqot* 66 (2011): 137–53.

Rey, Emmanuel. *Les colonies franques de Syrie aux XIIe et XIIIe siècles*. Paris: Alphonse Picard, 1883.

Reynolds, Susan. "The Historiography of the Medieval State." In *Companion to Historiography*, ed. Michael Bentley, 117–38. Abingdon Oxon: Routledge, 1997.

Richard, Jean. "Agricultural Conditions in the Crusader States." In *A History of the Crusades*, ed. Kenneth Setton, Norman Zacour, and Harry Hazard, 253–94. Vol. 5. Madison: University of Madison Press, 1985.

———. *The Crusades, c.1071–c.1291*. Cambridge: Cambridge University Press, 1999.

———. "La culture juridique de la noblesse aux XIe, XIIe et XIIIe siècles." In *Nobilitas. Funktion und Repräsentation des Adels in Alteuropa (Veröffentlichungen des Max-Planck Institut für Geschichte, 133)*, ed. Otto Gerhard Oexle and Werner Paravicini, 53–66. Göttingen: Vandenhoeck & Ruprecht, 1997.

———. *Le Royaume Latin de Jérusalem*. Paris: Presses Universitaires de France, 1953. [English translation published as *The Latin Kingdom of Jerusalem*, trans. Janet Shirley, 2 vols. New York: North-Holland Publishing Company, 1979.

———. "La seignuerie franque en Syrie et à Chypre: modèle oriental ou modèle occidental?" In *117e Congrès national des sociétés savantes, Clermont-Ferrand, 1992. Histoire medieval*, 155–66. Paris: CTHS, 1994.

Riley-Smith, Jonathan. *The Crusades, Christianity, and Islam*. New York: Columbia University Press, 2008.

———. *The Crusades: A History*. 2nd ed. New Haven, CT: Yale Nota Bene, 2005.

———. *The Feudal Nobility and the Kingdom of Jerusalem, 1174–1277*. London: Macmillan, 1973.

———. "Government and the Indigenous in the Latin Kingdom of Jerusalem." In *Medieval Frontiers: Concepts and Practices*, ed. David Abulafia and Nora Berend, 121–31. Burlington, VT: Ashgate, 2002.

———. "Some Lesser Officials in Latin Syria." *The English Historical Review* 87 (1972): 1–26.

Rodriguez, Jarbel. *Captives and Their Saviors in the Medieval Crown of Aragon*. Washington, DC: Catholic University of America Press, 2007.

Rose, Richard B. "The Native Christians of Jerusalem, 1187-1260." In *The Horns of Hattin*, ed. Benjamin Z. Kedar, 239–49. Jerusalem: Yad Izhak Ben-Zvi, 1992.

Roth, Norman. "Bishops and Jews in the Middle Ages." *The Catholic Historical Review* 80 (1994): 1–17.

Rubenstein, Jay. *Armies of Heaven: The First Crusade and the Quest for the Apocalypse*. New York: Basic Books, 2011.
Rubin, Jonathan. *Learning in a Crusader City: Intellectual Activity and Intercultural Exchanges in Acre, 1191–1291*. Cambridge: Cambridge University Press, 2018.
Runciman, Steven. *A History of the Crusades*. Vol. 2. Harmondsworth: Penguin, 1972.
Salamé-Sarkis, Hassan. *Contribution à l'histoire de Tripoli et de sa région à l'époque des croisades problèmes d'histoire, d'architecture et de céramique*. Paris: P. Geuthner, 1980.
Sauer, James A. "Syro-Palestinian Archeology, History, and Biblical Studies." *The Biblical Archaeologist* 45 (1982): 201–209.
Schenk, Jochen G. "Nomadic Violence in the First Latin Kingdom of Jerusalem and the Military Orders." *Reading Medieval Studies* 36 (2010): 39–55.
Schick, Robert. *The Christian Communities of Palestine from Byzantine to Islamic Rule*. Princeton, NJ: The Darwin Press, 1995.
Schryver, James G. "Identities in the Crusader East." In *Mediterranean Identities in the Premodern Era*, ed. John Watkins and Kathryn Reyerson, 173–89. Farnham: Ashgate, 2014.
Shagrir, Iris. "Urban Soundscape: Defining Space and Community in Twelfth Century of Jerusalem." In *Communicating the Middle Ages. Essays in Honour of Sophia Menache*, ed. Iris Shagrir, Benjamin Kedar, and Michel Balard, 103–20. London: Routledge, 2018.
Shatzmiller, Maya. *Labour in the Medieval Islamic World*. Leiden: Brill, 1994.
Sidelko, Paul. "Muslim Taxation under Crusader Rule." In *Tolerance and Intolerance: Social Conflict in the Ages of the Crusades*, ed. Michael Gervers and James M. Powell, 65–74. Syracuse: Syracuse University Press, 2001.
Smail, R. C. *The Crusaders in Syria and the Holy Land*. Southampton: Thames and Hudson, 1973.
———. *Crusading Warfare (1097–1193). A Contribution to Medieval Military History*. Cambridge: Cambridge University Press, 1956. [2nd ed. 1995].
Smarandache, Bogdan. "Frankish-Muslim Diplomatic Relations and the Shared Minority Discourse in the Eastern Mediterranean, 517–692 AH/1123–1292 AD." PhD dissertation, University of Toronto, 2019.
———. "A Reassessment of Frankish Settlement Patterns in the Latin Kingdom of Jerusalem, 493-583 AH/1099-1187 AD." In *Minorities in Contact in the Medieval Mediterranean*, ed. Clara Almagro Vidal, Jessica Tearney-Pearce, and Luke Yarbrough, 285–335. Turnhout: Brepols, 2020.
Smithline, Howard, Edna J. Stern, and Elizer Stern. "A Crusader-Period Bathhouse in ʿAkko (Acre)." *ʿAtiqot* 73 (2013): 71–108.
Stern, Edna J. "Ceramic Ware from the Crusader Era in the Holy Land." In *Knights in the Holy Land: The Crusader Kingdom of Jerusalem*, 259–65. Jerusalem: Israel Museum, 1999.
———. "The Crusader, Mamluk and Early Ottoman-Period Pottery from Khirbat Dinʿila: Typology, Chronology, Production and Consumption Trends." *ʿAtiqot* 78 (2014): 71–104.
———. "The Excavations at Lower Horbat Manot: A Medieval Sugar-Production Site." *ʿAtiqot* 42 (2001): 277–308.
———. "Excavation of the Courthouse Site at ʿAkko: The Pottery of the Crusader and Ottoman Periods." *ʿAtiqot* 39 (1997): 35–70.
———. "The Last Years of Crusader Acre (ʿAkko) and Resettlement in the Ottoman Period: Archaeological Evidence from the *Boverel* Quarter." *ʿAtiqot* 103 (2021): 141–86.
Stern Edna and Ayelet Tatcher. "The Early Islamic, Crusader, and Mamluk Pottery." In Nimrod Getzov et al. *Horbat ʿUza the 1991 Excavations Volume II: The Late Periods*. Jerusalem: Israel Antiquities Authority, 2009, 119–90.

Stern, Edna J., and S. Y. Waksman and A. Shapiro. "The Impact of the Crusades on Ceramic Production and Use in the Southern Levant: Continuity or Change?" In *Multidisciplinary Approaches to Food and Foodways in the Medieval Eastern Mediterranean*, ed. S. Y. Waksman, 113–46. Lyon, 2020.

Stow, Kenneth R. *Alienated Minority: The Jews of Medieval Latin Europe*. Cambridge, MA: Harvard University Press, 1992.

Syon, Danny, and Edna J. Stern. "Excavations at the Dar el-Gharbiya Neighborhood of Kafr Yasif: A Crusader Estate in the Territory of ʿAkko." *ʿAtiqot* 79 (2014): 233–61.

Talmon-Heller, Daniella. *Islamic Piety in Medieval Syria: Mosques, Cemeteries and Sermons Under the Zangids and Ayyubids (1146–1260)*. Leiden: Brill, 2007.

———. "Muslims and Eastern Christians under Frankish Rule in the Land of Israel." In *Knights of the Holy Land: The Crusader Kingdom of Jerusalem*, ed. Silvia Rozenberg, 43–47. Jerusalem: The Israel Museum, 1999.

Taragan, Hana. "The Tomb of Sayyidna ʿAli in Arsuf: The Story of a Holy Place." *Journal of the Royal Asiatic Society*, 3rd series, 14 (2004): 83–102.

Thorau, Peter. *The Lion of Egypt: Sultan Baybars I and the Near East in the Thirteenth Century*. London: Longman, 1992.

Tibble, Steven. *Monarchy and Lordships in the Latin Kingdom of Jeursalem, 1099–1291*. New York: Oxford University Press, 1989.

Tyerman, Christopher. *God's War: A New History of the Crusades*. Cambridge: Belknap Press, 2006.

Vorderstrasse, Tasha. "Archaeology of Medieval Lebanon: An Overview." *Chronos: Revue d'Histoire de l'Université de Balamand* 20 (2009): 103–28.

———. "A Port of Antioch under Byzantium, Islam, and the Crusades: Acculturation and Differentiation at Al-Mina, AD 350-1268." PhD dissertation, University of Chicago, 2004.

———. "A Port Without a Harbour: Reconstructing Medieval al-Mina." In *Studies in Archaeology of the Medieval Mediterranean*, ed. James G. Schryver, 15–39. Leiden: Brill, 2010.

Vryonis, Speros. *The Decline of Medieval Hellenism in Asia Minor and the Process of Islamization from the Eleventh Through the Fifteenth Century*. Berkeley: University of California Press, 1971.

Waksman, Yona, Edna J. Stern, Irina Segal, Naomi Porat, and Joseph Yellin. "Elemental and Petrographic Analyses of Local and Imported Ceramics from Crusader Acre." *ʿAtiqot* 59 (2008): 157–90.

Weinberg, Gladys Davidson. "A Glass Factory of Crusader Times in Northern Israel." In *Annales du 10e Congrès de l'Association internationale pour l'histoire du verre: Madrid-Segovie, 23–28 septembre 1985*, 305–16. Amsterdam: L'Association, 1987.

Weitzmann, Kurt. "Icon Painting in the Crusader Kingdom." *Dumbarton Oaks Papers* 20 (1966): 49–83.

———. "Thirteenth Century Crusader Icon on Mount Sinai." *The Art Bulletin* 45, no. 3 (1963): 179–203.

Wilson, James. "The Ransom of High-Ranking Captives, Tributary Relationships and the Practice of Diplomacy in Northern Syria 442-522/1050-1128." *Journal of the Royal Asiatic Society* 32, no. 3 (2022): 635–69.

Zimo, Ann E. "Baybars, Naval Power and Mamlūk Psychological Warfare Against the Franks." *al-Masāq* 30, no. 3 (2018): 304–16.

# Index

Abbasid(s) 4–5, 35, 52, 64, 122, 161, 164, 211n5
Acre 5, 23, 53, 118
  administration of
    diplomacy 49, 120–22, 125, 126, 175–76
    intelligence 152, 154–55, 156–57
    legal 18, 100, 103, 105,
  agriculture 71, 72–73
    raids against 76–77, 80–81
  archaeological findings in 95, 205n32
  industry 61, 62–63
  intellectual life of 144, 196
  Jewish population 13
  literary depictions of 184, 188
  mercantile interests 59–60
  Mamluk conquest of 7, 17, 114, 133
  Muslim population 28, 31, 44–47, 55–56, 57
    villages surrounding 42, 43–44
  religious sites 38, 40, 42
  treaties concerning 65, 112, 119
  treatment of prisoners in 48, 52, 138, 139
  War of St. Sabas (1250s) 6
al-'Adil (Sultan of Egypt) 112, 122, 128, 159,
adib [man of letters] 16, 52, 160, 182, 190, 191
adhan [call to prayer] 172, 178
Aleppo 4, 5, 17, 35, 51–52, 64, 122, 131–32, 147, 159,
  cultural importance of 89, 182, 190
ambassador(s) 17, 59, 114–15, 123, 125–26, 138, 140
amir 151, 190, 193, 196
amir al-silah (Mamluk) 152, 161
Antioch, Principality of 5, 97, 148, 156, 191–92, 196
  Armenian rule over 131–32, 153

Bohemond of. *See* Bohemond VI of Antioch-Tripoli
Christian population of 27
conquest of (1268) 7, 126, 169–71
culture 157, 189–90
defeat at Inab (1149) 4, 182
founding of 3, 6
glass production in 61
qadi's presence in 88
Turcoman attack (1247) 82
al-Aqsa mosque (Jerusalem) 38–39, 183
Arabic (language) 30, 35, 45, 48, 88, 116, 144, 194
  cultural exchange in 155–58
  as "Saracen" language 156, 157
  sobriquets 118
  sources 2, 15, 16–19, 21, 22, 23–24
  translators of 175, 176
  use for espionage 146, 147–49
Arabs 77, 129, 135, 143, 193–94, 195–96. *See also* Bedouin
archaeology 15, 16, 34, 42, 63, 200, 202
Armenia 64, 78, 79, 126, 153, 183, 196, 200
  Leo, king of 81, 117, 131, 224n150
Armenian Christians 15, 99, 100, 101, 143, 148, 200. *See also* Christian(ity)
Ascalon 3–4, 5, 29, 35, 40, 99, 138, 189
Ayyubid(s) 5–7, 46–47, 122
  administration 21, 35, 121, 141
    intelligence 153
    legal 88, 109
  literary culture 167, 168, 184, 187
  medical advances under 159–60
  military campaigns 40, 51, 110
  treaties concerning 60, 77, 112–15, 118, 128, 132

Baldwin I of Jerusalem 3, 149
Baldwin II of Jerusalem 156, 191
Baldwin IV of Jerusalem 5, 159
Baybars, al-Malik al-Zahir 7, 17, 115, 128, 175
Baybars al-Mansuri, Rukn al-Din 17, 19, 58, 78, 117, 132, 139, 147, 169
Bedouin 30, 70, 77, 150, 197
    description of 193–96. *See also* Ibn Munqidh, Usama
    intelligence networks 147, 154, 155
Beirut 6, 7, 49, 51, 103
    conquest of 32, 56
    industries 61–63
    Isabel of. *See* Ibelin, Isabel of
    Muslim population of 54
    religious sites 38
    treaties concerning 112, 119
Bethlehem 3, 6, 112
Bohemond of Taranto 3, 146
Bohemond VI of Antioch-Tripoli 79, 117–18, 126
    letters concerning 169–72, 175
Bohemond VII of Tripoli 59, 65, 114, 117–18, 126, 130–32, 188
Byzantium/Byzantine Empire 3, 20, 23, 28, 64, 124, 158

Caesarea 7, 20, 33, 62, 72, 100
Cairo 46, 71, 73, 89, 97, 116, 168, 193, 194
captivity 46, 59, 64, 65–66, 124, 172. *See also* slavery
ceramic(s) 20, 56, 60, 61–63, 200, 218n27
Charles of Anjou 51, 59, 114, 138, 156
Christianity 2, 30, 50, 104, 148, 152
    converts to 78, 158, 160
    religious sites 38, 41
Christian(s) 5, 8, 15, 27, 45
    Armenian. *See* Armenian Christians
    burial customs 33
    conflicts between 50
    converted 149, 150
    Eastern. *See* Eastern Christians
    Jacobite. *See* Jacobite(s)
    Latin (Western). *See* Latin Christians
    legal status 85, 100, 101
        slave trade 102–3
    Melkite. *See* Melkite(s)

merchants 58, 71
Muslims and 13–14, 29, 38, 40, 48, 52
    agricultural work 75
    cultural exchange 144, 145, 160
    treatment of Muslim captives 51, 66, 78
    Nestorian. *See* Nestorian(s)
    religious sites 36, 37, 183
    "rough tolerance" policy. *See* MacEvitt, Christopher
    Syrian. *See* Syrian Christians
    treaties with Muslim powers 111
    violence against 81
Church of the Holy Sepulchre 89, 186
commerce 18, 21, 46, 57–58, 68, 98, 104, 105
condominia [jointly held land] 21, 50, 109, 127–36, 140, 141, 227n21. *See also* munasafat
conversion/converts 32, 45, 52, 78,
    forcible 66, 82
    as informants 149–50, 155, 158, 160, 161
    legal status of 98–99, 104
    to Islam 26–27, 29, 30, 32, 48, 148
Crac des Chevaliers 7, 70, 76–77, 78, 79, 126, 132
    1271 conquest of 129, 169, 172, 173
crusader(s) 1, 3, 10, 24, 29, 113, 114
    intelligence networks 153, 156
    scholarship on 2, 8, 28
    violence against Muslims 7, 45, 55–56
    threat of 192
crusade(s) 1–4, 6, 51, 112, 113, 115, 117, 161
    cultural effects of 143–44, 157
    economics of 56
    European roots 15
    Fifth 40
    First 28–29, 38, 61, 63, 107, 124, 146, 148
    Fourth 152–53,
    historiography 7–10, 14, 25, 27, 108, 116, 165
        gaps in 12, 19, 111, 165, 205–6n36
    legal history 86
    King Louis IX's crusade. *See* Louis IX of France
    literary depictions of 164, 166, 178–80, 184, 189,
    primary sources 201,
        Arabic 17–18, 191

## Index

Third 5, 42
 violence against Muslim civilians 6,
  208n63, 214n68
cultural production 22, 89, 145, 165, 181
Cyprus 5, 10, 16, 49, 59, 116, 125, 157, 218n17
 archaeological evidence in 62
 Hugh III of. *See* Hugh III of Cyprus
 Mamluks and 138–39, 173
 shipwreck (1271) 47, 75, 94, 114

Damascus 4, 71, 78, 91, 121, 127, 147
 administration 60, 76, 92, 96–97
 culture 89, 94, 158, 159, 162
 literary depictions of 179
 refugees from 51–52
 treaties concerning 112–13, 114, 120, 122
 treatment of prisoners in 49, 65–66
dhimmi [protected minority] 15, 186, 225n5
diplomacy 5, 6, 138, 139, 140–41
Dome of the Rock 39–40, 163, 183, 185

Eastern Christians 1, 12, 14–15, 21, 22, 156
 archaeological evidence of 10–11, 35
 assumptions about 26–27, 50
 as informants 154, 155
 economic status of 53, 83
 legal status of 99, 104, 105, 106
 medical expertise of 158–59, 160, 161–62
 Muslim populations alongside 25, 30–31,
  37, 38–39, 43, 52
 religious sites 41
 *See also* Christian(s); Jacobite(s);
  Melkite(s); Nestorian(s); Syrian
  Christians
Edessa, County of 3, 4, 27, 147, 182
Egypt 3, 15, 24, 38, 66, 85, 121, 139
 cultural life 145, 175, 178, 182, 191, 192, 194.
  *See also* Ibn Munqidh, Usama
 diplomacy 122–23, 141
 espionage 149, 153, 155, 156, 160, 161
 fleet 173
 legal system 94, 97, 106
 Louis IX's crusade 6–7, 17, 147
 medical advances in 158–59
 mercantile interests 59, 64, 65, 71, 73
 refugees fleeing to 51–52, 53
 Saladin's conquest of 4–5

treaties concerning 110, 112–14, 119–20
treatment of captives 79
treatment of nomadic groups 150
Ellenblum, Ronnie 11, 14, 20–21, 22, 31, 38,
 53, 141, 201
 *Frankish Rural Settlement in the Latin
  Kingdom of Jerusalem* (1998) 12,
  25–26, 28–29, 42, 47, 140
 importance of archaeological evidence 43,
  200
emir(s) 65, 126, 138, 151–52, 153, 154
 as emissaries 122, 123, 124, 125, 139
 household of 49–50
 laws concerning 96
 as military leaders 147
England 5, 79, 114, 128, 149–50, 153
espionage 145, 146, 149
 counter- 152, 153

fada'il al-Quds [merits of Jerusalem]. *See*
 literature
Fatimid(s) 3, 4, 159, 160, 161, 193
 period 60, 61, 63
fatwa(s) [nonbinding legal opinion] 19, 76,
 93–97, 104, 106
France 1, 5, 8, 13, 51, 69, 119, 142
Frankish States 1, 3
 administration 109, 128, 140–41, 201
 diplomacy 115, 176, 178
 agriculture 68
 commerce 57, 69
 historiography 9, 107
 literary depiction of 186
 Mamluk conquest of 81, 183
 medical establishment 158, 159
 sources for 15, 16
 *See also* Kingdom of Jerusalem; Latin East
Frederick II Hohenstaufen 5, 6, 69, 88,
 112–13, 124, 128, 153,
French (language) 10, 16, 18, 45, 73, 88,
 157–58, 176

Galilee 26, 28, 31, 37–38, 42–44, 52, 70
 agriculture 71, 72, 73
glass 57, 60–61,
Godfrey of Bouillon 3, 88
Greek (language) 30, 166,

hadith(s) 46, 85–86, 94, 179. *See also* Islam; Qur'an
Hama 4, 17, 64, 77, 152, 195–96
Hanbali 18, 32, 72, 90, 91, 92–93, 210n97, 221n79, 226–27n20
Haram al-Sharif (Jerusalem) 53, 88, 89, 113. *See also* Temple Mount (Jerusalem)
al-Harawi, 'Ali ibn Abi Bakr 18, 35–37, 39, 43
Hattin, battle of 5
Hospitaller(s) 19, 71, 76–79, 100, 122, 129, 152–53
   castles and lands of 62, 73, 74, 130, 169, 173, 187
   treaties 65, 110, 119,
      with Baybars (1267) 58, 114, 118, 124, 133–37
   treatment of captives 46, 63, 64, 67
   *See also* Revel, Hugh; Templar(s); Teutonic Knights
Hugh III of Cyprus 5, 79, 114, 117, 125–27, 128, 130, 139
   1271 letter 75, 169, 173, 175. *See also* Baybars, al-Malik al-Zahir
   *See also* Cyprus; Lusignan

Ibelin, Isabel of 50, 58, 59, 117
   diplomacy with Baybars al-Mansuri 125–26, 127, 137
Ibelin, John of 23, 46, 58, 120, 123
   legal writing 9, 18, 87, 88, 99–100, 125
Ibn 'Abd al-Zahir, Muhyi al-Din 17, 23, 41, 55, 75, 94, 115
Ibn al-'Adim, Kamal al-Din 'Umar 18, 36, 65
Ibn al-Athir, Diya' al-Din 166–67, 177, 178
Ibn al-Athir, 'Izz al-Din 17, 147, 151, 153
Ibn al-Furat, Nasir al-Din Muhammad 17, 46, 64, 66–68, 70, 117, 121, 124–25, 128–29, 169
Ibn Jubayr, Muhammad 28, 67, 68, 78, 105
Ibn Munqidh, Usama 22, 28, 38–39, 65, 95, 147, 150
   *Kitab al'I'tibar [Book of Contemplation]* 17, 64, 165, 191–97, 198
Ibn Munir al-Tarablusi, Ahmad 182
Ibn Shaddad, 'Izz al-Din Muhammad 17, 36, 47, 65

Ibn Wasil, Jamal al-Din 17, 40, 64, 65, 70, 82, 89, 113, 123, 131–32, 152–53
Islam 2, 23, 26, 71, 80
   charitable system 49
   conversion to 12, 27, 30, 98–99, 148, 150, 158
   Islamic law. *See* law
   literary depictions of 182–83
   religious sites 33–42, 43, 200
   *See also* Muslim(s); Qur'an
Isma'ili 5, 77, 122, 130, 135–36, 149–50

Jacobite(s) 14, 99, 100, 200. *See also* Christian(s); Eastern Christians
Jaffa 5, 7, 41, 67, 70
   Baybars' conquest of 81, 126
   Burgess Courts in 100
   Count of. *See* Ibelin, John of
   Treaty of (1229) 6, 51, 112, 208n63
Jerusalem (city) 1
   administration 88–89, 93, 156
   Ayyubid conquest of 5–6
   Christian population 27–29, 139–40
   converts 149
   Frankish conquest of 32, 214n68
   literary depiction of 179–87, 189
   medical establishment 158–59
   Muslim population 26, 31, 33, 53
      archaeological evidence of 35, 95
   religious sites 27, 38–42, 43
   treaties concerning 112
   Turkish conquest of 113, 163. *See also* Khwarazmian(s)
Jerusalem, Kingdom of 1, 3–7, 191, 201
   administration 107, 108, 109, 142, 156
   agriculture 69, 75
   Christian population 53
   historiography of 8, 10, 21–22, 23, 25, 140, 141
   industrial production 60
   Jewish population 12–13
   joint kingdom with Cyprus 138–39
   legal system 87, 97, 99, 100, 105, 210n90. *See also* Ibelin, John of
   mercantile interests
      slave trade 64
   Muslim population 20–21, 42, 50

legal status of 85, 86, 88–89
violence against 55–56
primary sources 16–17, 32
treaties concerning 110, 112, 119–20, 137, 139
treatment of captives 124
Jew(s) 1, 32, 35, 83, 143
glassmaking 61
historiography of 12–13, 14, 15, 26–27, 28, 211n2
intellectual life 144, 145, 163–64, 167
legal status 85, 86, 88, 99, 100–101, 105, 106
gender implications 95, 96
slavery and 102, 103
mercantile interests 58
naming conventions 45
religious sites 36, 37
political status 109
rural populations 30
urban populations 29, 33, 38, 40
wine-making 71
jihad [holy war] 41, 42, 108, 110, 179–80, 192, 193

al-Kamil (Sultan of Egypt) 6, 88, 112–13, 123, 124, 132, 139, 153
Kedar, Benjamin 8, 11, 13, 27–28, 29, 89, 104, 143, 156
Kerak 47, 68, 187
Khwarazmian(s) 6, 82, 113, 163, 185–86, 187, 190
knowledge 2, 22, 144–46, 150, 161, 163, 227–28n40
archaeological 61
cultural 189, 192
exchange (of) 153, 154, 155, 165, 199
epistolary 168
terrain 147
languages 149, 156, 157
medical 157–58, 160, 162
religious 45, 181

Latin Christians 22, 40, 50, 172, 200
cultural exchange 163,
information networks 143, 155, 160, 161

legal system 85, 97, 98
*See also* Christian(s); crusade(s)
Latin East 1, 6, 69, 114, 200–203
administration 140–42
information networks 154
Christian population 24
diplomacy 122, 123
historiography 2, 7, 9–10, 11, 12, 15, 18, 108
intellectual life 143, 144, 160, 175, 178–79, 182
legal system 85, 86, 97
Mamluk conquest of 76
mercantile interests 101
Muslim population 13, 14, 26
sources for 17, 19, 191
treaties concerning 116–17, 118
*See also* Frankish States; Kingdom of Jerusalem
Latin (language) 8, 13, 16, 45, 158, 166
Lattakia 126–27, 130–31, 153
law 9, 78, 85–86, 104–6, 137, 142
Frankish 18–19, 66, 87, 97–103, 210n90.
*See also* Ibelin, John of
Latin ecclesiastical (canon) 45
Latin secular 103, 128
inter-sovereign 109, 111, 115, 127, 131, 133 141
Islamic 21, 88–93, 94, 95, 96–97, 135. *See also* fatwa(s); qadi
Lebanon 1, 11, 16, 24, 27, 31, 54, 70, 159
letter(s) 2, 55, 92, 120, 127, 164–78
diplomatic 67, 75, 118, 122, 123, 124
from captives 47, 68
legal advice 106
as literary exercise 22, 160, 197, 199, 240n18
man/men of. *See* adib [man of letters]
to Europe 51, 76–77, 79, 119. *See also* Revel, Hugh
Jacques de Vitry 50, 148
Levant 8, 10, 12, 110–11, 123, 201
cities of 120
coast of 7, 31
culture 158, 164, 196, 199,
economy 56, 57, 127–28. *See also* condominia; munasafat

literature 13, 202
   Arabic 18, 19, 22, 43, 46, 93, 191, 197,
      faḍa'il al-Quds [merits of Jerusalem]
         179–87
      poetry 165–66, 178, 189
   French 10
Louis IX of France 6–7, 17, 69, 114, 119, 122,
   123, 147, 153
Lusignan 5, 16, 75, 112, 169, 173, 203n7

MacEvitt, Christopher 14, 68, 86, 104, 200,
   201
   "rough tolerance" policy 14–15, 22–23, 37,
      147, 211n2
madrasa [school] 35–36, 89
mamluk(s) [enslaved soldiers] 7, 24, 52,
   63–64, 82, 224n143
Mamluk(s) (Sultanate) 1, 7, 21, 24, 71, 109,
   141
   administration 116, 123, 125, 126, 127,
      232n42
      legal 136, 138, 139
         use of shared land 130, 132. See also
            condominia; munasafat
   archaeological evidence of 32, 33, 61, 72
   cultural life 161, 166, 167, 168, 172, 174, 197
   diplomacy 175, 177
   fleet 47, 94
   intelligence networks 146, 148, 150, 154–55,
      156–57
      used against Mamluks 151–52
   literary depictions of 187–89
   mercantile interests 58–61
   primary sources from 17, 55
   raids against Franks 44, 46, 56, 57, 77, 81
      as strategy 75–76, 80, 82, 83
   raids against Mongols 120–21, 227n37
   religious sites 41
   treaties with Franks 6, 50, 73, 110–11, 116,
      133
      comparison with Ayyubids 112, 114–15
      formalities of 117–18, 119
      treatment of captives 65, 80
maqam [mausoleum shrine] 33, 34, 38, 41–42,
   43, 44, 215n80
al-Maqdisi, Diya' al-Din 18, 32, 90–91, 92
marriage 5, 65, 85, 87, 101–2, 112

medicine 24, 144–45, 157–59, 160, 161
Mediterranean 13, 19, 91, 108,
   archaeological exploration 34
   culture 10, 23, 143, 164–65, 166, 179
   religious tensions in 91, 92
   trade 63, 69
   travel narratives of 35
Melkite(s) 14, 15, 88, 200. See also Christian(s); Eastern Christians
Mongol(s) 6, 17, 64, 79, 120, 121, 122, 187
   1272 embassy 59, 138, 139
   cultural exchange with 168
   Franks impersonating 155
   refugees from 51–52, 53, 91, 105
Montfort (castle) 7, 44, 126, 156, 169, 173–74
   Teutonic knights of 47, 49, 75
Montfort, John of 128, 139
Montfort, Philip of 66, 82, 149, 154
Mosul 4, 35, 151
al-Muʿazzam ʿIsa 40, 112–13, 159, 184
munasafat [jointly held land] 21, 50, 109,
   127–28, 130, 132–33, 227n21. See also
   condominia
Muslim(s) 1, 2, 5, 8, 19–22, 24, 53–54, 108,
   199–202
   archaeological evidence of 11, 35
   Christians and 13–14, 140, 208n63
      knowledge exchange 145–46, 163–64
      shared lands. See condominia;
         munasafat
   economic participation 57–60, 83–84
      agriculture 70, 71, 72, 74–75
      industry 60–63
   envoys 123, 125, 141
   forced relocation of 79, 121
   Hanbali. See Hanbali
   integration under Frankish rule 15, 192,
      211n2, 226n12
   intelligence networks 147, 148, 149–50, 153
   Ismaʿili. See Ismaʿili
   legal status of 85, 86, 87, 104–6
      "inter-sovereign" law. See law
      Islamic law 88–97
      Frankish law 97–101, 228n61
   literary culture 178, 179–80, 185, 190
   medical advances 158–61
   military campaigns 80, 139

raids against peasants 76, 81
naming conventions 48
population 25–26, 27–31, 32–33
  rural 42–44, 50, 51
  traveling 51–52
  urban 44–47, 176, 187, 214n55
primary sources 16, 18, 19, 144, 228n58
religious sites 36–42, 213n34
Shiʻa. *See* Shʻia
Sunni. *See* Sunni
treaties with Frankish holy orders 77–78
treaties with Frankish rulers 109, 120, 128–29
violence against 7, 13, 55–56, 155, 157, 195
  enslavement of 49, 63–68, 82, 102–3

Nablus 3, 26, 28–29, 31, 60,
  agricultural production 70
  Frankish legal records from 87, 97
  Hanbali community 18, 32, 72, 90, 91, 92–93. *See also* Hanbali
  literary culture 183
al-Nawawi, Muhyi al-Din Abu Zakariyya Yahya 94–96
Nazareth 6, 27, 28, 36–37, 38, 71
Nestorian(s), 14, 100, 103. *See also* Christian(s); Eastern Christians
Nirenberg, David 13–14
Nizam al-Mulk 153–54
nomadic peoples/nomad(s) 27, 28, 31, 38, 53, 77, 82,
  economic participation 70–71, 129,
  as informants 146–47, 161
  legal status of 135
  literary depiction of 194, 195. *See also* Ibn Munquidh, Usama
  paganism among 30
  *See also* Bedouin(s); Turcoman(s)
Nur al-Din 4, 110, 147, 182

Orthodox Church. *See* Eastern Christian(s); Melkite(s)
Ottoman Empire 20, 44, 70,

Palestine 1, 24, 88, 165
  agricultural production in 69
  archaeological sites in 34, 42

historiography of 12, 15, 20, 25, 89
Muslim communities in 26–30, 33, 47
religious sites 36
Turkish invasion of 6–7, 120
peasant(s) 16, 68–69, 74–75, 84, 91
  forced displacement of 75–83
  legal status of 86, 93, 96–97, 103, 105, 235n120
  sources for 18, 90
  under treaties 115, 128, 129, 133, 135, 136
  violence against 21, 64, 152, 224n146
  conquest of Tyre (1291) 45, 55–56
pilgrimage 35–37
  Christian 11, 31, 70
  Muslim 18, 26, 41, 105, 158
poet(ry) 164, 165, 178–90, 191, 199
  debates regarding 166
  depictions of Franks in 197–98
  quotation in letters 167, 170
Prawer, Joshua 8, 9, 11, 12–13, 14, 27, 69, 86, 100, 103, 104, 199–200

qadi [judge] 65, 76, 93–95, 96–97, 104, 105, 223n132. *See also* raʼis
  administration of oaths 124–25
  description 87, 88–90, 91
  literary production 184–85
Qalawun, al-Malik al-Mansur 7, 17, 56, 59–60, 83, 132, 157
  espionage networks 154–55
  literary depiction of 188
  succession 175–76
  treaties with holy orders 65, 118
  treaties with individual rulers 50, 114–15, 117, 130, 133, 135
  treaty with Latin Kingdom (1285) 45–46, 81, 137
  *See also* Ibn ʻAbd al-Zahir, Muhyi al-Din; Mamluk(s)
al-Qalqashandi, Ahmad ibn ʻAli 19, 116–17, 124, 167, 177
Qurʼan 36–37, 39, 85–86, 101
  literary allusions to 179, 183
  quotation in letters 167, 170, 171, 175

raʼis [headman] 11, 48, 87, 88, 90, 103, 105, 106, 137. *See also* qadi
  of condominia 134, 136, 235n110, 240n30

Revel, Hugh 67, 76–77, 79, 118, 124–25, 135, 169, 172. *See also* Hospitaller(s)
ribat [frontier outpost] 40, 41, 89
Riley-Smith, Jonathan 8, 9, 12, 15, 48, 86, 104, 129, 156

Safad 7, 32, 48, 49, 80, 113, 139
   1266 capture of 66, 148
   Templar castle 46–47, 53, 67
Saladin [Salah al-Din Yusuf] 9, 12, 23, 35, 42, 83, 147, 158
   conquest of Antioch (1188) 88
   conquest of Jerusalem (1187) 2, 4–5, 38, 87
   ideology of jihad 110. *See also* jihad
   literary depictions of 180–81, 183–84
   patronage 40, 89, 164, 191
   children of 132
   treaties 128
Samaritan(s) 27, 30, 31, 100–101, 102, 103, 143
'Saracen'. *See* Arabic (language); Muslim(s)
science 157, 158, 161,
Seljuk(s) 3, 52, 64, 122, 124, 147, 151, 153, 161
serf(s)/serfdom 15, 68, 86. *See also* peasant(s)
servants 45, 49, 78, 102, 130, 172, 189
shari'a. *See* law
Shayzar 191, 196
Shi'a 92
ship(s) 49, 94, 137, 154, 172, 174
   seizure of 138, 173
   wreck(s) 47, 58–59, 75
   *See also* law(s); trade
Sicily 9, 69, 91, 111,
Sidon 7, 51, 56, 72, 112, 113, 119, 120, 128, 138
slavery 46, 47, 66, 67, 68, 102. *See also* captivity; mamluk(s)
Smail, R. C. 6, 8–9, 27
Sufi 40, 88, 89, 153
Sunni 35, 91, 96, 226–27n20
sugar 56, 57, 70, 72–73, 74, 200,
   vessels 63
Syria 6, 15, 24, 38, 66, 130,
   administration 52, 138, 141
      diplomacy 193
      information networks 153, 155, 156, 160, 161
      legal 89, 94, 95, 97, 105–6
   agricultural production 68–69, 73

Ayyubid rule of 4–5, 35, 40, 110, 113, 197
Frankish rule of 3, 79, 136
Franco-Syrian society 8
intellectual life of 17, 144, 145, 191,
   literary culture 163, 165, 175, 178, 179–82, 186–87
   medical knowledge 158–59
Jewish population in 12–13
Mamluk rule of 7
mercantile interests 46, 53, 59–60
Mongol invasion of 64
Muslim population in 20, 33, 85, 150
   historiographical assumptions about 26–28, 207n48, 208n63
   raids against Franks 193, 195, 196
   religious sites 36
   treaties concerning 119–20, 128–29
Syrian Christians 48, 88
   legal status of 99, 100, 101, 102, 103, 105
   mistrust of 147–49, 150
   *See also* Christian(s); Eastern Christians

tax(es)/taxation 12, 50, 60, 68, 71, 74, 77, 129, 140
   in treaty negotiations 130, 131, 133–34
   *See also* dhimmi; jizya
Templar of Tyre 16, 43, 45, 46, 55, 56
   accounts of captives 67
   depiction of Baybars 81, 82, 120, 121
   depiction of informants 150, 151–52, 154, 155, 156–57
   suspicion of Syrian Christians 148, 149
   translation from Arabic 175–77, 197
Templar(s) 39, 53, 74, 126, 130, 183
   condominia 129, 132
   espionage 146, 151–53, 156–57, 161
   treaties concerning 118, 119, 122
   treatment of captives 46–47, 58, 66, 67–68
Temple Mount (Jerusalem) 40, 53, 88. *See also* Haram al-Sharif
Teutonic Knights 19, 44, 47, 73, 119
   control of Montfort 49, 75, 174
Tiberias 3, 61, 63, 113, 128, 203n7
trade 68, 72, 98, 105
   slave 63. *See also* slavery
translator(s) 53, 147, 150, 156, 175
treat(y)(ies) 5–6, 110, 112–20, 126, 159, 231n20

broken 56
espionage and 153
formalities of 232n33, 233n66, 234n72
impact on villages 32, 50
of Jaffa. *See* Jaffa
legal implications 88–89, 111, 133–40, 201, 226n11, 235n109
as primary sources 18, 19, 21, 109, 141, 167, 232n27
role of captives 48–49, 64–65, 67–68
role of envoys 122, 124, 125
territorial considerations 73, 127, 128, 129–31
peasantry 77–78, 79, 81, 82, 224n150
trade considerations 46, 58–60, 83, 132
Tripoli 59, 62, 76, 79, 114–15, 116, 119, 131, 155
Bohemond VII. *See* Bohemond VII of Tripoli
county of 3, 5, 6, 126–27, 156, 159
cultural life of 157, 182, 188, 191
Mamluk conquest of 132–33, 151–52
refugees from 52,
Turcoman(s) 41, 70–71, 77, 82, 129, 147, 150
Turk(s). *See* Khwarazmian(s); Turcoman(s)
Tyre 3–4, 5, 6, 7, 56, 82
agricultural production 69
cultural life 159

industries 61, 72
mercantile interests 57
Muslim population of 47–50, 51, 53, 54, 103
Philip of. *See* Montfort, Philip of
primary sources 16, 32, 69, 74, 144, 154
Templar of. *See* Templar of Tyre
treaties concerning 117, 119, 128, 133–34, 135, 139
treatment of captives in 66–67
William of. *See* William of Tyre

'Umar ibn al-Khattab 39, 41

Venice 6, 19, 57, 72, 116
occupation of Tyre 3–4, 32, 47–48, 69, 74–75
slave trade in 63
Vitry, Jacques de 45, 50–51, 148, 150

William of Tyre 16, 82, 120, 147, 160

al-Yunini, Musa ibn Muhammad 77, 79

Zengi, 'Imad al-Din 4, 178, 182, . *See also* Mosul
Zorzi, Marsilio 19, 32, 48, 50, 69, 72, 74. *See also* Tyre; Venice

## *Acknowledgments*

When it comes to historical scholarship, there is this image of solitary souls squirreled away in barely lit rooms consulting books and writing their magnum opera far away from the rest of the world. I'm not sure why this is or whether it ever corresponded to reality. For my own part, this project would have been impossible to complete without the interaction and support of numerous people and organizations. The writing of this book, which developed from my doctoral dissertation, was anything but solitary.

From across the University of New Hampshire, I wish to thank my colleagues who made the effort to attend various workshops and talks that I have given related to this project and offered thoughtful and valuable feedback. I cannot overstate my gratitude to Islam Karkour for taking time away from single-handedly running UNH's Arabic Program in order to help me translate some of the Arabic poetry I got stuck on. It is simple fact I have been unbelievably fortunate to be a part of the Department of Classics, Humanities, and Italian Studies. The support of my friends, colleagues, and students has been unstinting and constant in what has been a fraught period in academia. I am forever grateful for the labors of Jennifer McCready, Colette Bazylinski, and Lisa Hartford, the departmental administrators for CHI, who time and again went above and beyond to make things happen. I owe particular thanks to Anna Wainwright and Paul Robertson for their insightful comments on chapter drafts.

From the dissertation stage of this project at the University of Minnesota, I also owe many thanks. My advisor Michael Lower enabled this project to happen at all by encouraging my pursuit of Arabic, and supporting my taking the time to gain the skills necessary to accomplish it. Many thanks also to Kay Reyerson, Jimmy Schryver, Ruth Karras, John Watkins, and Daniel Schroeter. Getting through the PhD program would have been impossible without the friendships of my many amazing graduate student colleagues whose conversation and company, in addition to intellectual support, made it possible to thrive. Thanks to Pat Baehler, Steve Bivens, Adam Blackler, Cameron Bradley, Lydia Brosnahan, David Crane, Rachel Gibson, Melissa Hampton, Brian Hill, Nate Holdren, Jesse Izzo, Katie Lambright, John Manke, Caitlin McHugh, Jecca Namakkal, Basit H. Qureshi, Chantel Rodriguez, Emma Snowden, Tiffany D. Vann Sprecher, Elizabeth Williams, and Alex Wisnoski.

In my travels, I've had the great fortune to forge collegial relationships and friendships who have all contributed to my understanding of the period and place. First thanks go to Reuven Amitai for his ongoing support and interest in my doings over the years. Thanks also to Edna J. Stern, Uri Shachar, Ben Goldman, and Jeremy Pearson for stimulating exchanges on crusades and other topics, feedback, and idea-sharing. The collegial participants of the intellectually rejuvenating 6th Advanced School in the Humanities on the crusades and the Latin East at Hebrew University to which I was invited by Iris Shagrir and Anna Gutgarts provided the final energy and push to bring this manuscript to completion. Finally, I can't forget to mention Jennifer Hower, whose hosting and organized adventures supplied much-needed fun and unforgettable experiences.

Generous financial and research support from a number of organizations also enabled this book to be completed. As a graduate student, fellowships from the Council for American Overseas Research Centers, the Bureau of Educational and Cultural Affairs of the U.S. State Department, the Social Science Research Council, the Andrew W. Mellon Foundation, the Council of European Studies, and the University of Minnesota supported research, travel, and writing. As faculty, support from the University of New Hampshire as well as a National Endowment for the Humanities fellowship from the W. F. Albright Institute allowed additional research and writing as I transformed the dissertation into this book. Thanks also to Maroma Camilleri and the staff at the National Library of Malta, Dr. Giuseppe Ciminello and the staff at the Biblioteca Apostolica Vaticana, and Mag. Friedrich Simander and the staff at the Österreichische Nationalbibliothek for allowing me to look at manuscripts in their collections.

I've had the privilege of staying at the W. F. Albright Institute of Archaeological Research in Jerusalem and being welcomed into the special community of scholars fostered there. Many thanks go to former directors Sy Gitin and Matt Adams and the Albright's unfailingly warm and generous staff. Special mention also to the scholars of all stripes who I met there whose comradery, conversation, and, frequently, mentorship helped guide me in this process: Andrea Creel, J. P. Dessel, Jennie Ebeling, Anthony Keddie, Sean

Kirkland, Jill Joshowitz, Vivian Laughlin, Lisa Mahoney, Shulamit Miller, Yael Rotem, Timothy Sailors, Debi Weisselberg-Cassuto, Hannah Ringheim, Yorke Rowan, and Laura Wright.

On the production side of things, I wish to express my deep gratitude to Jenny Tan, Lily Palladino, and the whole team at Penn Press for their guidance through the process of publication. I also want to recognize John Wyatt Greenlee and Kavita Mudan Finn for being outstanding collaborators in creating the maps and index. Much thanks also to the anonymous readers for their helpful and generous feedback and commentary. The book is all the better for their efforts; of course, any mistakes are my own.

Finally, I would never have started let alone completed this book, some thirteen years in the making, without the love and encouragement of my family. When times got tough in recent years, Alex and our dog Finn kept me going with compassion, love, and demands for belly scritches (Finn). Thank you, thank you, thank you for being my home. My interest in the Middle Ages was sparked from an early age and my parents, Steve and Deborah Zimo, would read to me the same books on Joan of Arc, Alfred the Great, and castles over and over again without complaint. They always encouraged me to follow my interests wherever they led, and so, as the culmination of that journey, this book is dedicated to them.

Printed in the USA
CPSIA information can be obtained
at www.ICGtesting.com
JSHW081043160724
66319JS00001B/1

9 781512 824896